BEING CHINESE IN CANADA

William Ging Wee Dere

BEING CHINESE IN CANADA

The Struggle for Identity, Redress and Belonging

Douglas & McIntyre

1 2 3 4 5 — 23 22 21 20 19

Douglas and McIntyre (2013) Ltd.
P.O. Box 219, Madeira Park, BC, VON 2HO
www.douglas-mcintyre.com

Edited by Cheryl Cohen   Indexed by Ellen Hawman
Cover design by Diane Robertson   Text design by Carleton Wilson

Printed and bound in Canada   Text is printed on 30% recycled paper

Douglas and McIntyre (2013) Ltd. acknowledges the support of the Canada Council for the Arts, which last year invested $153 million to bring the arts to Canadians throughout the country.

Nous remercions le Conseil des arts du Canada de son soutien. L'an dernier, le Conseil a investi 153 millions de dollars pour mettre de l'art dans la vie des Canadiennes et des Canadiens de tout le pays.

We also gratefully acknowledge financial support from the Government of Canada and from the Province of British Columbia through the BC Arts Council and the Book Publishing Tax Credit.

LIBRARY AND ARCHIVES CANADA CATALOGUING IN PUBLICATION

Dere, William Ging Wee, author
    Being Chinese in Canada : the struggle for identity, redress and belonging
/ William Ging Wee Dere.

 Includes bibliographical references and index.
Issued in print and electronic formats.
ISBN 978-1-77162-218-9 (softcover).--ISBN 978-1-77162-219-6 (HTML)

    1. Chinese Canadians--History. 2. Chinese--Canada--History. 3. Chinese Canadians--Social conditions. 4. Chinese--Canada--Social conditions. 5. Chinese Canadians--Social life and customs. 6. Chinese--Canada--Social life and customs. 7. Chinese--Race identity--Canada. 8. Canada--Race relations. 9. Dere, William Ging Wee I. Title.

FC106.C5D47 2019   971'.004951   C2018-905046-2
                                                C2018-905047-0

CONTENTS

INTRODUCTION

This book is a voice from Chinese Canada. It is a voice from the margins and firmly plants itself in the soil of Canada and Quebec. It explores my selective memories as a Chinese Canadian activist; my motivations and my conscious and subconscious desires to seek my true identity, culture and place of belonging. I don't consider myself a witness to history. I was too involved to be able to step back and give an objective testimony of pivotal events involving Chinese Canadians from the 1960s to today. This is a personal account of how events affected me and perhaps how I might have had an influence, however small, on them.

As the chapters that follow will make clear, the infamous and hefty head tax that Canada chose to levy only on Chinese immigrants has been a particular focus of many of my years in this country, including my participation in the head tax redress movement. The long-lasting effects on families caused by the Chinese Head Tax and Exclusion Act (HTEA) are incalculable. For sixty-two years, an entire community was prevented, by law, from integrating into Canadian society. The Chinese community did not develop in a normal fashion since the law prevented families from reuniting or starting in Canada. A total of 81,000 Chinese immigrants paid a total of $23 million into the coffers of the Canadian federal and provincial governments. Those governments indeed showed that they could profit from racism.

I was born in China. I spent the first five years of my life there with my mother and siblings, and the next two in Hong Kong. My father and grandfather sent money from Canada, where they had both immigrated before Canada brought in the legislation that made it impossible for them to bring their wives to join them. My father's last trip back to China was in 1947. I discovered that detail only after his death, through his head tax certificate. He had held on

9

to it, along with other papers he kept safe for fear of being deported if any of them were lost.

On a personal level, *Being Chinese in Canada* explores why my father and grandfather decided to immigrate to Canada and how they survived in an unwelcoming society. But the personal is only a small part of a broader picture that became clear to me, during my research for this book, as I looked through the General Register of Chinese Immigration—a thousand volumes that Canada used to record and control Chinese immigrants. It's a little known Canadian artifact that lists information about each Chinese person who was made to pay the head tax to come into the country.

I originally set out to write about my involvement in the redress movement for the HTEA. The Chinese Immigration Act of 1885 levied the head tax— which started at $50, rose to $100, and eventually settled at $500 per person— on those Chinese immigrants allowed into the country. The tax was replaced in 1923 by another Chinese Immigration Act, this one banning all Chinese immigration until 1947. It would be another twenty years before Chinese people were treated like others wanting to immigrate to Canada. Obtaining government redress was a further long battle. It was a defining period in the history of Chinese Canadian reality in this country and I was engaged for twenty years of my life in this struggle.

As I tossed the idea of my book to my daughter, Jessica, she lobbed back another suggestion: "I love it when you and mommy tell me about what you did in the Party. Why don't you write about that?" As she was growing up, I dragged her to countless head tax meetings. She helped me organize workshops, study groups and concerts. She even appeared in *Moving the Mountain*, the 1993 documentary about the HTEA that I co-directed with Malcolm Guy. To her, the redress campaign was old hat. But she thought it was so romantic that her mother, Gillian Taylor, and I had met and fallen in love as comrades. I thought about all this and the redress book I was planning to write gradually grew.

Knowing my culture—Chinese Canadian culture—is the key to understanding and defining my identity in Canada and Quebec. It is a lifelong quest. I am talking about a stereotype-breaking, in-your-face kind of culture, the kind of social understanding and feeling that reflect the everyday struggles and experiences of living in Chinese Canada. The kind of social understanding and feeling that establish our place and identity in this country.

During periods in my youth, I grappled with my sense of identity and belonging in Canada, and as a founding member and full-time organizer of the Workers Communist Party, I felt a powerful sense of identity and belonging. Only years later did I come to the painful realization that political and ideological kinship was not the same as personal and emotional connection.

The decade of the 1970s was a turbulent time in Quebec and around the world. The revolutionary and popular movements of the '70s honed the Québécois tradition of militant activism, and the province became a North American hotbed for resistance against the authority and repression of the state following the War Measures Act of 1970. Quebec activists learned how to organize within this atmosphere.

I was inspired by the national liberation struggles throughout Asia, Africa and Latin America, especially the worldwide movement to oppose American aggression in Vietnam and in Southeast Asia.

Throughout this period there was a beacon, a model: the People's Republic of China led by Mao Zedong. Many progressive youth of the West were inspired by the slogans of China's Great Proletarian Cultural Revolution and Chairman Mao's "Little Red Book." The Chairman exhorted the youth, "It is right to rebel" and "Bombard the headquarters." Mao's dictum, "Let a hundred flowers bloom and a hundred schools of thought contend," had a quixotic air for the youth searching for solutions. In the early 1960s, the Communist Party of China criticized the policies of the Soviet Communist Party and by doing so launched the New Communist (Marxist-Leninist) Movement, which became a global phenomenon and caught the imagination and enthusiasm of the disaffected young intellectuals, students and workers of the West.

I was one of them—questioning things and not just accepting "truths" for granted. Throughout my university years in Montreal, and for a decade and a half following them, I was caught up in the New Communist Movement.

Two years after the breakup of the Workers Communist Party in Canada, my marriage with Jessica's mother also ended. Without the ideological and political discipline of the Party guiding my way, I defaulted to the traditional Chinese cultural values learned from my parents. The year 1985 was a time of awakening as I began the search for my identity and my cultural terrain.

At that time, I knew nothing about Chinese Canadian history. Imagine: I knew about the history of the workers' movement in Quebec and Canada and the struggles that took place in Canadian history, but I knew virtually nothing about the struggles of my own people and nothing about the history of my own family here in Canada.

In the course of searching for identity and belonging I became involved in the Montreal Chinese community. Through this involvement, I finally discovered some aspects of my father's life here in Canada.[1]

When the Head Tax and Chinese Exclusion Act campaign started, I threw myself into it. Here was a unifying struggle against injustice and for equality, and it was personal. The struggle was not just for society in general as during the Marxist-Leninist years, but this time it was for myself and my family, and it was for the families of all the *lo wah kiu*, the pioneers of our community. There were small meetings, awareness-raising sessions, petitions, mass education meetings and concerts. During this period I made two documentary films to bring the message to a wider audience.

As an "insider," I went through the ups and downs as in any political campaign. However, the HTEA issue was fundamental to the development of our community. The discriminatory laws resulted in the unequal way the early pioneering families and the community interacted with the larger society and we needed to expose this history. The twenty-two-year redress struggle transcended any factions within the community. The HTEA was a historical wrong that had to be recognized and redressed. In 2002, I formulated with the Chinese Canadian Redress Alliance a two-stage redress proposal that some in the community feel gave the government too easy a way out.

When the government of Canada finally apologized to Chinese people in the country in 2006, it was far from the end of my cultural odyssey—an odyssey that in 1990 had led me back to China, where I met the love of my life, Dong Qing Chen, who agreed to come to Canada with me, and who became so significant in my continuing personal quest for identity and belonging.

Being Chinese in Quebec is not like being Chinese in Canada. My participation in a 2012 documentary film, *Être chinois au Québec*—Being Chinese in Quebec, which explored the legacy of the HTEA in Quebec, exposed the fault lines between our community and the larger society. It is still an arduous uphill struggle for the Chinese minority to stand up for our own identity in Quebec.

Trying to sum up my ongoing quest for identity and belonging in this book has led me to realizations that I never anticipated—realizations that are now part of *Being Chinese in Canada*.

* * *

Note: To help readers, in the chapters that follow I refer to Chinese immigrants by the names they were given by Canadian immigration, occasionally making it clear as well what their original names were. I use the Western nomenclature of placing the family name last where appropriate.

PART ONE

Family

Chapter 1

Coming to Gold Mountain

"For actually, the earth has no roads to begin with, but when many men pass one way, a road is made."
—Lu Xun, *My Old Home*, January 1921

My grandfather had a very tough time after first arriving in Canada. My mother once told me that when his money ran out, he was a beachcomber in Vancouver and survived by eating crabs that he dug out of the sand.

I was born in the village of Fong Dang in Toishan County, Guangdong, China during the seventh moon in the Year of the Rat 4646 (Western calendar 1948), in the house built with money that my grandfather (Tan Suey Der) and my father (Hing Dere) sent from Canada. As a boy, I was brought to Canada to live in the back of my father's hand laundry in Montreal. I knew I was different from other kids in school, and I didn't want to be different. I just wanted to be the same as the others. But Father always reminded me, "You're Chinese." These words expressed his understanding of not just identity but where he stood in Canada. Having this understanding was his first step in forming a strategy to cope and survive here.

It would be years before I understood that my father's words came from his experience navigating life in a country that systematically discriminated against him as a Chinese person. The discrimination started the moment he arrived here. The Canadian government made my father and, before him, my grandfather pay $500 each to enter the country—a fee that was written into the third Chinese Immigration Act (1903) as the "Head Tax." It was directed solely at the Chinese to discourage them from coming to Canada. Chinese immigrants saved and borrowed from fellow villagers and overseas compatriots to raise the head tax plus the passage and other travel expenses. At the time my grandfather arrived in Canada, the $500 he was forced to hand over on arrival could have bought two houses here or two hundred acres of prime land.

Still, despite the hardships and financial burden, people like my father and grandfather came. The reasons why are intertwined with a backdrop of upheaval and poverty in China due to feudal oppression by the decadent and moribund Qing Dynasty and the imperialist exploitation of foreign powers. In the nineteenth and early twentieth centuries, the peasant Taiping revolt claimed millions of lives and the original drug lords of Britain declared war on China after the Chinese burned a large supply of illegal opium on the beaches of Humen in Guangdong. This Opium War resulted in the first of many unequal treaties between a weak and powerless China and foreign imperial powers which led to Hong Kong being ceded to Britain and the forced opening up of markets for trade, including opium. The Boxer Rebellion, a major anti-feudal and anti-imperialist uprising, ended with eleven foreign countries forcing China both to pay a massive amount of money (US$333 million) that further impoverished the country, and to allow the foreign troops to occupy the country.

Southern China was also a hotbed of rebellion. My family's home province of Guangdong was in the south and produced Dr. Sun Yat-sen, the revered leader of the 1911 Revolution, which led to the end of the Qing Dynasty and the creation of the sovereign Republic of China. Many Gold Mountain men, including my grandfather, supported Dr. Sun and came from this tradition of standing up for one's rights.

During the days of the Qing Dynasty, the emperor forbade any migration to foreign lands but there was no other choice if a family was to survive. A large number of courageous Chinese left for the far corners of the earth to earn a living.

Why choose North America? Word had spread to the impoverished villages of Guangdong province that you could literally pick up gold off the ground in California. Many Chinese came in search of wealth, but they encountered violent racism from the whites competing for the same ounce of gold. In the 1850s, many Chinese gold miners migrated from California to join the Fraser Canyon gold rush in the British colony farther north. Other Chinese followed them from Southern China. They all came to seek their fortunes in the gold fields, and thus began the name Gold Mountain.

Besides the attraction of the gold fields, there were jobs to be had on the railways. One of the conditions for British Columbia to join the Canadian Confederation in 1871 was the building of a railway that would bind Canada from west to east. Chinese railway workers had built the western portion of the American transcontinental railway, and their industriousness and willingness to work at half the wages of white workers made them the model minority for recruiters looking to build the western section of the Canadian Pacific Railway (CPR). Despite the dangerous and near-starvation working conditions, fifteen thousand Chinese workers came and completed the CPR in 1885. More than one thousand of them perished during the construction.

Once the Chinese workers had driven in all the other spikes, Donald Smith (Lord Strathcona), one of the owners of the CPR, ceremoniously stepped up to drive in the last spike at Craigellachie, BC, at 9:22 a.m. on November 7, 1885, to complete the railroad. Yes, they recorded the exact time that Smith struck the hammer. It was a grand photo op. But if you look at a copy of the photo in one of the many historical archives that display railroad memorabilia, search as you might, you will not see a single Chinese face in the crowd.[2]

As the CPR neared completion, people became anxious about the Chinese presence in BC. The Chinese population made up the largest number of non-European immigrants in Canada. It was common knowledge that the Indigenous people and Chinese outnumbered the whites at the time.[3] The white colonial rulers could not let this stand so in 1885, the Royal Commission on Chinese Immigration was formed to respond to the anti-Chinese agitation and at least four Chinese Immigration Acts followed, from 1885 to 1923, the last of which was an exclusion act. Prime Minister John A. Macdonald set the tenor when he said in 1887, "It is not advantageous to the country that the Chinese should come and settle in Canada producing a Mongrel race."[4]

This is the historical context under which my grandfather came to Canada. He had no awareness of the odious social atmosphere that the government had induced against Chinese immigrants.

* * *

My grandfather and father weren't the first members of my family to come to Gold Mountain to try to provide food and clothing for their wives and children back in their impoverished village in Guangdong, and they weren't the first in our family to encounter racism in Gold Mountain.

As the story goes, in the early 1880s my paternal great-grandfather, my *Bak Gong*, travelled about eight thousand miles to Boston from Fong Dang village—which lies ninety miles in a straight line west of Hong Kong—to work for a few years with a couple of village cousins operating a hand laundry. The laundry was in a rough neighbourhood and the laundrymen were constantly harassed and threatened by the local ruffians.

Around that time, the United States took aim at Chinese people, passing the Chinese Exclusion Act in 1882. The hateful attitude the US policy created towards the Chinese might have fuelled the murderous sentiments of the thugs who harassed my great-grandfather. Or maybe they were still bitter that a company owner had brought in Chinese workers to break the strike at the Sampson Shoe Factory in North Adams, a factory town west of Boston, in 1870. It was a classic tactic: pitting one set of workers against another. The added factor of racism was effective in diverting from the real problems of low wages and bad working conditions created by the owner. As history has it, the strike was not broken by the Chinese workers but by mechanization. However, the general atmosphere provided an excuse for the hate and exclusion of Chinese people.

One evening, as my great-grandfather lay on the ironing table trying to fall asleep, he heard a group of men outside saying this was the laundry that they wanted to torch to "burn the chinks out." The very next day, the three laundrymen packed their meagre belongings and left for the west coast. My Bak Gong went back to China shortly after and he never returned to America.

He had started a family trend, though.

The money my great-grandfather made in Gold Mountain financed the education of my paternal grandfather, my *Ah Yeh*, who was born in 1884. At the age of sixteen, my grandfather married a sixteen-year-old woman from the Yee clan who lived in a neighbouring village. They had their first son the following year, in 1901—my uncle Chew Lip. My father, Hing, was born in 1903. In 1905, my grandparents' third son died shortly after birth. My grandmother also died due to complications from the birth. She was twenty-one.

In 1908, with two young sons to care for, my grandfather, then twenty-four, married his second wife, Yee Yue Ngau, from the same village as his first wife.

Yue Ngau was nineteen. Grandfather was a teacher, but the dismal situation in the village forced him to think about the future for himself and his family. Encouraged by his father, my Ah Yeh decided to look towards Gold Mountain. He had heard from friends and village cousins that if one could work hard and endure adversity, then one could make a living there. He got some money from his father and borrowed the rest from fellow villagers. He raised about $800, enough to pay the $500 head tax and passage to Canada.

In April 1909, Grandfather bid a tearful farewell to his wife and sons as he left the village to head for Hong Kong to seek passage to Gold Mountain. He arrived in Hong Kong in time to book a steerage ticket on the ss *Ningchow* to Victoria, British Columbia.

In my imagination, my Ah Yeh is standing on the deck of the ss *Ningchow*, peering into the morning fog as the ship cuts through the choppy, foamy waves. The moist sea air is slapping his face and pasting his black hair above his forehead. It's a pleasant feeling. He muses whether any ships under the command of Admiral Zheng He, the legendary fifteenth-century Chinese Muslim explorer, sailed these waters. As the mist starts to clear, Grandfather sees a solitary gull flying overhead. *We must be getting close to land,* he thinks. Grandfather feels he is being relentlessly carried towards an unknown undertaking over which he has no control. He is apprehensive, wondering whether people

ss *Ningchow* carried my grandfather from Hong Kong to Victoria, BC, in 1909. The cargo vessel was launched on August 21, 1902, at D&W Henderson Ltd. in Glasgow. (University of Glasgow Archives & Special Collections, Papers of James Adamson & William Robertson, GB248 DC101/0439.)

in Canada will be as threatening as the Americans his father encountered. *I don't have much choice,* he reflects. *I have two sons and my family to support. This is my mission.*

On May 15, 1909, after three weeks at sea, Grandfather's ship berthed in Victoria harbour. It seems that he did not spend time in detention. He was registered in the General Register of Chinese Immigration as entering Canada and paying the $500 head tax on the same day.

My grandfather lived in British Columbia to start with. He did odd jobs at first, including being a houseboy for a wealthy family, and then he settled into laundry work with his friend Kee Jang in Vancouver. I haven't found much more information about Grandfather's early years in Canada. Due to the forced separation of our family, there was not a continuation of recorded family history, only fragments of information related by my mother and my siblings or found in government archives. The only document I discovered was his CI 9 (Chinese Immigration 9).

One thing I do know is that Grandfather returned to China on July 24, 1912, after he presumably saved enough money for the voyage. The next year his first daughter, Yu Gim, was born. He returned to Canada shortly after the baby's first month celebration in June 1913.

I discovered the few facts I know for certain about my grandfather's arrival in Canada when I started poring through the General Register of Chinese Immigration, an important relic of Chinese immigration to Canada that is housed in the depths of the National Archives of Canada in Ottawa.

* * *

The General Register of Chinese Immigration contains over 1,000 volumes in ledgers that have tan-coloured covers and individually measure about 15 inches in height and 18 inches in width, or 3 feet across when opened. Each opened page contains handwritten entries (some have better penmanship than others), twenty-five lines going down and nineteen columns going across. Each immigrant's life story at the time of entry into Canada is reduced to these nineteen columns.

The Chinese Immigration Act of 1885 originally gave the Department of Customs the responsibility for its administration. The customs officers at each port were appointed as the local controllers and were the first line of defence against Chinese immigrants. They interrogated the Chinese, through an interpreter, and ensured the payment of the head tax before releasing them from the detention centres where immigrants could be incarcerated for up to three months. Each month, the controllers sent their lists of Chinese immigrants to Ottawa to be centrally registered in the General Register of Chinese Immigration.

The register contains 97,123 entries on Chinese immigrants who entered Canada between 1885 and 1949.[5] The aim of the controllers was to keep track of all Chinese travels into and out of Canada. No other immigrants were subjected to such control. Today, this historical artifact offers a glimpse into the life of each Chinese person entering Canada. At first, my family didn't know when Grandfather came to Canada. It was only through the register that I discovered when he actually landed here and the English transliteration of his name.

In the register, my grandfather's family name was written "Jay," and his full name was written as "Jay Man."

To Westerners already confused by Chinese names, my grandfather's name must have been doubly perplexing: his given first name was Man and his courtesy or style name—his *zi*, a name that is usually given when a person reaches adulthood—was Tan Suey.[6] To Grandfather, his family name in Chinese was all he cared about; whatever the immigration officer wrote in English was of no great concern to him. Upon arriving in Canada he gave his family name, 謝. At that time, both Jay and Der were used in North America as the English transliteration of our family name and my grandfather used them both interchangeably. Der is the spelling more commonly used in Western Canada. Later, my father's family name became Dere, as spelled by the immigration officer when my father arrived in the country.

It took me a while to find my grandfather's name because at the time of his arrival, a number of transliterations of the name Der were possible, including Tse (Cantonese), Hsieh, Xie (Mandarin), Dare, Dear and Sia. (Today, Chinese names are standardized by the Pinyin transliteration system developed by the Chinese government.) Established Chinese families are stuck with the family names written in the register. But no matter how you spell it, our family name means "Thanks." It is the twenty-fourth most common surname in China.

I could not find any of my grandfather's papers, including his precious head tax certificate. When he passed away in 1966, the family did not keep any of his documents and they were lost to history. So it was a poignant moment when, after months of searching, I finally found the entry in the General Register of Chinese Immigration that contained details about my grandfather (there is more on this in Chapter 12). His life had been reduced to a single line that read as follows:

- Column 1: Ottawa Serial Number; Port C.I.4 Number; or Port Number Statement and Declaration—**56321/31663**
- Column 2: Names—**Jay Man**
- Column 3: Port or Place Where Registered—**Victoria**
- Column 4: Date of Registration—**May 15, 1909**
- Column 5: Certificate Issued C.I.5—**49835**
- Column 6: Certificate Issued C.I.6 or File Number—**150439**
- Column 7: Fees Paid-Amount—**$500**
- Column 8: Sex—**Male**
- Column 9: Age—**25**
- Column 10: Place of Birth: City or Village—**Wang Lang** [*Should be Wang Kai*]
- Column 11: Place of Birth: District—**Sunning** [*Toishan*]
- Column 12: Place of Birth: Province etc.—**China**
- Column 13: Title, Official Rank, Profession or Occupation—**Labourer**
- Column 14: Last Place of Domicile—**Hong Kong**
- Column 15: Arrival in Canada-Port or Place of—**Victoria**
- Column 16: Arrival in Canada-Name of Vessel, Railway or Other Conveyance—**S.S. Ning Chow**
- Column 17: Arrival in Canada-Date of—**May 15, 1909**
- Column 18: Physical Marks or Peculiarities—**Scar above left temple. 5'4-½"—mole & pit on forehead—mole rt. Cheek-pits**
- Column 19: Remarks—[blank]

Upon further research into the archives to confirm his identity, I discovered my grandfather's "CI 9 certificate," which had his photo. It gave me an additional glimpse of Jay Man's history. The CI 9 (Chinese Immigration 9) was issued to all Chinese who wished to leave Canada temporarily. They needed the certificate to return to Canada within two years or they would lose the right to re-enter the country. According to my grandfather's CI 9, he had lived in Vancouver for three years, from 1909 when he arrived in Canada until July 24, 1912, when he took the Empress of India to Hong Kong. He was a laundry worker for most of those three years. The certificate also had the date stamp of when he returned to Canada, June 8, 1913. I found no other official records of him leaving Canada again.

* * *

By 1920, Grandfather had worked his way east to Quebec. I know this from the notarized letter I found in my father's papers. The letter, dated December 20, 1920, attested:

> DER MAN, laundry-owner, No.1423 Wellington Street, in the City of Montreal, declare and say: That my son, DER HING, about fourteen years old, is coming to join me in Canada; that he will attend school and not be engaged in any wage earning occupation; and that arrangements have been made by me for his care and maintenance while in attendance at school.
> Sworn before Notary G.A. Bourdeau.

Claiming that his son was coming to Canada as a student was an attempt to get an exemption from paying the head tax. Nevertheless, when my father arrived in Canada five months later, he had to pay the $500 tax.

At about the same time, Grandfather's eldest son had gone to Japan to study. Grandfather had sent money for Chew Lip (which is the English transliteration of his Chinese name) to get an education instead of bringing him to Canada for a life of hardship. My uncle returned to China from his studies and became the village head. Being the first-born son, he also bore the responsibility for the family in his father's absence.

In 1920, Grandfather was listed as part owner of the Wong Sing Laundry in Verdun, which these days is a borough of Montreal. It didn't take much capital to start a laundry, just an ability to swallow your pride, and a willingness to work hard and long hours washing other people's dirty laundry. It wasn't so much a business as a livelihood; a means to make some money so that my grandfather and the family back home could eat. There was no need to buy equipment as long as you had your hands. It was called a hand laundry because all the work was by hand—going door to door to collect the dirty clothes and linen, sorting and marking the laundry, washing and drying, starching and ironing, packaging and dispensing. The Chinese euphemistically called such a laundry *yi seng guan,* "clothing store," instead of the less glamorous name "wash house."

Why did my grandfather and so many Chinese immigrants gravitate towards laundry work? It was a question of survival. They could not find jobs in the mainstream due to class and racial oppression. They came largely from peasant backgrounds and lacked any language skills. At first some thought about bringing their wives to Canada, but the head tax discouraged that and the Chinese Exclusion Act of 1923 banned Chinese immigration altogether. For decades the men took on what had traditionally been women's work, washing and cooking. As long as you were willing to put in the long hours, Chinese family associations were there to help with credit in starting a laundry operation. A family association was made up of people from the same clan who had bonded together for mutual support and welfare. Restaurants required more capital, which is why many of those started as partnerships. There was self-reliance and mutual protection in such work.

Montreal at one time held the greatest concentration of Chinese hand laundries in Canada. There were 434 Chinese laundries in the city in 1915, and 553 in 1921.[7] The proliferation of these laundries prompted the Quebec government to pass a special laundry tax in 1915. The tax was $50, to be paid annually, and it was aimed at the Chinese without stating so explicitly. The law exempted laundresses, who worked out of their home and were the direct competition for male Chinese laundry owners. It also exempted religious institutions and incorporated businesses. The Chinese did not fit into any of those categories. Grandfather's partner, Wong Sing, gained notoriety when he challenged the new laundry tax in court in 1915. The judge ruled against him and condemned Wong to pay the $50 tax along with a $20 fine.[8] Wong Sing's resistance to this early systemic racism in Quebec was part of an organized resistance to the laundry tax. Seven laundry workers were sent to prison for refusing to pay the discriminatory tax.[9] The tax was repealed only in 1983. As Kwok Bun Chan wrote in his book, *Smoke and Fire: The Chinese in Montreal,* the Chinese laundryman paid higher taxes proportional to their revenue than other small businesses in the city.

From Lovell's Directory, a Montreal yearbook of businesses, I was able to obtain a history of the Wong Sing Laundry's existence. Wong took over the laundry from Kee Chin, who established the Kee Chin Laundry on Wellington Street at the corner of Gordon, in what is present day Verdun, in 1909. That same year, the name was changed to Wong Sing Laundry.

In 1921, the laundry relocated to a larger space at 245 Gordon St.,[10] perhaps in anticipation of my father's arrival from China. Wong Sing Laundry remained listed in Lovell's until the 1960s.

By 1926, my grandfather and father felt that it was time for them to venture out on their own. A few years later the Depression was under way. Business fell off drastically as many in the working-class sections of town simply could not afford to pay for laundry service, and many Chinese hand laundries went out of business. Those that remained faced stiff competition from the non-Chinese mechanized laundries and dry cleaners with modern equipment and telephone pick-up services. The corporate laundry businesses tried to drive the Chinese laundrymen out of the market. In 1932, they lobbied to increase the hand laundry tax from $50 to $200 but failed.[11] By 1941 the number of hand laundries in Quebec had fallen to 291 from 358 in 1931.[12]

My grandfather and father would nevertheless work for three decades at Buanderie Wing On, the laundry they started together just before the Depression in the working-class east end of Montreal at 4484 Parthenais, near the corner of Mont-Royal. They chose the one-floor structure because the rent was cheap and the owner was willing to rent to Chinese occupants. The building appeared to have been a workshop or a dilapidated warehouse, measuring 50 feet deep by 20 feet wide with a rough wooden floor. The windowless interior was dark and dismal. The only daylight came from the two storefront windows.

Like most laundries, the layout was simple: it was divided into three parts. The front was used to do the ironing and the business transactions of receiving and dispensing the laundry, with the packaged clean laundry stacked on shelves. The men built a counter with vertical wood slats six feet high and only a three-foot opening at counter level, to discourage robbers; they erected the shelves to hold the packaged laundry, and the ironing tables along the windows. The middle part was the living quarters where the men cooked and ate on a makeshift table with crates for chairs—that same dining furniture was still there when I visited the laundry thirty years later. The beds were behind curtains for a bit of privacy. The rear was used to wash and dry the clothes. There was a potbelly stove, fired by coal, to dry the clothing hung on lines. This was the only source of heat during the winter. The heat wasn't that much since the area was shut off with heavy curtains to preserve the temperature and dry the clothes quicker. But the heat became suffocating during hot summer days.

Despite a lack of documents showing his travels in the 1920s and '30s, I was able to work out that my grandfather returned to the village twice more in that period. In 1924, at age forty, he voyaged back to China, and his fourth son, Gim Bong, was born the following year. Grandfather returned to Canada, alone, in 1925. The Chinese Exclusion Act was passed in 1923, and even if he wanted to, he was not allowed to bring his family to Canada. Grandfather went back again in 1931 for the final time to see his wife and family. His last child, a girl, Wan Wah, was born in 1933. He returned to Canada that year, as the Japanese were consolidating their occupation of Manchuria and preparing to invade all of China.

During the years of Chinese exclusion, my grandfather, like most men without wives and families, led a lonely life of drudgery—long hours of work for little financial gain. The *lo wah kiu* (old overseas Chinese) had a saying, "A dollar a day," which about summed up the kind of money they were making. They worked fifteen-hour days, six days a week. Sunday was the only day of rest, which many spent trying to find companionship, either through the family associations or through gambling in the hope of making a quick return on their hard-earned cash. My grandfather knew gambling was a fool's dream and decided to spend his day off in more productive pursuits.

* * *

My grandfather was known in the general community to be mild-mannered. But I remember the one time he got very angry with me. Shortly after I came to Canada, I was staying in his laundry visiting my brother. I walked into the dim back room, which was used to wash and dry the clothes. Ah Yeh was standing in a laundry tub giving himself a bath. He glared and yelled at me, "You dead boy! You have no manners, get out." He was an angry man and he had lost his dignity and felt humiliated having his grandson see him naked.

Ten years later, when he was dying, I visited him at the Louis Hypolite Lafontaine Hospital in the east end of Montreal. The lifelong anger he had shown to his family had withered away. He had no more fight in him and he was resigned to his fate.

It was long after my grandfather's death that I discovered I had harboured an illusion about him for most of my life. I had thought he was a simple peasant; it was a great revelation to learn that he was a scholar. In the early 1990s, when I was making the film *Moving the Mountain*, I spoke with some of the old-timers in Montreal's Chinatown to get a glimpse of Grandfather's life during the Exclusion Years. Hum Yue Teng, an elder in the Hum Family Association (Hum Quong Yea Tong), told me, "I remember your grandfather used to tell me a lot of old stories. Your grandfather and father worked together in the laundry. When there was free time, your grandfather taught students. He taught students to write poems. Now in Chinatown, there is an old man from the Lee Family Association, Do Wan Lee, he was a student of your grandfather. The student [Lee] sometimes wrote poems and sent them to me to read. Your grandfather's intellect was exceptionally high. Your father's intellect was not bad either."[13]

This is one of my grandfather's poems:

Today Is My 60th Birthday[14]

As in past years, I am lucky to be alive to celebrate my birthday.
    Time passes as the water flows.
I am grateful to have friends like Kwok and Lee,
    Our friendship mutually supports each other like Liu and Chen.[15]
Regretfully, I could not be successful in my own country.
    Ashamed for your friendship, I feel unworthy.
I respect your spirit and philosophy,
    I honour everything you've taught me.
We come together to hope for the prosperity of our country.

           —Der Tan Suey, translated by Dong Qing Chen

Other people in Chinatown told me that my grandfather had a reputation of being a well-educated gentleman who took on the responsibility of teaching others. Some of the more ambitious men sat in on the classes that my grandfather taught at the Chinese Young Men's Christian Institution (YMCI, to distinguish it from the YMCA), focussing mainly on reading the Chinese classics and writing.

I can understand that Grandfather lived a life full of frustrations, which nurtured anger within him. As an educated man full of pride, he saw his life slipping away, year after year, without wife and family, doing menial work washing other people's dirty laundry and being treated as a non-person, without citizenship rights, by the Canadian government and society in general.

When faced with such hate, why did he not pack up years ago and go back to the village? This is a question that can be asked of all the other Gold Mountain men. The only answer I can think of is that Canada had become their home and source of economic livelihood, and they defied anyone to push them out.

When Canada repealed the Chinese Exclusion Act in 1947 and allowed the Chinese living here to become citizens, Grandfather took the opportunity to bring his youngest son and two grandsons to join him in the laundry. With the Liberation of China in 1949, he had to re-evaluate his life in Canada. He had planned to retire in China with his wife, so he was ambivalent about bringing her to a country that he still considered so unforgiving. However, going back to China now was out of the question. Yue Ngau managed to go to Hong Kong, and he supported her with regular remittances, so he didn't see an urgent need to uproot her. He was now over sixty-five. He had considered himself a *Gim Shan Haak*—Gold Mountain Guest. It was a lifelong stay; but after forty years he still felt insecure in Canada. And he had an overriding desire to be with his wife.

In 1962, at the age of 78, my Ah Yeh decided he had worked long enough. He wanted to give the laundry to my brother, Ging Tung, and his wife (my

Ah Yeh with his three sons (to his left, right and behind) pose in front of Wing On in 1957. I am the one looking menacing with the toy pistol and cowboy hat standing in front of Grandfather. (Dere Family Collection)

father had left to start his own laundry), but they insisted on paying him or at least giving him monthly payments in return. Grandfather finally agreed on payment in the form of a one-way airplane ticket to Hong Kong to satisfy his longing to be with his wife.

My third sister, Pui Yung, told me the story that shortly before she came to Canada in August 1964, she went to see Grandmother—our *Ah Ngeen*[16]— in Hong Kong to say goodbye. Ah Ngeen was so excited, because she had just received a letter saying that Ah Yeh was coming home after thirty years of separation. She started washing the floors and cleaning the home in great anticipation. Through the autumn of 1964, both Ah Ngeen and Ah Yeh were

Ah Yeh and his great grandson, Peter, pause for a photo
at Wing On Laundry in 1960. (Dere Family Collection)

preparing for their happy reunion. They were both as excited as newlyweds. He wanted to spend the remaining years of his life with his wife, whom he had not seen for three decades. It was a chilly October day when my father received news from relatives in Hong Kong that his stepmother had passed away at age seventy-five. Grief-stricken, he didn't know how to tell his father, whose heart was full of joy, expecting the fulfillment of his life-long dream to be with his wife again. My sister-in-law took on the sad task and waited until after supper to inform him. Upon hearing the news, Ah Yeh collapsed and had to be carried to his bed. His heart was broken. He'd lost all hope. After a life-time of hardship, his remaining years had become even harder. He entered into an illness from which he never recovered. He died from complications due to diabetes, which had been left untreated because he could not afford medical care. Tan Suey Der finally re-united with his wife, Yue Ngau, in death on August 4, 1966, at the age of eighty-one.

Chapter 2

My Father, Hing Dere

Time passes by, year after year
Living in this foreign land. Nothing changes.
As the world is turned upside down, I can only sigh.
My life is so unsatisfied.
The scenery remains the same, as I grow old.
I have no talent for money, as I remain poor.
If heaven grants my wish
I will ride the wind blown sail to distant shores.
—Hing Dere, "Feelings of a Guest"[17]
    (translated by Dong Qing Chen)

Once in Montreal, my father constantly thought about having his wife and family with him. "You would make my life easier and take away my loneliness," he wrote. Mother knew the hard work that he had to perform. He added, "I am afraid that life would be too hard for you here. There is little money, maybe it is best that you stay home."

The little I know about the childhood of my father, Hing Dere, *zi* name Chew Yip, is what my mother told me. He was born in 1903 in Fong Dang village, Toishan. His mother died when he was two. His father raised

Married again

him until he was five, then my grandfather remarried and, a year later, left the village for Gold Mountain. This event would forever uproot the family and entwine Toishan wistfulness with the severe realities of Canada.

Father was still a teenager when, in 1921, he received a letter from Ah Yeh asking him to come to Montreal. Perhaps anticipating the exclusion law, my grandfather wanted to bring my father to Canada before it was too late. My father couldn't see a future in the village, where he attended school and did various odd jobs tending the fields. The family ate whatever was grown and survived on the remittance that Ah Yeh regularly sent home. Father's older brother had just left to study in Japan, and he was now the oldest male left to look after the household. Nevertheless, Ah Yeh decided that my father could better serve the family by working in Canada.

In April 1921, Father bid a tearful farewell to his sister and stepmother and headed off to Hong Kong via Guangzhou. In Hong Kong, he stayed with a trusted village cousin who gave him the money that his father had forwarded; it was needed for the sea voyage and the entry fee into Canada. The cousin had already purchased the $50 steerage class ticket on the Canadian Pacific ship *Empress of Russia*,[18] set to sail at the end of April.

On May 16, 1921, after three weeks at sea, Father arrived in Vancouver. The Vancouver Detention Centre[19] was his first stop; he was locked up there for three weeks, and finally released on June 9. Despite showing the immigration

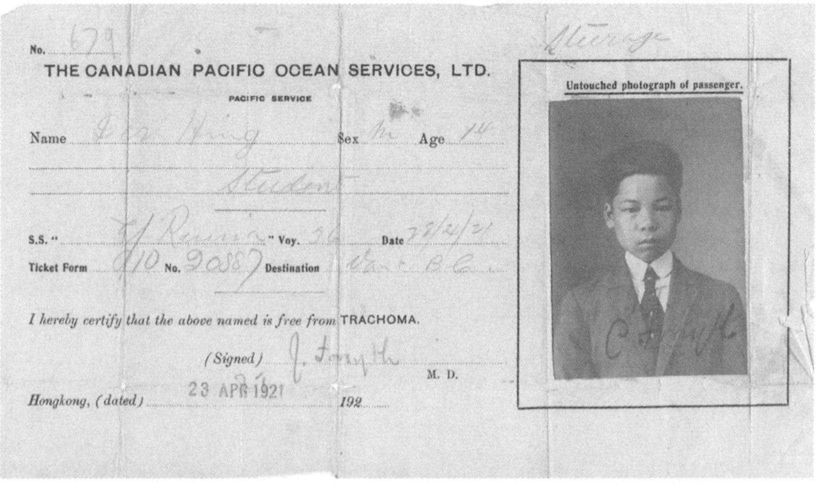
No. 679

THE CANADIAN PACIFIC OCEAN SERVICES, LTD.

PACIFIC SERVICE

Steerage

Untouched photograph of passenger.

Name .... Sex M Age 14

Student

S.S. " .... " Voy. 36 Date 28/4/21

Ticket Form .... No. 90587 Destination ....

I hereby certify that the above named is free from TRACHOMA.

(Signed) .... M. D.

Hongkong, (dated) 23 APR 1921 *192*...

This is my father's tattered steerage class ticket which he kept among his documents. (Dere Family Collection)

officer the notarized letter from his father attesting that he was a student, he was ordered to pay the $500 head tax. Grandfather was so smart that he had anticipated this.

Once released, Father made his way to Chinatown to look for Grandfather's friend, who would help him on the next leg of his journey. The friend bought him a ticket on the CP transcontinental train to Montreal and four days later, my grandfather met him at Windsor Station. This was the start of my father's bittersweet life in Canada.

Just two years after Father's arrival, the Canadian government brought in the Chinese Exclusion Act, banning Chinese immigration to Canada. The head tax had been punishing, but it was only money. By preventing families from joining the Gold Mountain men, the Canadian government hit at the heart of the Chinese raison d'être—the family.

Chinese in Canada campaigned to stop the immigration bill from being passed into law. On April 29, 1923, over one thousand Chinese from across the country attended a rally in Toronto's Victoria Hall.[20] Unions, such as the Chinese Shingle Workers Federation and the Chinese Produce Sellers Group, spoke up against the legislation.[21]

This is my father's head tax certificate, which attests to his payment of $500.
(Dere Family Collection)

But all attempts at protest failed. The Fourth Chinese Immigration Act (also known, more aptly, as the Exclusion Act) was passed and came into effect July 1, 1923, which the Chinese dubbed "Humiliation Day." The Chinese in Canada had been deprived of civil rights and were politically powerless. The act prohibited all Chinese, including family members of those already here, from immigrating to Canada.

And so it was that soon after my father arrived in Canada, the Chinese in this country entered into a dark and somber period. The community was frozen in time, with no opportunity for natural growth. It began to stagnate and die. The Chinese community became a "married bachelor" society where the ratio of males to females was eight to one in 1941.

The "married bachelors" revealed little to their children and families. The Chinese, excluded and unacceptable to white society across Canada, lived under a repressive atmosphere. Within a year of the passing of the Exclusion Act, all Chinese, even those born here, had to register with the Department of Immigration and Colonization. Activities of the Chinese going in and out of Canada were closely monitored and documented.

With all this going on, there was still a living to be made. For three ardu-

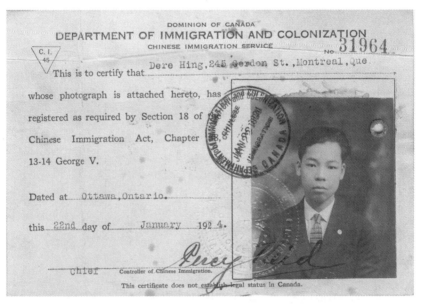

My father's "passbook." This was akin to the passbook in apartheid South Africa.
Failure to produce this paper could result in immediate deportation.
(Dere Family Collection)

ous years after my father's arrival, he and Grandfather lived and worked in the laundry with Wong Sing. Father would go to Sunday school at the Chalmers Church on Church Street, present day Verdun. It was not to hear about Jesus but to learn English.

"They had good English teachers with big classes of thirty to forty Chinese," Eileen Chang (Hum), one of the earliest Chinese women to be born in Montreal, recalled when I interviewed her in 1992. "Your father was one of the younger ones. The teachers really liked teaching the Chinese because of the Christmas parties. The Chinese students made all the food, because there were people who worked in the restaurants, so they prepared all the turkey, the trimmings, the cakes, pies and ice cream. They would have singsongs, and then games. They really would have a good time."

Grandfather was a strict man. He taught my father the Chinese classics and all the practical aspects of operating a laundry, including keeping the books with an abacus. My father was a stoic man and it seems he absorbed everything that his father taught him. He was responsible for writing the laundry tickets. Each laundry ticket was created on a four-by-six-inch piece of brown paper cut from the scroll of paper used to wrap the clean laundry. On each half of the pieces of paper, my father used a brush to write a Chinese character taken from the classical "Eighty Character Poem" as well as a number from one to one hundred. As the customer brought in the dirty laundry, the ticket would be torn in half. One half went to the customer and the other half was stuffed into the laundry, which was tied together by the sleeves of a shirt or the corners of the sheets.

Some customers were nice and cordial but others were brusque and condescending. The Chinese laundrymen learned how to accommodate them all. Nevertheless, there were occasions when BBs were shot through the window or garbage was smeared on the door. The laundrymen never bothered calling the police because they knew nothing would be done and they feared the police would start hassling them. They learned to minimize any dealings with authority as they feared and distrusted any government agencies.

Towards the end of 1924, my father turned twenty-one and his father told him it was time to go home to get married, despite the fact that Father would not be able to bring his bride to Canada. Grandfather hadn't been home in twelve years so he decided to accompany his son. He had saved enough money for the journey and he prepared my father to return to the village to marry a girl already chosen by the matchmaker. Father was obedient and carried out his father's wishes without question. The two men crossed Canada by train and took the ship to Hong Kong to make their way back to Fong Dang. My father married my mother in 1925. Dong Sing Yee was nineteen and she came from the same village as her mother-in-law, my grandmother.

Grandfather returned to Canada shortly after the birth of his fourth son in 1925. After a year and a half in China, my father also returned to Canada, disembarking in Vancouver on May 17, 1926. Oddly, there were no records of his CI 9 but I know the date of his return because it was stamped on the back of his head tax certificate. After the marriage, my mother wanted to come to Canada with my father. My father had to explain that Canada was not allowing any more Chinese to enter,[22] but he reassured her, "I will send you money and I will come back to see you, every time I save enough." This sentiment summed up the purpose of his life.

When Father got back to Montreal, my grandfather had already decided that they would start their own laundry. While his son was away, Ah Yeh had scouted various areas of town that he thought needed a laundry. It had to be a low rent district; he roamed through the east end of Montreal, a predomin-

Hing Dere returns to the village to marry Dong Sing Yee in 1925.
Hing is the man standing on the left. The other man is his brother, Chew Lip.
Dong Sing is seated on the right in white. (Dere Family Collection)

ately French working-class area where there were few laundries. He settled on a rundown, open space on rue Parthenais.

Father never thought about working outside the laundry. He knew that in a time of economic depression, there were no jobs for a "Chinaman." It would be useless to compete with the *lo fawn*[23] (white people) for any kind of work. Many sectors were legally closed to the Chinese, such as professions like law or medicine, even if one was lucky enough to get an education.[24] Economic exclusion went hand in hand with social exclusion. Toiling as a laundryman with his father was really the only choice for my father. They were independent workers, self-employed, resourceful and self-reliant. The laundryman worked, ate, or, if not, went hungry along with his family back in China.[25]

Life in the laundry was isolating, tedious and mind numbing.[26] Grandfather and Father only spoke a smattering of English and French, whatever was needed to receive and dispense the laundry. They were deaf and mute when it came to communicating with the outside world. There was very little social life due to the long hours and there were no other Chinese in the area. In Paul Chan Pang Siu's *The Chinese Laundryman – A Study of Social Isolation*, one nameless laundryman describes his life:

> "People think I am a happy person. I am not. I worry very much. First, I don't like this kind of life. It is not a human life. To be a laundryman is to be just a slave. I work because I have to. If I ever stop work, those at home must stop eating. … I am not an old man yet, but I feel old. How can a man feel good when he is forced into an occupation he doesn't like? But I get used to it. After you are at it for so many years, you have no more feeling but to stay on with it. You can't get rich but you don't have to worry about money as long as you can work."[27]

Father and son had only half a day off every week. They worked sixteen hours a day from Monday through Saturday, staying open on Sunday mornings because customers complained that they wanted to pick up their laundry on the way home from church. On Sunday afternoon, the two men locked up shop and took the Number Seven streetcar along Mont Royal and transferred to the Number Fifty-Five down St. Laurent, towards the river, to Chinatown.

The gathering place was the Young Men's Christian Institution (YMCI) at 189 Dorchester West, near St. Urbain. I got some details about the YMCI through conversations with James Wing (whose original Chinese name was

Ng Wing Wah), an old friend of my father who was also a student in the classes
my grandfather held there. Today, it is the site of Complexe Desjardins. The
YMCI was inaugurated on October 4, 1911, by a group of Chinese Christians
who wanted an organization in which to socialize with other Chinese. Because
it was not just a religious society, many lonely Chinese men were attracted to
its activities and it became a Sunday refuge from the grind of working in the
laundries or restaurants. It also provided a bed and shelter to those who were
down on their luck and needed a place to stay temporarily.

The "married bachelors" talked about the latest gossip and rumours, discussed the situation in China and in Canada, and read the Chinese papers. In
addition to conducting Chinese classes each week for those willing to learn,
my grandfather and my father wrote and read letters for those who were illit-
erate, so that everyone could communicate with their families back home.
Others played cards, dominoes and mah jong. The men would shop at the
Chinese grocers for the week's supplies. In the evening, before they left the
YMCI, they would cook and share a meal. For those who worked alone, this
was the only meal of the week they ate with companions. Men who suffered
the same hardships understood each other and enjoyed each other's company.
My father and grandfather looked forward to these weekly social activities.

The YMCI at 189 Dorchester in 1936. To show that it was a vibrant community,
the YMCI gathered all the children they could find to pose at its front door.
(Dere Family Collection)

Eileen Chang Hum's father Hum Hue (Thomas Hum)[28] became known as the "social worker" of Chinatown. He was a grocery store owner and a Christian who helped found the YMCI with other young Christians from Chinatown. I met Eileen when I first came to Canada. The Hum family was one of the first families that my father brought my mother and me to visit. Her father was very close to my father and grandfather through their activities in the YMCI. Eileen told me some stories of her father visiting the Chinese laundries around Montreal in the '20s and '30s.

Her father used to make a lot of deliveries, she said, and he would visit the laundries and deliver things to people who were unable to go out freely to do their shopping. "He used a horse and wagon, and he loaded his wagon with dry goods and vegetables, to go from door to door, laundry to laundry to sell these goods," she told me. "As he goes in, he talks to them and he finds that some of these people in the laundries are very lonely and sometimes they are sick and they don't even know it. He would ask them to go see the doctor and most of the time they refuse to go because they don't want to leave their work. So sometimes when it was so bad that he just had to take them and they didn't use taxis, he would bring them to the hospital with his horse and wagon. At that time the hospital was in Chinatown. That's how he did his social work, and that's how he knew people were sick, and when they needed anything, he was always ready there to help them."[29]

In discussing the life of Chinese in North America at this time, John Kuo Wei Tchen, director of the Asia Pacific American Studies Program at NYU and co-founder of the Museum of Chinese in America, has written:

> The Chinese, restricted from free immigration, gaining citizenship, and having families, created hand laundries. In turn, this institution protected—but also isolated [them]. ... Those Chinese workers who chose to stay resisted anti-Chinese racism by clawing out some turf for hand laundries, and this dynamic created the socially isolated sojourner attitude.[30]

My father was never a "sojourner"[31]—a controversial term—in the sense that has been used to describe someone who came to Canada to make money with the intention of returning to China. But, like most of the sojourners, he worked and lived for the day when he had saved enough money for a trip back to China. He may have yearned for an ideal life back in the village, but his reality was in Canada and in the end he never seriously desired to move back to China, even in old age. He chose to live in Canada and devoted his whole adult life to this country, but the Chinese Exclusion Act imposed the perception of sojourner on the Chinese. This thinking was pervasive, and it was maintained by the larger society to perpetuate the belief that Chinese immigrants did not belong here.

In 1928, Father told my grandfather that he wanted to return to the village. My mother told me his feelings were: "It is not right that my wife is alone without a child. I must go back to her." In 1930, my parents' first daughter, Pui King, was born. Father returned to Canada on April 23, 1930. He journeyed back to China three years later. During this two-year stay, my parents were quite productive. My number two sister, King Sin, was born in 1934. Shortly after Father returned to Canada in 1935, my mother had twins, number three sister, Pui Yung, and brother Ging Tung. At thirty, my mother was left in the village with four young children to rear.

My father never told me about this period in his life. He preferred to tell me things that were joyful. I think in his mind it would be too sad, painful and humiliating to talk to your son about such a lonely time in your life. The little I know is from my mother—through the letters she received from him.

"He said ironing clothes all day long was hard," she told me. "He had to collect clothes in winter like a beggar, walking miles and miles to pick up a bundle of dirty laundry and walk back the same distance to deliver the clean packages and collected only 50 cents. He had to climb the outside winding staircases covered with snow. He had to climb upstairs no matter how high the building was and he had to carry the bag all the time no matter how heavy.

"The *lo fawn* devil kids followed and taunted him and in winter they would throw snowballs at him, sometimes with rocks inside. If he put the bag down, they would take the bag away. If they took the bag, he would not have the money to compensate. He even had to crawl under the beds to collect the dirty, smelly clothes. Making the little money was not easy."

Towards 1940, Father received a letter from Mother that the Japanese were advancing towards the Toishan area and many villagers had fled. It was not possible to send letters and, more importantly, money back to China. My father and grandfather were very concerned for those back home.

The following is one of the poems my father wrote in the 1940s, during China's resistance war against the Japanese invasion. After a long day of washing and ironing, he would sometimes try to relax by writing poetry in the classical style but with a contemporary theme. (He must have had a genteel spirit; on his right pinky he grew a scholar's nail. Growing all his nails would be impractical; he would not have been able to work.)

Overseas for so many years.
So lonely and sad.
I can do nothing in this foreign land.
I look back to the village—such turmoil.
Can't go back.
No land, nothing left. No rights, only sorrow.
When will peace come?
On that day I will be on the next passage home.

—Hing Dere, translated by Dong Qing Chen

I believe it was around this time, in the 1940s, that my father's appendix burst. Eileen recalled that her father "took him out from the laundry and brought him to the hospital." My mother told me that Father had an operation for his appendix but they botched the procedure by not giving him enough anesthetic and when he started waking up they had to quickly close him up.

When World War II ended with victory being declared over Germany and then Japan, there was an air of optimism in the Chinese community. The returning Chinese Canadian war veterans were agitating for citizenship rights and the repeal of the Chinese Exclusion Act. My father and grandfather joined this campaign. They thought this was their chance to gain their rights in this country, including the ability to bring their families to Canada.

In hindsight, events moved quickly, but I am sure my father did not think change could come fast enough.

The Exclusion Act was repealed in May 1947. In August of that year, Father embarked on his last trip to China. This time he went through the United States, visiting friends and village cousins in New York, Los Angeles and San Francisco. He left San Francisco for Hong Kong on September 6, 1947. I was born during this visit. Father stayed until I was ten months old and he arrived back in Canada on July 6, 1949.

Father got his Canadian citizenship the next year, on May 21, 1950. Immediately, he set his plan in motion to bring his family to Canada. Later that year his first son, Ging Tung, arrived in Montreal. Fourteen at the time, my brother

This photo of the Dere family was taken in 1947, shortly after
my father's arrival back in the village. (Dere Family Collection)

was not as lucky as I would be and did not get much of a formal education; he
started working in Grandfather's laundry right away. He did not have much
time to go to school. Although he attended Rosemont High School for a year,
with the workload at the laundry, he was just too tired to study at the end of
the day.

The Dere family gathers for another picture in China, this time in 1949, shortly
before my father's return to Canada. My father is holding me. My number one sister,
Pui King, is holding her daughter. (Dere Family Collection)

Through his work in Chinatown, Father became a founding member of the
Montreal branch of the Chiu Lun Gong Sol in 1953. Hum Yue Teng, president
of the Hum Association and elder in the Gong Sol, explained to me in an interview in 1992 that this was a family association joining together four historical
clans: Hum, Tam, Hui and Dere.

"Legend tells us that 2,600 years ago [the Warring States Period], mem-
bers of the four clans fled south from war and starvation in Northern China to
Guangdong," he said. "They banded together and were protected by the Yuen
clan. The written names of the original four clans start with the radical 'Yan.'
The Yuen clan joined the four families because its name sounded like 'Yan.'
Today the five family names are united in the Chiu Lun Gong Sol."

The Chiu Lun Gong Sol still exists as an international fraternity of the
five clans. My father was the Chinese secretary and later the chairman of the
Montreal branch.

After my brother came, Father started preparing applications for my
mother and me to come to Canada. Father wanted to buy his own laundry
business before my mother and I arrived, and through the family association
in Chinatown, he learned about a laundry owner in Verdun who wanted to sell

the business he had started in 1951 and move back to Hong Kong. Father knew there were only three laundries in Verdun, one at the east end, one at the west end, and this one, in the centre of Verdun—Harry's Laundry at 526 Fourth Avenue.

The two men negotiated a fair price. The going price for a laundry was $1,000 to $2,000 depending on the how good the business was. Father was a frugal man; he sent money back home and saved whatever was left. He had some money to start the laundry and borrowed the rest from the Chiu Lun Gong Sol credit union (*woi*[32]). The *woi* allowed members of the family association to borrow money at low interest rates.

In 1955, my father took ownership of Harry's Laundry. He stood at the door and surveyed the premises to see what he needed to do. The previous owner had already constructed the partitions, shelves and the ironing tables so he didn't need to do any renovations. There was only a cot in the sleeping area, so he bought a double bed in preparation for the arrival of his wife and youngest son. He left Ging Tung working in Grandfather's laundry, because at the beginning, he didn't have money to pay and feed an extra person.

Hing Dere lived his adult life in this country. Canada and the brutal racial oppression he faced, his father faced, and his family faced, shaped him. He was self-reliant, a stoic man, a Confucian man who accepted life as it came. He was mild and sometimes timid when it came to dealing with the larger hostile society. But he endured and he derived personal strength from keeping true to himself and his life's mission—to care for the wellbeing of his family, which he accomplished well. In this, he was triumphant. He helped others and made a difference whenever he could. He left me a lasting value and legacy: "Whatever you do in life, make a contribution."

My father would have to wait until 1956, when he was fifty-three, to finally be reunited with his wife, my mother Dong Sing, who by then was fifty. They had lost their youthful years to the Chinese Exclusion Act.

Chapter 3

The Turbulent Exclusion Years (1923–47)

"I fancy we do not want them here. ... make it absolutely clear that Chinese women cannot come in under any circumstances."
—John Baxter, MP, St. John-Albert, NB, second reading of Chinese Exclusion Act, April 30, 1923

Chinese people in Canada commemorated every July 1 as Humiliation Day. On that day, they would gather across the country to denounce the Exclusion Act and call for its repeal. Some white church groups and progressive labour unions influenced by the Co-operative Commonwealth Federation or the Communist Party sometimes joined the protests.

The two and a half decades after the Canadian government banned Chinese immigration were extremely difficult for thousands of Chinese people, including my family, both because of Canada's treatment of the Chinese and because of international events.

In Canada, the government achieved its desired sinister effect with the passage of the Chinese Exclusion Act in 1923. Although the Chinese community protested against the law before it was passed and gathered every

July 1 to mark Humiliation Day for the twenty-four years the law was in effect, the population of Chinese in Canada during those years tells the real story. According to the Canadian census, the Chinese population dropped by 30 per cent between 1931 and 1951, from 46,519 to 32,528. The majority of the Chinese who left Canada went back to China. During that time, only forty-seven Chinese[33] were allowed into Canada under special categories, such as diplomats.

During this period the Chinese in Montreal and across Canada were extremely anxious about political developments in Asia. It was a time of tremendous turbulence, upheaval and division. By 1931 the threat of a Japanese invasion of China had turned into the reality of the Japanese occupying Manchuria in northeast China and preparing to invade the entire country.

There was a great political divide in China, which two organizations in Canada reflected: the Kuomintang, or KMT (Nationalists), and the Zhigongtang, or ZGT (Chinese Freemasons). In Montreal, while my father and grandfather most often sought out the company of other Chinese men in Chinatown at the Young Men's Christian Institution and the Montreal headquarters of the Hum Association, there were other mutual support organizations at hand, some with strong political associations, most notably the Chinese National-

The Hum Gong Yue Tang (Hum Family Association) meets for its Eastern Canada Conference, March 3, 1940. Hing Dere is standing sixth from the left in the front row. (Dere Family Collection)

ist League (KMT), which had opened its doors in 1918 at 139 Clark, and the Chinese Freemasons (Hong Men) at 78 La Gauchetière. Other organizations in Montreal at the time included various other family associations and the Chinese Benevolent Society, which had started in 1915 at 6 La Gauchetière.

The KMT and its newspaper, the *Shing Wah Daily News*, had a strong influence on the Chinese community in Canada. My father and grandfather were lifelong supporters of the KMT due to their respect for Dr. Sun Yat-sen, who had founded the party in 1912 to unite the nationalist forces and establish a republican government in China. That support was reciprocated: before Canada introduced the Chinese Exclusion Act, Chinese in Canada appealed to the Chinese government to make representation to Canada, which led Sun Yat-sen and his flamboyant Canadian bodyguard, Morris "Two-Gun" Cohen, to cable the Canadian government asking for a halt to the proceedings.[34] (To no avail, of course.)

In the 1920s, the KMT had sought the political and material support of the Soviet Union and the Comintern, or Communist International, an organization that united the world's communist and workers parties. The Comintern ordered the Chinese Communists to join the KMT and form a united front to tackle the reconstruction of China. After the death of Dr. Sun in 1925, Generalissimo Chiang Kai-shek took control of the KMT and began a purge of Communists in China, which led to a mass slaughter in Shanghai in April 1927. Ten thousand communists were killed throughout China within twenty days. This brought an end to the first united front and sparked the Chinese Civil War, which would last the next twenty years.

The history of the Zhigongtang (Hong Men) is more convoluted. It was founded as a secret society in Guangdong province in 1674 to overthrow the Manchu Qing Dynasty. In Canada, a branch was formed in 1862, during the Gold Rush, in Barkerville, BC. Its Canadian members were workers, gold miners and small merchants.

As historian Kin-ping Kam said proudly at the Twenty-third Assembly of the Chinese Freemasons in Canada, held in Toronto in September 1985: "It was neither the Kuomintang nor the Communist party that had overthrown the Qing Dynasty [in 1911–12] and built the Republic of China." Instead, "opposition against the Qing Dynasty ... fell on the shoulders of brothers of Hong Men overseas. This spectacular achievement shines as brightly as the sun and moon, and deserves the admiration and respect of thousands of generations to come."[35]

During the time of Sun Yat-sen, the Hong Men in Canada had a social and political agenda: to raise funds across Canada for the nationalist cause in China. They became bitter rivals with the Kuomintang after Dr. Sun's death in 1925 and Chiang Kai-shek's ascendance to the KMT leadership.

That rivalry endured throughout the 1930s and '40s. The Hong Men were sympathetic to the Chinese Communists, whereas the KMT members in Canada represented Chiang Kai-shek.

In the Montreal community, the Zhigongtang was well respected as a social welfare organization; its activities included organizing busloads of people to go to Mount Royal Cemetery to honour the ancestors for the Qing Ming festival, and it was active in establishing the original Montreal Chinese Hospital founded in 1920 in a former synagogue at 112 La Gauchetière in Chinatown.

The Hong Men, though, had an image problem in North America. Due to their origins as a secret society, authorities in the US and Canada associated them with Triad criminal gangs. The Montreal media sensationalized disputes between the ZGT and the KMT—including one physical altercation in 1933—calling them the "Tong Wars."

* * *

During the Depression, there wasn't much help from the provincial government for the Chinese in Montreal. It was the clan associations, the YMCI, the Benevolent Society, the Hong Men, the Chinese Catholic and Presbyterian missions and other organizations that came together to provide some form of relief to those who needed it.

The overseas family or clan associations were organized for mutual support following the principles of Confucian social formations. In Montreal, the major family associations were for the Hum, Lee, Wong and Chin clans. The Dere clan was not numerous enough to form its own organization, so it associated with the Hum Family Association and used its premises on La Gauchetière Street. The family associations were led by the merchants, who had the financial resources to back their activities, making loans for business ventures, and transferring funds to China. They also performed other functions, such as organizing the Qing Ming festival—and even sending bodies from Montreal for shipment back to the village for burial.[36] The merchants, although they only made up 5 per cent of the Chinese population across Canada,[37] were economic leaders of the community. But even they had little or no political clout when fighting unvarnished racism and human rights violations. This is the outcome of state-sanctioned repression.

During the Depression, the unemployment rate in the general population of Canada was 30 per cent. In Vancouver, 40 per cent of the Chinese were unemployed.[38] But it was not clear what percentage of the unemployed across Canada were Chinese, since they did not normally count in the general statistics. What was clear was that Chinese Canadians did not receive the same relief that was given to the white population.[39]

In Vancouver, the provincial government gave the Chinese Anglican Mission 16¢ a day, per person, to set up a soup kitchen in Chinatown. Many Chinese got sick from the poor quality food, which the Communist paper BC Workers News claimed was only worth 3¢ per meal.[40] In areas catering to whites, those who needed relief received meal tickets worth 15¢ to 25¢. Similarly, in Alberta, relief payments of $1.12 per week were given to the Chinese, less than half of what was given to others.[41]

On May Day, 1935, the Chinese Workers' Protective Association and the Unemployed Chinese Association, with the support of the Provincial Workers

This Dere family photo, circa 1937, shows the Gold Mountain "widows" and children left in the village. My mother is seated on the left with my three sisters at the left and in front. My grandmother, seated in the centre, is holding my brother in her arms. (Dere Family Collection)

Council, demonstrated in Vancouver, demanding that Chinese Canadians receive relief equal to that of jobless whites.[42] The Chinese Workers' Protective Association was founded in 1923 to fight for jobs and the rights of Chinese workers, and existed until the mid-1950s. It had some fraternal affiliation with the Communist Party of Canada.[43]

During the decade of the Depression, the Chinese population in Canada, without any fresh inflow of immigration, decreased by 26 per cent. Some decided to go back to China believing things couldn't be worse back in the village. In Vancouver, the local government urged destitute Chinese to leave. Paying for their passage was cheaper than giving relief to people who were becoming increasingly militant. For a promise to never come back to Canada, four hundred Vancouver Chinese decided to return to China with a government subsidy in 1935.[44]

The laundrymen in Montreal, despite their self-reliant form of economic livelihood, were also seriously affected by the global capitalist crisis. With the slump in business, my father and grandfather decided to take turns going to China, thinking it would be easier to maintain a one-man laundry operation with one less mouth to feed. Grandfather went back in 1931 and when he returned, Father left in 1933. When he came back to Canada in May 1935, he saw things were not that much better.

* * *

In the late 1930s, international events took centre stage. Japan waged an all-out military invasion of China in 1937. Canada entered World War II in September 1939 when it declared war on Germany; two years later, after Japan attacked Pearl Harbor, Canada declared war on Japan.

During the war years, the Montreal Chinese formed their own united front against Japan—the Chinese Patriotic League[45]—which included the KMT, ZGT, the YMCI and other organizations. Altogether, the league in Montreal raised over $400,000.[46] Across Canada, the Chinese bought $10 million in Canadian Victory Bonds to support Canada's war effort.[47]

My father and grandfather got involved in fundraising as the Japanese were advancing towards our home county in China. Their concern led them to become active in the patriotic campaign to raise funds for the anti-Japanese war effort. My father had brought news to Montreal of the impending Japanese onslaught when he got back from his visit to China in 1935. He knew that if the Japanese were not stopped in Manchuria, they would eventually reach our home province of Guangdong.

In 1937, Japan began its wholesale invasion of China in an undeclared war, after consolidating its occupation of Manchuria. People were eager for news from home. In Montreal, a large bulletin board was erected at the corner of La Gauchetière and Clark where Chinese articles about the war were posted daily. The *Montreal Gazette* reported that, during the same year, $10,000 was raised in the Chinese community for Red Cross work in the war-torn areas of China.[48] This is one of the few times that an article from the mainstream press did not deal with Tong wars, gambling, prostitution or other illicit activities in Chinatown.

(The more frequent type of sensationalized news included the press reporting that on a cold Saturday night in January 1934[49] the Montreal police, in an early incarnation of racial profiling, raided every single Chinese laundry, restaurant, club and some private homes in the city. Out of the hundreds of locations searched, only seven Chinese were arrested for possession of weapons and four for possession of opium. This was typical of the dramatic French and English press coverage, which often labelled Chinese as "inscrutable celestials."[50])

Hing Dere, standing behind the man seated at the far right, takes part in a fundraising campaign to support the war effort against Japan on July 7, 1942.
This is part of the photo he hung in Wing On Laundry and preserved throughout the years. (Dere Family Collection)

In the laundry, Father eventually hung a two-foot-wide group photo taken in 1942 after a fundraising procession through downtown Montreal. In the photo, he proudly stood behind the seated dignitaries—the leaders of the Chinese community as well as some white civic officials.

Newsreel footage of that procession showed a group of a dozen young Chinese women holding a large, spread-out KMT flag to collect donations. Father felt it was his patriotic duty to support the KMT and the Republic of China to fight against the Japanese invaders. Without the hindsight of history, he did not understand that the KMT under Chiang Kai-shek was far different from the KMT under Sun Yat-sen—the new leader devoted most of his energy to fighting the Chinese Communists instead of the Japanese.

Many Chinese Canadians volunteered to go to war. At first, the government of William Lyon Mackenzie King did not conscript Chinese or Japanese for two reasons: first, racial intolerance was not amenable to camaraderie with the white soldiers; and second, as historian Patricia Roy has written, with Chinese and Japanese serving in the war effort, "Canada would concede them a claim for equality and for all privileges of citizenship including the franchise."[51]

By 1943, however, when there was a need for additional manpower, Canada decided to conscript the Chinese, almost all of whom were born in this country. For one thing, many whites were complaining that the Chinese were not being conscripted.

Ken Lee, a Chinese Canadian war veteran I spoke to in 1992, explained events this way: "We were conscripted and we said, 'Why should we fight for this country when we have no rights?' So they said: if we would fight for this country, they would right all these wrongs."[52] Ken actually enlisted in the air force in 1941 because he wanted to fight Japan.

From 1923 onward, Chinese in Canada continued to agitate against unjust Canadian immigration policy, most notably by gathering across the country each year to commemorate July 1 as Humiliation Day. These were twenty-four years of struggle and resistance to systemic and institutional racism.

The struggle had also found support back in China.

"China feels that Canada has inflicted an injury on her prestige in the circumstance and spirit of the immigration act," Louis K. Lee, former editor of the *China Critic* an English-language newspaper in Shanghai, wrote in August 1943 in a contribution to the *Montreal Gazette*.[53] He called the official name, the Chinese Immigration Act, "a misnomer. It is really an act of exclusion rather than immigration."

Lee pointed out that, in the time of war, China and Canada were allies in the fight against German fascism and Japanese militarism. "The exclusion discriminates in a manner that is offensive to the racial and national dignity of the group excluded," especially so "when the exclusion is based on the principle of 'ineligibility to citizenship,' which conveys the obnoxious implication that the people are biologically inferior."

Lee continued,

> Since 1923 not a single Chinese laborer has been admitted to Canada. … as a nation of nearly five thousand years civilization (China) does resent the implication of inferiority! It is absolutely irreconcilable with her revolutionary principle of freedom and equality which was enunciated by Dr. Sun Yat-sen … and for which the present war against Japan is fought. Now Canada and China are among the United Nations fighting hand in hand for the common cause. It goes without saying that if such laws as exclusion of Chinese were allowed to continue that would constitute a constant source of friction between China and Canada and also reduce China's confidence in Canadian sense of justice as well as her hope of a better world after the war.

The *China Critic*[54] was published in Shanghai from 1928 to 1940, and also in 1945, with a weekly circulation of eight thousand. It supported the United Front of the Communist Party and the Kuomintang against Japanese aggression.[55] (Mao Zedong, who would become the founding father of the People's Republic of China, had originally developed the idea of the United Front back in the 1920s.[56])

* * *

The end of World War II was the beginning of the end for Chinese exclusion in Canada. Chinese Canadians who served in the armed forces demanded equal rights upon their return.

George Mar, a Chinese Canadian war vet who saw service in Asia, told me, "We figured we'd paid our dues to be full citizens. It's pretty hard to deny you full citizenship after the guys have gone to war for you. … We had offered our lives for our country and it's pretty hard for the country to deny you full citizenship and the rights everybody else has."[57]

Canadian opinion towards China, and by extension to the Chinese here, was becoming more favourable. China was an ally in the war and Chinese Canadians had enlisted in large number for the war effort. The government could no longer ignore the legitimate demands of these war veterans for citizenship and full rights including the right to vote. International pressure was brought to bear with the UN Universal Declaration of Human Rights forbidding discriminatory practices. Canada had joined with other countries to formulate the declaration.

After a lengthy debate in Parliament, the Canadian government finally repealed the Chinese Immigration (Exclusion) Act of 1923 on May 14, 1947, thus ending sixty-two straight years of official state racism against the Chinese.

However, the parliamentary debates were not without enduring sentiments of racism, with Prime Minister Mackenzie King setting the tone. "Large scale immigration from the orient would change the fundamental composition of the Canadian population," he said. "The government, therefore, has no thought of making any change in immigration regulations which would have consequences of the kind."[58]

During the debate to repeal the exclusion legislation, MP James Sinclair (Vancouver North), grandfather of Prime Minister Justin Trudeau, said:

> We have never separated the Chinese question from the Japanese problem for the same reason that we have found during our experience that they cannot be assimilated or blended into the national life as other groups—Caucasian groups—have been in the past.... The fact that in twenty-three years so few of them have intermarried shows the difficulty of ordinary biological assimilation. ... but after long experience with them, we do not want more oriental immigration, apart from the families of these men.[59]

Few MPs spoke with magnanimity towards the Chinese. During the 1947 debate, the Co-operative Commonwealth Federation (CCF) was the only party that stood unequivocally for the repeal of the act. CCF MP W. Ross Thatcher,[60] (Moose Jaw) called the Chinese Immigration Act "an insulting and unwarranted slur against a fine race of people." The act, he said, had been passed "in an era of prejudice. Having allowed thousands of Chinese men to come to Canada, it then deprived them of the society of their wives and their children. To this group such action seems contrary to the principles of morality, humanity and social welfare."

When the Chinese Exclusion Act was repealed in May 1947, there were still more battles to fight. The Chinese would have to wait another twenty years before they were put on an equal basis with others who wanted to immigrate to Canada.

What others (all others?)

Chapter 4

Family Reunification (1950s)

"When family ties are disturbed, devoted children arise."
—Laozi, *Tao Te Ching*

My mother and I arrived at Central Station late in the evening. We had travelled four days by train from Vancouver to Montreal, after sailing from Hong Kong to San Francisco and then catching a bus to Vancouver. As the train slowly looped its way through Pointe-St-Charles, I stared out the window into the darkness lit only by the dim incandescent lights of the row houses along the track. I knew we were nearing our destination and I felt anxious to meet my father—the Baba that Mother had spoken of for so many years.

You would think that by the middle of the twentieth century it would have been easier for Chinese people to immigrate to Canada. But even after the Exclusion Act was repealed in 1947, there were obstacles to family reunification and general Chinese immigration. Order in Council (PC) 2115 stipulated that only Chinese who were Canadian citizens could bring their wives and unmarried children under eighteen into Canada. Europeans were able to bring their families to Canada without being citizens. To make it more obviously unfair, large numbers of postwar refugees and immigrants from Europe were accepted without any family sponsorship.

A.R. Mosher, president of the Canadian Congress of Labour and a prominent member of the Committee for the Repeal of the Chinese Immigration Act, was among those who testified before the Senate Standing Committee on Immigration and Labour in March 1948 to denounce the government's discrimination against the Chinese.[61] His testimony included the following:

> To what other conclusion can one come when the law says on the one hand you can bring your wife and children into Canada provided you are of European, South American or United States parentage, so long as you are *resident* of the country (Order-in-Council 695). And, on the other hand, you must be a Canadian *citizen* before you can bring your wife and children into the country if you are of the Chinese or Asiatic race (Order-in-Council 2115). If this is not discrimination against people on account of their race then the word discrimination has no meaning.[62]

With representation by an active group of articulate second-generation Chinese Canadians, including many war veterans and some open-minded white Canadians, the government grudgingly made small changes to PC 2115. It raised the age of unmarried children to twenty-one, then to twenty-five before PC 2115 was finally repealed in 1956. Although the raising of the age did not directly affect my mother and me, it did make it possible for other Chinese to join families in Canada.

Changing the law was only part of the equation. Fear of illegal Chinese immigration led in 1960 to one of the biggest police and security operations in Canadian history, comparable to the raids that would take place under the War Measures Act a decade later.[63] Early on the morning of Sunday, May 24, 1960, the RCMP simultaneously raided Chinese communities in sixteen towns and cities across Canada. In Prince George, BC, the RCMP apprehended the entire Chinese population of two hundred and ordered them to complete questionnaires.[64] Of the thousands interrogated in the Canada-wide raids, only twenty-four Chinese were charged, with fifteen being fined or imprisoned.[65]

The Chinese communities were in a state of shock and anger. A month later, organizations from eleven cities across Canada came together to make representation to Ottawa. The delegation met with Davie Fulton, minister of justice, and Ellen Fairclough, minister of immigration, and had a two-hour meeting with Prime Minister John Diefenbaker. Foon Sien Wong, head of the Vancouver Chinese Benevolent Association (CBA), drew the prime minister's attention to the gross violation of human rights by the RCMP, who "freely arrest and detain Chinese ... they could not see the lawyer retained by the CBA. The situation resembles a country under martial law."[66]

The community protests had an effect on the government; it declared an amnesty for all Chinese who had entered Canada illegally before July 1, 1960. The Chinese Adjustment Statement Program was not altogether altruistic on the part of the government; it was more about regulation than atonement. It allowed any Chinese who had entered as "paper sons" to have their case reviewed so these "illegals" could become legitimate and gain Canadian citizenship.

The continued restrictions on Chinese immigration had given rise to the "paper son" phenomenon, which was an ingenious attempt to reunite extended family members separated by the Exclusion Act. When a child was born in China, the father upon his return to Canada would register the child in the hope that the government would eventually allow his family into this country. "Paper sons" were brought into Canada as a way to get around immigration requirements. During the Exclusion Years, when a daughter was born to a Gold Mountain man, the father would register the child as male. After the repeal of the Exclusion Act, many young men or boys in the extended family were brought into the country using these papers. When I was little I heard my father use the term, commenting that the paper son was sometimes more filial than the natural son. All was forgiven in 1960 when the Canadian government instituted the amnesty program to make the "paper sons" legal. Surprisingly, there was also a small number of "paper daughters," as I learned from the documentary film *Paper Sons and Daughters*, whose executive producer was Vancouver cultural activist Sid Tan.[67]

But it was not until 1967 that Chinese immigrants to Canada would be put on an equal footing with other immigrants under the "points system" and independent immigrants could apply to enter Canada. Between June 1960 and July 1970, the status of 11,569 "paper sons" was adjusted and legalized.[68] Altogether about 12,000 people came forward before the amnesty program ended in October 1973.

* * *

My mother and I came to Canada in 1956. After travelling the thousands of miles via Hong Kong, San Francisco and Vancouver, we finally reached Montreal's

Central Station and ascended the escalator to the concourse. Mother was carrying the suitcase that contained all our belongings in one hand and she held on to me with the other. As we entered the station, I saw two Chinese men, one older and the other much younger. The younger man, who I later found out was my mother's nephew, rushed over and took my mother's suitcase.

As the older man approached, I held on to my mother's leg, but she pushed me forward towards him and said, "Go say hello to your Baba." For the first time I nervously called my father "Baba."

My parents were in their early fifties when they started to share the joys and sorrows of living together again. Government legislation had robbed them of their youth as a couple. Now they would have to get to know each other again as they embarked on the next phase of their simple and remarkably pragmatic life. This was the start of our family reunification.

Age had been catching up to a large number of the Gold Mountain men; by 1951, 34.5 per cent of the Chinese in Quebec were over fifty-five. This was one of the pressing reasons to bring their wives and children to Canada. Many of the elderly men were ailing and they longed for their wives to comfort them in their remaining years. The Chinese population in Quebec grew from 1,904[69] to 4,794[70] in the 1950s, an increase of 152 per cent.

My mother, my brother and I were part of those statistics. Ging Tung, my brother, had arrived first in 1950 as one of the 1,036 Chinese—all women and children—who were permitted to enter Canada that year.[71]

Now that he had his youngest son in Canada too, my father wasted little time in making up for the lost years. Shortly after I arrived in Canada, he began taking me on twice-weekly walks to drum up business. One hand holding mine, and the other holding a dirty white canvas gunnysack over his shoulder, he would tell me about what life would be like in Canada and encourage me to go to school and get a good education.

The gunnysack was big enough to hold a child. It had brass riveted loops strung with a thick, strong cord to tie in the contents. He carried this sack up and down rue Willibrord and the avenues of Verdun, Fourth, Third, Second and First, cutting through the back lanes as he walked from one street to another. He climbed the spiral outdoor staircases, with the wrought iron railings, and knocked on the glass pane in the middle of the wooden framed doors, asking if there was laundry to be washed and ironed. He rolled up the dirty clothes with the sleeves of a shirt or the corners of a sheet and slipped in the knot a piece of paper with the address of the customer.

On our walks, he would tell me how cold and snowy the winters are. Never having seen snow, I asked what it was like. He said snow is white, cold and wet. I released his hand and ran ahead. I asked, how white, is it as white as the fence, as white as the window frame, as white as this car? He would always say, "whiter." This was April; I would have to wait another eight months to see for myself.

Father was very thoughtful in not enrolling me in school right away. He wanted time for me to adjust to this strange and foreign environment. He tried to enroll me in the nearby French school (École Notre-Dame-de-Lourdes), on Fifth Avenue behind our laundry, but they would not accept me.[72] My father, with his limited knowledge of French, couldn't understand why and only said to me, "Because we're Chinese." It could also have been because I was not Catholic. However, he managed to enroll me at an English school, four blocks away—St. Willibrord—that was also Catholic.

After a lifetime of experience in Canada, Father would use that simple phrase, "because we're Chinese," to explain away the many obstacles that stood in the way of advancement for the Chinese in this country. Father's outlook was shaped by his Confucian beliefs and his life experience in Canada. He was Canadian and Chinese at the same time—a Chinese Canadian. As someone who had never thought about retiring in China, he brought his family here to be Canadians.

My father enrolled me in grade 1 at St. Willibrord since I didn't speak any English. I was eight when I went to my first class there in September. Because of this, throughout my life I've always been two years older than my contemporaries. I'd already had two years of schooling in Hong Kong, and the non-language subjects, like math, were a breeze. My ability to pick up languages was put to the test, though. When I arrived in Montreal, everyone in Chinatown commented that my mouth was full of Cantonese. Within half a year, the Cantonese was replaced with English, and with Toishanese at home and in Chinatown.

In the 1950s, the people in the working-class Verdun area of Montreal were evenly split in speaking English and French. The students in my class represented the immigrant population. They were mainly postwar Europeans, Irish, Scottish, Italians, Ukrainians and Lithuanians. I was the only Chinese boy in the school from grade 1 to grade 7.

St. Willibrord divided the boys and girls into two buildings. There was a Chinese girl at the school, Germaine Wong, who later became an executive at the National Film Board. With the division of the sexes—separate entrances and schoolyards—we never saw each other at school. But in a display of the obvious, the school placed us side by side to walk down the church aisle for our First Communion.

Germaine's parents had a laundry in the eastern part of Verdun near Regina and Ethel streets. Germaine and her mother came to Canada at about the same time as us. My mother occasionally visited her mother and to hear my mother talk so glowingly of Germaine, I was sure they were planning our matrimony.

As the reunification of my family meant that we were one of the few families in the Montreal Chinese community, my father would bring us to Chinatown every Sunday to show us off. I met many of the old-timers, the *lo wah kiu*, who knew my father from the early days. Many of them were still alone. They would pat my head and stroke my face just to remember what the smooth skin of a child felt like.

My grade 1 teacher was Elizabeth Power. She took me under her wing and became my godmother. One day she spoke to my father about having me baptized since I was the only non-Catholic in the class. I was learning my catechism and preparing for First Communion and Confirmation. My father

My First Communion in 1958. I am second from the left.
Jimmy Hughes, my best friend, is at left. (William Dere Collection)

agreed. In my parents' traditional Chinese view of pleasing all the gods, to have another god to protect their son was a good thing.

After my First Communion, I became a fervent Catholic. Every Sunday, I went to Notre-Dame-de-Lourdes Church at the corner of Verdun and Fourth Avenue, across the street from our laundry. I felt mortified as everyone stared at the little Chinese boy walking up the aisle to sit in the front pew. I sat in the last row once, but the priest motioned me to come up front. Adding to the embarrassment, he reserved the front seat just for me. My faith sustained me through the ordeal. I was so zealous that I later became an altar boy at Verdun's St. Thomas More Catholic Church.

As an adventurous eight-year-old kid wandering around a strange neighbourhood, everything was new and fascinating. When I think about the neighbourhood today, I can appreciate its multicultural nature. Across the street from Harry's Laundry, the name my father continued to operate under, was the Italian Sisto Shoe Repair; next to him was the French Canadian Paul's Barber Shop. The first time he cut my hair, Paul told me that he'd never cut hair so thick and coarse; he proceeded to give me a brush cut. There was the English Verdun Wool Store, too, and around the corner was the rotund Scottish woman's Ross Fish and Chips; next to her was a Jewish haberdashery where my godmother bought me the suit for my First Communion. They all got to know me as I wandered in and out of their shops.

The Neighbourhood 1¢ to 5¢ Store was a wondrous place and it became my favourite hangout. It had aisles of knick-knacks on display tables, and against the walls were shelves stuffed with goods from floor to ceiling. The elderly European man with an accent of unknown origin let me browse for hours, allowing me to touch and smell the trinkets and toys in the store.

I walked the four blocks to school. In winter, when it was especially cold or snowy, my parents gave me the nickel for the bus fare. As the only Chinese boy in the neighbourhood, I was a familiar sight to the local residents. A few times, I was harassed by some of the bigger boys. One day, I was chased through the lanes by a group of three or four of them, yelling "*ching, ching, maudit chinois.*" As they cornered me, a larger boy stepped between us. He shouted something in French and drove them away. The teenager's name was Pierre Chatel. He lived on our street and his father was a customer of our laundry. He became my protector.

No Chinese childhood in those days was complete without going to Chinese school. I had to do double duty. On Saturday, I went to the Chinese

A Chinese Catholic School outing to Granby Zoo in 1960. I am at the far right,
and Germaine Wong is at the far left. (William Dere Collection)

Catholic school, and on Sunday, I had to attend the Chinese school at the YMCI.
My father continued his weekly tradition of visiting the YMCI that he started
thirty years before. The language of instruction was Toishanese at the YMCI and
Cantonese at the Catholic school. The textbooks came from Taiwan or Hong
Kong with the lessons consisting of morality tales about filial piety, friendship
and service to the community. Not much of the Chinese stuck with me.

There was little space to play whenever I brought friends home to the laundry. Eventually, I ended up hanging out at my friends' houses until after supper; then I returned home to do my homework on the ironing table. During
the summer when I wasn't bicycling around town or playing baseball with the
neighbourhood kids, I whiled the time away at the Verdun library. Books fascinated me. A few years before, when I was in Hong Kong, there was a reading
library on the ground floor below our apartment. It was literally a hole in the
wall—a storefront without the store or the front and with no depth. Wooden
shutters opened exposing shelves of books along the wall. These were graphic
novels, with torn pages taped and blackened from overuse. My mother gave
me the 5¢ to pay the owner for the privilege of spending an hour reading the
comics while sitting on a small wooden stool. My favourite books were *Monkey King* and stories of martial artists like Wong Fei Hung.

The Verdun Library was located on the second floor of the new City Hall situated on Verdun Avenue between First and Willibrord. I have fond memories of sitting down to read books on geography, which took me to places otherwise inaccessible. They formed a sense of wanderlust in me at an early age. I read the complete Hardy Boys series that was available at the library—some twenty-odd books. After that I got into the Nancy Drew series, until some kids laughed at me for reading girls' books.

* * *

My parents had difficulties learning to live together. They were set in their own ways after being apart for so many years. But the common economic struggle and the ingrained desire to keep the family together provided the motivation. I have happy memories and can only be thankful for my parents' ability to sacrifice for the sake of the family.

Life in a Chinese hand laundry was tough. There was the gruelling work and the cramped living conditions inside the laundry. But it was also the place that my parents and I bonded and forged our sense of family, as we shared a common, unique experience. At the same time, what we had was representative of many Chinese families that eventually re-established during those years.

Daily life in the laundry began around 6:30 a.m. After a breakfast of steamed bread and coffee or tea, my parents set to work ironing and, on Tuesdays and Thursdays, preparing the clothes for washing. They sorted the dirty laundry—smelly underpants soaked in dry urine or caked with excrement; crumpled sheets stained with menstrual blood—it was a messy job but that was what a laundryman or laundrywoman was expected to do.

My parents washed the clothes with an old round wringer washer and by hand in a large galvanized steel tub. The washing was done in the kitchen, or, rather, my mother cooked in the back room used for washing. The smell of bleach and hot steam overpowered the smell of food cooking on the stove. My parents worked until past midnight on wash nights. My mother took on some other work outside the house, so I can imagine how tired she must have felt.

It was just the three of us. In winter, I looked forward to wash night, because it meant there would be warmth coming from the coal burning pot-bellied stove used to dry the clothes. There was no other source of heat.

My father did not want me to learn the laundry business, although he did teach me to use the abacus. Making the laundry tickets was one chore

Father asked me to do. I did it the same way that his father taught him. I used a brush with ink from an ink stick. There was a series of eighty Chinese characters. I would write the numbers one to one hundred under the character at the two edges for each series of tickets. These would be the customers' tickets—half torn off for the customer and half tucked into the pile of dirty laundry. Father hoped that I would learn some more Chinese by writing the characters.

My father never asked me to do any of the physical work in the laundry. He was adamant that I would work hard to study for school and get good grades. He wanted my mind to think about university and getting a professional job. But there was one other thing that my father asked me to do to earn a little spending money: I delivered the packages of clean laundry on our street. The women of the house smiled as they answered the door and rewarded me with a tip of a nickel or a dime.

At the time, Harry's Laundry charged 17¢ for a starched and ironed shirt, and 15¢ for a sheet.

My family was poor but we were not impoverished. I never felt a sense of poverty. Being Chinese, I sensed that we simply did not have or do the same things as white people. My father didn't have money to buy a car. Conditioned by a life of exclusion in Canada, my father never thought about owning property.

My school friends told stories about their summer vacations at the cottage in the Laurentians, or at the beach in Maine. My parents never took a vacation. I spent my summers bicycling around Montreal—taking journeys like the nearly twenty-mile ride to my grandfather's laundry in the east end—and playing baseball, until I reached fourteen. That year, my father felt it was time I got a job, not just to earn money but to appreciate what it was like to work and be responsible for myself.

In the summer of 1962, there was talk on the street that a hiring hall, at Atwater just below St. Antoine, was taking on casual labourers to deliver flyers. I went with a friend at 6:30 a.m. We were selected with a group of four or five others. My friend and I were the only kids. We got into the back of a panel truck, which drove north to Rosemere. After ten hours, we got back to the office. The boss doled out the money—pay for six hours. I protested. I had worked at least eight hours, not counting the time of travel. "You only worked six hours, kid. Take it or leave it." The pay was $4, for the day's work. This was my first lesson in exploitation and the surplus value of labour.

I refused to be deterred from joining the working class. I got a job as a busboy at Ruby Foo's through my brother-in-law, Jackson Ing, who was a waiter there. Ruby Foo's was a famous Montreal landmark. It was a Chinese restaurant, owned by Jews, on Décarie Boulevard, not far from the old Blue Bonnets racetrack. The restaurant was elegant with red velvet–covered booths and carpeted floors. The smell was different from the restaurants in China-town. It smelled clean with a whiff of French wine. The customers were the upper crust of Montreal society. Celebrities and sports stars came to be seen with other celebrities. It had all the accoutrements of a five-star restaurant: a sommelier to promote the best wines; a chef who pushed around a cart where he could cut roast beef or make flambés; a Eurasian cigarette girl in a form-fitting *cheongsam*.[73] Sometimes I scored the breadboy shift. The breadboy carried heated rolls and bread in a metal box hung around the neck in front of the body. The breadboy shift got you out of the heavy lifting of the busboy. The busboy was the gofer; he had to clean and set the tables, and then take the heavy stack of dishes, with cups, glasses and cutlery packed onto an oval tray carried on the shoulder into the kitchen for the dishwasher. Not a few times, a tray slipped and fell making a crashing noise, which for some inexplicable reason drew applause from the restaurant clientele.

After a couple of summers, I defected from Ruby Foo's to move up to a waiter's position next door at Bill Wong's, another upscale Chinese restaurant. The owner, Bill Wong, was born in Montreal, and his Toishanese parents had paid the head tax. He was the father of Jan Wong, whom I knew later at McGill University before she went on to become a journalist. Although my father had exiled me from laundry work, I kept up the tradition of Chinese Canadians by working in restaurants. I financed my university education by working as a waiter during summers and weekends.

Working at these jobs, I experienced the class nature of society. The owners and most of the customers were of a different class from those that served them. My coworkers were mainly immigrants, Greeks and Chinese, who had families to support. Most of them worked in the restaurants as their lifelong job, like my brother-in-law, who worked for thirty years at Ruby Foo's to raise six children and finance their university education. Those of us who worked there part-time while going to school looked forward to graduation, to get away from the drudgery of restaurant work.

It was only in my university days that I really got a sense of how little money my father made operating the laundry. When applying for a student loan, I asked him for his annual income. He thought about it and said, "Oh, maybe $1,000." I didn't believe he made so little. It didn't seem right, so I wrote $5,000, the median Canadian income, on the application.

My father managed his expenses from week to week. I don't remember him doing income tax returns, so he must have earned less than the amount required to pay income tax. I later discovered that he cleared about $25 a week. My mother often chastised him for his parsimonious ways. She said he had no ambition for the future. This was a source of friction between them.

Father's personal frugality was built up over a lifetime of saving money, either for a trip back to China or to send money back to the family. He never spent anything on himself. Much of his clothing came from customers who never came to pick up their laundry. Despite that, my father was a generous man when it came to community service. He contributed and participated actively in the war effort. He was generous with his time and money in the Chiu Lun Gong Sol. One of the few times he travelled, he went with my mother to Vancouver to take part in the opening of the new headquarters of the Gong Sol in 1971. Years later, when I was perusing my graduation yearbook from Loyola High School, I was surprised to find my parents' name listed as donors and patrons of the school.

My father did something else for me that changed my life. For my high school years, this kid from working-class Verdun, son of a poor Chinese laundryman, got to go to Loyola High School, a prestigious Jesuit private school that served the English elite in Montreal. Ed Kirk was my grade 7 teacher, and he must have seen something in me because he tutored me and three other students to write the Loyola entrance exam.[74] I was the only one of the four accepted. I later learned that my father had asked Father Thomas Tou of the Chinese Catholic Mission to write to the school. Every time he saw me in Chinatown, Father Tou beamed with pride that I was attending Loyola. I know now that my father did not have the money for the steep tuition, so I must have received a scholarship or bursary. It was the four years at Loyola that opened up my view of the world.

My father never talked about the past with me. He preferred to tell positive stories of his work in Chinatown with his fellow clansmen. Now I understand why he was reticent to speak about the past. The period of exclusion and separation from family was lonely, painful and humiliating. Why would a father tell these things to his son? He did not have any bitterness. He accepted his fate with stoicism. He endured, survived and triumphed. My father had suffered for years from thrombosis in his legs from standing at the ironing table all his life, and he finally retired in 1976 at age seventy-two.

During the 1976 Montreal Olympic Games, my father wanted me to take him on a road trip in my new Saab. It was just the two of us. As the world came to the Games, we left town during the construction holidays, the last two weeks of July. At every roadside diner where we stopped for lunch, he ordered a fried egg sandwich; it was the only Western food that he liked. By then I was involved in political activities and had not spent much time with him in the past few years. The road trip provided us an opportunity to catch up. He told me that he wanted to see some relatives, friends and village cousins that he hadn't seen in a long time, in New York City and in Washington, DC. He didn't tell me at the time but he had been diagnosed with cancer.

My father never said so but I knew he was proud of me. Despite pleas from my father and mother, I didn't get a graduation photo taken, nor attend the commencement ceremony when I graduated from McGill with a bachelor of engineering degree. I felt a tinge of filial piety when I graduated from Carleton University, and I had my grad photo taken resplendent in my master's cap and gown. I gave the photos to Father. A few months later, I visited the Chiu Lun Gong Sol and, to my astonishment, he had framed and hung my grad photo on the wall alongside those of past Gong Sol presidents and elders. I was angry with him for putting me on display and demanded the photo be taken down, but he never did. It was only after his death, when my mother retrieved his belongings from the Gong Sol, that she brought the photo home.

Father died in October 1982 at age seventy-nine. His death broke my connection with the past and the Chinese community in Montreal. When he was alive, he was my link to Chinese Canadian society. At the time of his death, I was deeply involved as an activist organizer outside the Chinese community, so I was not conscious of my Chinese-ness and what the community meant to me. It would be a few years before I felt the need to reconnect with his past and to search for my own identity. I didn't realize how little I knew about his past until he died. I needed to find out how he lived and to discover his legacy. I would begin to touch his past when I became involved in the head tax redress campaign, and when I made the film *Moving the Mountain*. It was only after his death that I felt such strong admiration for him.

Chapter 5

My Mother, Yee Dong Sing Dere

"I express my deepest gratitude and my appreciation to Mrs. Dong Sing Dere as well as her family whose past sacrifices and contributions have significantly shaped the social, economic and cultural development of the City of Montréal, the province of Québec and Canada."
—Gérald Tremblay, Mayor of Montreal, Feb. 27, 2005

My mother took matters into her own hands when she realized the laundry in Verdun was not making enough money. She went out and got a job in a hat factory. She worked in the factory during the day, then after getting home she ironed in the laundry, made dinner, and on wash nights carried on working in the laundry until the early hours of the morning.

Yee Dong Sing was born in October 1905 in Shui Ben Hang, Toishan. She had two siblings. When she was young, her older brother left his young family at home and went to the Philippines to seek his fortune. He was later killed when the Japanese bombed Manila. My mother and her younger sister, Shao Chun, were left in the village to look after their parents. At that time, few girls attended school, but Dong Sing was a good learner, so her aunt, a teacher, taught her at home. When Dong Sing was nineteen, her mother told her that an auspicious marriage had been arranged for her with a *Gim Shan Haak*, a Gold Mountain Guest.

Would she have thought it auspicious if she had read a poem like this, I wonder:

Right after we were wed, Husband, you set
out on a journey.
How was I to tell you how I felt?
Wandering around a foreign country, when
will you ever come home?
You are wasting many joyous years of our
precious youth.
My spring heart has turned to ashes.
Poverty does not allow me the luxury of a choice.
But let it be known to all my sisters:
Don't ever marry a young man going overseas!

Unknown author[75]

Dong Sing left the Yee clan and entered the Dere clan in 1925. "At that time, I wanted to go to Canada," she told me. "I asked your father to ask about bringing me to Canada. But he said the government did not allow it. He had to leave after a year and a half." My father returned to the village three other times after they were married. By 1935, Mother was left at home to raise four young children and to look after the household including her mother-in-law.

Decades passed.

* * *

One of my earliest memories is of my mother and I leaving our ancestral village to go to Guangzhou, the capital of Guangdong province, to stay with my second sister. She had recently married and was living there with her husband, also from a head tax family. It must have been 1951. It was early morning with a misty breeze blowing across my face as we walked out of the village past the old banyan tree that guarded the entrance. The last image as I turned my head for one last look was the "mountain"—a low hill that I climbed as a toddler. We walked to take a small boat to cross the Tanjiang River, one of the tributaries flowing into the Pearl River Delta. I recall sitting at the bottom of the wooden boat and seeing the water skimming by. The boat was controlled by a man at the rear providing both motion and direction with the to and fro movements of his paddle. On the other side of the river, we took a bus to the city. In those days, there were no bridges crossing the river; today, there are modern highways taking people from Toishan to Guangzhou.

In China, it was traditional at the time for parents to find decent men with proper families for their daughters to marry. On his last trip back to China in 1947, my father thought long and hard about this.

Pui King, my eldest sister, would end up getting married later that year. My father had met her future father-in-law on the ship back to China; the two men spent the month-long voyage planning the marriage for the number one son and the number one daughter. But when my father broke the news to my sister, she was shocked. She was in her last year of high school and hadn't thought about marriage. "Marriage is an affair arranged by the old people, it was none of my business," she told me much later.

When the prospective mother-in-law came to visit our family, Pui King refused to see her. "How can I allow my son to marry a girl that I've never seen?" Madame Fong persisted.

My mother was not enthusiastic about the marriage since Pui King was still in school and only seventeen, but people in the village encouraged her. "You have three daughters, times are hard. Give your eldest daughter an opportunity to go to *Gim Shan*." Mother agreed but acquiesced to her daughter's rebellion at not letting her future mother-in-law see her before the marriage. "If this is a blind marriage, then let them be blind," Pui King insisted. So the battle of wills between the future mother-in-law and daughter-in-law began.

My mother compromised and allowed the mother-in-law to see her second daughter. King Sin was only fourteen. "They both look the same," Mother said reassuringly. The mother-in-law approved when she saw King Sin, accepting my mother's assurance that the older sister was as beautiful as the younger one.

It was a festive, boisterous affair with palanquins carrying the bridal party and the parents. Pui King was allowed to finish high school after the marriage and she had her first child shortly after. It was a marriage made in heaven. As I write this, my sister has been married to the same *Gim Shan Haak* for seventy years.

Marriage for my mother, of course, had meant becoming a "Gold Mountain Widow," as she described herself. She told me late in her life[76] that she always used to hope my father would come back safely and have a smooth journey. "I took care of the children and planted vegetables, grew rice to support life in

This is my one and only baby picture, taken in 1948. My mother
got indignant whenever my brother told the story that I was crawling
on the ground eating chicken poop. (William Dere Collection)

China. When the kids grew up, they could go to school and it needed money."

My mother asked my father to send back more money, but understood he
could only make a little money out of working in the laundry. "Life was hard
for him. He took good care of the family and sent back money even though
he made little. Some village relatives had some fields but they did not have
money. So, I used $400 [money sent by Father over the years] to buy the land,
about 3 mou [half an acre]. The harvest provided us with half a year's food. At
that time, I had three daughters and one son.

"Your father could not return because of the Japanese invasion. [Japanese
troops began occupying Guangdong in 1938.] With four children we needed a
lot of food; life was fine if we have the land to grow food.

"Meanwhile, Father sent back some money. Your uncle [my father's older brother] was the village head and he smoked opium. He took all the money Father sent, even when I was sick. During the Japanese war, we suffered and my health wasn't good. I got sick when I didn't have proper meals. I was sick for many months in 1944–45. There was no money from Father because of the Japanese. Luckily, I recovered with help from my neighbours. I ate the bad food and saved the good rice to cook rice soup for the children. We did not have rice to eat for months—until the harvest."

My mother recalled the women in the village being close, "like sisters," and sharing what they had. "It was mostly women left in the village with our children. We all knew that life was hard for our husbands in Canada. When we sat together, we would talk about whether they had sent money and some of them would say they received money.

"Father knew it was hard in the village and he felt sorry for me," she told me. "When the war was over, Father sent back money immediately—a few thousand Chinese dollars—to Toicheng,[77] where his brother operated a publishing company." With rampant inflation, such an amount would not have been large. But my uncle took it all.

"Since I had no money, I had to borrow money from my relatives," my mother said. "I told them that I would give them back the money when Father sent some. Life was hard. When I asked my brother-in-law to give me back the money, he didn't. He did not even tell me that he received the money. Father sent me a letter asking if I have received it. I asked brother-in-law to give me the money, he told me he had spent it all. So, there was nothing I can do."

With the defeat of the Japanese in September 1945, Toishan was still in turmoil. There were natural and man-made disasters. A typhoon tore through Toishan in 1946, leaving many dead and devastating the fields. The KMT government drove the local economy to bankruptcy. Mother was desperate to join Father in Canada.

"When I received money at the time, it was okay," she said. "But when I didn't, life was very difficult. I was very worried. I had four children. To raise them I had to worry about the school fees, the clothing, the expenses, and I was lonely at the time to think about all these problems by myself."

When it came to power with the Liberation of China in 1949, the Chinese Communist Party developed a policy to collectivize the land. Our family had purchased some land in the village with money my grandfather and father sent back over the years. The family was categorized as landlord class since my mother had hired someone to work the field, which consisted of two plots, about half an acre altogether.

"During Liberation, my second daughter didn't get married yet. And my youngest daughter was very bright. I sent her to Guangzhou to study and we stayed there. When the Communists came, we had to go back to the village. You were very little then, I had to carry you on my back. I was almost crazy with fear, and constantly crying in the streets.

"I was so scared and I cried a lot because the Communists have to make you work and I was so miserable at the time. The District Leader was very kind to me and explained what will happen, but I was afraid. He explained why they took the land." He explained the Communist concept of the collectivization of land for the greater good but Mother didn't understand.

After the war, my father wanted to sponsor my mother to come to Canada. It was only with the rescinding of the Chinese Exclusion Act that my father was able to obtain his citizenship in 1950, after twenty-nine years without civil rights in his adopted country. He had begun planning to reunite his family in Canada, and he brought my older brother, Ging Tung, to Canada first to join him and work in Grandfather's laundry; then he worked to bring my mother and me. Ging Tung left China in 1950. After sending my brother off in Hong Kong, my mother and I returned to the village because she was worried about my three sisters.

"Your father wrote that we should join him. Your brother had already left and now it was our turn to go. I thought, life is difficult here; maybe it'll be better in Canada.

"Those years at home were very difficult. No money was getting through since it had been sent to Hong Kong. Brother-in-law was already there and he kept the money.

"I wanted to go to Canada to be with your father. But even if I wanted to, I couldn't. That's why it made me so miserable. We were using all kinds of methods to come to Canada. Your second sister had married and we decided to go to Guangzhou to stay with her husband's family. We stayed in Guangzhou for two years, and then we went to Hong Kong. This was about 1953.

"In Hong Kong we stayed with my eldest daughter's family on Portland Street. She had already reached Hong Kong. My second daughter joined us the same year. My third daughter didn't want to leave China. Her head was full of communist songs. But later, I persuaded her to come because we needed to keep the family together. On Portland Street, we had four households living together. The house was full of young children. You played with your little nephews and nieces. I wanted to come to Canada and experience how life was elsewhere. I wanted to be together with the family here but your brother didn't want me to come. He wrote that it would be too cold and too difficult for me."

In 1956, my mother received the letter saying that she had been approved to come to Canada.

"I felt so happy and relieved," she said. She would be travelling with me and she knew it was a long distance, but she felt certain that life in Gold Mountain must be better than life in Hong Kong.

"You were about seven," she told me. "We went to the Immigration office and you even showed me how to get there and how to use the elevator. We were very happy because you were going to see your father soon."

Mother broke the news that changed my life forever. "*Ah Wee*," she said, "you are not going to school today. Tomorrow, we are going to Gim Shan to be with Baba." Even though she had prepared me months earlier that we would be going to Canada, it still came as a surprise when the actual day arrived. This was April 1956.

Father booked passage for us on the ss *President Wilson*. The fare for an economy class cabin was $345 per person, but I don't know if he got a reduced fare for a child. The ship left Hong Kong for San Francisco in early April 1956. My mother made friends with the woman in the next cabin. She was travelling to Boston with her six-year-old daughter to join her husband who operated a hand laundry there. I remember Mother being seasick. The little girl and I went to the cafeteria to get some *jook* (rice porridge) for her.

At the pier in San Francisco, a Chinese agent met the Vancouver-bound passengers. He took us to a Chinese restaurant for dinner and put us on an overnight bus to Vancouver. Third Uncle[78] met us in Vancouver and brought us to the train station for the trans-Canada trip to Montreal.

Mother reminisced about the trip, "Do you still remember Third Uncle? He was very kind to us. He bought you some playing cards for the train when you were seven. I saw him again in 1971 when we went to Vancouver. He passed away a few years ago."

* * *

My mother's experience was similar to that of other Gold Mountain widows. My parents were young enough to create a new life together in Canada. However, others were in their sixties or even seventies and those women came to nurse the elderly husbands they hardly knew. Some complained that life in China was easier than in Gim Shan.

Recalling her early days in Montreal, my mother said: "Remember? Your father picked us up in a taxi and right away, we went to the laundry. We did business in the laundry and we lived in the laundry. At that time, I only went out on Sundays and sometimes I saw some friends. They said, 'You should rent some place to live instead of staying in the laundry.' Your father lived in the laundry all his life and he was too cheap to pay rent for another place.

"The day after we arrived, I started to help your father in the laundry, ironing clothes. It was very hard work, the iron weighed eight or ten pounds, and the weather was very cold. When I first came, I didn't know any English. I just hid in the laundry; I didn't go anywhere. Your father taught me some English when we were ironing—the days of the week, numbers and a few phrases to take the bus to visit friends."

After working for about two years and realizing they weren't making enough money, she thought about the fact that some of her children were in Montreal too and that she didn't have a house for them. So my mother exerted her independence by working outside the laundry, despite Father's objections.

"I went out and met with Mr. Chang and asked him if he could find me a job," she recalled. "After about two weeks, I met him again, and he said that a hat factory needed people and asked me if I wanted to work in a factory. So, I went to Chinatown to meet him. I went with another lady to work in the hat factory. There were about five or six Chinese women who worked there. I made friends with the Chinese women. Their husbands had laundries and gambled away their money. That is why they had to work."

She left my father alone at home to iron clothes. "He complained that I didn't need to work in the factory. It was harder for me, not for him. But I said if I stayed at home, I couldn't make enough money. ... I was thinking about the future and my children. I wanted to give them a house to live in. The only way was to work outside the laundry."

Apparently my father thought differently. He believed that as long as we had enough to eat, it was okay.

"He complained that I was not helping him," my mother said. "But I was. I finished work at four and got home at five or six. As soon as I got home, I plugged in the iron and started ironing clothes, bed sheets, pillowcases and other things until seven or eight. Then I had to cook dinner. It was worse on wash nights; sometimes we had to work until two in the morning to finish washing all the clothes. I was so tired the next morning when I went to the factory. I really felt bad at the time. I wanted more for the future.

"I saved all my money, about $5,000 and after a few more years, $10,000. Your brother also saved some money so we bought the house on Second Avenue with a loan from the family association *woi*. It cost $20,000 and we paid it off in two to three years." The house was typical of Verdun at the time and "had six numbers," in my mother's words (it was a six-plex). So, she said, "we collected some rent to pay the expenses."

When her children had their own lives and their own homes, she sold the house.

Like my mother, many of the women that came to Canada at the time did triple duty as wife, mother and worker in the laundry, restaurant or factory. Many were isolated, lonely and dependent on their husbands. None of them had any language skills in English or French, so they were grateful for whatever money they made outside their husband's laundry. Like my mother, many were ambitious for the future of their family and their children. My mother was a strong and capable woman and she was the force that held our family together. She worked hard to get Father to sponsor other members of the

My mother, who worked at the laundry for seventeen years, joins my father for a photo at the ironing tables in October 1956. (William Dere Collection)

family to Canada. There was my third sister, my mother's younger sister and husband, and several of her nephews and nieces.

"I worked in the laundry for seventeen years," my mother said. "I had gallstones and I was always in pain. In 1968 I had the operation to remove my gall bladder and I felt better. In the winter, the weather was cold. I did the ironing and the draft from the cracks in the wall made my legs cold. My legs were bleeding from being so chapped. My hands were sore with calluses from holding the heavy iron.[79] I had no choice but to go outside to work. At the time we were trying to get your aunt, my sister, over from China. So we needed to have some money in the bank. I gave the money to your father to put in the bank. He didn't take any of my money and he never asked for any."

She met "some Western ladies" in the laundry. "There was one woman who always greeted me with 'How are you?' and I also greeted her with 'How are you?' She invited me to her house once. It was on our street. She had three rooms and a lot of stuff on the balcony. There were other ladies who were kind to me. When I had my operation they asked about me.

"It's not good to complain, people will look down on you. It's better to say good things than bad things. But your father was grumpy with me. He

Though life was hard, Mother and Father worked together for the family.
This photo was taken during a relaxing family gathering in the 1970s.
(William Dere Collection)

MY MOTHER, YEE DONG SING DERE · 83

was very kind when he was in Toishan—here, he was different. He didn't care about anything but the laundry. He just worked from day to day but I never held that against him."

My father took care of the shopping, she added, going to Chinatown every Sunday to buy the rice and vegetables. "Sometimes, he would treat us to roast pork or *char siu*. However difficult it was, we worked together for the family. Everything is good now."

Still, my mother said, "I like Canadian people [meaning whites], but equality is not really equality; it's still for them, sometimes depending on the situation, it's still to their advantage, right? It's not very fair, but it's a lot better than before. In the past people had to endure a lot, a lot of suffering. Now life is considered better. It is better now."

After Father's death in 1982, Mother went to Edmonton to live with my second sister, King Sin, and her two sons. King Sin's husband had died a few years earlier. After a year, Mother returned to Montreal and got a subsidized apartment operated by the Chinese Catholic Mission on St. Urbain Street. For the first time in her adult life, she was not responsible for anyone but herself. The convenience of living in Chinatown allowed her to communicate in her own language. She did her own banking, took care of the rent, shopped and cooked her own meals. She found peace and serenity in her retirement years. In the apartment building there were many elderly widows who lived similar lives. She quickly made a wide circle of friends—a sisterhood—and organized mah jong groups with them. They talked about their children and grandchildren and how well they were doing.

Mother attended the same Chinese Presbyterian church where James Wing, my father's YMCI friend, was an elder. The church or the old age club would take them for outings and organize elaborate Chinese New Year celebrations. My mother attended the church for the social companionship. But it was an old, worn, dog-eared copy of the *Tao Te Ching* that she brought from China and kept throughout her lifetime that inspired her life philosophy of balance and harmony. Mother practised this balance in her cooking where she tried to maintain the body's equilibrium of yin and yang. This entailed making bitter broths made with ginseng and other herbs, which I was forced to consume as a kid.

She achieved contentment in her later years. In 1995, she talked about being happy that her children all had families. "You married a wonderful wife and have two bright children," she told me.

"My heart is content. The government gives me a pension, about $1,000. I don't need any money. The rent is $200. I buy some materials and make my own clothes and knit scarves and sweaters for my grandchildren. You and your brother and sisters visit me every week, sometimes twice a week. You bring me food, sometimes too much food for me to eat, so I share it with the neighbours. Some don't have children to visit them. I don't worry now. I feel calm, on lock."[80]

Mother lived in her apartment until 1998. When she wasn't able to cook for herself any longer, she moved in with my family. She enjoyed her time with a young grandson—Jordan was five when she moved in—and a daughter-in-law who dutifully and patiently listened to her tales of village life from so many years ago. We celebrated her one hundredth birthday in October 2005, attended by her five children, twenty-one grandchildren, seventeen great-grandchildren, and one great-great-grandchild. They came from around the world. With other relatives and friends, altogether over one hundred people celebrated her birthday.

In February 2005, Yee Dong Sing Dere was recognized by the City of Montreal with a Certificate of Commemoration presented by the mayor, who expressed his gratitude to my mother and our family for "past sacrifices and contributions" to Montreal, Quebec and Canada. My daughter, Jessica, received the award on behalf of her grandmother. The certificate could not make up for my parents' pain and suffering caused by the racist and hateful laws, but it did recognize their history and contributions to Montreal.

In 2006, two days before Prime Minister Stephen Harper made his apology in Parliament for the Chinese Head Tax and Exclusion Act, Mother suffered a stroke. I informed her at the hospital of the apology. Even though she was paralyzed on the right side of her body, she smiled and said, "I am happy. You worked hard for this."

On July 13, 2006, Yee Dong Sing passed away in her 101st year. She lived her first fifty years in China and her second fifty years in Canada. She was a true Chinese Canadian.

As much as I admire my father, my admiration for how my mother lived her life is more profound. She was a woman warrior, determined to succeed despite all the obstacles. She was caring with an overwhelming love; she wore her emotions on her sleeve. Her effect on me is immeasurable.

Certificate of Commemoration

*The present certificate
is to recognize and honour the*

Mrs Dong Sing Dere (YEE, Tung)

*whose husband was one of the early Chinese Canadian pioneers that
settled in Montréal, Québec, Canada before 1923 as labourers
and who were affected by the
Chinese Head Tax and the 1923 Chinese Exclusion Act.*

*In the name of the City of Montréal and on behalf of all Montrealers,
I express my deepest gratitude and my appreciation to Mrs Dong Sing
Dere as well as to her family, whose past sacrifices and contributions
have significantly shaped the social, economic and cultural development
of the City of Montréal, the province of Québec and Canada.*

February 27, 2005

Gérald Tremblay
Mayor of Montréal

Scan of Dong Sing Dere's Certificate of Commemoration.

PART TWO

Political Consciousness

Chapter 6

Getting Organized

"It is not the consciousness of men that determines their existence, but
their social existence that determines their consciousness."
—Karl Marx[81]

---

*"The whole world is watching! The whole world is watching!" I was lying in
bed, trying to doze off, listening to the small transistor radio on the pillow
next to my ear, when I first heard the chants. I was now wide awake. It was
a muggy Montreal night in late August 1968 and CBC Radio was covering
the US Democratic Party's National Convention in Chicago. The commentator was giving a blow-by-blow account of the running skirmishes between
the protesters and the police. I was twenty and the events in Chicago stirred
something inside me.*

A CBC reporter, doing a piece on racism in Quebec, recently asked me,
"Have you ever been affected by systemic racism?" I answered, "Yeah,
my whole life." When I was younger, I would not have been able to offer such
a categorical response. Yet, as the immigrant son of a Chinese laundryman, I
felt the race and class oppression of Canadian society from an early age. All the
hardworking Chinese of my father's generation were aware of this mistreatment. They may not have been able to articulate this consciousness as well as

Marx did in the quotation above, but they fought against the way they were treated and matched wits with their oppressors through their everyday practice of resistance against authority—a form of resistance that was a natural reaction to state racism.

Ever since I'd arrived in Canada as a child, people had been more conscious that I was Chinese than I was myself. Common culture, developed over decades of discriminatory legislation, painted the Chinese as different and apart. My father felt and lived this difference, but it would be years before I could come to intellectually understand how my father felt. I am still trying to articulate the profundity of my father's consciousness and his experience, over six decades, of negotiating the contradictions of life in Canada. My own consciousness of these contradictions began in my teens as I began to open my mind and question my place in society, and to gain some maturity in my political and intellectual interpretation of life. This questioning led me to explore radical revolutionary explanations for the class and racial inequalities that I felt around me.

I entered high school during the 1960s. It was a decade of international upheaval. In Canada, the idea of the Quebec nation was emerging in people's consciousness. But despite these political developments, which turned out to have a crucial effect on me, my world view had not yet taken shape. I was mainly focused on my studies and playing sports when I first started attending Loyola High School in the fall of 1963.

It wasn't a big school, only five hundred students—all boys. It was located in the leafy west end of Montreal—on the campus of Loyola College, before the college merged into Concordia University. The high school was housed in a three-storey gothic building at the northeastern corner of the bucolic campus. The school has since moved into a new, bigger complex across Sherbrooke Street at the corner of West Broadway. (Coincidentally, today, the old building is the home of Concordia's Psychology Department, where my daughter, Jessica, studied for her PhD in Clinical Psychology.)

Loyola catered to the English Catholic elite of Montreal. Many of the students became successful and well-known businessmen, academics and politicians. The school had high-calibre sports teams, too; the hockey and football teams were consistent winners. However, it was the high-calibre teachers that had an impact on me. Most of them were Jesuits with PhDs. They lived up to the reputation of Jesuits, who promoted independent liberal thought, putting them in frequent conflict with the established order.

Perhaps it was the times that brought together some liberal-minded members of the Society of Jesus to teach at Loyola. They reflected the attitude of the '60s. There was Norm Lawson, my English and Latin teacher. He challenged me not to be so cynical when I was thinking critically. Richard Haughian was my coach on the senior basketball team and my history teacher. As time went by, he also encouraged me in discussions on the Cuban revolution. Open my mind and question authority; think critically but not cynically; accept other cultures as they are; learn from the world. These were some of the concepts that I was nurturing and they have stayed with me throughout my life.

At the time, most of my fellow students parroted the position of the US on world events, especially after the assassination of J.F. Kennedy in November 1963, which seemed to have had a spiritual effect on the school.

In 1967, I wrote my final year history paper on the Cuban revolution, entitled "Castro's Cuba." In it, I quoted liberally from Fidel Castro, who in 1961 had said: "Revolutions, real revolutions, do not arise through the will of one man or one group. Revolutions are remedies—bitter remedies, yes. But at times revolution is the only remedy that can be applied to evils more bitter." Those words moved this seventeen-year-old student to explore more about social revolution and its meaning.

The theory and practice of revolution and social activism had not yet fallen into place for me. I was still questioning why and how events happen in the world. I was not fully aware of the social and economic differences due to class. I was just dipping my toes in the vast ocean of social protest, national liberation and revolution. Nevertheless, my political ideas and understanding were taking shape as I began to read "revolutionary" literature.

Then, in the fall of 1967, I entered McGill University, where I had chosen to study mechanical engineering out of practicality. My father had steered me into seeking an education that would get me a decent job, a professional job. He had once pointed out the fenced, spacious McGill campus behind the Roddick Gates as we rode the Sherbrooke Street bus.

As I walked through these gates, the proverbial freedom in thought and action of those heady days overwhelmed me.

Within days of starting the engineering program, I began running into one protest after another; it was the heyday of the New Left and there were protests throughout my university days. One evening in 1968, I was in bed when I heard a CBC report on protests in Chicago against the Vietnam War. I knew that I needed to be involved. I identified with the young people protesting against both the war and the political system that fed the war. I stayed up most of the evening pondering what I had to do to help stop the war. McGill too was the venue for protests calling for an end to the war in Vietnam, as well as for nuclear disarmament. There were sit-ins and occupations for a democratic university, and a massive demonstration for the nationalist McGill français movement that wanted to transform McGill into a French university.

But while others were turning to the European Marxist philosophers like Louis Althusser or Jean-Paul Sartre, I was reading books like *Wretched of the Earth* (1961), by Martinique Marxist psychiatrist Frantz Fanon, and *Revolution in the Revolution?* (1967) by the French journalist and philosopher Régis Debray, who had fought at the side of Argentine Marxist revolutionary Che Guevara.

Fanon introduced me to colonial oppression and exploitation in the Third World.[82] What an introduction! Through reading Fanon, I began to understand that colonial oppression relied on violent repression of the native culture and way of life. The only way to overthrow the oppressors, liberating the nation and the people's cultural thought, was also by force. He taught me to stretch Marxist thinking. Fanon, the psychiatrist, exposed the psychological violence of the settlers. But the native population never stood still. In Fanon's words: "He is overpowered but not tamed; he is treated as an inferior but he is not convinced of his inferiority. He is patiently waiting until the settler is off his guard to fly at him."[83]

Fanon talked about nationalism as well as colonialism, and so gave me a new way of looking at the political movement developing in Quebec at the time. He warned against bowing to "bourgeois nationalism." It could mislead poor workers and peasants to get behind the nationalist cause, only to be betrayed by the ruling class, which wants to gain power for its own class interests. It was through reading Fanon's work that I came to understand that nationalism in fighting against colonialism and foreign occupation is progressive, whereas nationalism to exclude others is regressive.

Fanon also issued an inspiring call to arms which I could not resist at the time, and which still rings with great appeal today:

> Let us waste no time in sterile litanies and mimicry. Leave this Europe where they are never done talking of Man, yet murder men everywhere they find them, at the corner of every one of their own streets, and in all corners of the globe. ... It is a question of the Third World starting a new history of Man.[84]

systemic isms

It was an indictment of those who went to the European schools and came away with a colonial mentality. I saw some of that at McGill—students who were there because of the parents' money and connections, and who wanted to use their degree to reinforce the neocolonial ruling class to lord it over the ordinary people of their countries. Neocolonialism, the continuation of dominance by the ex-colonizers, took the place of open colonialism to keep the countries of Asia, Africa and Latin America within the economic and cultural sphere of European and North American imperialism. I began to understand the concept of *How Europe Underdeveloped Africa*, the title of Walter Rodney's 1972 book,[85] which summed up colonialism and neocolonialism and how the exploitation of the Third World enriched the economically advanced countries.

Debray tried to put the Cuban revolution within the context of orthodox Marxist-Leninist concepts, and explained why each struggle must be waged within the historical concrete conditions of the country. He opened my eyes to the pitfalls of intellectualism. Writing in *Revolution in the Revolution?* Debray suggested that intellectuals will try to understand through preconceived ideas from books and live life through these books. Such intellectuals think they have all the knowledge they need through their reading and become less flexible and practical.[86]

Debray addressed the paradox of the Cuban revolution, where the worker-peasant alliance overthrew the US-backed government to achieve state power, without seemingly being led by a Marxist-Leninist party. Unlike the Chinese or Vietnamese revolutions, where the Marxist-Leninist party formed the liberation armies, the Cuban Rebel Army "learned revolution by waging revolution" under the political leadership of Castro and his comrades. Debray claimed that the core of the political leadership was within the Rebel Army, hardened by armed struggle. This leading core, or vanguard, later coalesced into the Communist Party of Cuba in 1965.

At the time, I did not fully grasp the concept of a vanguard Marxist-Leninist party. This understanding would come later when I began to study the Chinese Revolution.

It was Edgar Snow's *Red Star Over China*—the first edition of which came out in 1938—that gave me the visceral appreciation for social revolution. The book gave me an idealized, quixotic view of the Chinese Revolution led by Mao Zedong. Snow wrote about the lives of the heroic Chinese communists who set up bases in northwestern China under Mao's leadership in the 1930s after their legendary Long March. Nearly wiped out by Chiang Kai-shek's Encirclement and Annihilation Campaign, the Chinese Workers' and Peasants' Red Army under the command of the Chinese Communist Party retreated and marched over 6,000 miles (more than double the distance between Toronto and Vancouver) in 370 days, with many deaths along the way. The US Army at the time doubted that such a march took place or was even possible, Snow wrote.

As with any pivotal historic event, there are disputes over facts and alternative facts, depending on which side of the fence you are on. But taking into account all the claimed numbers, 85,000 to 130,000 Red Army soldiers started the march and 8,000 to 20,000 survived to set up their bases in Shaanxi. It was a turning point in the revolution. It was in these bases that Mao and Zhou Enlai consolidated their leadership of the Communist Party of China. I came to see that Mao understood the nature of China's revolution to be agrarian, with the peasantry as the driving force, both in the resistance to the Japanese and in the eventual victory over Chiang Kai-shek. All the while he avoided erroneous directives from Stalin and the Communist International (Comintern).

Snow offered a romantic view of the Chinese in the liberated areas where new selfless men and women were being shaped. He wrote the stories of how and why these men and women took part in "the long struggle to carry out the most thorough-going social revolution in China's three millennium of history."[87]

In 1936, Snow visited the Chinese soviets in the liberated areas to write about the ordinary people who accomplished extraordinary feats. He met and interviewed Zhou Enlai and Mao. I learned from Snow that Mao's favourite book was *Water Margin*, the Chinese classic that was my father's favourite book and whose stories he had ingrained in me as a boy.

From the time I came to Montreal at age seven, my father had told me stories from *Water Margin*, which is about 108 outlaws who used their martial skills to fight against feudal tyranny, only to be betrayed in the end by the same feudal ideology that they fought against. Father applied his nineteenth century Chinese view of the world to twentieth century Canada—even his spoken Toishanese was from an earlier period. Most of the time he succeeded; it allowed him to make sense of the new world. This was the early education I received from my father; he was educating me to take extra care in dealing with power because the system was against us, and to this day, I remain disdainful of authority.

Snow perceived a gentler side of Mao during the time he spent with the Chairman, calling him "a humanist in a fundamental sense; he believed in man's ability to solve man's problems. ... [H]e had probably on the whole been a moderating influence in the Communist movement where life and death were concerned."[88]

What most provoked me, though, were the stories of the ordinary men and women who gave up everything—including, many, their lives—for the revolution. Snow described the role of women in the liberated areas and how they played a vital role in the revolution, long before the Western feminist concepts of women's liberation saw the light of day. "Equal pay for equal labour" was the slogan of the Chinese soviets, to eliminate wage discrimination against women. Policies were instituted for maternity leave and childcare. These stories stirred me to action!

Snow's enthusiasm for the Chinese Revolution was unmistakable and infectious, at least for this young incipient "revolutionary." I gladly loaned the book to a Singaporean student at McGill named Pang. He told me that these books were banned in Singapore. When he returned home he kept the book; he must have smuggled it into the country. In a small way, I contributed to Communist thought in Singapore. My reading of the book also coincided with momentous events in China at the time: the Great Proletarian Cultural Revolution. The name Cultural Revolution itself invoked extraordinary, earth-shaking transformations taking place. China gave me pride to be Chinese. Red China became my model.

* * *

The struggle for decolonization was taking place throughout the Third World at the time, and as an impressionable young student, these battles of the underdog against the powerful foreign colonial occupiers were inspirational.

The peoples of Asia, Africa and Latin America were throwing off the yoke of rapacious colonialism. Many nationalist leaders—such as Eduardo Mondlane of Mozambique and Guinea-Bissau's Amilcar Cabral—were assassinated in last-ditch attempts by the European powers, including Britain, France, Belgium, Spain, Italy, Portugal and the Netherlands, to retain the colonies. If countries did not acquire independence after years of pacifist struggle, as India did, armed national liberation struggles in countries like Zimbabwe, Mozambique, Angola, Guinea-Bissau, East Timor and Eritrea were the only methods that the colonial authorities understood. Then there was the struggle of the Vietnamese people against the military might of the US.

I wasn't the only one inspired by all of this.

In 1960s Quebec, decolonization was *de rigueur* ideology.[89] The idea of the Quebec nation emerged in people's consciousness through the politics of the Quiet Revolution, a period of intense political, social-cultural and economic change that took place between 1960 and 1966. Quebec nationalism had evolved since colonial times when French settlers occupied the Indigenous people's territories and dubbed it New France in the sixteenth century. Contemporary nationalism gave rise to the Quiet Revolution's motto of *Maîtres chez nous* (Masters of our own house), to reflect the desire for self-determination of the Quebec nation and control over its own destiny. Among other things, the class nature of Quebec society began to develop in people's thinking. The Quebec national bourgeoisie as a class began to exert itself to take control of economic power with the help of the state, through nationalizing private power companies to create Hydro-Québec, for example. The Quebec left struggled to keep up, and the rudimentary class-consciousness was expressed through nationalism.

Quebec nationalists claimed Quebec had Third World status and sought the decolonization of their own nation. In doing so, they appropriated the term and affronted those in the Third World fighting for genuine decolonization. The real decolonization struggle of the Indigenous peoples in Canada was ignored and trampled on by the original colonizers of Quebec—the *Québécois de souche* or *pure laine*, the "White Niggers of America."[90] This title of Pierre Vallières' book muddled the concepts of race and social and economic status in society. It was as if they did not see the class nature of their own oppression so they needed to borrow the reality of racial and colonial oppression from others. The decolonization theory of Quebec was discredited and began to wane when people realized the true nature of the fight against colonialism was to be seen in the Cree people's struggle for self-determination in Northern Quebec.

* * *

At this time, I was having many new experiences and meeting many new people, including a good number of the foreign students who came to McGill and introduced me to their world. Even the foreign students' views of McGill were an eye-opener for me: for many of them, the further from Canada they had come from, the better McGill's reputation.

Devinder Garewal was a Sikh from India. He was an imposing figure, well over six feet tall, fully bearded and turbaned. But he was soft-spoken and patient in his explanations, even in the finer points of dialectical materialism. He was a couple of years ahead of me in engineering. I got to know him as he was passing out leaflets at an antiwar protest, and he invited me to attend a Marxist-Leninist study group. By then, I had abandoned the casual and loose politics of the New Left and begun the study of the theory of revolutionary Marxism-Leninism, also known as scientific socialism. Marxism-Leninism is the synthesis of Marx and Lenin's theories as applied to revolutionary practice. It is the guiding ideology of Communist parties throughout the world. Mao further integrated these theories to apply them to the Chinese Revolution and thus developed Marxism-Leninism-Mao Zedong Thought.

The pieces started coming together for me, as the theory explained so much about why and how capitalist society maintained itself through exploitation of workers and the Third World.

Devinder and I took over the *Plumber's Pot*, the engineering newspaper. We dubbed it the "best red paper on campus," as we mocked the New Leftism of the *McGill Daily*. (One of the editors of the *Daily*, Mark Starowicz, Loyola alumnus, went on to become an executive at the CBC.)

Then, one icy December evening in 1968, I walked briskly along La Gauchetière and slipped through a small wooden door next to the Sun Kuo Min Café. I walked down the dimly lit corridor with the sound of mah jong tiles click-clacking in small rooms on either side, and through the pungent redolence of Chinese herbal soup simmering on some stove. At the end of the corridor, I went into a small meeting hall, the gathering place of the East Wind Club, organized by the Hong Men (Chinese Freemasons). The club had monthly showings of films from the People's Republic of China. People went to these events surreptitiously, looking over their shoulder before entering from the street. The Kuomintang was still strong in Montreal's Chinatown and who knows, maybe the RCMP was watching the place.

This evening, the club was showing *Dr. Norman Bethune*, a black and white Chinese production starring American Gerald Tannebaum, who overacted his role as Norman Bethune, the selfless Canadian communist doctor who gave up his life for the Chinese Revolution. Preceding the feature film was a newsreel of Red Guards at Tiananmen Square waving the "Little Red Book" and shouting "*Mao zhuxi wansui*" ("long live Chairman Mao"). The feature film was my introduction to Bethune. The visual dramatization of his life and death made a deep impact on me and explained why people, even from the West, made revolution. I went home that evening and read Mao's *In Memory of Norman Bethune*.

The audience was mainly restaurant workers who had just gotten off work. I respected and had sympathy for these workers who were so easygoing and down to earth in their view of the world. I was the only student there, but since I was still working as a waiter, I spoke their language—which included some colourful swear words focusing on your mother's genitals. They had an avuncular sentiment towards me and jokingly called me "*Mao doy*" (Mao boy).

Politics was only part of my life. Economic survival was also important, as I needed money to continue in university.

In 1969, I was walking along University Street with my friend and fellow Verdunite Richard Orawiec, and looking at companies that might be hiring summer students. We saw a sign for "Saguenay Shipping." As a lark, we said to each other, let's get a job on a ship. Sure enough, Saguenay, a subsidiary of Alcan, had a student employment program but no students had applied because the pay was so pitifully low—$185 a month. We took the job for the adventure. The company flew us to Kitimat, BC, my first plane trip, to board the ss *Sunek*, a fifteen-thousand-ton ocean freighter. The *Sunek* made the run between Kitimat and Port Esquivel, Jamaica, to pick up alumina for the Alcan smelter in Northern BC. Kitimat was a company town designed and built by Alcan in the 1950s to take advantage of the hydroelectric power.

The *Sunek* plied the route between Kitimat and Jamaica along the Pacific coast of North America, through the Panama Canal, and occasionally across the Atlantic to an aluminum plant in Norway. The hierarchy of class and race on board ship was unambiguous. All ten officers were white and the thirty-member crew was Jamaican. It was a lesson in class and racial division. The officers were mainly British, with the exception of the Greek assistant engineer and two Canadians—they had well-maintained cabins to themselves on the upper deck. The Jamaicans, on the other hand, lived four to a cabin on the dingy lower deck. Richard and I shared a guest cabin with bunk beds on the officers' deck.

Naturally, I hung out with the Jamaican crew and worked alongside them chipping away at rust and repainting various spots of the ship. They passed the days doing their marine duties at sea with an easygoing attitude as they chewed ganja to preserve their mellow mood. The Jamaicans did all the heavy lifting when the ship was docking or undocking and when it took on or offloaded the cargo; these operations could take all day or all night. Most of the crew were young; there was a burly, bearded one named Chung, whose father was a Jamaican-born Chinese. I learned from Chung that Chinese labourers settled in Jamaica at about the same time that they settled in Canada. Posters of Che and Fidel hung in many of their cabins alongside reggae musicians Bob Marley and Peter Tosh.

Richard and I ate in the officers' dining room complete with white tablecloths and crisp white napkins as the two dignified Jamaican stewards served

With three of my Jamaican buddies on my last day on the ss *Sunek*, before disembarking in San Pedro, California. (William Dere Collection)

the meals. The Jamaican cook prepared the delicious food. The crew ate below deck in their segregated mess hall; once I asked if I could eat with them and they all laughed. Their meals were simple fare but the main reason was that there was barely enough food at each meal for the ravenous crew. If open class struggle were to happen, this was the epic setting for it.

Nevertheless, Richard and I enjoyed our time on the ship. When not chipping and painting I did engine watch as well as night duty on the bridge. I particularly savoured the sultry sea breeze and viewing the abundance of stars in the clear night sky. During the day, we watched the flying fish sailing across the bow or the dolphins jumping alongside the ship through the azure blue water. On our last trip down to Port Esquivel, Richard and I fantasized about being sailors and we debated whether to stay on the ship and sail to Norway from Port Esquivel. Richard was the first to come to his senses, as he reminded me that we were the first in our families to go to university and it would be a great disappointment for our immigrant parents if we became sailors. I agreed. Richard later became a dentist.

Back at McGill, I was about to meet my political mentor.

Devinder took me to the lab of Daya Varma, an MD with a PhD in pharmacology who was a professor at McGill, and introduced me. The lab was a hangout for progressive students. Daya was the leading force on campus of the Third World Marxist-Leninists; he had joined the Communist Party of India during his student days in the 1950s. Apart from becoming my political mentor, he would become a lifelong friend.

The Marxist-Leninist study groups of Third World people were an alternative to the New Left, nationalist and decolonization movements in Montreal in the late '60s. Through the network of Third World students and study groups, I began to organically understand the fight for national liberation and the need to make a break from colonial mentality through socialist thought.

In the Marxist-Leninist study groups, we examined classical works such as Lenin's *Imperialism, the Highest Stage of Capitalism* and *The State and Revolution*; Mao's *New Democracy*, and *On Contradiction*; and Marx's *Communist Manifesto*. The texts furthered my understanding of the world, especially the Third World. It was a new language and I quickly became proficient in it.

Having knowledge of Marxism-Leninism was like having a passport into understanding the oppressed peoples and countries of the world—it was a different world outlook. When you think you have the solutions to change the world for the better, you tend to have an air of arrogance. I've been accused of this more than once.

I am not an orator. I don't move and inspire people through speech. My skill is in organizing. This ability to mobilize people put me behind the scenes and allowed those more talented, who can articulate the cause, a platform to inspire people through oration. I resisted attempts by Daya to get me to address meetings. After I refused his many invitations to be a speaker, he became frustrated and accused me of "false modesty."

* * *

With the core of people from the Marxist-Leninist study groups, Daya formed the Afro-Asian Latin America Peoples' Solidarity Committee (AALAPSC) as a mass organization to broaden the support for Third World struggles—struggles we deemed to be at the vanguard of world revolution. The AALAPSC, also known as the "Afro-Asians," created different support groups for the struggles in areas such as Palestine, South Africa (Azania), the Portuguese colonies in Africa, and the Caribbean and Latin American struggles in places like Haiti, Trinidad and Tobago, Guatemala and Venezuela.

Two of the more renowned members of the Afro-Asians were Hidipo Hamutenya of Namibia and Mtshana Ncube of Zimbabwe. Hidipo would become a minister in the SWAPO[91] (South West Africa People's Organization) government and he was almost elected president of Namibia. Mtshana was a member of the Patriotic Front–ZAPU[92] (Zimbabwe African People's Union).

The Afro-Asians published *Third World Solidarity* and later the semi-monthly journal *Third World Forum*, both of which Daya funded. We distributed the literature and set up book tables at community functions, trade union conferences and Third World solidarity rallies. Literature tables were a good way to communicate with people who dropped by out of curiosity and allowed us to do our agitation and propaganda. I sat behind many of these tables and enjoyed my conversations with those who stopped—especially the ones that did not agree with our points of view—and lively debates ensued. On these tables we had pamphlets from the national liberation movements, Marxist-Leninist texts, and of course, literature from China. We met fellow travellers and recruited many to our cause.

The insular movement of Quebec nationalist renewal was beginning to turn international, as members of the Afro-Asians—especially the French-speaking Haitian and North African members—started to link up with the Québécois community groups and the solidarity committee of the Confédération des syndicats nationaux union. World events and local Third World activists helped to turn the homegrown nationalism into a global internationalism.

Today, there is much discussion on whether we have ethnic, linguistic-cultural or territorial nationalism in Quebec. However, in the 1970s many on the left saw Quebec nationalism as a progressive force challenging the status quo, but this nationalism became internationalism with the influence of Marxist-Leninist thought.

* * *

On Daya's suggestion, I was assigned to create the Canada-China Friendship Association. The international network of China friendship groups was essentially a united front of trade unions, community organizations, political groupings, academics and common people from all walks of life who had an interest in China. Many of these friendship groups were mass organizations and seen as fertile grounds for Marxist-Leninists to recruit people who were sympathetic to China—and by extension to socialism. Friendship work was productive in promoting a friendly awareness of People's China, and it spurred on a broad spectrum of people to get a first-hand look at the "miraculous" changes taking place in the new workers' paradise.

I took on the task with Alan Silverman, whom I befriended in a study group, and we've remained friends ever since. Alan and I were roommates in the mid '70s, sharing a flat on Drolet, half a block up from Carré St. Louis. He introduced me to gefilte fish, the bland Jewish delicacy. He kept a cupboard full of cans of this stuff, which he often ate as a quick meal.

Winning support for China prior to Canada establishing diplomatic relations with the People's Republic in 1970 was a "revolutionary" task. We saw China as the model, the beacon of world revolution; it was important to gain sympathy for China to counter the anti–Red China sentiments emanating from the US. The KMT was still strong in Canada and they were fighting a rearguard battle to discourage Canada from recognizing the People's Republic of China.

Alan and I published newsletters and organized public meetings and film screenings of revolutionary classics, like *The Red Detachment of Women*. While I was still a student at McGill, I was able to book rooms and even take out audio-visual equipment without charge for these meetings and presentations on China. To get around any censorship from the administration, I presented the purpose of these meetings to be travelogues on China. In 1970, we invited notable speakers, such as Rev. James Endicott, an international peace activist, long-time friend of China and supporter of the Chinese Communist Party. Endicott founded the Canadian Peace Congress and received the Stalin Peace Prize in 1952. Another speaker was Ted Allen, who fought in the Spanish Civil War and was a friend of Norman Bethune. He was asked to speak about his book on the life of Bethune, *The Scalpel. The Sword*. Allen later wrote the screenplay for *Lies My Father Told Me*, for which he received an Academy Award nomination.

William Hinton, another old China hand and author of *Fanshan*, also spoke in Montreal in 1971. I remember checking him into the old thousand-room

Laurentian Hotel, a utilitarian lodging which has since been demolished for an office complex, at the corner of Dorchester and Peel. He spoke glowingly of the agrarian revolution in China's countryside, but years later Hinton would become an outspoken critic of economic reforms in China. We also organized talks with the knowledge we gleaned from pro-China books and magazines like *China Reconstructs* and *Beijing Review*. Alan gave a talk on the true nature of Lin Piao,[93] which shed some light on the internal intrigues of the Chinese Communist Party during the Cultural Revolution.

People in Quebec had great interest in People's China. A few years later, when I knew and worked closely with Roger Rashi, he told me that while he was working in a furniture factory in 1972, the union called a general assembly at the shop to deliver a report on a Quebec labour delegation to China. Three hundred of the five hundred workers in the plant attended.[94]

Our friendship association lasted until 1974, when we merged with Prof. Paul Lin's Canada-China Society, which had a more respectable clientele of academics, politicians and business people.

* * *

The 1970s—the decade in which I would graduate—were a tempestuous time in Quebec and around the world. But I can't discuss that further without mentioning an event that took place in Montreal as the '60s were coming to an end.

Racism in Canada has taken on many forms. We had the early naked state racism against the Indigenous peoples and the Chinese immigrants, but racism became more subtle and insidious as history progressed. I came to realize that the politics of racism required some intellectual understanding of how the economic system perpetuated racist ideas—both to exploit and divide people, and to maintain the system among oppressed and marginalized minorities.

The stark lessons of racism were clearly demonstrated in Montreal in 1969. The anti-racist struggles of the First Peoples, Blacks and other minorities had not yet entered the consciousness of the Quebec nationalist left. Vallières' book used the concept of "white niggers" to paint a misleading picture of Quebec as an oppressed colony. In doing so, he clouded over Black Quebecers' fight against racism. The anti-racist struggle in the province was crystallized by the occupation of the Sir George Williams University computer centre in support of Black Caribbean students' claims of discrimination by a white biology teacher. Without any sensitivity to the grievances of the Black students, the university went into a public relations mode to absolve itself and, after a hearing, found the teacher to be not guilty of racism. In response to the original grievance, the students staged one of the largest student occupations in Canadian history with over four hundred taking part.

I remember standing on de Maisonneuve Boulevard, looking up as the occupying students threw out computer punch cards and printouts from the ninth floor, like confetti, covering the street below. The occupation was peaceful until the riot police were called. A fire broke out in the computer centre in the ensuing "riot."

There was a substantial racist backlash to the burning of the computer centre. With black smoke spewing from the ninth floor windows, whites on the ground chanted, "Let the niggers burn." The Quebec left was jolted by the reality of racism at home; it wasn't a struggle of Blacks in the us South or in far-away South Africa, but in downtown Montreal. This open anti-racist rebellion was a fitting close to the turbulent '60s.

The Quiet Revolution of the early '60s had given the Quebec people the burgeoning confidence of being *Maîtres chez nous*. We lived through the results of the terrorist bombings perpetrated by the Front de Libération du Québec (FLQ) and the state repression in response, imposed under the War Measures Act after the FLQ kidnapped British trade commissioner James Cross and kidnapped and assassinated Pierre Laporte, a Quebec government minister. Our group at McGill opposed the terrorism of the FLQ. We viewed terrorism as a political tactic, devoid of any mass participation and support, to be counter-productive.

The declaration of the War Measures Act in October 1970 had a blanketing effect on us. The military was everywhere, even on the street in front of the McGill campus. Police repression was palpable. Many political activists were rounded up, and others were forced to work in a semi-clandestine manner.

One of Daya's graduate students was picked up by the police and thrown into the Parthenais Detention Centre. Our collective was indignant but felt powerless for fear of being seized. Daya encouraged us to continue the agit-prop work. We had flying squads of people distributing leaflets denouncing the state repression.

I went to Daya's office to pick up a bunch of stickers with the famous image of the old Québécois Patriote stepping in a forward lean with a musket in his hands, a corncob pipe in his mouth and a tuque on his head. The slogan "A

Bas Le Fascisme!" ("Down with Fascism!") was emblazoned on the sticker. People posted this sticker around town, including on campus.

I felt the nervous tension. We were in an atmosphere of "apprehended insurrection." It cast a pall over our political work. Granted, it was nothing like the repression faced by the Third World revolutionaries and anti-colonial fighters in their life and death struggles, but it still came as a shock to most of us who had been taught to expect civil liberties, freedom and democracy in Canada. One day, running between floors in the McConnell Engineering Building, I sensed someone following me. I quickly dodged into a washroom and sat down in a stall. That person pursued me and entered the toilet but seeing I was there, doing my business, he left.

There was an acute economic crisis in the early '70s. Unemployment was high, wages low, and inflation was rampant with soaring prices. In response, workers' study groups, community organizations and social movements were sprouting at the grassroots. General strikes were called; union leaders were jailed. The dead-end nationalism of the Parti Québécois was driving people to seek a broader solution to the many problems facing Quebec society. During that time we participated in some of the major struggles in the Quebec anti-imperialist movement—rallying people against the Vietnam War, and in support of the Palestinian and South African struggles—and we also mobilized support for the labour battles that were rocking Quebec society.

After writing my final exam in May 1972, I went with a comrade to the east end Maurice Richard Arena where a union rally was being held. The assembly came on the heels of a province-wide general strike and legislation ordering the workers back to work. The arena was full of striking workers, union militants and community activists listening to speeches from their leaders. The strength of unity and solidarity was awe-inspiring. Music added to the festive and rebellious atmosphere. The Cuban song "Guantanamera" rang in my ears. I was truly inspired by José Marti's words and felt I was casting my lot with the poor of the world.

The three union leaders of the Front commun[95] were at the forefront of the popular struggles in Quebec and each was sentenced to one year in jail for defying the legislation to return to work. Each union issued a manifesto putting forward a fledgling class analysis, but they still saw Quebec society as a colony of Anglo capitalism and US imperialism. The manifestos revealed the class-consciousness growing among Quebec workers. This trend of thought could not help but have a powerful influence among the left in

Quebec, which would lead to a more radical rupture from the decolonization politics of the '60s.

Upon my graduation in 1972, I set out to find work. Many of my fellow engineering students were offered employment even before they graduated. A few months of pounding the streets and knocking on doors produced no results. Was it because I was Chinese, as my father said, or was it due to the economic recession? By this time, I knew that I wasn't the main source of my own misfortune. The reason I was unemployed was due to the system that offered few opportunities for immigrants and minorities. *and women*

I decided to enter graduate studies, with the hope that a master's degree would open some doors. I enrolled at Carleton University and moved to Ottawa. While there, I was restless, so along with a group of like-minded science students, I organized a Science for the People chapter. I left behind my Third World comrades in Montreal. I've always been a solitary man—a loner—but I missed the companionship and the camaraderie of the like-minded friends who came from all over the world to congregate in Montreal.

Chapter 7

Life of the Party

"You don't join the Communist Party without carrying a burden of morality—which is a burden, not a gift—and playing the role of a moralist."
—Howard Fast, *Being Red*[96]

In the 7 a.m. light of dawn, I put my glasses on. When I looked over to the bunks two rows over, I saw a half-nude woman comrade stretching her arms. I could not see her face, as the upper bunk was blocking her. I only saw her breasts and midriff. Free of encumbrances, she was not embarrassed to stand bare-breasted as she took her time to put on a T-shirt. I never found out who she was, but her open, relaxed demeanour formed a lasting impression and was one of the memorable highlights of the founding congress of the Workers Communist Party.

I returned to Montreal in 1974 after two years in Ottawa. Many of the friends and comrades I knew at McGill had graduated and gone back to their countries or off to graduate schools in Europe or elsewhere. I kept in touch with some of them for a while. Devinder went to Imperial College in London; some went back to Trinidad, Guyana or South Asia, to take part in the popular movements in those countries; Amin Kassam, a former editor of the *McGill*

Daily, went on to become an editor for a daily paper in Nairobi, Kenya, and a well-known poet. This is one of Amin's poems:

how kind

compassion
has changed
meaning

first
starve
maim

kill
in the name
of peace

then
allow
a little food

and call
it mercy
so kind

Amin Kassam[97]

My friends' sojourn at McGill and in Canada proved to be good training as they sought to change things for the better in their home countries. In 1975, following a trip to China, I visited some of these comrades in Pakistan, India and East Africa. Shortly after, I lost touch with them due to distance, time and preoccupation with other endeavours.

I rejoined the Afro-Asian Latin American Peoples' Solidarity Committee. The membership had changed. Many of the new members had intellectual interests as students in Asian or African studies. Debates and discussions within the Afro-Asians took on a more academic tone rather than the impatient tone of the departed young people who wanted to change the world now.

At this time, the political terrain in Montreal was undergoing a major shift to the left and many of us in the Afro-Asians could not resist the groundswell taking place around us.

With financial support from Daya Varma, a physical Third World Centre was founded in Montreal. It started out in a dilapidated triplex at the corner of University and President Kennedy; we then moved to a stately greystone on Prince Arthur in the McGill ghetto; lastly, we moved to a third floor cold flat on St. Laurent near Sherbrooke Street. Some nights it was so cold that we held meetings in our winter coats, and only the heated debates prevented us from freezing.

However, within the Afro-Asians, there was a battle brewing—a two-line struggle (the "revolutionary" pro-China vs the "revisionist" pro-Soviet lines). There were those around the journal *Third World Forum* that wanted a softer, New Left intellectual approach to Third World struggles. At that time many progressives looked to the Third World as a fertile ground for their anti-corporate theory. The editors of the *Forum* had affiliations with other like-minded organizations and journals such as *Latin American Perspectives, Review of African Political Economy* and *Latin American Working Group* out of Toronto. Nevertheless, the study of Marxist-Leninist thought in the Afro-Asians continued with appropriate texts like *Imperialism and the National Question.*

I was part of the group that wanted a more radical approach. We felt that those around the *Forum* held a reformist academic attitude to anti-imperialism, but in the interest of not causing a split, we did not openly call them "revisionist," while we were the "revolutionary" anti-imperialists.

* * *

Around this time, the labour movement took the lead for social change in Quebec society with the three Common Front unions issuing manifestos calling for the movement of the struggle from "narrow" nationalism to the broader perspective of class exploitation. Community and labour activists quickly absorbed lessons from the 1972 general strike of 250,000 workers across Quebec, and the jailing of the three union leaders in 1972–73. Militants turned away from decolonization politics to study Marxism.

While many were influenced by the European politics of the 1968 student movement and the writings of Louis Althusser and Nicos Poulantzas, the most impact came from the internationalist politics of the Third World and the anti-revisionist pronouncements of the People's Republic of China.

In 1972, Charles Gagnon, jailed for more than two years for his earlier activities in the Front de Libération du Québec, broke ranks with fellow *felquiste* Pierre Vallières and "bourgeois nationalism" when he wrote *Pour le parti prolétarien (For the Proletarian Party)*. This booklet was an important clarion call to organize a revolutionary party based on Marxism-Leninism. It was a polemic against the "independence first" strategy promoted by left Quebec nationalists carried over from the '60s. Gagnon formulated that the immediate task of activists was to build an ideological and political alternative to capitalism and create the conditions to build a revolutionary party to lead the working class and Quebec society to socialism.

Other organizations that began to articulate this trend were the Mouvement révolutionaire des étudiants du Québec—in which my old McGill friend Alan Silverman had become a leading member—as well as Agence de presse libre du Québec and Mobilisation. Many militants were recruited from political action committees into Marxist-Leninist study circles. A strategy known as implantation—going into the factories and workplaces to bring Marxist-Leninist politics and ideology to workers—was taking hold, as many students and middle-class youth looked for work in industries (e.g., at Dominion Engineering) and in the service sector (e.g., in hospitals).

Alan had studied in France in 1969 and was inspired by the fervent student upheavals there. Back at McGill in 1970, he became involved with the Afro-Asians as well as the burgeoning student movement. I remember the two of us marching in an anti–Vietnam War demonstration along Côte-des-Neiges to the US consulate on Pine. Police on horseback broke up the demonstration, waving batons as they chased and taunted the protesters. Alan and I managed to get away from the overexcited horses and the even more excited cops. Somehow, Alan also got involved with the Movimento progressista italo-quebecchese,[98] an Italian working-class organization in Montreal, which lasted a couple of years in the early 1970s. Alan introduced me to one of its leaders, Alfonso. I was suitably impressed when he told the story of how he obtained free copies of the selected works of Mao after writing a letter to the Foreign Languages Press in Beijing.

Alan was a "red diaper baby." His father, Herman, was a member of the Communist Party USA in the 1930s. Herman left the Party when the Soviet Union signed the Soviet-German Non-aggression Pact in 1939, after the Western countries refused any alliance with the USSR. The pact created a state of confusion for those in the international communist movement who had worked to build the united front against German fascism. However, the pact bought the Soviet Union two additional years to prepare for the German invasion that came in 1941.

This was Alan's first lesson in the possibility of division within the international communist movement, as the debate on the Soviet-Chinese split forced many of us to take sides at the time.

Alan's mother, Hilda Pollack, seems to have had a bigger influence on him politically. She was an active member of the Voice of Women, an international feminist peace organization. He remembers her reading the selected works of Mao; he also remembers her using some quotations of the Chairman to scold him when he misbehaved. She reminded him: "Just because someone is a member of the Party, it doesn't mean he is a good person."[99] Hilda was a kind woman. I remember she visited me in the hospital after my surgery for a burst appendix in 1988.

For months, at the chilly Third World Centre on St. Laurent, the twenty-five-odd members in the Afro-Asian organization focused on discussing the Three Worlds Theory and the role of China and the Soviet Union in support

These covers from the *Third World Forum*
show the hot topics debated at the time.

of Third World struggles. This was the winter of 1974; we were passionately engaged in this debate, which was a line of demarcation between the "revolutionaries," who supported the theory, and the "revisionists," who opposed the theory, in Third World support work.

The Three Worlds Theory as formulated by Mao divided countries up this way:

- The First World was made up of the two Superpowers, the Soviet Union (Social imperialism) and the United States (us imperialism).
- The Second World was the advanced capitalist countries of Europe, Japan, Canada, Australia and New Zealand.
- The Third World was the developing countries of Asia, Africa and Latin America.

In terms of Mao's theory, the Chinese were applying their united front tactic—learned during the anti-Japanese war—to the international situation. Social imperialism was China's principal enemy, and the world dominance of the First World could be challenged through the unity of the Second and Third Worlds, as characterized by the slogan, "Countries want independence, nations want liberation and the people want revolution."

Opposition to the Three Worlds Theory came from the left and the right, depending on how one viewed Marxist orthodoxy. On one hand, some people were not convinced that the Soviet Union had restored capitalism and become an imperialist power; they maintained that the USSR was still playing a progressive role in helping the liberation struggles, especially through its support for Vietnam in its fight against the "only" superpower, the United States. There were others who maintained that, in opposing us and social imperialism, you couldn't unite with capitalist countries, such as those in Europe, or the reactionary regimes in the Third World.

This debate paralyzed the Afro-Asians. However, *Third World Forum* continued to be published for another two years thanks to the dedication of the "revisionist" faction.

* * *

During this time, even with a full-time job at C.D. Howe Consulting Engineers in Montreal, I was engaged in the vibrant political atmosphere—attending union rallies; establishing contacts in the progressive and revolutionary organizations in the city; and organizing Third World support demonstrations, information meetings, and literature tables in universities and the CEGEPs (Quebec's general and vocational colleges between high school and university, or between school and the work force for those students studying for a vocation).

In the spring of 1975, members of the Mouvement révolutionaire des étudiants du Québec organization who were active in the Canada China Society approached me to take part in a delegation to visit China. It was to be one of the first Canadian friendship delegations to China since the establishment of diplomatic relations between the two countries in 1970. The delegation was a true united front, composed of people from a wide spectrum of Quebec society. For example, the leader was Denis Lazure, a psychiatrist, who later became a cabinet minister in the Parti Québécois government, and members included Jean Paré, later an editor at *L'Actualité* magazine. Five members of the delegation became members of the Canadian Communist League (Marxist-Leninist), the precursor of the Workers Communist Party. Alan was the assistant leader of the delegation.

Four days into the trip, Lazure came down with appendicitis and was hospitalized for an appendectomy in Changsha, China. We all wondered if he had acupuncture anesthetic during the operation. No, he told us when he rejoined the tour five days later in Beijing.

As we crossed the bridge at Lo Wu into China from Hong Kong, I was a wide-eyed idealist thinking I was setting foot into the dream socialist society depicted in Edgar Snow's book. Banners hailing the liberation of Vietnam on April 30, 1975, greeted us as we crossed the river; such banners were hoisted throughout the areas that we visited in China. At the Shenzhen train station, we met people from the New Zealand–China Society who were on their way out. They spoke glowingly about what they'd seen. I wrote in my journal, "Hopefully, this trip will change some stereotypical opinions of China shared by some members of our delegation."

During the trip, some in the delegation tested the stereotypes. A photojournalist had a right-angle lens that took photos around a corner, and he and another journalist tried to verify the much-reputed honesty and morality in socialist China by leaving packages of cigarettes, small amounts of money and other personal belongings in their hotel rooms when they checked out. They waited to see if the hotel staff would return their property to them; the Chinese did, often chasing after the bus to give back their insignificant items. In

The 1975 Canadian Delegation to China gathers for a photo at Dr. Norman Bethune's Mausoleum, Shijiazhuang. I am the fourth from the left, front row. Herman Rosenfeld is to the right. Alan Silverman is the bearded one in the second row. Denis Lazure, absent from the photo, was in a Changsha hospital recovering from an appendectomy.
(William Dere Collection)

another test, when we transferred from the train to a bus, they purposely left a pair of shoes on the train; sure enough, a breathless attendant chased after the bus to return the shoes. Alan and I smirked at these pranks.

Mao's Cultural Revolution, which began in 1966, was not yet officially over but the exuberance of the Red Guards—the young people that Mao urged to "bombard the headquarters"—had long died down. Many of them returned to school to make up for the decade they had lost. Others went back to their work units. There was an uneasy truce among the factions within the Chinese Communist Party; the Gang of Four had not yet been exposed, so Jiang Qing was still using the prestige of being Mao's wife to carry on with her activities; the revered, pragmatic Zhou Enlai, first premier of the People's Republic of China, was ailing with cancer; the once deposed party leader Deng Xiaoping was brought back by Zhou to try and revive the economy, which had suffered ten years of decline, until he was again deposed by Mao after Zhou's death in January 1976. Mao was also ailing at this time; he was becoming more and more reclusive.

The Cultural Revolution lingered—I felt the ideological purity in the presentations of the cadres at the various locations we visited, and I was moved by the revolutionary slogans emblazoned on banners as we travelled through the country, such as "Serve the People" and "Dare to Think, Dare to Act."

We spent three weeks visiting factories, communes, schools, nurseries, revolutionary and ancient sites as well as tourist locations like the Ming Tombs and the Great Wall. One of the highlights was a meeting with Chai Zemin, president of the Chinese People's Association for Friendship with Foreign Countries. Chai was China's ambassador to Guinea and Thailand; he later became China's first ambassador to the US in 1979. It was of particular interest to me to hear him expand on socialist construction in China and the country's foreign policy at that time. My notes on what he said included the following:

> Socialism in China is a new thing. We are in the process of constructing Chinese socialism and socialist ideology. Friends who visit China should compare the new China to the old China. You can't cut off bound feet and replace them with new feet. There is much left over from the old society.[100]

Chai expounded on the Three Worlds Theory and surprisingly answered in detail when I asked specific questions on topics such as the role of the Shah of Iran, the liberation struggle in Dhofar and Oman, and China's position on the three liberation movements in Angola. My notes on his answer to the Angolan question include these words:

> The Soviet Union supports liberation movements out of its own interest. There are three groups in Angola: The USSR is supporting only the MPLA [People's Movement for the Liberation of Angola]; the Soviet Union takes a different attitude towards the other two. It wants to get its hands on Angola. This way leads to civil war among the movements in Angola. A civil war would be detrimental to the Angolan people. China supports all three movements and urges them to unite. We have invited all three groups to China. They should not fall into the hands of the Superpowers by disagreeing among themselves.

The other two movements (apart from the MPLA) that were fighting to liberate Angola from Portuguese colonialism were UNITA (National Union

A chance encounter with a peasant family at a Chinese Commune in 1975.
(William Dere Collection)

for the Total Independence of Angola) and the FNLA (National Liberation Front of Angola). Unfortunately, Angola did fall into a devastating civil war that lasted from 1975 to 2002; the MPLA emerged victorious, but five hundred thousand Angolan people died.

While the rest of the delegation headed back across the Pacific to Canada after the tour, I headed west to India, Pakistan, Kenya, Zambia and Tanzania to visit former members of the Afro-Asians who had gone back home. Dar es Salaam, former capital of Tanzania, was the centre of the exiled anti-apartheid community from South Africa. I visited the office of the Pan Africanist Congress of Azania, the other major South African liberation movement, which we supported because of its policy of armed struggle and its pro-China stance. In Lusaka, Zambia, I remember walking into the African National Congress office and Oliver Tambo, leader of the ANC, was casually sitting behind the front desk. I introduced myself and explained the support work we were doing in Canada. We had a good thirty-minute talk and he encouraged me to keep up the good work.

When I arrived back in Montreal in July 1975, there was excitement in the air. I felt the political enthusiasm of those involved in the Marxist-Leninist circles. The ideas of Charles Gagnon in *Pour le parti prolétarien* had percolated among

The 1975 Canadian Delegation visits Shaoshan, Mao's birthplace. Denis Lazure, head of the delegation is seventh from the left, front row. I am third from left, second row, resplendent in my Red Guard garb. (William Dere Collection)

the broad left in Quebec. Gagnon formed *l'Équipe du journal* (The Newspaper Team) to publish *En lutte!* in French at first, but later an English edition called *In Struggle!* came out too. Gagnon went on to create the Marxist-Leninist Organization of Canada, In Struggle! (En lutte!) after uniting with smaller groups in English Canada. En lutte! was not able to penetrate the English milieu in Montreal as much as the Mouvement révolutionnaire des étudiants du Québec, which began among students at McGill; however, it was strong at the Université du Québec à Montréal among the left nationalist students and intellectuals.

In my circle, unity talks were underway among three of the Marxist-Leninist groups in Quebec—the Mouvement révolutionnaire des étudiants du Québec, the Cellule ouvrière révolutionnaire and the Cellule militante ouvrière. Herman Rosenfeld, my roommate during the China trip, was a member of the MREQ as well as the Afro-Asians. He presented me with a copy of the unity document. After reading the points of unity and a couple of discussions with Herman, I was ready to join the unity process.

The politics and ideology of the unity document corresponded with my understanding and assimilation of Marxism-Leninism-Mao Zedong Thought and I was eager to participate in an organization that reflected my principles of social equality and compassion, and that wanted to prepare the working class for revolutionary change in Canada.

In the fall of 1975 the three organizations announced the creation of the Canadian Communist League (Marxist-Leninist) which in French was called the Ligue communiste (marxiste-léniniste) du Canada. The average age of the members of the three founding organizations was twenty-one.[101]

The League was structured according to the orthodox Comintern instructions for a Leninist party passed at its third congress in 1921.[102] The basic units were the cells, either around a factory if the numbers warranted, or an industry; for those who worked in the *quartiers* (neighbourhoods), there were community cells.

Each cell was composed of eight to ten members led by a cell leader, who reported to the district. The cell leader organized the weekly cell meetings, with the general agenda from the district. Members, or preferably sympathizers, offered their homes for such three- or four-hour meetings. The locations were anywhere around town; for this reason, we joked that we all got to know the city better than a taxi driver.

People pejoratively called it a Stalinist party; that would be giving Stalin too much credit. It was under Lenin that the Comintern laid down the directions on the organization and structure of Communist parties throughout the world based on the discipline of Democratic Centralism, where the party membership must carry out the decisions of the leadership once an issue has been thoroughly discussed and adopted.

The cell meetings began with a discussion of current events and directives from the leadership, and there would be a study of Marxist texts. Other discussions dealt with the agit-prop topics for the week, articles from the party newspaper the *Forge*, the week's plan for distribution of the paper, and the cell's participation in activities organized by the League or mass organizations. I felt a lively atmosphere of study and discussion; it was not at all tedious attending cell meetings. Each of us was assigned tasks for the week. My cell members were Québécois Francophones. I struggled at first with my high school French, but as time went on, I picked up the political expressions and the working-class slang. I've never spoken better French since then.

Once a month, there would be the collection of dues, which came to 25 per cent of income. At the beginning, I was giving $300 a month from my engineer's salary. This came as a shock to many in my St-Henri quartier cell since most of the members were either on welfare or had minimum wage jobs. Even with paying the monthly dues, I was able to save enough to buy a $5,000 Saab, which was recommended by an Afro-Asian comrade from Trinidad, Kenny

Charles. The car was immediately borrowed by League cadres for travel to the different regions of Quebec, such as Val d'Or and Chicoutimi.

My *nom de guerre* in the cell was Ti-Guy. I was probably the first Chinese Québécois that my fellow cell members had known, and they accepted me as a comrade and became protective and patient as I struggled with my French. It was at this time that I felt integrated into Francophone Québécois society, discovering first-hand how my fellow cell members lived in the working-class districts of St-Henri and Pointe-St-Charles by going into their kitchens and hanging out with them as we prepared our activities of distributing leaflets or getting together to make placards for pickets and demonstrations. I felt I was part of something larger than myself, in a family of equals where equality and compassion prevailed.

* * *

One evening in the fall of 1975, I received a phone call. "Hi, it's Roger. Can we meet tomorrow?" Who, I thought, was Roger? He spoke as if I should know him. "Okay," I said, and we set up a time and place to meet.

I arrived at the restaurant at the designated time and waited. And waited. I had a bag full of pamphlets and I read them all twice to pass the time but I kept looking at my watch. Half an hour, forty-five minutes; finally a stylish, swarthy man with coiffed hair and a thick black mustache arrived, introduced himself as Roger Rashi, and apologized profusely for being late. This was the pattern as we regularly met over the next six years. The running joke among the comrades was if Roger was half an hour late, he was early. I had this incurable habit of being on time, so I learned to take work with me when I was to meet Roger. We held our meetings at all hours of the day and night in restaurants. I got to know almost every greasy spoon in Montreal's Plateau district.

At this first meeting, Roger explained what was expected of me—to head up the anti-imperialist "fraction" of the League. Fractions were groupings of League members within the Confédération des syndicats nationaux or Fédération des travailleurs et travailleuses du Québec trade unions, community mass organizations such as SOS Garderies (daycares), health clinics, the Comptoirs food co-ops and other areas.

The anti-imperialist fraction would develop an internal plan to educate the membership on the international situation and to mobilize support for the anti-imperialist, anti-colonial struggles in the Third World. I felt honoured by this heavy responsibility to bring anti-imperialist politics to the working class of Quebec and Canada. I would report to Roger and he would be my go-to person on the work of the League on the international scene. I quickly discovered that Roger was the Spokesman, and de facto Chairman, of the League.

Roger Rashi, an Egyptian immigrant who arrived in Quebec at fifteen, was charming and charismatic. He was one of those people who would turn heads as he entered the room. He was self-assured and warm, and you had his full attention as you spoke. He had thick black hair combed into a pompadour à la Elvis. He spoke French at home, which was essentially his mother tongue. This was a carryover of the French occupation of Egypt in the nineteenth century. He later told me[103] that he felt like an outcast when he first arrived in Montreal, and not part of the Quebec majority. He went to English schools and attended McGill. It was at McGill that he became politicized through the anti-war student movement, particularly that part that turned towards Quebec nationalism. He was active in the "McGill français" campaign as he gradually adhered to left nationalism. He started identifying himself as a Québécois and he eventually became part of the revolutionary socialist movement—moving away from nationalism—that was sprouting in Montreal in the early 1970s.

His odyssey to Marxism-Leninism was typical of the time. The early-twentieth-century Marxist philosophers Antonio Gramsci and Rosa Luxemburg, with what Roger saw as their "less authoritarian" politics, had an early influence on him. But the War Measures Act and the ensuing repression brought him to see the value of the "more authoritarian" politics of Marxism-Leninism. His intellectual influences came from France—Louis Althusser and Nicos Poulantzas. The mass movement of the French youth fascinated him, as did the national minority movements in the US—the Black Panthers, the Young Lords and the Students for a Democratic Society. He turned to studying Mao and the Chinese experience, which had a vision of socialism different from that of the Soviet Union, and he started connecting with the Maoist critique of the USSR. After the unions issued their manifestos on class struggle in Quebec, he joined workers study groups, he told me a little while ago, "in order to translate highly intellectual revolutionary concepts into practical everyday class struggle. This was an important factor in moving closer to the workers' movement. The main Marxist textbooks in the universities were Maoist—the anti-colonialist nationalists were sympathetic to the Chinese experience. It was a complex conjuncture of many influences."

When I spoke to him in 2015, Roger expressed respect for Charles Gagnon, with whom he waged fierce polemics in the heyday of Quebec Marxism-Leninism over Gagnon's political line and understanding of M-L ideology.

"Charles Gagnon had an influence on me when he came out of prison in 1971," he said. "The movement to study Maoism had begun in many of the groups in Quebec. Charles reflected and strengthened that. His book *Pour le parti prolétarien* (*For the Proletarian Party*) was a reflection and a further assimilation of trends already in play. I always maintained that the key influence in launching the M-L movement in Quebec was Charles Gagnon's text. I think his aura as an activist, the years he spent in jail, a very sincere approach towards questions in the rejection of nationalism and towards a revolutionary stance influenced and gave early credibility to the M-L strength that would probably be not that high without him."

* * *

Back in 1975, the League established the anti-imperialist fraction to show the importance of "proletarian internationalism"—solidarity work that supported international struggles and demonstrated unity of the world revolutionary movements. The Comité anti-impérialiste (CAI) recruited people from the cells who had experience or an interest in international affairs, including those in the Afro-Asians and in China friendship work, as well as students who had returned from attending Beijing University, members of immigrant mass organizations, and university professors and students studying world affairs. We also led a group of like-minded non-party people, many of them Third World immigrants, who would help to organize anti-imperialist and anti-racist activities such as conferences, demonstrations, and setting up literature tables in schools and union meetings.

The League managed to turn the Afro-Asians, ostensibly an independent mass organization, into a front group. We did this by rallying its members—winning people over to the League's positions or implanting League members and sympathizers. The "revisionist" members gradually left and the *Third World Forum* published its final edition in May 1977. The independent members who remained were adherents of the Three Worlds Theory and sympathetic to Marxism-Leninism.

A new Third World Centre was established at 11 Maguire St. in Mile End, closer to the working-class and immigrant areas of Montreal.

We adopted a less unwieldy name for the Afro-Asian Latin America Peoples' Solidarity Committee (the Afro-Asians): Comité anti-impérialiste des peuples du tiers monde (CAPT), or Third World Peoples' Anti-Imperialist Committee. Daya Varma maintained his steadfast leadership in the organization.

There were several other mass organizations under the umbrella of the CAI[104] and other ad hoc committees to support the struggles in Asia, Africa and Latin America. An anti-racist organization to support the rights of immigrants was created—Organisation de lutte pour les droits démocratiques des immigrants, or Organization to Fight for the Democratic Rights of Immigrants. It was led by a woman comrade who remained a clandestine member since

adhérez au

COMITÉ ANTI-IMPÉRIALISTE DES PEUPLES DU TIERS MONDE

join the

THIRD WORLD PEOPLES' ANTI-IMPERIALIST COMMITTEE

CAPT

This CAPT brochure shows the militancy of Third World struggles in the 1970s.
(William Dere Collection)

her husband was working as a secret member in a factory cell. A clandestine member worked among the workers and mass organizations not as an open member but as someone who was sympathetic to the politics of the Party. This style of work also came directly from the organizational structure of the Comintern, which believed that in times of repression, clandestine members would continue the work of the Party when the open members were arrested or eliminated.

I was becoming a full-time organizer. I was in my twenties; I was tireless; I ate and slept the political activism. I had my weekly cell meetings, weekly or bi-weekly meetings with Roger, weekly meetings of the CAI, weekly meetings of the CAPT, and weekly or bi-weekly meetings with comrades I led who were working among immigrants and other mass organizations. Aside from other Party activities, I was writing articles for the Party paper and internal documents. It was a frenzied, 24/7 existence, and I was going on about four hours of sleep.

Those years were intense, stimulating, intoxicating, exhilarating and romantic. I felt alive as never before.

Starting at midnight, I would roam the neighbourhood of the Plateau—I lived in the area, on Waverly near St. Viateur—to deliver the agenda and the location of the next day's meetings. Luckily, most of the comrades also lived in the vicinity. Once a week, I distributed the *Forge* at the gates of the Canadian National Railways main shops on Leber Street in Pointe-St-Charles. It was a sprawling complex of shops, which at one time employed over one thousand workers, building and repairing rail cars and locomotives. The owner of the café across the street thought my partner and I were dedicated but crazy when we showed up each week as he opened at 6 a.m. for a cup of coffee or hot chocolate. We would catch the workers leaving the night shift and those going to the day shift.

For those driving, we often only had time to shout slogans and pass the paper through the car window. With those who took the bus and got off at the gate, we had a few minutes to engage in discussions on issues affecting the shop and the rail industry. The prize for the day would be a name and contact number of a worker who wanted to continue the discussion. These names would be passed on to the comrades who worked inside the plant. (Twenty years later, I returned to these same shops as the manager of engineering; there were no more militants at the gates passing out leaflets or newspapers.)

My state of hyper-activity was the norm for League members. We were driven by the notion that the Canadian revolution was just around the corner—we felt we needed to create the vanguard party to lead the working class and masses to fight for socialism and a society free from exploitation and want.

We also adopted an underground style of work, thinking that the state police—the RCMP—constantly monitored us. Coming off the heels of the War Measures Act and the resulting repression, this kind of thinking was not far-fetched. The 1977 Quebec Keable Inquiry and the later McDonald Commission on the RCMP exposed its various illegal activities of breaking into organizations, such as the Parti Québécois and the Agence de presse libre du Québec, that they deemed subversive and dangerous, and stealing their membership lists and other documents, tapping telephones and opening private mail.

Sometimes we took comical precautions. I always carried a pocketful of dimes since we could not make phone calls from home—only from public pay phones. Luckily, in those days Bell still had pay phones at almost every major street corner. No Party conversations could be held inside the house or in the car. If you were driving to cell meetings, you needed to take a circuitous route to include deserted industrial areas to make sure you weren't being followed.

As an example of the absurd precautions, one cold February day I went to the apartment of a member of CAPT, an American graduate student named Steve, to talk to him about joining the League. He lived on Drolet Street, near St. Joseph, where each apartment had a small balcony facing the street. His was on the second floor in plain view of everyone. I said, "We can't talk inside." So we put on our coats, grabbed two stools and sat on the balcony to talk about the League program for over an hour. I am sure the passersby regarded us with great suspicion. He never did join the League for reasons other than this crazy episode, but operating in such a manner did not help convince people that we were normal.

Our precautionary measures also meant that I ended up doing night guard duty at the *Forge*.

The paper had moved into the offices of the Agence de presse libre du Québec after the APLQ joined the League in 1976. The spacious building was at 2074 Beaudry, and had been home to a children's wear manufacturer in the 1960s. It was strangely located in the middle of a residential neighbourhood with typical Montreal working-class housing of quadruplex cold-water flats. The production and editorial offices were located on the third floor; the second had other offices and bunk beds; the ground floor was used for storage of newsprint, books, leaflets, picket signs and banners.

APLQ offices at another location were broken into in 1972, and documents and files were stolen. Officers from the RCMP, Sûreté du Québec and Montreal police were exposed and pleaded guilty to the break-in but were given an unconditional discharge. So League members had reasons to be suspicious of the police.

Then one night in 1978, the *Forge* offices were broken into and typewriters were stolen. Naturally, the League security, *service d'ordre*, suspected the worst. Since I was a part-time *Forge* staffer—I vetted the articles written on the international situation—I was assigned to be part of the night guard duty immediately afterwards. On a one-off basis, I had the midnight shift; it was not a production night, so I eventually ended up alone in the building. I was given a number to call in case of trouble. I was on edge all night, listening intently for any sound that could have been made by an intruder. I did not sleep well and you can imagine how elated I was when the sun rose.

This state of apprehension only fed our idealism that revolution was imminent and the enemies of the revolution were doing everything to maintain their hold on state power.

The CAI went on to become the main force for anti-imperialist work in Montreal. The Marxist-Leninist members of the CAPT all rallied to the League and as a result, the League's influence among the different Third World support groups—such as the Filipinos, South Asians, Haitians, Latin Americans, South Africans and Zimbabweans—strengthened. We brought the message of Third World liberation struggles into the trade unions and community organizations with the help of comrades working in these areas.

We often met at the Mazurka Restaurant, 64 Prince Arthur, near the corner of St. Laurent. Apart from being one of our hangouts, many leftists, Afro-Asians, and students from McGill and CEGEP Vieux-Montréal would congregate there. It was across the street from the Ho Chi Minh bookstore. The Mazurka was a Polish, family-owned restaurant, and it introduced me to perogies, cheese and meat blintzes and cabbage soup—comfort food. At that time, we met to plan our activities and discuss the affairs of Quebec and the world over a full-course meal for $1.75. We would sit in the upper level of the split-level restaurant so we could keep an eye on the door. It was a warm and comfortable place, although the waiters would clear the table to get us out after overstaying our limit of two hours.

Alan was on the first central committee of the League. He got a job in a hospital and Gilles Duceppe, future leader of the Bloc Québécois, was in his cell, which was composed of workers in the hospital sector. As an intellectual, Alan found the work in the hospital gruelling. At the same time, the central committee was waging a campaign against intellectualism since most of the leadership was middle-class intellectuals. Alan was demoted and appointed to work as a district cadre to organize the regions around Montreal.

He continued to suffer from intellectualism—abstract concepts through studying texts that might not be applicable to the concrete situation. After his second demotion from the district, Roger came to see me to ask that Alan join the anti-imperialist fraction. I was delighted to have Alan working with me again. I understood his style of work—once he saw his way through a clutter of intellectual texts, he was a very effective organizer.

One incident underlined both his intellectualism and his capacity to innovate and adjust. We had organized a demonstration to denounce the Vietnamese invasion of Kampuchea, and halfway through the march, Alan decided to lead the demonstrators into a snake-like formation, zig-zagging from one side of the street to the other. He had seen this done in Europe and in Japan. However, the Europeans and the Japanese prepared and rehearsed the formation with long poles that the rows of marchers held to keep in step, which we did not do. We ended up in a state of disorder and confusion and quickly returned to the normal straight formation.

By 1977 the CAI had spread to Ontario, with the help of English-speaking comrades who had been sent from Montreal to organize mainly in the auto industry. Toronto was a hotbed of Third World activity, with people coming from the English-speaking Caribbean, South Asia and Latin America. Our plenum meetings of the CAI were held on the last Saturday of the month in Kingston with comrades from Toronto and Montreal each driving three hours to meet in a motel off the 401. The meetings were still in French to respect the rights of our Québécois comrades. The Toronto comrades were used to it since all the meetings in Montreal were held in French. The meetings took a little longer with translation for the unilingual speakers. This close-knit group of about a dozen people helped organized the Canada-wide Third World support work of the League and later the Workers Communist Party.

* * *

In December 1977, we were preparing for a cross-Canada tour of two Pan Africanist Congress members—Mzonke Xuza and Trofomo Sono—when our plans suddenly appeared to be in jeopardy.

Mzonke was a student leader who had worked with Steve Biko, the Black Consciousness Movement leader who had been murdered in police detention in apartheid South Africa two months earlier. Mzonke was forced into exile and became the assistant representative of the PAC at the United Nations. Trofomo had been a young leader in the Soweto uprising in 1976, and president of the Soweto Student Representative Council.

I went to Dorval airport to meet them on the flight scheduled to arrive from New York at 10 p.m. I waited until midnight, with no sign of them. I inquired and was told that all passengers had gotten off the plane. I knew something was wrong and phoned the League lawyer who in turn gave me the telephone number of Juanita Westmoreland.[105] Juanita was an activist lawyer, supportive of our work to build solidarity with the struggle in South Africa. It was way past midnight when I called her but she snapped into action right away and asked me to pick her up at her home in Verdun to drive her to the airport.

Down the road from the airport was a motel where they detained people considered to be illegal. I waited in the lobby while Juanita went inside the motel to talk with the authorities. Around dawn, I could see the smiling faces of two young Black men; I immediately knew they were Mzonke and Trofomo. They were travelling on UN papers but had still been detained. Juanita did her job to free them.

I accompanied the two PAC comrades across Canada—to Montreal, Quebec City, Hull, Ottawa, Toronto, Regina and Vancouver. We held thirteen public meetings that had been organized by the Azanian People's Support Committee and the CCL (M-L) with the support of trade unions and community and anti-imperialist organizations—forty organizations[106] in all. Over three thousand people attended the meetings and we raised $18,200 for the PAC struggle. It was one of the more successful campaigns organized by the CAI of the League.

I got to know the PAC representatives to the United Nations. First, there was David Sibeko, a big bear of a man. I was devastated when I heard in 1979 that he had been assassinated in Dar es Salaam. Then there was Henry Isaacs, who replaced Sibeko. I remember visiting Henry, a good-looking, dapper and friendly man, at his apartment on Roosevelt Island in New York City. He was

Cover of the League's brochure in support of the struggle in South Africa
against apartheid. (William Dere Collection)

a gracious host and took me to the UN to attend the General Assembly session
discussing sanctions against South Africa. In some minute way, I felt I helped
to contribute to the liberation of the Azanian people.[107]

We held similar campaigns with representatives of the Zimbabwe African
National Union and the Palestine Liberation Organization. There were also
the comrades from the Argentine Communist Party (Marxist-Leninist) who
were in a life and death struggle with the Videla regime, which "disappeared"
up to thirty thousand political activists in its five-year reign of terror, 1976–81.

I was always amazed at how Third World people were, in one way or another, connected with people in the metropolitan Second World. We once hosted a tour of Canada by David Abdulah, the general secretary of the Oil-field Workers' Trade Union of Trinidad and Tobago, and he stayed with me in Montreal. David was a comrade of Ram Ramharack, an old Afro-Asian who went back to Trinidad to organize workers into a revolutionary party. Ram helped arrange David's tour of Canada. This must have been the summer of 1979.

One Sunday, at the end of his tour, David asked me if I could drive him to visit his grandmother who lived in one of the large apartment buildings on Walkley Avenue, in the Notre-Dame-de-Grâce borough of Montreal. David was a tall, handsome man with bronze skin. I was completely stunned when his grandmother answered the door; she was a tiny Japanese woman. David's hug completely engulfed her. They both had a big chuckle at my expense. The petite woman's joy at seeing David was infectious. "Yes, I am David's grand-mother!" she said.

* * *

The League and Charles Gagnon's organization En lutte! waged an intensive struggle for the "unity of Marxist-Leninists" and to win over independent M-L groups. The League rallied groups like APLQ and Mobilisation and four or five others in Quebec[108] after exhaustive criticism and self-criticism sessions. This process proved remarkably successful as more organizations followed suit, including ones in English Canada such as Workers' Unity in Toronto and the Regina Marxist-Leninist Collective.

One group that did not join the League was the Black Study Group (BSG) in Toronto. It wasn't because of disagreement over Marxist-Leninist princi-ples. I feel it was due to white chauvinism on the part of the League leader-ship. The League had a four-person politburo, all male and white, although you could consider Roger to be a minority person as an Egyptian immigrant. They did not like the way the BSG defined itself, believing this definition was not adequately Marxist. Members of the BSG rightly felt that they should be able to define themselves any way they like. They voiced this point of view, criticizing the League for great-nation chauvinism.[109]

* * *

With one day's notice, I was told to get ready to attend a very important League conference. On the Friday evening, without knowing where exactly I was going—but making sure that I was not being watched or followed—I was to pick up three other comrades, none of whom I knew. They were told to wait at specific locations, where they could not be mistaken for anybody else but League people, at different areas around Montreal.

I drove through isolated industrial areas in the southwest of Montreal and the east end, where it would be noticeable if there were any other cars around. It was very cloak-and-dagger. As I picked up the last of the comrades, I got driving instructions from someone I knew in the *service d'ordre*, the Party's security apparatus, to go to the next checkpoint. I drove towards Boucherville, on Montreal's South Shore, in complete darkness. The two-lane road did not have lights and there were no houses or buildings to act as beacons in the night; I could see no stars through the overcast sky, and the black pavement was illuminated only by the car's headlights.

It was near midnight as I drove through the deserted part of Boucherville looking for the next checkpoint. All of a sudden, I saw a pair of headlights in the rear-view mirror. The car was speeding faster to catch me as it flashed its high beams. I pulled over to let the car go by. As the car pulled alongside, the driver said in French, "Comrade, you are driving too fast."

I countered with, "Are you cops?"

One of my passengers interjected, "It's okay. He's a comrade from Trois-Rivières." I got the final instruction to a *camp de plein air* (fresh air camp) in the Estrie. To this day, I don't exactly know where we went.

We finally arrived at the *camp de plein air* and entered a large, dark hall with many bunk beds and I dropped my exhausted body down on the first empty bunk I could find. It was morning when I next woke, to the sound of people getting up—and the sight of a woman comrade getting dressed.

There was much excitement as we sat in the opening session of the Founding Congress of the Workers Communist Party. This was the culmination of four years of hard work, struggle and sacrifices. We had prepared the conditions to create the revolutionary party of the Canadian working class. The overthrow of the exploiting class could not be far off; the socialist revolution was just around the corner. I am not being facetious—we actually thought that. Since we had implanted ourselves in the workplaces and the trade unions, we believed that we had fulfilled the three Leninist conditions to form the Party: (1) develop the Party program, (2) unite communists (Marxist-Leninist) and

(3) rally the working class.

There were seventy-five delegates from all sectors of the League's work, and from across Canada, along with a team of support staff, mainly women comrades, who worked efficiently and tirelessly to produce the documents and provide simultaneous translation. I was the delegate from the anti-imperialist fraction.

The deliberations on the Party documents and program took place over the course of the weekend. The organization, as usual, went off without a hitch as all the documents were translated into French and English and distributed for discussion.

The Workers Communist Party was officially declared on September 2, 1979, with the introduction of the Central Committee; Roger Rashi was elected Chairman and Ian Anderson, Vice-Chairman. A rousing rendition of "The Internationale" closed the Founding Congress.

In the excitement of the founding of the Party, there was one glaring error made that did not register with the delegates. While women made up about 50 per cent of the general membership, only four women were chosen for the seventeen-member central committee. There were no minorities chosen for this leading body of the Party; I was the only person of colour there. Of course, this was 1979 not the twenty-first century.

A comrade who knew my work nominated me for the central committee from the floor; this intruded into the slate already chosen by the leadership. The pre-selected central committee members had prepared their self-criticisms in advance. The leadership did not support my nomination, saying I was too liberal. They were probably right. I tend to prefer the softer, humanist side of Marxism. I was destined for middle management, and I would suffer the same fate during my corporate career. I was just not ruthless enough to be senior management material. (As Gillian, my first wife, would later tell me, this was probably to my credit.)

After the WCP was created we continued fighting the day-to-day class struggle; defending the rights of the workers, immigrants and minorities; and teaching the masses the merits of internationalism in order to see the new world just over the horizon. The membership of the Party reached its height in 1980 with 1,020[110] members and as many organized sympathisers in study or readers' groups; 80 to 85 per cent of those were from Quebec. The circulation of the Party paper, the *Forge*, reached as high as 14,000 copies with an average of 10,000 per week (counting both the French and English editions).

The Party also produced *October*, a quarterly "Theoretical journal of Marxism-Leninism-Mao Zedong Thought," with French and English editions. It

This *Forge* ad shows the reach of the League across Canada. (William Dere Collection)

had an internal propaganda journal, *Drapeau Rouge/Red Flag*, so members could study current events and theoretical thought more deeply. The Party had an annual budget of over $500,000 collected through dues and fundraising campaigns. It operated three Norman Bethune Bookstores, in Montreal, Toronto and Vancouver.

We could mobilize three thousand people to our rallies. I remember the commemoration meeting we held on the death of Chairman Mao—three thousand people jammed into the ballroom of the Queen Elizabeth Hotel in Montreal. Patrick Brown, the CBC reporter covering the event, was astounded; he sat next to me and kept asking, "Where did all these people come from?"

En lutte! had about six hundred members. Altogether, the two leading Marxist-Leninist organizations could mobilize up to five thousand people for their united causes, such as spoiling the ballot during the 1980 Quebec referendum on sovereignty association. The work of the two organizations in the lead-up to the referendum vote had such an impact that the PQ partially blamed *"les Maoistes"* for their loss.[111] Mathematically, that was not possible; however, it was not known how many left nationalists were influenced to abstain from voting. The influence of the WCP and En lutte! on Quebec intellectuals, mass organizations and the trade union movement was undeniable.

The founding of the WCP gave us a new burst of energy. The years 1979–81 were the most productive in Maoist activities in Quebec and Canada, and by 1982, Party activists were able to organize five hundred workers into a left caucus within the Confédération des syndicats nationaux, a feat not since repeated.[112]

The WCP tried to recruit people from the various minorities. It worked with some Acadian fishermen in New Brunswick. At its May Day rallies, many visible minority organizations were invited to attend. At the Toronto rally in 1979, information booths were set up by Filipinos, the Indian Peoples Association in North America, a group co-founded by Daya Varma, and the Chinese Canadian magazine *Asianadian*.

The May Day supplement of the *Forge* came out in a dozen languages, including Chinese. However, like the CCL (M-L), the WCP was never a multiracial, multinational organization. I was the only Chinese Canadian member of the Party. There were no Blacks in the organization. I was one of two visible minority members; the other was a Bangladeshi comrade in Toronto.

By 1978, I was working at Pratt & Whitney as a test engineer. However, my activist workload was getting to be too much, and even with taking time off from my job, I did not have enough hours in the day to carry out my organizational activities. I quit my day job and became a full-time paid organizer. I was now a member of the Bureau d'organisation of the WCP. In 1978, it was located in an apartment on Jean Talon above an Italian bakery, and later moved into a more spacious location on the second floor of a triplex on St. Denis near Jarry. At the bureau, I was given the *nom de guerre* "Moose." The day-to-day functioning of the Party was run from the bureau with a staff of mainly women comrades who literally acted as secretaries for the four male members of the politburo.

I was getting paid $125 a week. By then I was living with my girlfriend and comrade Gillian Taylor, who luckily was waitressing at the time, and she supported us from that job. Roger told me later that all the full-time cadres including himself were getting $125 per week, a raise from the $100 that he started with.

I had first set eyes on Gillian at a chalet in the Laurentians in January or February of 1977—when I woke up in bright sunlight, she was there, a brunette with the beauty and dynamism of youth, in a pair of baby blue long johns, throwing a log of wood into the fireplace to stoke the flames. Antonio Artuso, a Brazilian immigrant, had invited a group of us involved in anti-imperialist work to his in-laws' cottage on a small, tranquil lake north of Montreal. The invitation spread to more people than the chalet could hold and many of us ended up sleeping on the floor in front of the fireplace. Gillian and I connected as the weekend unfolded.

A week later I invited her to a now defunct Chinese restaurant at the corner of Jeanne Mance and Dorchester, the Shanghai, to eat moo shu pork. The Maoists hung out there because we were impressed with the rudeness of the waiters.

Gillian was at the time organized in a League study group at McGill. She was a "*bleuet*"—born in Quebec's blueberry country, Chicoutimi. Her father was an engineer with Alcan in the town of Arvida in the Saguenay. Arvida was named after **Ar**thur **Vi**ning **Da**vis, American president of Alcoa (Aluminum Company of America) which morphed into the Aluminum Company of Canada (Alcan). The aluminum smelter was one of the first American penetrations into the regions of Quebec. The Saguenay region, with its cheap source of hydroelectric power and labour force, attracted the American capitalists.

Gillian had been studying physiology and women's studies at McGill. In 1975 she had also studied in Cambridge, at the Technical College. "I met Trotskyists, anarchists and I saw the clandestine videos taken from the stadium in

Chile," she reminisced recently, "and that's how I became politicized, actually in England, around the resistance in Chile."

She recalled having "a feeling that I was being recruited at McGill by people in the League. In some ways, I was more drawn to the people that I was meeting than the organization. It was not the class struggle. Class struggle didn't mean much to me." Her entry point into the movement at McGill, she said, was a group called Science for the People. "It was more linked to social issues, Grassy Narrows Reserve and mercury poisoning; native issues. I read *Diet for a Small Planet* and saw how corrupt the food industry was. I was drawn to those issues and Third World stuff. I hadn't read Marx; I started from a broad critique of society."

She was introduced to Marxism-Leninism in about 1976: "I was looking for an identity, being a product of a middle-class, sheltered environment. ... It was more at the level of relationships, meeting people, hanging out with them, having talks with them in the kitchen. It was a funny overlap of people and activities. I started reading Mao, Lenin and Marx in the study groups. All the meetings were in French; I became bilingual translating for people. What attracted me was being with something much larger than myself."[113]

The M-L student movement at that time was one of the largest political groupings on Montreal campuses.

Gillian was comfortable being involved as a sympathizer. She distributed the *Forge* at Pratt & Whitney at 5 or 6 in the morning. "I felt like a fraudster, actually," she said in looking back, "because I didn't have much to offer as a middle class young woman giving papers to men in their thirties and forties driving out in their cars, having just worked all night, and handing them a communist newspaper. I was reading the paper and studying the theory; that world of the workers, the unions, that was also a huge new world for me. I was learning about it through the study groups, which was probably not really adequate." This was the reason why many intellectuals adopted the practice of implantation—working in factories.

I asked her about life in the Party. "Those years, I was making new friends, I was a student then not a student, I was working as a waitress, I met my future husband, I was a sympathizer for a very long time. I did postering, distributing the paper and leaflets, demonstrations. Being a sympathizer was a comfortable place for me because I wasn't buying into the whole organization."

What really piqued her interest was the international solidarity movement. As she later told me, "What I was doing at the same time was going to the activities of CAPT. El Salvador, Nicaragua, Latin America support work was really hot. I remember the office on Maguire. I went to meetings in the evening and heard speakers that came. I remember the Argentinian comrade who came to talk about the struggle against Videla. I remember the people, Steve, you, and the organizations and the countries. There was so much going on in the world. That always made more sense to me—the positions I was to take, and how I could do something. The CAPT anti-imperialist stuff felt more real to me. We were talking about something genuine that I could understand."

Gillian lived on St. Viateur in the Plateau, above the bagel factory, for a year—you can't get more Montreal than that. Eventually, Gillian and I moved together into a cold second-floor flat in a duplex on Waverly, between St. Viateur and Bernard in the Mile End section of Montreal. We were both very occupied and immersed in political activities, she with her student and community work and I as full-time anti-imperialist organizer. We only saw each other late in the evenings. When I wasn't working, she supported me through her waitressing job at the Magic Pan.

One late evening in December 1977 or early January 1978, I was anxiously waiting for Gillian to come home. She had left early that day to join other League members and sympathizers to board buses headed for Ste-Thérèse, located an hour north of Montreal. The mainly women immigrant workers at Commonwealth Plywood in Ste-Thérèse were organizing a union and they had been on strike for a few months; the plant continued to function with scab labour and the League was mobilizing support to strengthen the picket line to prevent the scabs from entering the plant.

I don't remember all the details of that day, but it remains a vivid memory for Gillian: "We went up in several buses. There were a lot of us students that went up from McGill. There were Party people and sympathizers. It was a pretty cold day. This was another world for me; it was the first time that I was involved in a strike. I was kind of exhilarated. Maybe that was a reflection of my age and level of development. I do remember these women all about five feet tall, all Portuguese women in their forties, fifties. They were salt of the earth women. They were right up there in front yelling in Portuguese at the Sûreté du Québec."

It turned out that she couldn't come home until late that night because they had all been arrested.

"It was a bit concerning to be arrested, herded with a lot of other people into the back of police vans," Gillian said. "It was a very powerful learning experience. We had pushed back the small number of police that tried to get a truck through because we were so numerous."

I was mesmerized when she recalled years later what ensued: "There weren't enough of them to push us around, so we blocked the truck from going in; and about forty-five minutes later, over the hill and out of a school bus came the riot squad. I don't know how many there were, but it was a privileged moment—I got to see what the power of the state looked like when they got the forces they need. They were totally pumped, banging their sticks on their shields and ready to bash a few people. It was scary but it also diffused very quickly because of the leadership—we had a very effective leadership.

"Immediately, the experienced protester people were saying 'Placards down! Stay silent! No resistance!' It was very quick, immediate—we were just doing nothing.

"The League *service d'ordre* handled it extremely well and wisely. It led to the Sûreté du Québec making a huge tactical mistake when they charged us with holding offensive weapons and there was no evidence of that. We offered them nothing to fight with. We were just all herded up into the trucks. Locked up and fingerprinted.

"I felt the benefit of being associated with an organization. At the end of the day, around 5 p.m., we were in a courtroom, about eighty-five of us League people, workers and union people; there were good lawyers there and the judge gave us some recommendations and we went home. Our lawyers called a meeting later that week. I was impressed with the organizational efficiency. We were taken care of. The charges were stayed because the judge said a stick with a piece of cardboard at the end of it could not be classified as a dangerous weapon. If they had charged us with mischief, we would have lost."[114]

The Ste-Thérèse strike was settled after fourteen months.

* * *

The League gave us two weeks of vacation each year—the construction holidays in Quebec, the last two weeks of July. For two or three years, Gillian and I drove to the Maritimes with two other couples who were also in the League. Alan and his wife, Yvette, were on their honeymoon in 1977, and we drove up to the Acadian town of Chéticamp at the western end of Cape Breton's Cabot Trail. Even there we couldn't resist getting involved. Gillian remembered one Sunday we were at a campground, listening to CBC Radio's *Cross*

Country Checkup program on China, which turned out to be a China-bashing exercise. Alan and I got very incensed about the things being said. We weren't near a phone to call in and we kept saying, "Come on, someone from the Canada-China Society should call." Sure enough, towards the end of the program, Steve—whom I had tried to recruit to the League—called and set everyone straight.

However, we were faced with a much more serious situation when we returned from the road trip. On July 22, security guards shot eight workers at Red Rose Flour. Though this happened near the start of the vacation period,[115] many of us remained away while the comrades in town organized pickets and demonstrations to denounce the shooting. We did not see the urgency of the situation, and for that we were severely criticized. The leadership was driven by the idea that revolution was primary and our personal lives secondary and we needed to live our lives subservient to that ideal.

My relationship with Gillian grew, and we married at the beginning of 1980 at the Anglican Christ Church Cathedral to please her parents. She was still working at the Magic Pan, but later returned to school. We talked about starting a family but under the existing conditions, it was difficult. At the Bureau d'organisation, some of the women comrades were getting pregnant as they were approaching thirty. There was a discussion that maternity leave would be taken in rotation so as not to deplete the resources. Taking this to heart, Gillian and I waited our turn to have our baby.

Many years later, when I asked Gillian whether she felt her time with the Party was a waste, she rekindled my memories of our involvement in work supporting the anti-apartheid struggle.

For her, she said, the South Africa support work was very meaningful. "My involvement was with the left, not just Marxist-Leninists. What I liked about CAPT was the collaborative ventures with other organizations or with the community of Latin Americans. It shaped what I would become in a very positive way. I didn't feel that I wasted the years with the Party. I don't feel any bitterness because in my career as a nurse, I have been one of the most political people in terms of being able to analyze situations. It gave me a sort of confidence to challenge authority when appropriate. That was a gift."

Then she generously added how I had contributed to her political development. "You were much more experienced than I was in terms of politics and analysis. You were patient and explained a lot of things to me. I realized at some point that I was the girlfriend of someone pretty high up in the organization.

Later I told people that I sort of married the Chairman Mao of the left. You were more conciliatory, more interested in the perspective of other people. Maybe that's how it should be; you were my sweetie...."

She was very perceptive to tell me, "You had a whole life-long experience of the ethnic questions. You lived personally through immigration as a young child, you had a lot of depth to you that these other people did not have in terms of their real lives. Our time together, as a couple, opened my eyes to the reality of you being a member of a visible minority."

Chapter 8

Life after the Party

"And when no model is or can be endorsed, the only solutions are uto-
pianism or cynicism."
—Manuel Vazquez Montalban, *Murder in the Central Committee*[116]

It was spring 1982. I had not met with Roger Rashi for more than two months, so there was no one in the leadership with whom to discuss my disillusionment with the direction of the Party. I was prepared to justify my stance and to present the reasons why I was quitting. The arguments had roiled in my head for quite a while and I was primed to argue them out with the Party. But no one came to see me, as if my membership in the organization did not matter. So I parted from the Workers Communist Party without a whimper.

McCarthyism, with its anti-communist witch-hunts and demagoguery, has survived long after the death in 1957 of the American it was named after, Joe McCarthy. Not much thinking is required to understand why. The 1917 October Revolution in Russia and the 1949 Liberation of China both challenged the supremacy of the capitalist system, and since then the Western establishment, especially in the US, as American writer Howard Fast observed, has poured millions, if not billions, of dollars into training security and intelligence personnel and an army of propagandists—indoctrinating those in popular media and culture, academia, teaching and politics in the fine art of anti-communist slander, hatred and fear. The general public absorbed the overriding premise that communism is evil. The Canadian government supported a proposal to build a $5 million grandiose monument in Ottawa dedicated to the victims of communism.

These emotions have so permeated our psychology that there are people who are still not willing to admit that they participated in the New Communist Movement during their youth—for fear of being publicly shamed for their political indiscretions a lifetime ago. I've agreed to withhold names or use only first names of some of these individuals. The only full names used are of those who gave their permission, were publicly associated with the Party or whose names were printed in Party literature.

There are many unacknowledged members of the Canadian Marxist-Leninist movement from the 1970s who went on to successful careers in academia, the media and politics. Gilles Duceppe, former leader of the Bloc Québécois, is probably the most prominent of the politicians who admitted to being a member of the Parti communiste ouvrier (PCO). There were other prominent members of the PQ, as well as in political parties in other provinces, who were Maoist members or fellow travellers that I won't name here. So much for "naming names," an act so despised during the McCarthy inquisitions.

* * *

The Marxist-Leninist phenomenon lasted about ten years in Quebec and in the rest of the Western world. Just as quickly as it spread in the '70s, the movement dramatically collapsed in the '80s. The reasons for the rise and fall of the New Communist Movement were manyfold, simple and complex at the same time.

The Workers Communist Party—Parti communiste ouvrier—dissolved itself at a special Party congress in Montreal in January 1983 following a year of acrimonious debates, finger pointing and finger wagging within the organization that pretty much paralyzed its work throughout 1982. This came in the wake of the dissolution of En lutte! in May of that year.

I left the Party in April 1982. I was thirty-three, out of work, broke, with Gillian attending university and a young infant to raise. My father was dying of cancer, and like my father, I took life as a natural progression, a passage.

Gillian has a strong memory of the time my—and her—days with the Party came to an end. "In the fall of '81, you were very disenchanted with the Party," she told me a few years ago. "We were very much involved in the South Africa work. We had the PAC [Pan Africanist Congress] guy, John Pokela, come and stay with us and I was very pregnant at the time with Jessica. I was very impressionable and kept saying, 'Oh my god, what kind of world are we bringing this child into?' I didn't know about everything you were distressed about.

"When you left the Party in 1982, I left. It was such a relief."

As a transition from the hectic life as full-time activists, Gillian and I threw ourselves into the solidarity work against South African apartheid. In a 2014 conversation, she reminded me: "We had the Azania Support Committee that started back in 1980. I remember all the pregnancy advice I got from Stanje and Louise [members of the Azania committee]. When you were analyzing South Africa you had a whole experience in how the Party viewed it—the politics of the PAC versus the ANC [African National Congress] and armed struggle."

Aside from the politics of the movement, Gillian said what she was most excited about was that we had joined forces with a couple of organizations in

The PAC delegation to Montreal, headed by its president John Nyathi Pokela,[117] third from the left. Next to him is Gillian Taylor who chaired the solidarity conference organized by the Azania Support Committee. (William Dere Collection)

144 · CHAPTER 8

the Black community. "This was very cool, it made a lot of sense … and was meaningful. We had meetings at the Negro Community Centre [on Coursol Street] at the Black United Front [in lower Notre-Dame-de-Grâce]. There was Beverly Walker and Esmeralda Thornhill, Black women we worked with. Years later, I was riding the 90 bus, an old Black guy got on and sat opposite me in the back and he goes, 'Ah, you're Bill Dere's wife—oh, from a long time ago.' I didn't recognize him but he remembered me from the South Africa support days."

Nevertheless, as I've mentioned previously, the WCP was never a multi-national, multiracial organization, despite its program calling for such a party. It botched the one opportunity to bring African Canadians into the organization when it treated the Toronto Black Study Group like any other "opportunist" collective and criticized its "Black nationalism." The League prematurely announced that the members of the BSG had dissolved their organization and individually joined the League in 1977,[118] but that was not the case. I felt uneasy, and perhaps it was my liberalism coming to the surface, about how the League was treating an oppressed minority.

The WCP's position on Canada's "oppressed nationalities" was borrowed straight from the Chinese Party's policies on "national minorities." Apart from the Quebec National Question (more on this later), the WCP's stance applied the concept of "regional autonomy," a form of self-government.[119] This would apply to First Nations as well as other areas where minorities congregated in adequate numbers, such as Chinatowns. Ian Anderson and I had long discussions on the question of the assimilation of visible minorities (the terminology that was used in the 1970s). We both agreed that visible minorities could not be assimilated due to racism and that they formed distinct minority nationalities. This became Party policy[120] but the WCP was not able to organize within the visible minorities, as there were only two racialized members, as mentioned in the previous chapter, and the Party did not have any concrete plans to work among these communities.

I was starting to take a more independent view of minorities and the role of the Marxist-Leninist movement, instead of simply viewing things from the M-L perspective when it came to the role of minorities. I started studying the literature of the minority nationalities in the US. I learned about the Black Liberation Movement through the writings of Amiri Baraka (LeRoi Jones); the nascent Chinese American organizations like the I Wor Kuen, which united in 1978 with Baraka's Revolutionary Communist League, and a number of

Chicano, Puerto Rican, Dominican and Japanese American organizations to form the League of Revolutionary Struggles (M-L), or LRS. Coincidentally, Reese Erlich, member of the central committee of the LRS and former writer for *Ramparts* magazine, stayed with Gillian and me during his visit to Montreal in 1979 or 1980. He enthralled me with stories of the multinational nature of the Movement in the US as I questioned him on the I Wor Kuen and the Chinese American struggle for equal rights. I also started reading Chinese American cultural writers like Frank Chin and Louis Chu. When you start to emancipate your mind, you never know where it will lead you.

Towards the fall of 1981, my Chinese Canadian consciousness started to stir which fed my feeling of uneasiness about the Party. With our activity in the South African anti-apartheid support work, Gillian and I had gotten to know many individuals and organizations in the Montreal Black community. I was moved by the commitment of these individuals and their tireless efforts in uniting as a community to fight against racial discrimination locally in Montreal and Quebec as well as supporting the struggle for liberation in far-away South Africa. I saw this as an inspiration and an example for the Chinese community. I felt disappointed that there was no such activity in Montreal's Chinese community at the time.

(Ten years later, in December 1990, I tried to unite the two communities in a conference under the rubric "Singled Out by Law for Unequal Treatment."[121] This conference, organized under the auspices of the Congress of Black Women of Canada and the Chinese Canadian National Council, got the attention of the federal multiculturalism bureaucrats who were concerned about such unity. They contacted our two organizations and asked to be invited to our future activities.)

The slow simmering of positions and attitudes that the Party took on China internally and externally started to boil over at the beginning of 1981. Until then, as Roger said, the WCP had "slavishly" supported the Chinese Communist Party (CCP) through the Cultural Revolution, the downfall of the Gang of Four and the rise of Hua Guofeng, who replaced Mao as Chairman of the CCP, but the Party hit a roadblock with the resurrection of the twice-deposed communist phoenix, Deng Xiaoping, who became China's paramount leader in 1978. Deng's economic reforms were not to the liking of the WCP leadership.

I saw China with a historical perspective of past, present and future. Mao and the CCP liberated China from millennia of feudal oppression and a century of imperialist aggression and exploitation. In thirty years of socialist construction, the Chinese had succeeded in wiping away hunger for half a billion people and as Xi Jinping, president of the People's Republic of China, said a few years ago, "The greatest contribution made to humanity by China was to prevent its 1.3 billion people from hunger."[122] The Chinese leadership judged that the economy had stagnated during the Cultural Revolution; politics was in command but it had not demonstrated that Chinese socialism was superior to capitalism in taking care of the people's material and cultural needs. I was attracted to political activism, having China as a revolutionary model; I wasn't going to give up on this model without a better intellectual understanding.

I saw the WCP's stand as that of an inexperienced group of Western youth criticizing tried and true revolutionaries who had changed the course of China. What right did they have, other than possessing their own interpretation of Marxism-Leninism? By this time, my disenchantment with the Party was complete and I felt my mind released from the confines of Marxist fundamentalism. The Party had met my M-L principles when I joined, and when it no longer corresponded to my politics, parting was natural.

After 1982, I had the South African support work to help me transition from the vigorous lifestyle of a revolutionary to a more manageable life as a family man, and to help maintain my identity as a progressive. When Nelson Mandela was released from twenty-seven years of imprisonment in 1990, I felt proud that I had been a part of the worldwide movement that supported the liberation struggle of the South African people. And I had not abandoned my intellectual belief in Marxism as an alternative to the evils of capitalist and imperialist exploitation.

* * *

Towards the end of 1982, nearly three-quarters of the members had quit. By October only $23,000 of the $150,000 annual campaign was raised; the organization was in deep financial trouble and the *Forge* ceased its weekly publication. As the WCP neared its end, its members held many "talk bitterness" sessions and denounced the shortcomings of the Party leadership. There were three main such topics of "denunciation": Stalinism, feminism (which I will get back to in a moment) and the issue of Quebec.

As in the days of McCarthy, Stalin reared his ugly head in the Canadian Marxist movement in 1982. When you engage in name calling, Stalinism is a catchall, because there is no comeback for that label. You are automatically on the defensive. Even leftists are conditioned to denounce Stalin quicker than you can say Pol Pot. As the argument went, the WCP was Stalinist because there was no democracy, no freedom of expression, no open debates; public or private dissent of Party positions was impossible; everyone was under the dictatorship of the politburo.

The WCP was in fact a Leninist party with the principles and functioning of democratic centralism, developed during a historical period by the Third International (Comintern). Dissident members rightly rejected the Leninist concept of organization for modern-day Canada. If you took a historical viewpoint based on objective analysis (historical materialism), you could understand that this type of centralized party was necessary in times of extreme repression and under wartime conditions. Even coming off the events of the War Measures Act, the leadership of the WCP did not differentiate between societies under the heel of fascism, imperialist invasion, occupation and war, and a bourgeois democratic society under peacetime, as in Canada. The subjective, intellectualist idealism of the leading group postulated that the revolution was imminent and needing a disciplined vanguard party, led by a strict hierarchy with an authoritarian leadership; this was at the core of the political, ideological and organizational morass. Even if the leadership was not conscious of the problems caused by its demands for tireless, 24/7 activism— allowing no time for study, debate or reflection—the rank-and-file members had had enough of the abuse and rebelled.

The Party leadership also fell into the de-Stalinization entanglement—the futile attempt to understand and explain Stalinism. In late 1982, they tried to buy some time and to deflect the inevitable by waging a campaign to debate Stalin. Bob, a member of the politburo, went to see Alan Silverman to borrow all his books on Stalin, of which he had many, to write a position paper for internal discussion. The debate on Stalin was used to attack the Party. The issue wasn't Stalin. If the leadership did not see that, it was indeed in trouble.

Social democracy then became a much easier alternative and many of the ex-members who remained active politically gravitated to this political orientation.

When it comes to feminism, even though I support feminism, I don't feel qualified to write about it. I can only produce here some of the criticisms of the WCP on this issue. The WCP saw the oppression of women as a secondary issue to the class struggle. It treated feminism as bourgeois or petit-bourgeois ideology, pitting women's struggles against male power and not against the

The WCP theoretical journal explains the Party's position on Quebec.

(William Dere Collection)

capitalist class. In the Party, women made up nearly 50 per cent of the members, but they were concentrated mainly in spheres related to domestic issues such as daycares, food co-ops, health care, and community organizing. The WCP leadership was 100 per cent male at the highest level of the organization, the politburo; women made up only 25 per cent of the central committee.

Because it didn't see gender issues as being just as important as the day-to-day class struggle, the leadership only paid lip service to fighting against male chauvinism. It did not see that women's oppression predated capitalism. In short, the WCP did not attack patriarchy as the source of women's oppression within the Party and in the larger society. It could not climb out of its institutional male chauvinism.

Another long-suppressed resentment of the Québécois members was the position the WCP took on the issue of the Quebec nation, especially its position to spoil the ballot during the 1980 referendum on sovereignty association, and its continued subordination of the nationalist struggle for independence to that of the class struggle. Many Francophone working-class members said they looked foolish when their fellow workers supported the PQ's call for independence and the "Yes" option in the referendum. The criticism of the leadership by the dissident members was over-simplified by the focus on the English–French divide. Some Québécois members blamed the anti-nationalist position on the "McGill Anglophone Clique"—the four members of the politburo. However, En lutte! took an identical position on the Quebec national question and the referendum, and the En lutte! leadership was Francophone, led by Charles Gagnon. This subtlety was lost on the social-nationalists. To be fair, the Quebec membership of En lutte! also denounced their leaders' call for spoiling the referendum ballot instead of supporting the "Yes" vote.

There was also a narrow nationalist attack on the Party's anti-imperialist work. Alain Saulnier, one of the leaders in Quebec, said in a presentation to a special Party meeting in November 1982: "The PCO favoured struggles that traditionally receive widespread support from Anglophones (ex. South Africa) while long neglecting the Quebec people's support for the Latin American and Irish peoples, for example."[123]

So it came full circle: in the early '70s the left nationalists of Quebec had started looking towards Marxism, rejecting the "independence first" strategy for a more inclusive class struggle and internationalist principles; the movement ended ten years later with the same "independence first" outlook couched in the rhetoric of "independence and socialism."

For ten years, as in the example of Charles Gagnon, Quebec leftist nationalists saw something larger and sought change in revolutionary class struggles in unison with Canadian workers. However, unlike Gagnon, many of these nationalists went back to what they knew and spawned a Union des forces progressistes (Union of Progressive Forces), a Québec solidaire and a Gilles Duceppe. Many ex-members of the PCO and En lutte! are active nationalist militants today in trade unions, media, academics and electoral politics. However, Charles Gagnon, until his death in 2005, remained true to his belief that nationalism in capitalist society is a bourgeois ideology; he maintained an outlook of humanist internationalism.

* * *

The crisis of the Western Marxist-Leninist movement was due to both internal and, to a lesser degree, external contradictions. The objective and subjective internal contradictions as outlined above were the determining factors here in Canada. But there were other factors as well. The New Communist Movement in Canada, especially in Quebec, was marked by its youthful membership; the average age of members of the three organizations that united to form the League in 1975 was twenty-one. There were no intergenerational members, with the tradition and experience of the struggles of the old Communist Party of Canada.

As the 1980s began, people approached their thirties. Family life suffered and children were abandoned to a series of babysitters as the parents spent endless nights at Party meetings and functions.[124] They had devoted a decade of their lives to the cause. People started thinking about family, jobs, returning to school to get the degree that they abandoned, and restarting their careers. Today we would say that they wanted a better work-life balance.

The objective organizational problems of the Party offered a convenient subjective excuse for three-quarters of the membership to leave.

The external conditions, which led to the collapse of the M-L movement in the West, were a unique conflation of historical events. The Western capitalist world was in the midst of another economic crisis in the early '80s with high unemployment, a drop in wages and high inflation. The neo-conservative, neo-liberal policies of Margaret Thatcher in the UK and Ronald Reagan in the US directly attacked working people and the trade union movement; this led to a decade of exuberant self-interest and unrestrained greed in corporate business and on the stock market. In Quebec, the PQ government dealt a devastating defeat to the Common Front unions in 1982 through legislating austerity cutbacks in the health services and education—rolling back wages for civil servants, such as nurses and teachers. Ten years earlier, the trade unions had responded to the attacks of the Liberal government with a general strike and the New Communist Movement was born, but now the mass movement was in disarray. The Marxist organizations were in collapse, unable to withstand the onslaught of neo-liberalism as represented by the nationalist PQ.

Internationally, the world order was in flux. The USSR and the Soviet camp were in the throes of disintegration due to numerous internal contradictions and external pressures; China had relinquished its role as the model for world revolution and started to implement economic reforms. The Marxist-Leninist movement lost its compass and its leaders did not have the experience or the dialectical thinking ability to analyze the profound changes taking place in China and around the world. The use of the same mechanical process to analyze either the existence of socialism or restoration of capitalism in China would not suffice in the 1980s or even today. Historically, Lenin solved the crisis of Marxism during World War I and Mao solved the problem of applying Marxism to a semi-feudal, anti-colonial China during World War II; the crisis of today's Marxism in the advanced capitalist world remains to be solved.

The WCP used China as the model. "We had a slavish attitude towards China," Roger Rashi recalled. "We had a lack of renewal of socialist thought. The weakness of our movement based on intellectuals and students was that of only looking at concepts rather than at concrete practice. The classic communist movement in the 1930s had deep roots in the working class and was able to continue. We were not in the same situation. The workers' movement in Poland in 1980 challenged state capitalism but turned into an anti-communist movement; it was way beyond the capacity of our movement to respond."[125]

Roger was demoted from his position of Chairman at the beginning of 1982 and went through a series of criticisms and self-criticisms. In conversation with me, he described 1982 as a "year of confusion—an unproductive year."

The crisis, he said, was a "subjective psychodrama, emotional, an unleashing of grievances and frustrations; a rebellion against any form of thought. The middle cadres were completely paralyzed and could not organize itself within the organization; top leadership was consumed with its own internal struggle and absolutely incapable of deciding or orienting anything."

Roger described the dynamics of a failing organization and how quickly it crumpled, and he finally explained why our weekly meetings ended: "I was demoted and stopped meeting with you; I stopped going to all meetings, I only went to central committee meetings. It was the bankruptcy of highly centralized leadership in a non-revolutionary situation."[126]

I had not realized when I quit the Party that Roger had been undergoing an existential crisis of his own and was being severely criticized at both the rank-and-file and leadership levels.

Roger dropped out of active participation in the politics of struggle after the WCP collapsed. He went back to his family textile business until 1996 when he emerged to work with one of the organizations that formed the Union des forces progressistes and later Québec solidaire.

I have since asked a number of people how their experience in the WCP affected them.

Roger said it helped him with the ability to analyze things and the ability to see the practical implications of a theoretical position. "As a result of the critiques levelled internally [at] the M-L groups in the past, we try to make left-wing organizations relevant and thrive in the new epoch. We need policies of gender equality, parties based on participatory democracy, in order to answer to the needs of the new era."

He concluded that he had "no resentment or nostalgia. I took it as an existing fact and moved on from it. The many years I spent travelling around Quebec and around the country, involved with meeting people from different countries, have made me what I am today and contributed to my development."[127]

Roger continues to be politically active as a leading member of Québec solidaire and with Alternatives, an international solidarity organization in Montreal.

Alan Silverman said he is not bitter—although "it took me a year or two to come to terms with the demise of the Marxist-Leninist movement." He felt his options in life "would have been larger" if he hadn't quit his teaching job at Dawson College in Montreal, but he didn't regret having worked at Ste-Justine Hospital, also in Montreal. "As a Jewish, middle-class, Anglo intellectual, it helped me understand what other people's lives were all about."

Alan said he had learned a great deal, "especially in meeting people like the PLO representative, Abdullah Abdullah, and the ZANU people. We played our little part in bringing down apartheid and [supporting] the Vietnamese people to defeat the Americans. It was enriching. My experience in the Party helped in my political understanding of how the world works."

His family moved to Toronto "after the party," in part because they didn't identify with the Anglo-Jewish community in Montreal, "and although we are bilingual, we were not assimilated; we did not feel Québécois."

When we spoke, Alan had recently read *Love and Capital*,[128] which had increased his admiration for Marx. "As a human being, a humanist, it was mind boggling what this man did. He was so committed, fundamentally, in serving the people and being for the oppressed; it was quite spectacular."[129]

Yvette Matyas worked as an administrator in the Party's Bureau d'organisation so she had a unique perspective on the functioning of the organization. Initially, she worked at the Jewish General Hospital in Montreal on the support staff and got involved in union politics as a shop steward. She met League member Julian Sher through his mother at the hospital, and Julian recruited her to the League in 1976.

"I got involved not so much from an intellectual background," she told me. "I didn't know much about Marxism-Leninism. I got involved from an anti-authoritarian, anti-establishment interest in social justice. I was part of the rebellion of the '60s against the system. I was happy to be part of a larger group fighting for social change."

She recalled working at the Bureau d'organisation as an administrator. "It was a place where very important people of the Party worked—where the leadership worked. It very much echoed women's traditional work of being secretaries. ... But I learned a lot of my skills from that period of time— leadership and organizational skills."

She had some regrets, "My son was born in 1979. It was very difficult being a parent then because I really believed that the priority was the revolution, which was around the corner. My son had many, many different babysitters, as I was going to meetings. If I saw this kind of parenting today, I'd be very upset."

She said that working at the Bureau d'organisation had involved incredibly long hours—fourteen hours a day. Early on, she was enthusiastic, but then that enthusiasm began to wane, for personal reasons related to the family. When she and Alan Silverman got married, they had a civil ceremony instead of a Jewish wedding "because we felt that religion was the opiate of the masses," which "very much upset" her parents, Holocaust survivors. "It was only years later that we had a Jewish ceremony."

Being in the Party, she said, "was difficult for us as a couple, since we could not share much of what we were doing; everything was top security."

She explained why she had such strong emotions towards the end: "When I lost my belief—losing faith in my ideals—it was very sad for me. I remember crying. It wasn't so much a loss of belief in the WCP, but I felt betrayed for having hoped so much for a better world and it wasn't there as I had imagined."

Describing her feelings about leaving, Yvette said: "The whole anti-imperialist movement was so strong—that's what attracted me. But 1982 was a painful year; I left the Party before it exploded. I was pregnant with my daughter and Alan was away at the last Congress. It caused a lot of tension as a couple. It was a sense that you are no longer part of a group that you had worked in. It was a sense that I had failed; I couldn't believe anymore. It wasn't an easy departure [from the party] and Alan hadn't departed yet. For a long time I was bitter about the Party but not now. I felt ashamed to leave the Party—it was such a close organization."

Looking back on her whole time with the Party, she acknowledged some of her positive experiences. "It took me a while to get over the bitterness and resentment—I realized that there were people who tried to do good," she said. "There's even a sense of nostalgia—having a sense of hope—that I don't see much of with young people nowadays. It was a larger collective, instead of individuals; there were good moments. I learned a lot of skills. Later in life, I got very high-level leadership positions and I think those skills came directly from things I learned in the Party. There was a strong sense of collective hope—you don't see that very often today."

Yvette rose to become the director of operations in a large Toronto hospital before her retirement.

Herman Rosenfeld, originally from New Jersey, attended McGill as a grad student in the early 1970s. After the founding of the CCL (M-L), he was sent to Toronto to work in the auto industry. He worked at the General Motors plant and became a union militant with the Canadian Auto Workers. He was the national staff representative in its Education Department for fifteen years.

As a militant member, "quite honestly, I was thrilled to be part of what I thought was a project to organize a political party that could win over the working class to socialism, and galvanize them into a mass movement to challenge the system. It was rooted in factory and workplace cells … I believed in the ideology."

He said he has "not an iota" of bitterness or resentment. "It helped me get into the world of the working class and trade union movement; it taught me how to do this; it gave me hope that it was possible to win workers to the idea of socialism. I still believe it. And the way that the WCP actually did educational work with workers is something I think was very positive then and I built on those lessons throughout my career as a socialist in the working-class movement. Even though it proved to be a failed experiment in how to build a socialist party and movement, it was a springboard for me to learn more about how to do it right: I went to grad school and studied Marxism more in depth and continued the work that was partly inspired by the M-L experience for the rest of my life."

Herman turned to the Euro-Marxist academics in the New Left tradition to try and explain the world in the twenty-first century: "There have been some extremely thoughtful and incisive Marxist political theorists," he said, naming Ralph Miliband—"not his sold-out sons"—and Nicos Poulantzas for their work on Marxism and the state and on revolutionary politics in developed capitalist countries, as well as Marta Harneckar and Mike Lebowitz, "both of whom worked in Venezuela and Cuba," and all of whom "helped put Lenin's work in a modern context.

"I think the Communist movement has run its course as a guide to a working class–based revolutionary transformation of capitalism, and other forms of Marxism need to develop as political movements that can operate in both bourgeois democratic political and economic systems."

This kind of thinking, Herman added, obviously meant "that I think the ultimate failure of the M-L movement ... had as much to do with its ideological roots in authoritarian and undemocratic forms of organization and politics, un-dialectical and idealist concepts of the bourgeois state, as with the changing times." What exists in Nepal today is "very different" than the original M-L movements, he noted.

Everyone I spoke with about life after the Party felt they did not waste those years. They learned the skills of political analysis, gained organizational abilities, and maintained their indomitable spirit of wanting to change the world for the better. For some, this experience even helped in career development.

James—who requested that his full name not be used—was someone I worked with in the anti-imperialist committee of the Party. He relaunched his academic career ten years later and obtained his doctor of philosophy degree at Oxford University. When he applied for a permanent position in a prestigious London university, the interviewer, Fred Halliday, questioned him about those missing years on his cv.

"I discovered years later," James told me, that "because I let my guard down in the interview and when asked what I had been doing during those years, I said I spent the years as a left-wing activist working in factories and around solidarity movements … that was what made me stand out from among the applicants and I got the job. So, on balance, I guess the whole thing was good for me."[130]

* * *

The Marxist-Leninist (Maoist) movements in Asia did not suffer the same fate as their counterparts in the West. The M-L movement in Nepal, which Herman mentioned, has interesting lessons for modern-day Maoism. The Communist Party of Nepal (Maoist) came to power in 2008 after a ten-year "people's war" that from 1996 to 2006 took the lives of seventeen thousand people. The Party chairman, Prachanda, was elected prime minister; he had been in office for less than a year when he resigned over his unsuccessful attempt to install civilian control over the army by trying to fire the army chief. The US-trained head of the army had the backing of the Nepalese president, India and the USA, which had maintained the Communist Party of Nepal (Maoist) on its list of terrorist organizations. The Nepalese Maoists tried to apply the principles of New Democratic Revolution as Mao laid out for China to the Nepalese situation.

When Hishila Yami—minister of public works in the new Nepalese government and one of two women members of the Communist Party of Nepal (Maoist) politburo—visited Canada in 2008 on a tour organized by Daya Varma, I asked her how the new democratic revolution would be carried out in a multi-party system if her party got voted out of power. She gave a non-answer. Her party subsequently lost the majority and split into different factions over questions of tactics and strategy. Some wanted to resume the people's war, others wanted to give social democracy a chance, and others wanted to apply Mao's theory of new democracy to Nepal. Nevertheless, the party was instrumental in abolishing the monarchy and setting up a republic.

The original party under Prachanda, going under the new name of Nepal Communist Party (Maoist-Centre) entered into an alliance with the Nepal Communist Party–Unified Marxist-Leninist and won 113 out of 165 seats in the December 2017 elections to form the government. There are thirteen different communist parties in Nepal with slight variations to the name. In Nepal, it seems "communist" is not a bad word. As the Nepalese Maoists lost and regained power, the remnants of the Marxist-Leninist movement and independent Marxists in the West fell all over themselves in denouncing, criticizing and advising the Nepalese Maoists on the best path towards socialism.

The way I see it, the struggle of the Nepalese people for socialism is in their hands as they work their own way through their new democratic revolution.

* * *

The Workers Communist Party here in Canada held an erroneous position on intellectuals and their participation in the progressive movement. It was understandable that the Party had a "workerist" attitude. The people who formed the Canadian Communist League (Marxist-Leninist) were mainly students and intellectuals who rebelled against their class nature and followed the road of implantation to get closer to the working class; they developed a disdain for intellectual work and were not able to accommodate intellectuals in the Party.

As an example, I tried to get Daya Varma to join the League. We met many times on the slope of Mount Royal across from his lab in the McIntire Medical Building to discuss the League program and its mass work. Daya was ready to join the organization; however, the leadership (I don't remember whether it was Ian or Roger) said Daya should be sent to Toronto to organize the East Indians there. I was taken aback. Here we had someone well established as a scholar and researcher with world-class credentials at McGill and we wanted him to give up all that and move to Toronto as a full-time organizer!

When I told this to Daya, he didn't say anything, but I saw in his eyes that he was in disbelief. We knew right away that the Party could not accommodate an intellectual and free thinker of his stature. Daya remained sympathetic to the Party. He later led an independent study to monitor the effects on pregnant women of the gas leak from the 1984 Union Carbide plant in Bhopal, India, where close to four thousand people were killed.[131]

Steve, with whom I discussed the Party program on his balcony in the freezing cold, was also treated with the cavalier attitude we had for intellectuals. (He asked that I not publish his last name.) A CEGEP professor and anti-imperialist activist with CAPT, he visited the liberated areas of Kampuchea in 1980 following the Vietnamese invasion and occupation of that country. Along with academics like Malcolm Caldwell and George Hildebrand, he was one of the few intellectuals who wrote about the Kampuchean agrarian revolution at the time.

The WCP held to the belief that all intellectuals should be sent to work among the working class in order to show their revolutionary commitment and reform their world outlook. Unlike the Old Communist Movement, we did not value the positive role that intellectuals could play in the organization.

Nevertheless, in its short seven-year existence, the League and the Party made significant contributions to Canadian Marxist political thinking and practice. I can break this down to four major items:

1. THE PRINCIPAL CONTRADICTION IN CANADA

"There are many contradictions in the process of development of a complex thing," Mao Zedong wrote in his famous essay "On Contradiction" (1937), "and one of them is necessarily the principal contradiction whose existence and development determine or influence the existence of the other contradictions."[132]

The WCP clearly stated: "The principal contradiction in Canada is between the Canadian bourgeoisie and the Canadian proletariat." The statement of the WCP had dispelled other constructions, which tended to camouflage Canada as an imperialist country in its own right, independent of the US.

2. QUEBEC NATIONAL QUESTION

It was a breakthrough in the 1970s to move away from the "big-nation chauvinism" of the Canadian left and the "narrow nationalism" of the Quebec left nationalists.

The WCP recognized Quebec to be an oppressed nation because it did not have the right to self-determination. (Whether it is oppressed today remains to be debated.) So the WCP recognized the right of the Quebec people to self-determination up to and including separation. However, in a break with the left nationalist tendency, the WCP called for the unity of the Canadian working class, including Quebec workers, in the struggle against its principal enemy, the Canadian ruling class.

It formulated that the separation of Quebec would only weaken the unity of the Quebec and Canadian working class and people, and play into the hands of the Canadian and Quebec bourgeoisie. En lutte! held a similar position on the Quebec national question.

3. THREE WORLDS THEORY

The WCP adhered to the orthodox communist practice of the international united front, at that time annunciated by Mao in the form of the Three Worlds Theory. However, in opposition, there were those fundamentalists that said that communists couldn't form this kind of unity—you stood alone, and you fell alone.

4. IMPLANTATION—AT THE WORKPLACE AND WITHIN WORKING-CLASS ORGANIZATIONS

However "workerist," implantation was a concept to get leftist intellectuals to go among the working class and learn concretely what it meant to survive against capitalist exploitation. The concept had been picked up from the Chinese Revolution and the "go among the peasants and workers policy" of the Cultural Revolution. The intellectuals of the WCP applied this principle to find jobs in factories and in the service sector to integrate with the working masses. It had significant embryonic results for the WCP within the trade union movement in Quebec and the auto industry in Ontario.

* * *

The decade of the 1970s—my twenties—felt very ordinary. I lived out my principles and my belief that a world of equality and compassion was possible, and I was part of an organization that allowed me to put my principles into practice. I went into it with my eyes and heart wide open. I felt no bitterness or resentment, remorse or regret. In fact, I was thankful that I associated with people who shared my quest for a better world, even though I did not connect back with them until many years later. However, there were many hard lessons to be learned from that period of my life, which have led me to quite a few awakenings. One of the hard lessons was that political and ideological kinship do not necessarily equate to personal connections or a source of emotional support.

Looking back with the rear-view mirror of history, one tends to fall into sentimentality and nostalgia, especially if one dedicated a lot of emotions and energy to the movement. I try not to do that as I look back at those years.

Until it was all over, it was not important that I was the only Chinese Canadian member of the Party. Once the Party ended, though, others—especially the Québécois comrades—returned to their roots and to a place of familiarity. What were my roots?

Chapter 9

The Question of China

"From antiquity to modern times, China had only two major external influences—Buddhism in the first few centuries and Marxism in the twentieth."
—Daya Ram Varma, *The Art and Science of Healing Since Antiquity*[133]

Two of us stopped at a farm near Dongguan, China, to pick up some fresh lychees in 2015. The farmer greeted us warmly and explained that the crop was doing well this year, but it was nevertheless hard work to look after the trees and harvest the fruit. As he was offering us some samples to taste, a large black SUV pulled up in a cloud of dust. Four men wearing crisp white shirts poured out. They all walked with the stride of bureaucrats and an air of arrogance. "Two crates of your best lychees and make it fast," commanded the driver as the others grabbed freshly picked lychees from a basket to sample. "These are probably government functionaries," my lychee-picking companion, Dong Qing, said. "They are rude and don't know how to behave." As in all societies, even in a socialist China, you have some people who feel they are entitled to lord it over others.

Chinese Canadians have mixed feelings about today's China. Some are staunchly anti-communist. Many are from the older generation that fled the civil war or the communist takeover, but even among those there is grudging admiration of China's standing in the world today. There are also those who are more politically aware and believe that Western democracy is the best course for humanity; they decry the lack of individual and political freedom in China. Then there are those who do business with China and take a more pragmatic view of the country's internal system.

A limited number of Chinese Canadians are sympathetic to the developments in China. They look at the fact that China has lifted 800 million people out of poverty since the 1949 revolution and that the per capita GDP has risen greatly—from $155 in 1978 to $7,950 in 2014.[134] Where do I stand? I am an unrepentant Maoist.

All of these differences in outlook, of course, would inevitably have an impact on the head tax redress movement, which I will discuss in later chapters.

The developments in China were something that my dear friend Daya Varma and I carried on an exchange of views about for many years before he passed away in the spring of 2015. Daya continued to support "socialist construction" in China long after it became unfashionable to do so in Western leftist circles. Sam Noumoff, who was a political science professor at McGill, and also an old friend of China, joined in our discussions on China via email correspondences. Sam passed away in the autumn of 2014, but in the months before his death, we debated the political and ideological basis of China's economic reforms.

It was through these exchanges, conducted by email, that I finally understood the theoretical underpinnings of China's socialist economic reforms.

I started the exchanges in 2013, after I had finally read *China's Socialist Economy*[135] by Xue Muqiao, who lived from 1904 to 2005. I'd bought the book three decades beforehand, soon after it first came out. Xue is seen as an architect for China's economic reform and the socialist market system. He got the ear of Deng Xiaoping, who put many of his theories into practice. After Liberation, Xue held many key posts in the Chinese government and gained first-hand experience in the economic problems facing China.

He outlined in the book how, since there was no other model for creating a socialist society, he drew from the experience of the Soviet Union, with Lenin's New Economic Plan and Stalin's Five Year Plans as guides. Soon Xue realized that the Soviet policy towards agriculture and the peasantry did not suit China and that the Soviet economic policies were too rigid and inflexible for the Chinese situation. The Chinese Communist Party had to blaze the trail to construct socialism after the destruction of the semi-feudal, semi-colonial society.

Xue adhered to the basic principles of Marxism-Leninism and Mao Zedong Thought, but pointed out that the construction of socialism was something entirely new in human history. Neither Marx nor Lenin had to develop any guiding theory for the construction of socialism. Mao was able to develop his theories on the New Democratic Revolution and initial stages of building socialism with Chinese characteristics by linking his theories with practice. Xue did not openly criticize Mao but his criticisms of the Great Leap Forward and the Cultural Revolution pointed out the ultra-left thinking that strayed from what he considered to be the basic or objective laws of socialist economics.

Xue forecast that building socialism in China could take more than a hundred years. Every step the Chinese took, he said, would have to adhere to "the objective economic laws of socialist relations of production corresponding to the productive forces" (human power, material resources, equipment and technology, where workers add value to create products), as well as the principle of compensating "each according to his work," the law of value (measuring the value of labour and commodities), and the socialist market economy of supply and demand. He also developed plans to reform the management and accounting practices of both the national economy and local enterprises. Xue wrote:

> In 1958 we began making quite a few errors because we lacked experience in socialist economic construction. ... If we do not quickly catch up with the advanced levels in capitalist countries, we shall not be able to prove the superiority of the socialist system to the people of China and the world. ... The aim of socialist construction is to satisfy the constantly rising material and cultural requirements of the nation.

He noted that China lacked a democratic tradition and that the issue of how to develop a people's democracy "as distinguished from bourgeois democracy" still had to be solved in both theory and practice. And he predicted that, with its low pay coupled with good workmanship, China would become the factory to the world.

Much has changed in China since Xue developed his theories of socialist construction in 1981. However, as I noted in my 2013 emails to Daya and Sam,

Xue's theories were still reflected in the Communist Party of China program, passed at the eighteenth Party congress of November 2012.

Sam and I agreed that ideological issues were not well developed in the book. Xue had been refreshingly frank, though, and did not get bogged down in ideological rhetoric. I noted that the insight I got from the book was that socialist construction was a new human phenomenon that would have both successes and serious reverses.

Countries like China, Vietnam and Cuba were at the time embarking on unexplored territory. Some people might say that they turned away from Marxism, but then again, Marx was never challenged with building socialism. He gave a good basic analysis ideologically, politically and economically of the evils of capitalism, but he contributed little to what socialism could be and how to construct it. I think that was the contribution of Xue: he was able to go beyond Marx.

Sam agreed "fully" that Xue had provided some refreshing analysis. However, he said he feared that Xue had "bent the bamboo too far in the opposite direction." When it came to the socialist market economy, Sam went on to say that he feared what Xue had "underestimated was how fast and deep the roots of petty capitalism can develop."

I also noted that many people in China and outside of China underestimate the dynamism and the allure of capitalism and its ability to regenerate itself.

For the purists on the left and the right, China is neither a socialist nor capitalist country and many have predicted or wished for the demise of the regime from the weight of all its internal contradictions. The new Chinese leader, Xi Jinping, has been quoted as saying "The Chinese dream is an ideal. Communists should have a higher ideal, and that is communism."

"Mao once commented that holding a majority is not equivalent to being right, having himself been suspended at times from the Party," Sam noted, writing too that:

There is no fixed model, but the river must be crossed by feeling the stones. In the final analysis, we must remain vigilant in examining the long term consequences of all policy initiatives. If the short term consequences are negative, but are rectified over time we can tolerate the temporary distortion.

Daya published our full email discussion online, on the website for the *International South Asia Forum Bulletin*. I had hoped that the email correspondence would continue into a discussion of China's foreign policy, but alas, Sam fell ill in late 2013 and that never happened. Nevertheless, after discussing Xue's book with my two good friends, I feel I have a greater understanding of the transformations happening in China today and how they fit within a general Marxist framework.

* * *

There is an unending slew of Marxist analysis to show how capitalism has transformed China into a class society full of hardship and exploitation for the country's people since China's rise as an economic power over the last thirty years.

An example of the numerous journals taking part in the "China is capitalist" viewpoint is the venerable US journal *Monthly Review*, which has published articles from leftists, academics and various "refugees" from the Cultural Revolution or the June Fourth Movement[136] to show how China has entered into the capitalist world order. The authors of such articles usually write from the position that the material, social and economic progress made by the Chinese people came from capitalist policies of the "market" led by a bureaucratic ruling class.

To be fair, *Monthly Review* has published a small number of articles that take a more sympathetic view of China. One of these was by Samir Amin, the director of the Third World Forum in Dakar, Senegal, and an avowed "Third-Worldist," even now that "Third-Worldism" has become a bad term among the elite Eurocentric left who feel they have regained the Marxist high ground and have given up on China. (The attempt to force the retreat of the "Third Worldists" like Samir Amin seems counterintuitive at a time when there is a dearth of diversity, creativity, innovation and originality in Western Marxist thought today.)

In his article "China 2013," Amin situates China among the emerging nations of the world and says the revolution has benefitted the Chinese people enormously. He writes:

> Some argue that China has chosen, once and for all, the "capitalist road" and intends even to accelerate its integration into contemporary

capitalist globalization. They are quite pleased with this and hope only that this "return to normality" (capitalism being the "end of history") is accompanied by development towards Western-style democracy."

He calls the question "Is China socialist or capitalist?" a poor one if one fails to consider that China has followed an original path since Liberation.[137]

Amin has a few choice words for those who criticize China from the academic left. "*China bashing* panders to the infantile opinion found in some currents of the powerless Western "left": if it is not the communism of the twenty-third century, it is a betrayal!" he writes.

Fidel Castro may have been addressing these academics when he said with brutal honesty in 2005, "Here is a conclusion I've come to after many years: among all the errors we may have committed, the greatest of them all was that we believed that someone ... actually knew how to build socialism."[138]

I won't go any deeper into the theory and practice of Chinese policies, or the various pedantic theories on the ruling class and the state under a socialist system, as an academic would. I tend to look more at the political implications to see what they mean for the people.

Criticizing China is easy, but the hard question is how to reform the country to better improve the people's standard of living and culture; this is what building socialism is all about. It is no accident that Cuba and Vietnam, two countries where the Communist Party is in power, are undertaking the same kind of economic reforms that China has been implementing. Is this the "end of history" as the critics perceive the rise of capitalism?

Western intellectuals have started to write more freely about what is happening in China. This is a welcome departure from the pack thinking of both left and right academics, who gleefully greeted China's entrance into the capitalist world. What I like about the Amin article is that he points to a third path for social development. Obviously, the so-called traditional Marxist socialist path of the Soviet Union and Eastern Europe did not work. Can China transition from an authoritarian Marxism to a more humanistic Marxism? Then again, what is socialism in the real world? Many who pronounce themselves on this question really don't know, beyond the doctrines they glean from Marxist texts. Daya Varma, in later years, starkly and honestly admitted, "I don't really know what socialism is."

Amin keeps true to his sympathies for the independent developments of Third World countries. The apologists of Western democracy like to promote their common thought on the evils of either Chinese communism or Chinese capitalism. They like to espouse the theories of Western democracy but they have not been able to resolve the inequities of their society in the practice of democracy.

However, sixty years of socialist education gives Chinese workers a class-consciousness that provides them with a powerful advantage over the ever-diminishing industrial workers of the West. I am not concerned about the class-consciousness and militancy of the Chinese workers. They have already won many battles against the bosses, including factory Party cronies. They know that their rights are guaranteed in the Chinese and the Party Constitutions. People I've spoken with in China do not back down when it comes to their fundamental economic and social rights.

As China carried out its 2011 five-year plan to concentrate on consumption instead of investment expansion, we saw more popular struggles as the gap between the middle class (working people) and the extremely wealthy one per centers got more acute. However, this may have been the plan of the Party leadership all along. The five-year plan in 2011 called for 6.5 per cent annual growth with 15 per cent increases in the minimum wage each year. Within this context, contradictions developed but that was planned so China could move to a more self-sufficient internal economy.

There is no sign that Chinese workers will be following the route of the Western working-class movements and their class-oriented parties as an alternative. The Western road leads to social democracy and dead-ends in Greece (Syriza, the Coalition of the Radical Left) or Spain (Podemos). I thought Marx and Lenin had put to rest the original strand of "revisionism"— social democracy. I suppose for the Western left, the social democratic reform of capitalism is more palatable than socialist reform in China. But then sometimes, a Bernie Sanders is simply better than a Donald Trump, or a Justin Trudeau is simply better than a Stephen Harper.

* * *

Something that commentators on China don't often address is the five-year plan, which centrally develops the different regions and sectors of Chinese society. The 2011 five-year plan called for the development of the interior and Western China with high-speed rail, solar and wind energy among other things. The plan called for the slowing down of the economy as China transitions from investment to consumption as the focus. China is moving from an external demand–driven economy to an internal demand–driven economy. Western observers see dire consequences, as the Chinese economy no longer grows in double digits. But it was *planned*.

China is extremely complex, and complicated to decipher. People tend to forget that the Chinese Revolution was a new form of revolution, a People's Democratic Revolution. It was not a socialist revolution. We can only take a long-term approach to see where it is going. The Chinese Communist Party's eighteenth congress document reiterated Xue's prediction that it may take China a hundred years to build socialism.

In 2013 I visited China for a month and while there, I sat down and wrote a long email to Daya and Sam about what I was seeing.

Who gets to determine whether China is socialist or not, I asked rhetorically. I had been asking the people I met "Do you think China is still socialist?" They responded that China is socialist when it comes to economic reforms or China is socialist with Chinese characteristics. These were ordinary people, workers, retirees, small-business owners, tour guides and bus drivers. I did not talk with academics, human rights activists and so on, who may have given me different answers.

The standard of living in China had developed tremendously over the five to ten years before I visited, and the people said that was due to the superiority of the socialist system. "Maybe this is Party talk, but the people in China seem to have more faith in socialism than the Western left who say that the economic achievements in China are due to capitalism taking over," I wrote. I thought this was ironic.

A bus driver in Changsha talked about the fact that China still had five-year plans. He told me that the twelfth five-year plan (2011–15) was targeting the development of central China after the eleventh five-year plan focused on the economic development of Western China. Despite all the news about entrepreneurial businesses booming all over China, the Chinese government still controlled the key sectors of the economy, such as finance and banking, telecommunications, energy, transportation and heavy industry.

Were all the accomplishments of the Chinese people over the previous twenty years due to the development of capitalist economy and not due to the centrally planned socialist economy with economic reform, I wondered. The people I spoke with didn't think so. Despite the fact that they did not express their economic achievements in ideological language, many still believed that the achievements were due to the superiority of the Chinese socialist system.

Had the Chinese gone beyond the ideology of doctrinaire Marxist-Leninist fundamentalism? Or had they moved more towards Marx's humanist approach to social development? During more than five decades of the Chinese socialist educational system, socialist and traditional values of respect were inculcated into the generations. Long gone were the days of the M-L revolutionary centre when one country served as the model of socialism. It seemed that the only people who wished to export revolution were the remnants of the M-L left and Trotskyites in advanced capitalist countries.

I still saw some billboards and posters exhorting the people to follow the CCP and to diligently study the documents of the eighteenth Party congress, but apart from that, there were few public displays of communist ideology. China Central TV showed programs to reflect the party line and dramas depicting the struggles and the history of the communist movement, the anti-Japanese war and the civil war, as well as progressive struggles around the world—including a special on the life of Nelson Mandela and the fight against apartheid in South Africa.

China came through the capitalist global economic crisis in 2008 relatively unscathed due to its centralized socialist planning system. When I visited China in 2013, a recent stock market slump in the West had been triggered by concern about the slowdown of the Chinese economy to less than 7.5 per cent growth.

I included the above thoughts in my email from China, and Daya responded: "It is very good and conforms to my own impression. I have developed some disdain for new age ultra leftists."

On all my trips to China over the years, I have tried to observe what the changes mean to the ordinary person on the street. These days, it certainly helps that my father-in-law is an old communist revolutionary.[139] He is in his nineties as I write. He has lived through the revolutionary changes, fighting against the Japanese invaders and in the civil war. His older brother and sister were revolutionary martyrs. Through the tumultuous Cultural Revolution and other political campaigns and rectifications, he has remained steadfast in his faith in the Chinese Communist Party and socialism. Sometimes I see China through his eyes.

A man named Jaxi, whom I met in the Tibetan region of Yunnan in 2015, revealed to me that the Tibetan people in that rural part of China had great

March 2015. With my Tibetan friend Jaxi at Tiger Leaping Gorge, Deqen Tibetan Autonomous Prefecture. (William Dere Collection)

respect for Mao and the CCP. I was surprised to see the hammer and sickle flying in front of many households along with the Tibetan prayer banners. Nowhere else in China did I see this kind of open affection for the CCP and Mao. Jaxi told me that the loyalty to Mao and the Party was due to the liberation of the Tibetan people in this area from feudal oppression and slavery in 1951. Since then, the standard of living had improved beyond their dreams and life expectancy for Tibetans had doubled in the last sixty years. They considered Mao on par with the lamas because he granted them special rights to promote their social and cultural life.

There were images of the Dalai Lama and the Panchen Lama in the monasteries I visited, contradicting Western media reports that idolatry of the Dalai is forbidden in China. Panchen is second to Dalai in the lama hierarchy but Panchen has a significant role in the process to select a Dalai. The Tibetans in the Yunnan region considered the two lamas as equals.

"Zhaxi Dele!"[140]

PART THREE

Redress

Chapter 10

Being Chinese in Canada

When my daughter was little, I read her bedtime stories—tales from China and Chinese Canada that I was discovering. There were books by Paul Yee (Teach Me to Fly, Skyfighter) and Laurence Yep (Dragonwings). They were about the Chinese experience in Gold Mountain and meant for pre-teens and teens, but nevertheless, Jessica got an early start on Chinese Canadian literature. As I read to her, we both learned about Chinese cultural values and morality. Due to the weightiness of the subject matter, after a couple of pages she quickly fell asleep. She never said "Again!" as she did with more traditional books like Goodnight Moon.

When a relationship or a marriage is freed from the political and ideological framework of the Movement, it has to stand on its own. The unresolved issues of culture and ethnicity have to be worked through. That was the hard lesson I learned. By 1985, the many differences and contradictions that affected us personally and as a couple came to the fore for Gillian and me. We decided to part ways. Once we'd agreed to the amiable terms, the divorce was simple and cost me the $80 filing fee after I prepared the legal document with the help of my lawyer friend Ian Wong. As Gillian and I stood before Judge John Gomery, he only had one question—whether our three-year-old daughter would be well taken care of. We told the judge that both of us loved Jessica so much that we would not let anything harm her. He granted us joint custody of our daughter, and the divorce.

During the process of the separation and divorce, I experienced a period of anguish. Gillian and I had been together for seven years. I went through the classical five steps of grieving the end of a relationship—denial, anger, bargaining, depression and finally acceptance. It took me a year and a half to two years to come out of my daze, and to come to terms with my new situation. Amazingly, at the end of this period, I felt free and energized.

For the first time in my life I had to dig deep into myself to understand who I was without the external influences of society, politics and ideology or the traditional Chinese values of the institution of marriage. I began to develop an awareness of being Chinese Canadian—I needed to find myself. But I was in for a rude awakening. In 1985, there was little in the way of Chinese Canadian culture—the culture that expressed our experiences in Canada.

I continued to search for that elusive identity and sense of belonging. At first I explored the influences from within the Chinese North American culture that I could connect with emotionally. But I also needed to bond with the cultural roots of my forebears. Since childhood, I'd heard stories of historical events from the time of the various Chinese empires, but I'd never read the four main Chinese classical novels, despite the fact that one of them was *Water Margin*, the book my father had so often quoted from.[142] The Chinese classics are to the East as the works of Homer, Shakespeare, Dostoevsky and Tolstoy are to the West, and they have influenced the cultural and literary thinking of the Chinese through the millennia. I wanted to dig into how those stories have crept into the psyche and influenced the cultural works of Chinese people around the world. In the end, I read the English versions of the four Chinese classics.

* * *

I read everything about Chinese North America and the Chinese diaspora that I could get my hands on. I attended Chinese film festivals wherever I could. In the 1980s there wasn't much overseas Chinese culture to be had, but there was enough to drive my interest and imagination. Lacking Chinese

Canadian materials, I took to the surrogate of Chinese American works. One of the first Asian American films was the 1982 film noir *Chan is Missing* by Wayne Wang, which left a lasting impression on me because it had a storyline situated entirely in the Chinese working-class community of San Francisco. This was ten years after I had been influenced by the Asian American civil rights movement, which came on in the wake of the African American movement: students went on strike in California universities for Asian American studies. Due to its greater numbers, the Chinese American cultural scene in general was much more developed and vibrant than what was happening in the Chinatowns of Canada. I felt a strong need to be aware of my identity and the need to feel proud of what I am.

I became a proponent of developing and promoting Chinese Canadian culture. I travelled to the Chinatowns of Vancouver and Toronto and met some of the pioneers of Chinese Canadian cultural expression. There was Barry Wong, one of the originators of *Pender Guy*, an English-language community radio program that offered local writers an outlet for their stories, satire and community action. *Pender Guy* is a play on words in English and Chinese. *Guy* is Toishanese for street. Barry was a community cultural activist and one of the few people I knew who could speak in grammatically correct paragraphs and in a mellifluous radio voice. There was the late Jim Wong-Chu, the author of a book of poetry, *Chinatown Ghosts*.[143] His poems had a strong influence on me. (Later, I would use his poetry in my 1993 documentary *Moving the Mountain*.) Jim came to Canada as a "paper son" and he lived through the experience of all that entails. He was a founding member of the Asian Canadian Writers' Workshop through which many Asian Canadian writers emerged. The prolific author Paul Yee is one of those writers that came through the workshop. I read his *Tales of Gold Mountain* to Jessica as a bedtime story.

I looked south of the border and was influenced by the writings of Frank Chin, a fellow railroader (he worked as a brakeman on the Southern Pacific Railroad). His writing was impatient and uncompromising—that was his appeal for me. This is one of his works:

The Year of the Dragon[144]

We'come a Chinatowng, Folks! Ha. Ha. Ha. … Happy New Year!
Fred Eng. "Freddie" of Eng's Chinatown tour'n'travoo.
"We tell Chinatown where to go." Ha ha ha. I'm top guide here.

Allaw week Chinee New Year. Sssssshhh Boom! Muchee muchie
fiery crake! Ha. Ha. Ha ...
But you're my last tour of the day, folks. And on my last tour of the
day, no hooey. I like to let my hair down. Drop the phony accent.
And be me. Just me.
I figure once a day, I have got to be me.

I was particularly provoked by Chin's searing criticisms of literary stars
Amy Tan and Maxine Hong Kingston.

Tan's *Joy Luck Club* made it big on the *New York Times* best sellers list and
in Hollywood with a white feminist portrayal of Chinese immigrant families,
in which the emasculated Chinese males were painted as insensitive misogyn-
ist louts. Chin regarded Tan's work as "fake," denigrating Chinese men and
playing to the stereotypical racist assumptions of Chinese Americans depicted
by popular white culture.

Maxine Hong Kingston's books, *China Men* and *The Woman Warrior*,
charmed me with the stories describing the early *lo wah kiu* (old overseas
Chinese) experience in *Gim Shan* (Gold Mountain) through which I tried to
situate the narrative of my father and grandfather. However, Frank Chin in his
brash style shattered my impressions with his scathing critiques.

In his influential essay "Come All Ye Asian American Writers of the Real
and the Fake,"[145] Chin lambasted Kingston, along with Tan and David Henry
Hwang (*M. Butterfly*), for perpetuating racist stereotypes in their works so
they would gain easy acceptance by white America. He wrote:

> These works are held up before us as icons of a Chinese culture ....
>   Amy Tan opens her *Joy Luck Club* with a fake Chinese fairy tale
> about a duck that wants to be a swan and a mother who dreams of her
> daughter being born in America, where she'll grow up speaking perfect
> English and no one will laugh at her.[146]

Chin accused writers like Tan of faking Chinese fairy tales to please Western appetites instead of using the real tales from China's mythical past. As for
Maxine Hong Kingston and David Henry Hwang:

> In *The Women Warrior*, Kingston takes a childhood chant, 'The Ballad
> of Mulan' ... and re-writes the heroine, Fa Mulan, to the specs of the

stereotype of the Chinese woman as a pathological white supremacist victimized and trapped in a hideous Chinese civilization. ... David Henry Hwang repeats Kingston's revision of Fa Mulan and Yue Fei, and goes on to impoverish and slaughter Fa Mulan's family to further dramatize the cruelty of the Chinese.[147]

Before you jump to your feet to accuse Chin of misogyny and professional jealousy, note that in his essay he touched on sexual politics and the emasculation of Chinese men in white popular culture. With a "stroke of white racist genius," he said, Kingston had attacked "Chinese civilization, Confucianism itself, and where its life begins: the fairy tale." Kingston, Chin wrote, "takes Fa Mulan, turns her into a champion of Chinese feminism and an inspiration to Chinese American girls to dump the Chinese race and make for white universality." American publishers, he said, "went crazy for Chinese women dumping on Chinese men." Chin cited the October 1978 issue of *Cosmopolitan* (after Kingston's *The Woman Warrior* had appeared in 1976), in which Lily Chang wrote: "Once we have broken away from the restaurants of Chinatown, we prefer lovers distinguished by a freer, more emotionally flamboyant style. In short, Caucasians" (from the article "What It's Like to Be a Chinese American Girl").[148]

All right, enough of going against the tide. Chin gets "real" with three other Chinese woman writers; he writes glowingly about them:

Unlike the pack of Chinese Americans, Sui Sin Far (Edith Eaton), Diana Chang, and Dr. Han Suyin write knowledgeably and authentically of Chinese fairy tales, heroic tradition and history. ... Chinese men who are not emasculated and sexually repellent in Chinese American writing are found in [their] books and essays. These three women are unique unto themselves, for they are Eurasians. Diana Chang and Dr. Han Suyin are the daughters of Chinese men. Sui Sin Far was the daughter of a Chinese mother and British father.[149]

Sui Sin Far is better known in the US than in Canada despite her Canadian upbringing. Her family moved to Montreal when she was little. Her early writings as Edith Eaton appeared in the *Montreal Star*, where she wrote about the plight of the Chinese working man in the early 1900s and criticized the burden imposed by the racist head tax. She later went to the US to write under her pen name, Sui Sin Far. Her writings were the only ones found at the time to be sympathetic to the Chinese as she used her pen to denounce the US Chinese Exclusion Act. There are at least two biographies of Sui Sin Far written by American authors. She died at age forty-nine, in 1914, and was buried in Mount Royal Cemetery in Montreal.[150]

In Chinese Canadian literary circles, the "Amy Tan effect" fortunately did not take hold. When I read *Disappearing Moon Cafe*[151] by SKY Lee, I was prejudiced by Frank Chin's critique of Chinese American women writers. However, SKY Lee, one of the first Chinese Canadian woman to be published, wrote with understanding and sympathy about the Gold Mountain men who were transposed from the Chinese villages to a hostile Canadian setting. Lee, who is also a feminist, wrote about the strong women who had to negotiate between Chinese and Canadian social mores while at the same time remaining true to their heritage, values and newfound sense of independence. She wrote real Chinese Canadian literature reflecting the racism encountered in Canada, and about both the early Chinese who fought to retain their feudal relations, and the younger generation that rebelled against these relations.

In a depiction of a more esoteric view of identity, the Chinese men and women of the era in SKY Lee's novel were governed by the cultural and moral values of the times. They clung to their identity as overseas Chinese because, indeed, they were inassimilable as determined by the laws of this country and by the colour of their skin. They all took pride in their Chinese-ness; since childhood they'd been taught that their culture was superior to that of the barbarians, even though in Canada, they were at the mercy of these same barbarians. As time went on, the thinking changed and Chinese identity started to become Chinese Canadian identity. This transition found expression in the cultural works of the other early Chinese Canadian writers.

The American Chinese found their cultural expression in the '60s and '70s and the Canadian Chinese cultural workers expressed their Chinese-ness a decade or two later. It is through these cultural works that my quest for identity got fleshed out, and when my search for clarity and belonging became political, it became a demand for a rightful place in the cultural makeup of this country.

* * *

The Malays have a word, *peranakan,* to describe the Chinese born in Malaysia, Indonesia and in Southeast Asia. The peranakan Chinese have acculturated into the indigenous society and gradually lost their Chinese language and culture. Assimilation was easier: after a generation or two, the physical racial features become indistinguishable. Since the reunification period in the 1950s, the peranakanization of the Chinese born in Canada, or who came at a young age like myself, has been a natural process. Assimilation of the mind if not the body has taken place. Many have fought to retain some degree of the Chinese cultural heritage implanted by their parents and the Chinese ancestors of an earlier period, despite the strong attraction of the dominant popular culture. In this process, a Chinese Canadian cultural identity has emerged. This identity is no longer governed by the millennia-old Confucian culture of the early Chinese. This Chinese Canadian identity was born out of the experience and reality of today's Canada.

Due to the immigration restrictions of the past hundred years, the Chinese community in Canada is still an immigrant one. The language patterns have evolved: first the majority dialect was Toishanese,[152] then Cantonese starting in the '70s, and now Mandarin is becoming the dominant dialect. The Toishanese villagers brought with them their culture and values of a hundred years ago; the Cantonese brought with them the more modern urban Hong Kong values; now the immigrants from Mainland China come with the values distilled from a socialist educational system over the last half century. Many of these came as professionals, in order to qualify for entry into Canada; some eventually joined the working class when they could not find jobs in their chosen field.

Interspersed over this period were the arrival of the Indochinese and Vietnamese Chinese, and the Taiwanese and Chinese from Southeast Asia and other exotic locations, like those coming to Quebec from the French-speaking islands of Mauritius and Réunion.

Then there is the intergenerational gap, as the Canadian-born Chinese educated in English and/or French, integrating with mainstream Canadian and Québécois cultural values, started to lose their ability to speak Chinese. Perhaps it is the members of this generation of Chinese Canadians who have the most questions about identity consciousness. Still, the ancient ancestral culture continues to gnaw at their souls. They can leave Chinatown, but Chinatown never leaves them. With all this diversity, Chinese-ness in Canada has many meanings and it is constantly shifting and evolving.

Identity consciousness for the Chinese in Canada invokes many contradictions and interpretations, and it presents a minefield each misstep can provoke division and scorn from all sides, and, worst of all, self-doubt. It is even more difficult to negotiate a Chinese identity in Quebec (see Chapter 17).

You build a cultural identity by being aware of your place in history and in staking your claim of belonging. This is not an easy task. The dominant society tries to assimilate your mind; it denies your race, your culture and your language. To fight back, you want the right to know your race, your culture and your language. You want the right to be proud of your cultural heritage. This is when that self-doubt becomes self-awareness and self-affirmation.

Chapter 11

Moving the Community

"No longer was there any fear, any doubt … ten thousand battles, ten thousand victories."

—Louis Chu, *Eat a Bowl of Tea*[153]

As a candidate in the school board election, I went to meet people on the street, which involved distributing flyers. I was doing so on Boulevard St. Laurent—the part of Montreal that locals know as "The Main." A Haitian Québécois man stopped, accepted one, looked at the photo and asked in French, "Who is this? Mao Zedong?" "No," I replied, also in French. "It's me." It was clear that I represented something more than the Ward 14 Chinese community.

It was the 1980s. Apart from the older generation of the *lo wah kiu* who had lived through those exclusionary years, very few of us were aware of the true consequences of the Head Tax and Chinese Exclusion Act (HTEA). But now the community could begin to unveil this dark history of unburnished government animosity towards Chinese immigrants. We saw the need to unravel these untold family secrets so we could come to terms with the past.

One of the first to step up was Dak Leon Mark, a Chinese Canadian who, following the proclamation of the Canadian Charter of Rights and Freedoms in 1982, felt it was time to resolve a long-standing human rights issue that had been irking him most of his life. Dak Leon Mark, also known as Mark Ark Liang on his head tax certificate, had come to Canada on February 27, 1919, at the age of eleven. Mark's father was a laundryman who saved to pay his son's head tax. In 1983, Mark was a retired International Woodworkers of America union member, and he knew his rights. He went to see his member of Parliament, Margaret Mitchell (NDP, Vancouver East).

I can imagine Mark, then 78, at a coffee party in Mitchell's riding office, with his hat in his hands, saying softly, "Miss Mitchell, now that Canada has entered a new era of human rights with the passing of the Charter of Rights and Freedoms, I think it would be time for the Canadian government to refund me the $500 my father paid as the head tax for me to get into Canada."

Mitchell realized that indeed this was an issue of fairness and equality since no other group of immigrants had to pay this punitive tax. Upon her return to Ottawa, she raised the issue with the government and, on September 6, 1983, she fired off a letter to Prime Minister Pierre Trudeau in which she wrote: "I ask that the federal government undertake to compensate those Chinese Canadian citizens who have proof of having paid the Head Tax by repaying it with interest." That was the first salvo in what would be a two-decade-long struggle for justice for the Chinese head tax payers and their families.

The Prime Minister's Office essentially ignored the issue. The ever-persistent Mitchell stood up in Parliament on February 6, 1984—Chinese New Year's Day—and many times afterwards, to keep the redress issue alive in the House.

With Mitchell's help, the Chinese Canadian National Council (CCNC)— the only national Chinese Canadian organization at the time—initiated a campaign on behalf of the head tax payers and their families in 1984.

It was in this year that the *ngin how shiu* (as I later learned to say head tax in Toishanese) finally entered my consciousness. My father had passed away two years beforehand, without ever telling me about the head tax or the Exclusion Act and how they had affected him.

The campaign for redress had really begun decades earlier. After World War II, the five hundred Chinese Canadian veterans returned and campaigned to be treated as full Canadians, with equal rights—including the right to vote—and the repeal of the Exclusion Act, all of which they won in 1947. Wong Foon Sien,[154] a leader in the Chinese Benevolent Association (CBA) in Vancouver and a Chinatown labour activist, started seeking redress for the two discriminatory laws, the head tax and the Chinese Exclusion Act, after the war.

The Chinese Canadian National Council officially launched the modern-day redress movement with a national conference in Toronto on May 6, 1984, in response to the strong interest expressed by the Chinese community across Canada. More than two thousand people across the country registered with the CCNC in just six months. In Vancouver, Hanson Lau, through CJVB Chinese Voice radio station, had already organized a registration of head tax payers in February and four hundred people had shown up in one weekend. "Everybody saved the (head tax) certificates because up until at least 1947, it was their only identification that would allow them to stay in Canada," Lau said in a newspaper interview. Describing the urgency faced by the aging head tax payers, he said, "If we wait 10 years, there won't be many people left."[155]

* * *

I began my tentative steps into Montreal's Chinatown politics in 1985, three years after the death of my father, who had been my personal link to the Chinese community.

Due to our father's high reputation, my brother, my sisters and I were well received by his family association. The president of the Chiu Lun Gong Sol asked me to follow in my father's footsteps and become a member of the board. I knew the politics of the family associations were very conservative and highly influenced by Confucianism—respect for patriarchy and authority. The heads of the different associations were the leading businessmen in Chinatown and the gatekeepers between the community and the outside world. Politicians campaigning for votes and police officials who wanted community co-operation would go to either these associations or the Chinese language newspapers to pass their messages to the community. I politely declined the invitation, citing my lack of understanding in the running of the Gong Sol and my weak fluency in Chinese. However, my third sister, Pui Yung, started working there as an administrator of the *woi*—the credit union. (Times have changed: in the past these associations were necessary for the welfare and protection of their membership, but today, outside of the *woi*, the associations do not offer much to young people other than a tenuous link to the past.)

Meanwhile, away from Chinatown, the Chinese Neighbourhood Society— an organization run by community activist Yat Lo that was the CCNC affiliate in

Montreal—started to register Montreal head tax families in 1985. It was smart of Yat to appoint a Québécois, Pierre Vaillancourt, as executive director of the neighbourhood society in order to gain easier access to Quebec's French government bureaucracy. The society's offices were located on Av. Du Parc, between St. Viateur and Bernard, at a time when the neighbourhood was still an immigrant enclave with Chinese, Portuguese, Latin American and some remnants of the old Jewish first-generation immigrants. I knew the area well since I'd lived a few streets east of Parc, on Waverly, during my early Maoist days.

Since 1985, I'd been working as a volunteer with the Chinese Family Service of Greater Montreal, which was located in Chinatown. I met with Yat to see if we could bring the two community organizations together to register more of the surviving head tax payers and their families. Altogether, about 350 head tax payers were registered locally. Through my participation as a board member (vice president), the Family Service applied to be a member of the Chinese Canadian National Council in 1986 to give us more clout in the redress campaign through a show of unity with the Chinese Neighbourhood Society.

All of us were neophytes in organizing a national campaign in the community. We had learned a few things from the anti-W5 movement, which activated young Chinese Canadians in sixteen cities across the country into a national coalition against the racist depiction of Asian Canadian faces in a W5 episode about Canada's universities. The CTV program suggested that foreign students were here to steal places from genuine Canadian students (read: white). The campaign forced CTV to admit that its program had been racist.

But the Head Tax and Exclusion Act (HTEA) was different. It touched our foundation in this country.

We had to reach deep into our collective consciousness to really understand and appreciate the profound history of the men and women who had lived through those foreboding years. Our only plan at the start was to seek out the head tax payers and families and to learn about the HTEA history from them. We really didn't have a good plan for three or four years, other than to lobby and meet with the different ministers of multiculturalism. We hoped that the government would do the right thing once they saw how wrong the head tax and Exclusion Act were. This naive political thinking was natural as the movement took its infant steps.

* * *

After a trip to Vancouver in 1986, where I met some of the members of the community radio program *Pender Guy*, I was inspired to start a comparable program at Montreal's Radio Centre-ville. Robert Yip also had a similar program in Ottawa called *Orientation*; he sent me material that he'd used on his program. These programs were in English and addressed the young generation of Chinese Canadians, with arts and culture expressing the everyday experience of the Chinese in Canada. It was through these programs that many young people began to develop an identity awareness.

I became involved in a group of young, single Chinese Montrealers; it was more of a social club of about twenty people who met over potluck meals and discussed Chinese culture and Chinatown events. There were one or two of them, like Ming Shyr, who already worked at Radio Centre-ville, and we developed an idea to produce a radio show for the mainly English-speaking Chinese youth of Montreal. We called it *Orientations*. We had a thirty-minute slot every Thursday night at 11:00 and every Saturday afternoon at 2:00. Our regular host was Leisa Lee. I don't know how many people listened in, but when we asked for listeners to call in, we always had one or two. I manned the mic a few times when no one else was available and I immediately discovered how difficult it was to coordinate your brain, to know what to say, and your mouth, to actually say it. I tried to infuse a little politics with the culture, playing music from Hugh Masekela to introduce people to the music of struggle in South Africa; but there was also Asian American music. I wore out a bootlegged copy of the tape *A Grain of Sand: Music for the Struggle of Asians in America* featuring Charlie Chin, Chris Iijima and Nobuko Myamoto with songs like "Imperialism Is Another Word for Hunger" and "Wandering Chinaman." Either Robert Yip or Jim Wong-Chu had passed the tape to me.

In the lead up to the 1986 Montreal municipal elections, we took a position not to endorse the Civic Party or the Montreal Citizens' Movement because neither had any representation from the city's ethnic communities. We asked listeners to consider a third party, the Democratic Alliance, uniting members from the Chinese, Greek, Italian and Black communities. Kenneth Cheung, mayoral candidate for the Alliance, appeared on the program to explain his platform.

(On a more mundane note, one of the more humorous episodes was when we recorded from my kitchen, a session on how to make *joong* as we told its history.[156] I had watched my mother make this festive treat when I was a kid, so I thought it wouldn't be that hard. *Joong* is a dumpling made of glutinous rice and stuffed with Chinese sausage, chestnuts, peanuts, salted egg yolk and whatever else you want. The whole mixture is wrapped in bamboo leaves and then boiled until the house is filled with the aroma of the concoction. Try as we might, we were not able to wrap the leaves properly around the filling without having the rice spill out. Then Brenda Lee, a member of our collective, told everyone in the kitchen that there was a mould we could buy to shape and wrap the leaves. So the show ended with this sound advice.)

Orientations lasted about a year before it died a natural death.

* * *

Through my participation with the Chinese Family Service, I soon discovered that the Chinese community was facing a myriad of issues, including housing, especially for the elderly; job discrimination and lack of opportunities for minority youth; access to services, health and mental health; little minority representation in the decision-making structures of government; and no support for immigrant kids and their parents in the school system.

In Montreal, Chinatown occupied prime downtown real estate and various developers wanted the land. Kwok Chan, a sociology professor at Concordia University, once told me that a survey was done to show that the Montreal Chinese community would be the least likely to protest urban encroachment by the different levels of government. To celebrate the Centennial of Canada in 1967, the Chinese community built a pagoda in a little green space at the corner of St. Urbain and La Gauchetière, dedicated to the "cause of peace and harmony among all Canadians." Fourteen years later, without consultation, the city decided to dismantle the pagoda to widen St. Urbain Street.[157] Don't worry, they said, we've kept all the pieces in case you want to rebuild it somewhere else. Even though we couldn't save the pagoda, more than two thousand people signed a petition to save the Lee Family Association building, which the city wanted to expropriate to widen the street. Today, the sidewalk on St. Urbain narrows as it passes La Gauchetière. We were successful in saving the historic Lee building.

However, Montreal's Chinatown came close to being totally destroyed in the 1980s. In 1984, the federal government proceeded to take up half of the old Chinatown to build the Place Guy Favreau complex of offices. In the 1960s, the building housing Hydro-Québec headquarters had already taken the block between St. Urbain and Clark streets, removing the area of Chinatown north of Dorchester where the Chinese YMCI, along with some housing units, were located; the Ville Marie Expressway blocked any southward expansion. Next came Complexe Desjardins in 1976 and finally the Palais des congrès in 1983. So by 1984, Chinatown was hemmed in with only the area east of St. Laurent for any possible growth. Former Mayor Jean Drapeau had pre-empted that possibility when he passed Bylaw 6513, forbidding all commercial development east of St. Laurent, in 1985.

I thought about the Workers Communist Party position on national minorities and the need for regional autonomy for Chinatown. If we had that autonomy, Chinatown would still be intact and the area would be used for the benefit of the Chinese community.

The commercial interests in Chinatown were incensed by such a blatant act against the community in Bylaw 6513. I supported their campaign to repeal the bylaw because it totally ignored the community's objections and imposed a regulation to limit Chinese economic participation. Kenneth Cheung was a vocal opponent and led a long battle against the bylaw.

On Sunday, March 10, 1985, more than one hundred Chinese protesters marched up and down La Gauchetière and St. Laurent shouting "Repeal Bylaw 6513 and protect Chinatown," and "Save Chinatown" in Chinese, English and French. The street demonstration, the first of its kind by an otherwise fairly quiescent community, was organized by Kenneth's Montreal Chinese Business and Professional People's Association and supported by fifteen other community organizations. The organizers hung banners across the streets of Montreal's tiny Chinatown denouncing the bylaw. It was a strange sight in Chinatown and onlookers stared. At the end of the march, the crowd sang "O Canada" and "Gens du pays" to show their allegiance to Canada and Quebec.

Kenneth's anti-bylaw tactics included "dogging" Drapeau on his trip to Hong Kong in 1985. According to an article in the *Montreal Gazette*, Kenneth sent a note from economy class to Mayor Drapeau, in first class, that read: "Dear Mr. Mayor, I would like to meet with you for a few minutes to discuss an urgent matter. I promise to be very nice, very polite and maybe very pleasant."[158]

Kenneth later ran for mayor in the 1986 elections in Montreal in order to bring some minority representation to city hall. Unfortunately, he came in third. Jean Doré of the Montreal Citizens Movement won the mayor's seat, replacing Drapeau. The fight to repeal Bylaw 6513 produced a pyrrhic victory. The bylaw was amended to allow businesses on La Gauchetière to set up one block east of St. Laurent, until St. Dominique Street—Chinatown gained an additional 175 feet.

Kenneth Cheung was a successful businessman in Chinatown and president of the Montreal Chinese Business and Professional People's Association from 1984 to 2005. He had run unsuccessfully for city council in 1982 before his run for mayor in 1986. Despite his business credentials, or maybe because of them, Kenneth was a combative activist in standing up for the rights of the Chinese community and other minorities. He had a long-time alliance with Dan Philip of the Black Coalition of Quebec. He always put his money where his mouth was by financially supporting many Chinatown causes. He was impatient with politicians and was always a thorn in their side.

Kenneth was involved in the head tax redress campaign and became president of the CCNC in order to "shake things up," and to break the Toronto-centric monopoly of that organization. Sadly, he passed away in 2008 at the age of seventy-one.

* * *

Education is always a high priority within the Chinese community, as with other communities. In the 1980s, there were virtually no services to integrate immigrant students into the school systems. Montreal teachers and school staff did not reflect the cultural, racial or social composition of the student population. Chinese parents who did not speak English or French were left confused and could not help their children. Many of them came to the Chinese Family Service for help.

The 1987 school board election was one of the first opportunities for the community to get involved in the electoral process. Faced with the problems concerning education for our kids, we decided to participate in the electoral campaign.

We formed an Ad Hoc Committee on School Elections '87 on April 23, 1987,[59] and discussed whether to support existing candidates or to run Chinese candidates. It was agreed that we needed to run our own candidates to highlight the problems facing the education system and to involve more people from our community in the political process.

For the next six months, the committee threw itself into an organized grassroots electoral campaign that the community had not seen previously and has not seen since. Subcommittees were set up to explain the importance of the election and the issues; to meet with other communities to explain our positions and gain their support; to recruit community workers to canvass voters to ensure that they were on the voters' list; to work with Chinese, English and French media to get our message to the larger community; and to raise funds. Jonas Ma and Johnson Choi were elected as campaign managers.

At an August 19 meeting, the candidates and ridings were chosen: Sandy Yep in Ward 2, LaSalle; T.Y. Hua, in Ward 10, Ville St. Laurent; and me in Ward 14, the large inner-city ward that included Chinatown.

In the previous elections (1983), Ivan Livingstone, once a football player for the Montreal Alouettes, had been elected to represent Ward 14. Ivan, from the Black community, had taken over from Carl Whittaker, the former school board representative and the founding executive director of the Black Community Council of Quebec. I was faced with a dilemma: Should I run against a Black incumbent? Although I had spoken with Ivan several times about Ward 14, when I made attempts to discuss running against him before finalizing my nomination he was out of town. Johnson Choi expressed the importance of selecting a ward that we would be capable of winning, regardless of who the other candidates might be. After much discussion, we decided to run in Ward 14; this was the ward that contained the most schools with which our community had the most problems, and we needed to respond to their need for help.

Our slate of candidates received widespread media coverage in the Chinese, English, French[160] and ethnic press. Many volunteers came out to work on the campaign for the three candidates in LaSalle, Ville St-Laurent and downtown. It was one of the first times that the Montreal Chinese community got enthusiastically involved in participatory democracy.

Despite my past decision to shun electoral politics, this was an awakening for me. Talking with people, explaining that there was something that they could do, and encouraging them to come out and vote; it was an opportunity to meet many minority people who inhabited the inner city. (Some encounters were gratifying, as the anecdote at the top of this chapter indicates.) This community interaction taught me lessons that I would soon put to use in the HTEA redress campaign.

School board elections usually get only about a 20 per cent turnout of voters. However, my mother mobilized about thirty people from her apartment building, Bo Ai Lo in Chinatown, to come out to vote on Election Day—Sunday, November 15—and that would end up turning into a media event.

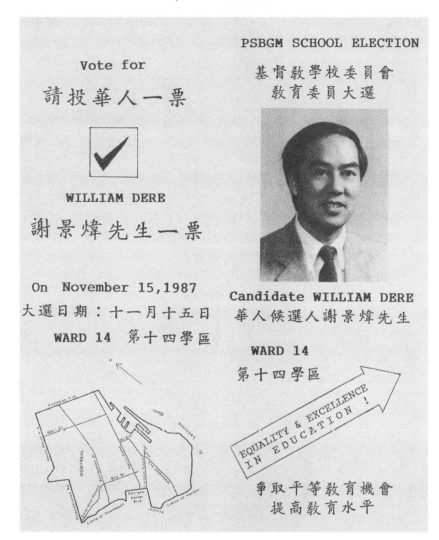

Mistaken for Chairman Mao, my Chinese leaflet for the 1987 school board elections.
(William Dere Collection)

The elderly women trudged their way from their residence to the base-
ment of the St-Charles-Borromée Hospital three blocks away. They all arrived
for the 9:00 a.m. opening of the polls, then sat patiently waiting for the poll
workers to arrive. They talked among themselves as they waited. Many of
them were voting for the first time. They knew my mother and, by extension, they knew me, so they thought it was safe to vote for "*Ngee mou goy leck
doy,*" which translates loosely as "Second aunt's smart boy." (In the Confucian

patriarchal system, "second aunt" refers to my mother since she was the wife of the second son of my father's family and the woman's title defers to the husband.)

Terrance Lau, one of our volunteers, had arrived at the polling station at 8:30 and, on seeing no one was there, phoned the office of Richard Jarvis, the chief returning officer. I arrived at 9:15 and made frantic attempts to reach the school board and the chief electoral officer, explaining that the polling officers had not arrived and there were many people waiting to vote at the Chinatown polling station. The man at the other end of the phone tried to calm me down by saying, "I'll see what I can do." Of course, these polling officers were all volunteers and perhaps they didn't feel like trekking down to Chinatown on a Sunday morning.

Feeling combative, I decided to alert the media. I called the city desk at the *Montreal Gazette* and asked to speak with the city editor. I made it sound as dramatic as possible, knowing full well that school board elections are seen as ho-hum affairs and that he might not be interested. I told him to hurry down with a reporter and a photographer;[161] there might be a riot here since some old ladies were very indignant and angry at being prevented from voting. I also called some contacts at the TV and radio stations.

Some of the old "aunties" waiting patiently for the polling officers to arrive with their enumeration papers in their hands. (William Dere Collection)

Finally, the polling officers arrived two and a half hours late and the remaining
people started to vote, many for the first time. My mother is in the photo holding
her enumeration paper. Young Chinese volunteers translated for the elderly women.
(William Dere Collection)

Sure enough, the media sensed blood in a story of injustice being perpetrated on a bunch of elderly Chinese ladies and rushed down to the hospital.
There was coverage in both the English and French media.[162] The *Gazette* did a
story complete with a photo of the smiling, uncomplaining grannies. By 11:30,
two poll workers finally arrived and set up the polling station. By that time,
many of the patient old aunties had left without being able to vote. Some lucky
ones had gone to meet their children or grandchildren for dim sum; others went
back to their apartment to prepare a bit of rice and vegetables for the noon meal
before going to the old age club for a round of mah jong, or to the concourse
of Place Guy Favreau to sit for the afternoon and talk with other seniors, where
the topic of conversation would be how the *lo fawn* officials didn't let them vote.

This was the first and probably the last time that these women participated
in the democratic voting process and they were deprived of their rights, either
by design or by omission. I lost the election by seventeen votes. If all the seniors had had the chance to vote, I would have been elected.

A few days later, the election team of the three candidates, along with
Kenneth Cheung, Jonas Ma, Johnson Choi and lawyer Ian Wong, met to sum

up the experience. We decided to appeal the elections in Ward 14 due to the irregularities. It wasn't the fact that I lost by seventeen votes. What stirred our indignation was that thirty seniors were deprived of the right to cast a ballot to which they were entitled.

Before the court hearing at the Palais de Justice, Ivan Livingston was not happy when I offered to shake his hand. He walked away. I followed him and started to explain that this was not personal. It was the principle of getting a fair shake for all. We only wanted justice. That is why we were in court that day. "It's nothing personal against you, Ivan," I said. "You should understand that the school board took away a chance for the Chinese community to be represented."

Ivan's stance softened a little when I explained that it was not a battle between the Chinese community and the Black community but the fact that people were not permitted to vote when they made the effort to do so. Ian Wong was my lawyer who pleaded the case brilliantly. Kenneth Cheung believed in the need for our community to stand up and be counted; in this case, we stood up but we did not get a chance to be counted. Although Ian worked pretty much pro bono, Kenneth contributed whatever expenses were needed to bring the case to court, including the $500 deposit.

On March 23, 1988, Judge Paul Beaudry ruled in our favour and ordered a new election for May 15. However, in April, Ivan and the school board appealed the judgment to delay the re-vote. Since almost a year had gone by, we did not see any merit in stirring things up at the school board and further aggravating Ivan, so we decided not to contest the appeal and instead let Ivan serve out his term. We had accomplished the objective to involve the community and to uncover the problems facing minority students in the school system. When it was all over, we sent out thank you notes to over one hundred volunteers who actively supported and participated in our campaign.

The 1987 campaign also prepared the groundwork for the next school board elections three years later. With Johnson Choi again as campaign manager, Queenie Hum became the first Chinese and the first woman elected to any office from our community. She became the school commissioner for Ward 14 in 1990.

The 1987 school elections also exposed how the mainstream media just doesn't get the struggle of minorities. They felt one minority candidate was interchangeable with another—so why have two running against each other?

After the *Montreal Gazette* ran a story that highlighted this angle, I complained. The initial story ignored the fact that my involvement would add to the number of voters rather than split the vote. It also omitted that I reached out to the Black incumbent and other minority groups. I contacted the reporter to lodge my objection to the tone of the story. I said: "We're not apologizing for running. ... There was no way we could involve the Chinese community without having a Chinese candidate."

A second short article with the headline "No apologies" further played up the supposed conflict between two minority communities. I argued in a letter to the *Gazette* ombudsman that the articles had "left the impression that we were arrogant and did not care what other communities felt." I called out the newspaper for its "negative perception concerning the ethnic communities and its reporters' lack of sensitivity and understanding of ethnic issues."

Clair Balfour, the *Gazette*'s assistant managing editor and ombudsman, in his column, defended their articles. Balfour concluded that, "on balance, I don't think the coverage was unfair to Dere, suggesting arrogance or unjustly emphasized conflict, although certainly a longer story could have contained more detail."[163]

To me, though, this was simply an example of how to whitewash a story by the mainstream media, which felt that one ethnic candidate—all being the same—was enough.

* * *

Towards the end of the 1980s, the political institutions were beginning to catch up to the demographic realities of the Montreal population. Urban Montreal had become a multicultural, multiethnic and multiracial society. However, the political makeup of the city, let alone the province, did not reflect this new reality. Through our efforts, the Chinese Family Service, the Chinese Neighbourhood Society (also known by its French name, Amitié chinoise de Montréal) and other Chinese community organizations participated in various consultation conferences as we tried to make our presence felt.

Throughout most of 1988, I was part of the Chinese Professional Group chaired by Ian Wong. There were about fifteen members, including Cynthia Cheung, Kenneth's daughter.[164] Our group worked alongside the Chinese Community United Centre and the Chinatown Development Consultation

Committee to provide a response to Montreal's master plan for development, which would include amending Bylaw 6513. We were also tasked with studying the site for the relocation of the Montreal Chinese Hospital from its upper St. Denis Street location back to Chinatown.

For the first time, we seemed to have the ear of city hall under the new Jean Doré administration, where we had direct input to John Gardner of the city's executive committee responsible for city planning. I don't know how much of our recommendations were implemented, but we did achieve the goal of having the new hospital built at the corner of Viger and St-Elisabeth.

Eleven organizations representing a cross-section of the Chinese community presented a joint brief to the Montreal Urban Consultative Committee on Inter-cultural and Inter-racial Relations on February 1 and 2, 1988. Major issues raised in the brief[165] included the police—we pointed out the problems of communications and collaboration between the police and Montreal's Chinese community, and we insisted the police take action to improve their communications and make their services known to the community. We asked for funding to build a cultural centre in Chinatown. Transport was another issue—we asked for Chinese-language signs and maps to be placed at the Métro station near Chinatown. We also asked for the station to be renamed Place d'Armes–Quartier Chinois. Hiring too was a major issue—we wanted an employment equity program introduced, to be monitored every six or twelve months, to deal with the underrepresentation of Chinese and other minorities in the work force at city hall.

During this time we had an active group of young people in the community who felt they could make a difference and actively participated in the community's development. We took advantage of the new Montreal Citizens' Movement administration in city hall that promised community involvement and renewal. However, as I write three decades later, we are still fighting for some of the same demands. The "Young Turks" that delivered these demands to the various levels of government have moved on and we are awaiting a new breed of young Chinese Québécois activists to take up the torch.

* * *

Starting in 1985, the Chinese Canadian National Council met with a succession of federal ministers of multiculturalism, beginning with David Crombie under the Conservative government of Brian Mulroney, without much progress. But apart from registering the head tax payers for possible financial redress, the redress campaign had not, as yet, fired up people's imagination. The *lo wah kiu*, conditioned by decades of official hostility, simply kept their heads down and advised young people not to get into trouble with the authorities. Nevertheless, in Montreal, we held meetings within the community with various associations to rally them to the campaign. There were other pressing issues, though, that still remain to this day: employment equity, access to government and health services, housing for seniors, and language training for new immigrants.

The redress campaign in Montreal started to get a toehold with the formation of the Committee to Redress the Head Tax and Chinese Exclusion Act in April 1989.

We trudged along with the work, one step at a time, one person at a time, one meeting at a time, thinking that every little effort gets us closer to the goal. One evening, as I was listening to the album *Back to Back*, which Sandy Yep had purchased for me on his trip to New York City, I got an idea. The album contained the music of Charlie Chin and Chris Iijima, which moved me every time I listened to it. My idea was to organize a benefit concert to raise funds and, more importantly, to increase awareness of the redress campaign, and Charlie Chin would be the special guest performer. I felt culture would touch people emotionally and move them to action.

People from the young adults social club, volunteers at the Chinese Family Service and the redress committee were all mobilized to organize the concert. We worked tirelessly through the summer right up to the night of the concert in November. There was much planning involved, from booking the hall (the Chinese Catholic Community Centre) to organizing the sound system (my Ukrainian Canadian buddy Perry Gingerysty volunteered to do the sound).

As 350 people started filing in on the evening of November 11, 1989, I knew the concert would be a resounding success. It was billed as a "Concert of Contemporary and Traditional Chinese Culture." The program included the Yuet Sing Chinese Music Club of Montreal, performance artist Ming Lee, a slide show on Chinese Canadian history by Raymond Foo and Roxanne Chan, and a sculpture exhibit by Mary Wong. I even wrote a humorous sketch, *The Immigration Game*, which was performed by the amateur players from the redress committee and included Minoo Gundevia, an actor with the Teesri Duniya, an Indo-Canadian theatre troupe.

The Montreal head tax benefit concert aimed to raise funds for the redress campaign.
(William Dere Collection)

James Wing, as one of the youngest head tax payers and an activist in the campaign, gave a rousing speech. Then Charlie Chin kept the audience enthralled with his monologues and songs about the poignant experiences of the Chinese in North America, with which many in the audience could identify. The concert got extensive press coverage locally and as far west as Vancouver where there was an article in the *Chinatown News*.[166] The concert raised more than $2,000 for the redress campaign, with financial contributions from ten Chinatown associations and businesses, including Les Aliments Wong Wing, whose president, Raymond Wong, was sympathetic to the redress campaign. More significantly, it gave a sense of power and achievement to all those involved. The redress campaign was gaining traction.

Chapter 12

Moving the Mountain

"Possessing both a clear purpose and an eye for the poetry in everyday life, *Moving the Mountain* is framed by the contemporary movement seeking redress from the Canadian government for the money exacted, and the humiliation that the head tax represents."
—Cameron Bailey, program note, Toronto International Film Festival, 1993[167]

When my grandfather came to Canada was a topic of intense research for the film. I spent months in a laborious line-by-line examination of the General Register microfilm that I had purchased from the National Archives. When I had almost given up, I came across a letter in my father's papers in which my grandfather's given name appeared as "Man." That gave me a clue as to what name the immigration officer might have entered for Grandfather. Looking up various transliterations of our family name in the General Register, I came across "Jay Man Shon" and "Jay Man," both born in 1884, which I knew from Grandfather's gravestone was the right year. Jay Man Shon, however, was born in Hoy Ping, the wrong district. Jay Man, though, was born in Sun Ning, the old name for Toishan. I let out an audible "Yes!" breaking the silence of the library. It was a eureka moment as I sat back and settled on Jay Man as my grandfather, finally discovering that he came to Canada in 1909.

Towards the end of the 1980s, despite the experience of the head tax and the Exclusion Act among the old timers, or *lo wah kiu*, I discovered that knowledge about Chinese Canadian history was scant among the younger generation in our community and among the general population. Canadian attitudes towards Chinese immigrants had long been shaped by popular culture and the pernicious depictions in government pronouncements and legislations. So you can imagine the uphill struggle to change these attitudes, to get non-Chinese Canadians to know the Chinese as individuals with the same dreams and aspirations as other Canadians.

What, I wondered, could I do to change this perception? I threw myself into the redress campaign initiated by the Chinese Canadian National Council (CCNC); I met head tax payers who were still alive and their families (there were still quite a few alive at that time). I went to talk with my mother and my family. My siblings were just as in the dark as I was. Father had never talked to them about those difficult years, but Mother opened up to me about that period, as if she had been waiting for me to ask or to give her permission to speak about those lonely times. She showed me Father's head tax certificate, citizenship certificate and immigration papers, which she kept safely in an almond cookie tin after his death. This was the untold story of my family and soon I realized that there were similar hidden stories of Chinese Canadian families across the country.

To tell these stories, I thought about writing a book. But it would be too solitary and too time-consuming. Besides, it would take an effort to read such a book about an unknown subject. Then I thought about making a video or short film, a medium through which I could reach a larger audience and move people emotionally by telling these stories using sounds and images.

At that time, there was little in the way of audiovisual documentaries on the Chinese community. What there was were stereotypical depictions, like the National Film Board's *Bamboo, Lions and Dragons,* a film the Chinese community roundly denounced when it was released in 1981.

My imagination went wild on how to go about producing a video. I had no experience in doing so. I went to the film board's offices in Montreal and watched about fifty documentary films; not many of them impressed me. I thought I could do as well if not better than most of them. As an engineer, I started to read about the techniques of filmmaking, but this was just an intellectual exercise. I quickly came to the realization that I needed help and this would be a good opportunity to organize and mobilize people around a common goal.

I remembered an old comrade from the *Forge* newspaper, Malcolm Guy. He had been responsible for producing the international section of the paper and we would meet every week to review the articles, so I got to know him. Later, Malcolm worked as a producer on CBC Radio and with his partner, Marie Boti, founded Productions Multi-Monde in 1987 to produce progressive films on immigration and the Third World. I turned to Malcolm for help. After the first meeting, we saw that we had a very good arrangement to make the film. Malcolm would provide the technical film production expertise and I would provide my knowledge of Chinese Canadian history and politics to write the script. I would have a free hand with the political and cultural content of the film. We would co-direct the film, and Malcolm would be the producer.

At first I wanted to make a short, thirty-minute film that could be used to animate head tax meetings. However, I eventually uncovered more than enough material for a miniseries. We decided to limit ourselves to ninety minutes. This would be Malcolm's first full-length feature documentary. For funding purposes, I registered a company called Gold Mountain Productions–Productions Montagne d'Or.

I did something else that was critical to the project—something I was good at. I was able to organize about a dozen or so members of our community to work on the documentary. They soon came to realize that it was a worthwhile film and they believed in it. They started to take ownership of the project, volunteering their time and energy in doing research, looking for subjects to interview, doing the interviews and translating and transcribing for the head tax payers and the widows who lived in Chinatown. I also reached out to the community in other cities. In Vancouver, I contacted my old friend Barry Wong, who threw his usual enthusiasm into the project and formed a group, Gold Mountain Productions–West. My contacts in the CCNC in Toronto also helped with possible head tax payers who were willing to be interviewed in other parts of Canada. The CCNC notified its twenty-seven chapters across the country and asked them to support the project.

The volunteers[168]—including half a dozen in Vancouver—were the unsung heroes of the film. One of them, Belle Kei Wing Wong, a lovely young woman from Hong Kong, was a volunteer at the Chinese Family Service while looking for a job after graduating from McGill. I recruited her and offered her the position of production assistant on the film. She excelled in her work as administrator, interviewer and translator (Cantonese, Mandarin and English). She organized the filming in China after skillfully negotiating with the Chinese authorities. Belle stayed with us for four years.

While I went about writing the screenplay and organizing people in the community to participate in the film, Malcolm set out to organize the film crew, the director of photography (the cameraman) and the soundman, all the while pursuing the funding. The film had the working title "It's Only Fair," which came from the slogan used by the CCNC for the redress campaign. About two years into making the film we decided to find a "million-dollar" title for the film. Malcolm and I settled on *Moving the Mountain*, a title that came from Mao Zedong's essay "The Foolish Old Man Who Removed the Mountains." It was one of Mao's most read essays in China. The mountain in our case was Gold Mountain. The cameraman for our film was an ex-comrade who had studied in China, Steven Griffiths. He was especially helpful during our filming in China, where he was able to navigate his way around our minder—Stella Bai, sent by the Guangdong film authorities—with a few choice Cultural Revolution invectives in Mandarin.

In June 1990, the first funding came through from the Canada Council—$26,229; shortly afterwards another $29,730 came from the Ministry of Multiculturalism. It was an opportune time: the government publicized its policy of funding more multicultural and diversified projects, and we took advantage of this shift in thinking. On top of that, a letter addressed to me accompanied the grant from Multiculturalism, and it was signed by Minister Gerry Weiner—so my work in lobbying his department for redress may have produced some immediate results. This provided the seed money to start filming. The major funding was obtained from Telefilm Canada and the Société génerale des industries culturelles, Québec, and broadcast licences from Vision TV and TV5. One of the major funding agencies wanted to remove me from the co-directorship, citing my lack of experience, but Malcolm insisted that I remain co-director or the film could not be made or would not be the same.

The film had a budget of over $350,000, although the final cost was higher, according to Malcolm. There were the countless hours of unpaid labour from our dedicated volunteers. The salary budgeted for my participation as co-director and writer was put back into the film. In addition, my erstwhile company Gold Mountain Productions put in $5,000 plus whatever expenses I incurred working on the project, which I never claimed. So it was a labour of love and an act of political involvement.

Moving the Mountain took four years to make, from 1989 to 1993. Malcolm

and I agreed that it was good to have had the time to allow the film to be nurtured and to mature. My research, with the help of the volunteer researchers,
opened up a whole wealth of knowledge on Chinese Canadian history. I knew
this would be a groundbreaking film, since no one else had made such a documentary. I began doing the research in a more general interest fashion with a
non-academic approach through oral and popular history. I became known as
the Montreal amateur expert on Chinese Canadian history and culture.

During slack periods, while waiting for funding, I made *Gens du pays: The
Chinese of Québec* a twenty-five-minute video that I shot with a Hi-8 camera.
The video was co-directed with Susan Lebrun, a graduate from the Concordia
communications program. Susan was a very able woman with an effervescent
personality, which made working with her such a joy. The funding for the video
came from another grant from Multiculturalism and the City of Montreal.

Gens du pays created a stir in the thin-skinned nationalist video circles
when it came out in 1993. They claimed that it was too one-sided and depicted
French Québécois as racists. It was true that the film put forward publicly,
for the first time in one production, the views of Chinese community leaders
such as Cynthia Lam,[169] Kenneth Cheung[170] and Queenie Hum;[171] these views
expressed the struggles of the Chinese in Quebec for equality in employment
and access to services. The video provided an outlet for these views, not those
readily available in the mainstream media, which had little diversity—a state
of affairs that continues to this day. So again, I claimed my terrain with no
apology for standing up to give voice to my community.

* * *

In making *Moving the Mountain*, I travelled across Canada to as far north as
Barkerville in central BC, where the early Chinese founded a settlement. I
introduced aspects of Chinese North American culture with poetry from the
early pioneers and from contemporary poets like Jim Wong-Chu; there was
music from Charlie Chin, Sook-Yin Lee, Sean Gunn and Number One Son.
I had to struggle with Malcolm to include Sean's music. Malcolm said that
Janet Lumb, our music director, did not like Sean's strongly worded songs. I
insisted on having Sean's music because I liked the politics and Sean was one
of the pioneering musicians in our community. (I would later receive a well-
deserved criticism from Kuan Foo, who played bass guitar with Sean in "Head
Tax Blues." I apologized to him for not including his name in the credits and

instead just listing the name of the band. The musician who performed with Sean and Kuan was guitarist Martin Kobayakawa. It is difficult enough for an Asian Canadian musician to make it on his own without my kind of help!)

The film also took me on my first visit back to my ancestral village in China. I was ecstatic to finally enter the family home that I had left as a young child forty years earlier. The occasion imprinted itself on my soul forever. And it was captured on film. I tried to learn as much about village life as I could—to get a sense of how my mother had lived. The sixty households there, about three hundred people, mainly engaged in small-time farming; others had left the village for employment in towns and cities throughout the province. I discovered that there were more Toishanese[172] living outside China than living in the county of Toishan. But as a rule, they are not emigrating today; unlike their forebears, there is no obvious need to leave their ancestral home.

Fong Dang village had a number of small lanes about five feet wide to allow two people to walk abreast comfortably. On both sides of the lanes were solidly built brick houses, including our family home. The sounds reminded me of the Montreal Chinatown of my childhood. Everyone spoke my Toishanese dialect and I was able to converse with village cousins without feeling

On location, 1991, in front of one of the famous Watchtowers (*Diaolu*) near my village in Toishan. With me are Belle Wong and our cameraman, Steven Griffiths.

(CREDIT: Dong Qing Chen)

self-conscious. Even though we'd never met, everyone said they knew me—through my mother's letters and her visit three years earlier. It was a feeling of returning home. The visit back to my village was a milestone in my journey of self-discovery.

Overall, the film project led me to get closer to my mother and my siblings, as I began to speak with them about the past, about our father and grandfather, and to learn things about our family in China before I was born. They told me that every Chinese New Year, when it was a time for families to be reunited and to celebrate together, Father was not there, but they always set a bowl and a pair of chopsticks for him at the dinner table, wishing he would be home for the next New Year.

The film also let me spend time with many of the old-timers in the Chinese Canadian community. The most notable was James Wing (Ng Wing Wah), the "star" of the film.

I first met James in 1988 at a head tax redress function. I soon discovered that he was a friend of my father and grandfather and knew my mother. Through his participation in the redress campaign, I easily recruited him as the main subject in *Moving the Mountain*. Not only was he one of the youngest head tax payers, having come to Canada at eleven, but he had a moving story to tell. He was articulate, too, and spoke with clarity and emotion in front of the camera.

When James first arrived in Canada, he and his father were strangers because Mr. Wing Sr. had left China for Canada before James was born. The young Wing could never address his father as "Dad" or "Papa"—"I don't know why," he said. "The word never got past my throat. It was some kind of psychological block."

The young James was actually raised by his father's restaurant business partner; he worked as a waiter in restaurants and was a houseboy in a wealthy Westmount home. James graduated from Montreal High School and went to night school at Sir George Williams University to get a degree in biology in 1947. Not able to find a job in that field, he studied electronics at a trade school and finally found work at Canadian Marconi, from which he retired in 1977.

James first married in 1933, and in the 1950s was able to bring his thirty-seven-year-old wife, Lee Guim Shong, and infant son to Canada. Two of his older children, a son and daughter, students at the time, decided to stay in China to contribute to the new society. The son who came to Canada died in a traffic accident. However, James's wife was young enough to give birth to another son, Simon, who grew up to become an endocrinologist (and my friend).

James was at the time, and would continue to be, an important and active figure in the redress campaign.

Important events were taking place in the campaign at the time *Moving the Mountain* was being made. The film and the campaign took up all my energy. I felt motivated and energized just as I'd felt ten years earlier when I dedicated myself to the Canadian Maoist movement. The film took four years of my life. I was proud of my effort and I beamed like a delighted father after the birth of his first son, which was actually the case—my son, Jordan, was born in the spring of that year, 1993.

The film had its Montreal premiere in October 1993 before an audience of more than three hundred, mainly from the Chinese community, including my mother and other family members, the film's interviewees—some of whom were elderly women who had bared their innermost feelings in the film—and all the volunteers and supporters, everyone who felt they owned a piece of the film.

* * *

Moving the Mountain received its world premiere at the Toronto International Film Festival in September 1993, with two screenings to packed houses. The film was also broadcast on various educational TV networks in Canada, and screened in film festivals in Vancouver, Edmonton, Hong Kong, Bombay, Rotterdam, New York and San Francisco. It was nominated as one of the finalists in the Best Political Documentary category at the Toronto Hot Docs Festival in 1994. However, it was never broadcast on the CBC.

Malcolm never told me why he couldn't get it past Mark Starowicz, the boss of documentaries at the time for the national network. Robert Yip, head of the Ottawa Redress Committee, and Priscilla Fong in Montreal were among those from the community who launched a letter-writing campaign to Starowicz demanding that the film be shown on the national network in order to live up to its mandate to have programming to reflect Canadian society. In the kind letter Fong wrote to the CBC and other media outlets about airing the film, she said:

As a first-generation Chinese Canadian whose father and mother arrived in Canada in 1898 and 1921, respectively, I found the documentary to be an enlightening and moving experience. I only heard vaguely of the $500 head tax a few years ago and was never aware that my parents paid this tax upon their arrival in Canada. This was brought to light by a family member just recently. Since my parents never spoke of the hardships and prejudice that they must have endured when they first arrived, it was not until I saw *Moving the Mountain* that I realized just how tremendous their suffering must have been.

I strongly feel that the film should be seen not just by the Chinese population, but by all Canadians.[173]

Despite not airing on the CBC, the film got Malcolm and me a free trip to Singapore, as it was shown at the 1994 Singapore International Film Festival with the sponsorship of the Canadian High Commission.

I subscribed to Abbie Hoffman's Yippie philosophy, expressed in the title of his book *Steal This Book*. I believed in spreading art to the masses. *Moving the Mountain* probably had limited sales numbers, about which I never bothered to inquire. I dubbed many copies myself and distributed them to all those who were interested in the subject. Malcolm later did the same. We probably distributed more free copies than we sold.

I was most gratified with the film when young people would come up to me and say that what they had seen in the film also happened to their family and that the film uncovered that hidden, unspoken past, as if the film had given them permission to talk to their families about their history in Canada.

When I undertook to make *Moving the Mountain* in 1989 to educate the public, I did not anticipate one surprising benefit: that it would inspire and attract community leaders and activists to a campaign that was already a decade old when the film was released. Kenda Gee of the Edmonton Redress Committee inspired this insight; he told me that after seeing the film, he was moved to actively engage in the campaign. May Chiu, a Montreal lawyer and activist, told me that she first heard about the Head Tax and Exclusion Act when she saw *Moving the Mountain* at the One World film festival in Ottawa in 1994. This heartwarming result revealed itself as I was interviewing people for this book, twenty years after the release of *Moving the Mountain*.

Jooneed Khan of *La Presse*[174] wrote a generous review after *Moving the Mountain* premiered in Montreal. He offered that the film was a "homage" to my father. It was, but I felt it was a homage to my mother as well.

* * *

Because of all the research I did for the making of *Moving the Mountain*, I have some further discoveries to share relating to the General Register of Chinese Immigration.

As I pored through pages of the register and looked at the name of each person, I tried to imagine what was going through their minds as they landed in Canada and were locked up in detention[175] before being allowed official entry into the country.

The distinction for being number one in the register went to Tyng Gong, who arrived in Victoria, BC, on September 1, 1885. The only other information entered was that he paid a $1 fee. I suppose this was a new process and the customs officer was not adequately trained for the job. However, he got it right for Mr. Ah Way, eighteen. Mr. Way was number two on the list and the first one to pay the head tax. He arrived in Victoria on September 2, 1885. Ah was not Way's first name, but a salutation, like "ah you." In the Chinese language, monosyllabic names sound awkward, so *ah* prefixes them. The officer did not know any better and wrote down "Ah" for eight of the names on page one of the register.

Way was the first arrival registered from "San Ning" (Toishan). He left China from "Canton" and arrived on board the ss *George W. Elder* via San Francisco. He was kept in detention, paid the head tax—$50 at the time—and was finally issued a CI 5 (the original version of the head tax certificate, without a photo) on June 18, 1887. The head tax was raised to $100 in 1900 and then to $500 in 1903.

The first woman in the register was Mrs. Ah Lee, thirty-five, who arrived in Victoria on September 8, 1885. She hailed from "Fat Shan" (Foshan) and paid a fee of $1, as the wife of a merchant.

In the east, Hum Jak, twenty-five, of Hoy Ping, arrived in Quebec City on August 13, 1909, from Liverpool, England, on board the *Empress of Ireland*. His listed occupation: "Laundryman." He paid the $500 head tax and was registered on January 17, 1910. He was expected to live in Ottawa. Although it is only a one-line entry, the information provided conjures up the image of an adventurous young man who literally travelled the globe to settle in Ottawa.

Some of the other interesting individuals recorded in the register were:

Li Yu and seven of his cohorts were logged as "Deserted from the Empress of Asia." Li's occupation was "Sailor's Cook." I imagine that Li, twenty-nine, and his seven young friends walked off the *Empress of Asia* and into the arms of Canadian immigration on February 25, 1919, and were held in detention until

March 4, when they all paid the $500 head tax and were ushered into a happy life in Canada. Or maybe they paid the $500, were arrested, thrown in jail and deported as deserters. All we know about these eight young men are their single line entries in the register.

There was an actress—Miss Kam Shu, a brave young woman of twenty-six. Yes, she brazenly (for that era) told the immigration officer that her occupation was actress when she arrived in Vancouver on board the ss *Monteagle* on October 15, 1909. She came from the village of Kam Chun, Sunning (now Toishan). She stood 5 ft, 4¾ in, and had a scar on the left corner of her mouth. There was no indication whether she travelled with a companion or made the perilous journey on her own. Nevertheless, she paid the $500 head tax and was allowed into Canada. My first thought was that she might have founded a Cantonese theatre troupe in Vancouver and gone on to become a successful artist.

Two more worldly actors also arrived on the shore of BC in October 1909: Gin Yung Ken, forty, and Wong You Sam, twenty-six. Both men hailed from Shanghai. Seattle was their last place of domicile before they arrived in Vancouver on October 20 on board the *Princess Charlotte*. Did they join Kam Shu and head off to Vancouver Island to found an artists' colony? Or maybe they all travelled east to Montreal to perform at the Gayety Theatre? [176]

Most of the Chinese immigrants had more mundane occupations, since their mission in coming to Canada was to establish a better living for themselves and their families. There was a class bias to the Chinese Immigration Acts, and merchants were exempt from paying the head tax; as today, those who could afford to pay taxes did not. Occupations listed in the register, where I estimated that over 90 per cent of registrants were male, and only 5 per cent were merchants, included labourer, farmer, cook, laundryman, grocer, merchant, druggist.

Prior to 1918, the occupation of more than 90 per cent of the men was listed as labourer. However, after 1918, something curious happened: the majority of those coming were listed as students. They were in their teens or early twenties whereas, a generation earlier, the ages of the labourers ranged from twenties to forties with some even in their fifties.

I think there were two reasons for the switch of occupations and ages.

First, the Chinese Immigration Act of 1903 allowed students to be exempt from paying the head tax. However, this was not the practice in reality. All the students I saw in the registers had paid the $500 head tax. This was the case for my father too, who was listed as a schoolboy. The law allowed a refund of the head tax if proof was provided that the payer was a student in a recognized institution. My father never got his refund, even though my grandfather submitted a notarized letter stating, "he will attend school and not be engaged in any wage earning occupation." I did not see any entry where a student's head tax was refunded.

The second, and the major reason for the switch of occupations and ages, was the passing of time. The first pioneers left their wives and children back in China when they initially came to Canada. After fifteen to twenty years of labouring on their own, they felt it was time to ease their loneliness and hardship by bringing a son to join them. In the months before the passage of the 1923 Exclusion Act, the register entries were full of young boys and teenagers, with a few housewives. Those in Canada who had enough savings wanted to beat the July 1 deadline.

The sixty-two years of state racism (1885–1947) affected people in profound and lasting ways. Decades have passed since the 1947 repeal of the Chinese Exclusion Act and even the redress movement that followed is starting to fade into history. However, up to the highest levels of society, Canadian attitudes towards the Chinese are still shaped by the institutional exclusions that were imposed by the state. It is important to put a human face to the victims and to listen to their stories. That was my aim in making *Moving the Mountain.* Sixty-two years of state racism does do something to you.

Chapter 13

Crying in the Wilderness (1984–93)

"The first thing you need to learn as a hunter is patience."
—Jiang Rong, *Wolf Totem*

The throng of 350 made a stirring sight on Parliament Hill: the mainly elderly Chinese men and women wore red "Redress Now" caps, and the younger men and women among them wore T-shirts too, emblazoned with "Que justice soit faite! / It's only fair!" The T-shirts carried an image of my father's head tax certificate, which was Sandy Yep's idea and Montreal's contribution to the rally. It was a poignant occasion, as for the first time in our community's history, the lo wah kiu *and youthful protesters demonstrating together shouted slogans calling on the government to give justice to our elderly head tax payers and their families. The passion of the crowd was a mixture of anger and hope.*

In September 1987, an astonishing thing happened: the us Congress passed the Civil Liberties Act, which offered us$20,000 to each Japanese American who had been incarcerated during World War II. The Japanese American redress movement had been struggling for internment redress since the sixties, inspired in part by the US civil rights movement. At this point in Canada, the National Association of Japanese Canadians (NAJC) had been campaigning—to no avail—for ten years for reparation for the confiscation of property and internment during the war.[177]

On October 29, 1987, the NAJC reached out to other Canadians and organized a "Multicultural Rally" in Toronto at which fifteen ethnic organizations, including the Chinese Canadian National Council, demonstrated their solidarity with Japanese Canadians in their redress effort.

On August 10, 1988, US President Ronald Reagan signed the Civil Liberties Act into law. The following month, Reagan's old friend Prime Minister Brian Mulroney followed suit, announcing a settlement with the NAJC on September 22 after a seventeen-hour negotiating session. The deal provided a payment of $21,000 for each Japanese Canadian affected. The NAJC had demanded individual compensation of $25,000. Descendants of deceased internees were also eligible for financial compensation.

The Chinese community followed the developments in the Japanese Canadian redress struggle with great interest and hoped that the government would use this example to settle with Chinese Canadians. There were good reasons to hope: Not unlike the history of Chinese Canadians' struggle for redress, the Liberal and then the Progressive Conservative government had previously used every trick in the book to stall any settlement with Japanese Canadians. First they had refused to negotiate with the NAJC, then they played divide and rule by promoting a "Survivors' Group" that did not want individual compensation redress for fear of a backlash. A Price Waterhouse report of May 1986[178] estimated the loss to Japanese Canadians from confiscation of property and internment to be $443 million in 1986 dollars; Conservative Multiculturalism Minister Otto Jelinek rejected the report as irrelevant as well as the consequent NAJC redress proposal.

Head Tax Exclusion Act redress was the perfect campaign to unite the Chinese Canadian community; almost every single Chinese who had family that immigrated to Canada before 1923 was affected. You would think it would be easy to get 100 per cent of Chinese Canadians aboard but it was not.

Between the start of the redress campaign in 1984 and the year 1988, Chinese Canadian activists failed to come up with any real plans beside using the CCNC to get the redress effort going. We held many educational and organizing sessions within the community; networked internally to get organized, and externally with progressive Canadians in social and labour organizations;

and we formed an alliance with the Japanese, Ukrainian, Italian and Indo Canadians who were also seeking redress for past injustices by the government. The government remained unresponsive.

But in 1988, buoyed by the sudden Japanese redress, we tried to take advantage of the political talk of the various Canadian parties and their candidates in the lead up to the November 21, 1988, general elections.

In Montreal, we organized the first public meeting on redress at the Kam Fung Restaurant and 250 people, including elderly Chinese head tax payers and their families, attended on November 3 to demand action from the invited politicians. James Wing spoke at the meeting in English and Chinese.[179] In Toronto, 500 people rallied at Toronto's city hall.

A month before the election, a CCNC delegation met with Multiculturalism Minister Gerry Weiner, who promised that the issue would be reported to the prime minister and then brought to the cabinet immediately after the election. Brian Mulroney was re-elected with a majority government. We were galvanized and felt the time had come for head tax redress.

We did the rounds of political lobbying. In Montreal, we met with Opposition MPs from Quebec—Raymonde Folco, Irwin Cotler and Marlene Jennings—and they all voiced their support. We got our old friend, Juanita Westmoreland-Traoré, as president of Conseil des Communautés culturelles et de l'immigration du Québec (Council of Cultural Communities and Immigration of Quebec), to write to Mulroney to expedite the redress. The CCNC initiated a national letter writing campaign to the prime minister, and articles and letters to the editor were sent to newspapers for publication. Many of the large newspapers took editorial stands in support of head tax redress.[180]

In April 1989, Montreal was one of the first cities to organize an independent Head Tax Exclusion Act Redress Committee outside of the CCNC. This committee was made up of some of the leading activists I had worked with—Jonas Ma, Sandy Yep, Cynthia Lam, Queenie Hum, Kenneth Cheung, Fo Niemi, Yat Lo, and later Walter Tom. We continued to work at the grassroots level and to establish contacts with other cultural communities, such as the Black and Jewish communities, and to consolidate the redress committee with regular information meetings. As an old time agit-prop strategist, I felt the longer the campaign took, the more time we would have to build up the movement and mobilize the community. However, even I didn't think it would take as long as it did.

To put things in context, 1989 was when I started work on *Moving the Mountain*. A month before the redress benefit concert (mentioned in Chapter 12) was held in Montreal in November 1989, Charlie Chin performed in front of an appreciative audience in Ottawa. This was at the CCNC National Conference of October 6–9, which was full of hope and optimism that redress was just around the corner. Two of the largest member organizations sent powerful delegates: Bill Yee, president of the Vancouver Chinese Benevolent Association, spoke, as did Lillian To and Wilfred Wan from SUCCESS, [181] a Vancouver community service organization. The keynote speaker was Noel Kinsella, the top bureaucrat from the federal Ministry of Multiculturalism. Cynthia Lam and I also spoke, representing the Montreal Chinese Family Service and the Montreal Redress Committee. We were still speaking in generalities about the head tax redress campaign, without getting any closer to developing our demands and strategies. We had the naive notion that the government would do the right thing on its own.

By now, though, the word on redress was spreading throughout community organizations across Canada and the issue was being talked about both at the grassroots level and in the family associations and Chinese benevolent associations.

We also reached out to other Canadians.

"It seems inconceivable that we are not prepared to admit that this was a dark racist chapter in our nation's history and commence negotiations for compensation," Bob White, president of the Canadian Auto Workers, said in a letter to Mulroney in December 1988. And in July 1989, George Erasmus, national chief of the Assembly of First Nations, told the prime minister: "On behalf of the Assembly of First Nations, I am writing to you and your government in support of the Chinese Canadian National Council and their demands for redress."

Others who came out in support included the Canadian Council of Churches, the Canadian Conference of Catholic Bishops, the Nova Scotia Human Rights Commission, and well-known individuals such as Pierre Berton, Margaret Atwood and June Callwood. Coverage in the mainstream media was sympathetic, with supportive editorials in the major newspapers, including *The Globe and Mail*, *Toronto Star*, *Vancouver Sun* and *Montreal Gazette*.

* * *

Despite all the support, the CCNC's work on the redress campaign was inter-
rupted following the clampdown of student protests in Tiananmen Square[182]
in Beijing, June 1989. The Chinese Canadian National Council previously had
not dealt with issues outside of Canada and Gary Yee, president at the time,
didn't want to deal with "home country politics" or tell the Chinese government what to do.[183] I shared Gary's point of view. The CCNC had been founded
as an anti-racist immigration and human rights organization focusing on
Canadian struggles. However, the CCNC board included members who immigrated from Hong Kong and held the pre-1997 anti-China political views of
the British colony and they wanted to take a strong stand against the Chinese
government.

The CCNC came out criticizing the Chinese government and became the
main clearinghouse for Ottawa's funding and assistance for visa students from
China who had been stranded in Canada due to the events back home.

The turn the CCNC took from concentrating on Canadian human rights
issues to commenting on international human rights politics would have far
more repercussions on the Chinese Canadian community than it would ever
have on the Chinese government.

Committees to support the democracy movement in China sprang up in
many cities across Canada. One of the more vocal ones, in Vancouver, was
where Raymond Chan, later a minister in the Paul Martin government, cut his
political teeth. I first met Chan in Vancouver in 1991. As I was trying to win him
over to the redress campaign, he was trying to win me over to the democracy
movement in China.

Flush with funding from the Canadian International Development Agency
(CIDA) to support the Chinese students, the CCNC produced a monthly *Bulletin*. In its inaugural issue of July 11, 1989, the CCNC publicized the services
that it was providing for the Chinese students—services that they had never
been able to get for Canadian human rights issues. The *Bulletin* said the CCNC
had established "information, counseling and referral services for Chinese
Visa students on their needs of immigration, employment, health and education." Further:

> The CCNC set up hot lines in five cities, Ottawa, Toronto, Montreal,
> Edmonton, and Vancouver. A Chinese Secretariat of CCNC was formed
> to coordinate this emergency project. An Advisory Committee from the
> national executive was formed to monitor and evaluate the program.[184]

Overall, CIDA budgeted $1.2 million to assist Chinese students in Canada through a contract with the Canadian Bureau for International Education, which subcontracted $354,106 to the CCNC to provide the services listed above and hire twelve intake contract staff. The CCNC, in the end, spent only $272,363 in helping 8,600 students by providing information, advice, referral, interpretation, workshops, and so on.[185]

Four days after the Tiananmen incident, Gary Yee and a delegation from the CCNC met Prime Minister Joe Clark in Ottawa to ask him to seek a motion in the United Nations Security Council that would condemn the "massacre" in China. On June 9, the CCNC was included in a full-page ad in *The Globe and Mail* that had been placed by a number of international human rights organizations and urged: (1) the UN to hold an emergency debate on the crisis in China; (2) the recall of Canada's ambassador to China; and (3) the temporary suspension of trade initiatives, credits, cultural exchange, and technical and education ties with China. The inclusion of the CCNC in this ad campaign would later draw derision from some sectors of the Chinese community.

Grumblings were emanating from Canada's Chinatowns about the role the CCNC was playing as an agent of the federal government. While there was support for the Chinese students in the community, there were many—especially those who had economic and cultural interests with the Chinese—who criticized the CCNC for taking an anti-China position. Cracks were starting to appear in the façade of the only national organization supposedly representing the Chinese Canadian community.

This excursion into "home country politics" fomented the divisions within the redress movement that successive Canadian governments would exploit.

Note that the CCNC traced its official start back to 1980, when it announced itself as the Chinese Canadian National Council for Equality. (It was created by the coalition of activists who had protested against the 1979 CTV *W5* program that depicted Asian Canadian students in Canadian university as foreigners taking up spaces that should have gone to Canadian [i.e., white] students.[186]) Somewhere along the way the word "equality" dropped from the name. Ironically, due to the twist of language, the common Chinese name for the CCNC remained Ping Kuen Hui—Equality Council.

Those who came together to form the CCNC were young university graduates with progressive leftist leanings similar to the New Democratic Party. Right from day one, there was a generational, cultural and linguistic gap between the CCNC and the long-established *lo wah kiu* grassroots organizations in the Chinatowns of Canada (such as the family associations and the Chinese benevolent associations), which represented the head tax generation of conservative, Confucianist, Sun Yat-sen nationalists. Members of the older organizations spoke Toishanese from the rural culture of China; members of the CCNC were young, second-generation Canadians who spoke mainly English or young, educated Asian immigrants who spoke Cantonese and Mandarin. Although a few of the regional *lo wah kiu* groups joined the CCNC at the beginning, the CCNC was not able to tap into the immense resources of established Chinese organizations that represented the older generation. The family associations, the tongs, had united across the world outside of China on a clan or district basis; they felt they had no need to be part of other large organizations.

* * *

The events surrounding the founding of the National Congress of Chinese Canadians (NCCC) in the 1990s remain somewhat murky.

Some say it was founded in reaction to the CCNC taking an anti-China stand. I don't subscribe wholly to that theory. The Tiananmen incident may have been a catalyst but the CCNC never represented the interests of the established conservative organizations. Times had changed, and the organizations that had served Chinese immigrants so well for so long now felt they needed to get themselves organized on a national scale—the CCNC, though, did not serve their purpose. They needed their own national congress to represent their views to government.

Two of the larger CCNC organizations from Vancouver—the social service organization SUCCESS and the Chinese Benevolent Association of Vancouver joined the congress at its founding.

Before the NCCC was founded, though, two national conferences of Chinese Canadians were held in 1991, in Winnipeg (March) and Toronto (May). The Toronto conference passed a resolution stating that it resolved to form the National Congress of Chinese Canadians "to act as spokesperson and to work for the redress of Head Tax."[187] Kai Tao, a Winnipeg delegate at the national conference in Toronto, explained why they did not call for individual financial compensation: "Some members of the community are afraid of racial backlash and negative reaction from other Canadians."[188]

In 1992, more than 500 delegates representing 280 organizations met in Vancouver to officially form the National Congress of Chinese Canadians. At the founding convention, the congress stuck with the resolution. It would seek redress in the form of an apology and community compensation; it did not call for individual compensation.

The stance of the NCCC would offer the succession of governments in Ottawa an opportunity to play the "divide and rule" strategy to impede any redress. The CCNC was still very much a going concern and animosity, sometimes very personal, developed between the two national organizations. They were also divided politically, to reflect the federal political parties: NCCC members were known as Liberal Party supporters, whereas the CCNC mainly supported the NDP (although some were Progressive Conservative supporters).

A fifteen-member delegation of the NCCC (Conference) had a meeting with Gerry Weiner and his officials on December 2, 1991. Weiner used the birth of the NCCC and its policy of not supporting individual compensation as an excuse to impede redress on the part of the Mulroney government.

Attempts were made to seek a rapprochement on redress between the two national Chinese Canadian organizations—the congress and the council. Gary Yee and the CCNC Toronto office finally arranged a meeting with the NCCC leadership, including Toronto lawyer Ping Tan,[189] on April 9, 1992. In his report on that meeting, Gary wrote:

> The NCCC representatives appeared to have different interpretations of the May 1991 redress resolution. It was unclear whether individual financial redress was possible under their resolution. ... As long as NCCC does not oppose individual financial redress in their statements to the media, public or government, then there really is no excuse for the government to delay.[190]

Shortly after, the NCCC began hardening its position against individual financial redress and clung to a position of community collective redress. Over the years, the NCCC invited representatives from the Chinese embassy and consulates across Canada to participate at its national conventions and other functions. Some critics even went as far as to claim that the NCCC was formed by the Chinese embassy to represent its interests in Canada. Red baiting of this sort is reminiscent of the old Soviet days with the embassy of the USSR seen as a source of international subversion.[191] (In 2016, as the outgoing head of CSIS and national security advisor to Stephen Harper, Richard Fadden would fire a parting shot of innuendo—widely reported in the mainstream media but without any explicit proof—that Chinese Canadian politicians and people associated with the NCCC might be spying for China.[192])

* * *

A little earlier, through a series of individual meetings with Minister Weiner, the CCNC and other member groups of the newly formed National Redress Alliance—such as the Italian Canadian Congress and the Ukrainian Canadian Congress—had come to one conclusion. All decided that putting pressure on Weiner to take action required homework, deeper grassroots consultation and organizing to develop a more concrete proposal to present to the government.

The CCNC organized a well-attended National Redress Conference in Toronto on March 16 and 17, 1991. The National Redress Committee of the CCNC was formed at this conference, a move that the community greeted with enthusiasm. However, a resolution was also passed regarding the redress campaign and, to the dismay of many outside of Toronto who did not attend the meeting, the resolution did not offer any concrete plans or demands to resolve the issue.

What may have influenced the decision to take a cautious approach was a March 12 letter from Vancouver that was issued to the CCNC and distributed at the conference. It was signed by five community luminaries, including lawyer Tommy Tao of the Chinese Benevolent Association. This letter offered a dissenting view to the CCNC's position on individual financial redress, suggesting that the demand for such compensation be dropped. The letter included the hard-hitting statement: "The views of the claimants are tainted by self-interest."

The letter named some of the organizations[193] that would later join the congress and presented their positions, going on to propose that individual redress should take the form of a "certificate of honour" or a gold coin to be issued to each head tax payer or family. This suggestion would come back to haunt us. The letter concluded:

With so many really serious problems that we now face globally and nationally, we sincerely hope that the headtax issue can soon be resolved and put behind us, so that we can channel our energy towards the other much more pressing issues.

By July of the following year—1992—Tommy Tao, then an NDP candidate in the federal riding of Vancouver Quadra, seemed to have warmed to the CCNC position. As reported in the *Vancouver Sun*, "Tao called on all Chinese-Canadian community leaders to unite and support the CCNC's proposal."[194]

But, in the spring of 1991, several community leaders began attacking the stance of the CCNC on redress and its work in support of Chinese students after Tiananmen with "behind-the-back letters"[195] to Prime Minister Mulroney openly criticizing the council. One of these leaders was Joseph Du[196] of Winnipeg, who claimed that the CCNC was not being fair by excluding Winnipeg from the funding to aid students.[197] In a letter to the prime minister, Du also criticized the leading role the CCNC was playing in redress, saying that the organization did not speak for the whole community. (Du, however, would later play a more positive role in the lead up to the 2006 redress struggle as co-chair of the NCCC.) Ping Tan, who became the founding national executive co-chair of the NCCC, also wrote a letter to Mulroney criticizing the CCNC on both the head tax and the Chinese student issues.[198]

This was the start of the personal animosity between the leadership of the CCNC and the NCCC.

Gary Yee, who had dedicated his time and energy to the redress movement for seven years, only to have some johnny-come-latelies to the struggle complain to the prime minister, was personally hurt.[199] These types of public criticisms only served to provide an excuse for the government to delay redress with the often-repeated admonition: "Your community needs to get together and let us know what you want."

Following up on the warm reception it had received at its founding, the CCNC's National Redress Committee sought feedback from community organizations across Canada so it could draft a meaningful redress proposal for government. In a June 25 memo to the committee's policy subcommittee, Yantay Tsai of Winnipeg, editor of the *Manitoba Chinese Post*, emphatically and boldly stated: "Those who do not consider themselves victimized have the freedom of choice to decline redress but they have no right to deprive other victims' right for redress."[200]

* * *

Activists in Montreal were seen as independent leftist hardliners. We had started to grumble internally among ourselves about the lack of strong leadership from the Toronto-centric CCNC, so we set about reinforcing our own local activities, such as uniting with individuals and organizations within the community, reaching out to other communities (Black, Jewish and Japanese), lobbying local politicians for their support, and educating the wider society through articles and interviews in the media. We stood by our principled position that the victims of racism needed to be individually redressed as an issue of justice and human rights.

Hoping to prop up the CCNC's hand in dealing with the government, I sent a letter to Gary Yee on December 5, 1990, saying that the CCNC must be "ideologically prepared to take on the government," and that

> Unless we settle this issue, it will be difficult for us to be taken seriously in other vital areas such as employment equity, race relations and immigration. If we cave into the government now, we would only reinforce government attitudes that the Chinese community is docile and easily won over.

Two weeks later, Jacky Pang, CCNC national executive director, mailed a letter to Chinese Family Service executive director Cynthia Lam calling for a need to "redefine the structure of the Montreal Redress Committee." Pang wrote:

> Since we are going to extend the membership of the Committee to all organizations and individuals, it is anticipated the executive of the enlarged Committee may need to go through a process of democratic nomination and election, rather than by default that William Dere is the Chair of the Committee.

Ouch!

Shortly after, the Chinese Neighbourhood Society—one of the two member chapters of the CCNC in Montreal—became more involved in redress. That was a good thing. Society board members William Lai and Walter Tom joined the redress committee. I was re-elected as committee chair.

Strengthened with the new forces, Montreal Redress Committee members Jonas Ma, Walter Tom and I met on June 25, 1991, with the Montreal Head Tax Action Committee, which had recently been created by the organizations that supported the National Conference of Chinese Canadians. In a July 2 memo to the CCNC–NRC, I wrote that the NCCC-affiliated action committee reflected an older section of the community who were associated with Chinatown businesses, restaurants and family associations. We should continue to reach out to this group since they were now committed to fighting for some form of compensation. However, it was up to us to set the agenda and propose concrete action. "We should organize a National Redress Rally on Parliament Hill this Fall," I suggested in the memo. "I am sure we can mobilize hundreds of elderly to participate."

I could see why the CCNC people in Toronto were not inclined to work with the NCCC. Some in the CCNC accused the NCCC of sowing division in the community over redress. The Montreal Head Tax Action Committee was only one of a number of head tax action committees that the NCCC had created in the major cities as a counter to the redress committees associated with the CCNC. The division in the community over redress now had an organizational form.

I am sure the government revelled at these developments to stall any settlement.

* * *

At the beginning of 1991, the CCNC sent out a survey to the three thousand head tax registrants. When the CCNC released the results   gathered from 867 returned questionnaires—it turned out that 90 per cent of the respondents came from three cities: Vancouver, Toronto and Montreal.[201] Also, 45 per cent were head tax payers and/or their spouses; 45 per cent were descendants of head tax payers; and 10 per cent came from organizations and other individuals. What the respondents wanted broke down this way:

- 90 per cent were strongly in favour of some form of compensatory redress; only 1 per cent was satisfied with just an apology.
- 38 per cent believed that redress should only go to the head tax payers or widows; 62 per cent wanted individual redress to go to the descendants (children and grandchildren), but only 30 per cent of the head tax payers and 21 per cent of the widows supported financial redress for descendants.
- 85 per cent wanted the $500 refund plus interest. But 75 per cent wanted more than $500 in financial individual redress. Just 30 per

cent of the respondents would be satisfied with the total amount of $23 million as a symbolic return of the head tax collected, while 70 per cent said the final amount should not be capped at $23 million.[202]

The survey results, released by June 1991, offered the CCNC–NRC powerful support as it tried to get the government to the negotiating table. However, the survey also showed that of the two thousand head tax payers who were alive in 1984, only nine hundred were still alive in 1991.

While the surveys were still coming in, there were developments on the redress front on the West Coast.

In March 1991, Victor Yukmun Wong and others, like Charles Mow of the Chinese Canadian Historical Society, formed the BC Coalition of Head Tax Payers, Spouses, and Descendants "to advocate on behalf of the BC head tax registrants." It was a time when the "established organizations in Vancouver were either reluctant or unable/incapable of furthering the redress campaign," Victor, co-chair of the new coalition, wrote.[203] Victor was an NDP activist; other well-known community activists, like radio personality Hanson Lau and cable TV's Sid Tan, later joined the organization. The coalition was credited with re-launching the redress movement on the West Coast, where it was able to draw more than one thousand people to meetings.

At the meeting held in Vancouver on July 28, 1991, with more than two hundred people in attendance, the coalition ratified demands and positions that included wanting the CCNC–NRC to adopt a position in favour of individual financial redress. They called for a payment of $20,000 per head tax certificate, going to the head tax payer, the surviving spouse or surviving descendants.

The BC organization disagreed with the CCNC position of a total compensation package topped at $23 million, saying the CCNC "should have gone to the grass-roots first before arriving at this position in 1988."

The BC coalition also called for an immediate national campaign to bring the government to the negotiating table. Public meetings were held in major cities across Canada—1,100 attended in Vancouver, 280 in Montreal and 350 in Toronto. Newspaper articles by Gary Yee, John Tang, Victor Wong and me appeared in both mainstream and community newspapers.

Then, on August 10, 1991, the Metro Toronto Redress Committee put forward its position in a memo to the CCNC–NRC: It called for a symbolic return of the $23 million—face value of the head tax collected. It wanted the CCNC–NRC to negotiate specifically for redress of the HTEA and to work in mutual support with the other communities seeking redress—Ukrainian, Italian and Sikh Canadians. The Metro Committee supported individual compensation to include the surviving head tax payers, widows or children based on one certificate–one compensation. Community compensation would focus on services and homes for seniors, anti-racism education and race relations.

A very interesting letter came out of another part of the country that year. I received a copy, dated May 14, 1991, and addressed to Prime Minister Brian Mulroney. The letter, signed by a number of influential Chinese Canadians—including *Manitoba Chinese Post* editor Yantay Tsai—called on the government to deal with the redress issue as a gross violation of human rights in Canada. As such, it "must be dealt with from a national perspective of all Canadians as opposed to a community perspective." The letter also said:

> We are deeply concerned that many Chinese Canadian community organizations, which have hitherto shown no interest in the Head Tax and the Exclusion Act issue, have suddenly in recent months taken positions and demanded community compensation.[204]

The letter called on the Mulroney government to start negotiating with the CCNC, the only national human rights organization in the Chinese community and to whom over three thousand head tax payers and families had given a mandate to negotiate on their behalf. The letter concluded by urging the government not to use a "divide and rule" strategy.

On the evening of October 8, 1991, Gary Yee called me to confirm that we would be meeting Minister Gerry Weiner on October 28, and asked if I could bring James Wing. We discussed finalizing our proposal so that we could present it to Weiner at the meeting. The next night, Victor Wong of the BC Coalition called from Vancouver to get me onside for their $20,000 individual redress proposal.

I immediately called a meeting of the Montreal Redress Committee to firm up our position. At this committee meeting, on October 16, 1991, we decided to take the positions that I outlined in the memo reporting on our meeting to Gary Yee: the main points included standing firm in support of compensation for the descendants of the head tax payers. We supported the Metro Toronto Redress Committee's suggestion of $5,000 per claimant, which would be part of the symbolic $23-million total compensation. We would propose a deadline of July 1, 1992, for a final settlement.

We all had an overly optimistic deadline—to negotiate an agreement by Canada Day, 1992, the 125th anniversary of Confederation.

* * *

Chinese Canadian war veterans had played a key role in repealing the Exclusion Act and winning the vote for the Chinese in Canada. However, they played a reactionary role when it came to fighting for redress for the individual head tax payers and their families.

In 1991, the hundred-member Chinese Canadian War Veterans Association voted by a slim majority to reject the concept of any individual compensation for the victims. They carried their loyalty to the country to such an extreme that it was not in the best interest of the actual victims of the Head Tax and Exclusion Act.

There were a handful of common objections to redress heard within and outside the Chinese community. Head tax claimants were motivated by self-interest and greed. Chinese immigrants paid the head tax willingly and now their families were successfully benefitting from Canadian society. The government had the legal right to restrict Chinese immigration to Canada and did not have the money or the legal duty to redress wrongs from the last century. There would be a backlash against Chinese Canadians from the mainstream media and the larger community for the aforementioned reasons.

To put things into context, the counter-arguments that we presented at the time included noting that when Dak Leon Mark first approached Margaret Mitchell in 1983, he was motivated by a sense of justice, equality and human rights; he wanted the $500 head tax refunded to him only because no other group of immigrants had to pay. Also, Chinese immigrants had not paid the head tax willingly—they were not given a choice. The government had the legal right to restrict and ban Chinese immigrants from Canada and now it must be held accountable.

The age-old argument that the government did not have the money was, in our opinion, merely a smokescreen. The $23 million the government had collected as head tax was equivalent to over $1 billion today. Essentially, Chinese immigrants contributed to paying Canada's debt and reducing the deficit with the head tax. The government should show that it cannot profit from racism. The backlash, we said, would come from those who did not understand. Our community and the government had the duty to explain our history in Canada.

The government was denying our history as long as it denied redress. There had been no backlash when the Mulroney government redressed the Japanese Canadian community for internment during World War II with over $400 million paid as compensation. The fact that a Conservative government in Ottawa and Ronald Reagan in Washington were justifying their redress of the Japanese took some of the sting away from any redneck objections.

* * *

Armed with the feedback and consultations from across the country and the survey from the head tax registrants, Gary Yee prepared for our October 28, 1991, meeting with Minister Gerry Weiner. Days beforehand, Ping Tan cancelled a meeting with Gary, so Gary and the CCNC–NRC went into the meeting with Weiner without any clarification from the NCCC.

On the morning of October 28, I drove to Ottawa with James Wing as the Montreal contingent of the CCNC–NRC. James was an energetic seventy-eight-year-old at the time and probably the youngest of the surviving head tax payers. He had been one of the first *lo wah kiu* to become active in the redress campaign. During the ride to Ottawa, he spoke about his friendship with my father and grandfather, giving me new insights into what life had been like during those years.

Delegates[205] from Toronto (led by Gary Yee), Ottawa and Halifax conferred with us in a Chinatown restaurant in Ottawa to prepare for the 3:30 p.m. meeting.

We arrived at the official meeting early and waited patiently in one of the wood-panelled parliamentary conference rooms. Weiner then came in with his entourage of half a dozen aides. We introduced James Wing, and James presented his poignant history to the minister. Weiner appeared visibly moved and said he would try his best to find a solution. When Gary presented our proposal, Weiner was more impassive; he was noncommittal and said he would study it.

Our main points included wanting an all-party parliamentary resolution to acknowledge the injustice and racism inherent in the Head Tax and Chinese Exclusion Act; a letter of acknowledgment and regret from the prime minister to each holder of a head tax certificate (including the descendants); and individual symbolic financial redress in the sum of $23 million. The proposal also demanded financial redress of $10,000 per head tax certificate to eligible children of deceased head tax payers without surviving spouses. Other demands included community financial redress of $5 million for a Chinese Canadian community trust.

All these demands were reasonable and fair. At the meeting I argued that the federal justice minister should also participate in the negotiations for a settlement since this was a question of justice.

On January 5, 1992, Gary Yee flew to Vancouver and addressed a meeting organized by the BC Coalition, attended by over 1,200 people. Weiner must have taken note; two weeks later, he met with Victor Wong in Vancouver and said he would present the CCNC–NRC proposal to the prime minister soon.

Gary Yee was open to collaborating with the National Conference of Chinese Canadians (the precursor of the National Congress of Chinese Canadians, which would be officially founded in September 1992). But, in a memo to the National Redress Committee on March 26, Gary wrote that he had tried to meet with the NCCC's head Ping Tan without any success. Gary added that he would continue trying to obtain a meeting with the Congress leadership to push for an agreement that financial redress for the elderly head tax claimants was a priority.

Members of the CCNC–NRC meet with Multiculturalism Minister Gerry Weiner,
October 28, 1991. Members of the CCNC–NRC delegation standing in front of Weiner
from left to right: William Dere, Gary Yee, Avvy Go, James Wing, Alan Li, Shana Wong,
Lewis Chan, May Lui. (William Dere Collection)

In a later face-to-face meeting, Minister Weiner assured Gary Yee that his department's redress package was almost ready to be sent to the prime minister. All member chapters were urged to send letters to the prime minister and to hold public forums to update the community on the progress of the campaign. Plans were underway to hold a Redress Rally on Parliament Hill on Victoria Day.

In a March 24, 1992 letter to Weiner, Gary expressed concern that funding for the Canadian Race Relations Foundation, which was to have been part of the Japanese internment settlement, had been deferred:

> It is offensive to the Japanese Canadian community and all their redress supporters. Furthermore, how can we expect your government to enter into good faith negotiations with us on Chinese Canadian redress if you fail to honour or respect past redress agreements.

Gary urged the minister to begin the negotiations on head tax redress as soon as possible. He also actively participated in the National Redress Alliance of other affected communities.[206]

A couple of months later—on Victoria Day, May 18—the redress rally on Parliament Hill was an extraordinary success (as described in the vignette at the top of this chapter).

A portion of the rally at Parliament, May 18, 1992. (Photo courtesy of CCNC)

"One of my personal highlights was the march, when we brought the seniors on the bus to Ottawa," said Montreal human rights lawyer Walter Tom, who travelled on the bus with his grandfather, Hum Wing Goon, a head tax payer who came to Canada in 1921. "We talked about the awakening of the community. That was something we've never done before. This was an active thing."[207]

James Wing spoke passionately on behalf of head tax payers; Mrs. Lee, a widow from Toronto,[208] spoke calmly in a moving speech on behalf of the spouses of deceased head tax payers; Walter Tom made a stirring speech in French on behalf of the Montreal Redress Committee. Japanese Canadian redress activist Art Miki, who flew in from Winnipeg to support our campaign, also spoke. The *Moving the Mountain* team travelled with the two buses from Montreal and filmed the rally. There were more than 350 people, mostly seniors.

Many saw this as a turning point in the redress campaign, as it was the first time that the Chinese Canadian community was taking such direct action and presenting itself before Parliament. The next day, a delegation that included head tax payers, spouses and widows remained in Ottawa to lobby MPs and attended Question Period, where they were acknowledged in the gallery by the Opposition. Some of the delegation met Gerry Weiner in the lobby of the House of Commons, where he confirmed that he had made his recommendations to the prime minister but refused to disclose any details.

We would not get to know the government proposal until a year later.

To maintain the redress pressure on the Prime Minister's Office, member chapters of the CCNC were urged to write letters to the prime minister demanding the government start negotiating an expeditious and fair settlement.

The National Congress of Chinese Canadians finally held its long-anticipated official founding conference on the same weekend as the CCNC rally on Parliament Hill. Gary Yee and Victor Wong wrote letters urging its leaders to clarify their position on redress and to not oppose individual redress. But there was no discussion on this at the conference. The newly formed organization also suffered an early split as the pro-Taiwan (Kuomintang) section of the Chinese Benevolent Association pulled out of the congress.[209]

Then, in the spring of 1993, articles began appearing in major Canadian newspapers to explain the nature of the head tax campaign and why it was so urgent to seek redress for the remaining elderly head tax payers. This media blitz by the CCNC–NRC was also designed to pressure the Mulroney government into starting redress negotiations with our community.

"Redress will enable our community to leap confidently into a new era as full citizens in an inclusive Canada. Redress will provide justice to our seniors," Gary Yee wrote in an op-ed article in *The Globe and Mail.* "Redress will help demonstrate that our government should not profit from racism."[210] Gary's grandfather had paid the $500 head tax on arriving in Canada in 1917, but had died in 1989—five years after Brian Mulroney had promised that if he were elected, his government would resolve the issue.

During 1993, Mulroney was about to leave office and we again put our hopes on politicians to live up to their promises made during election campaigns or in a period of legacy building. Mulroney never lived up to his promise; seeing his popularity sinking in the polls, he resigned from office on June 25, 1993.

The redress campaign experienced its own change of leadership.

In September 1993, Gary Yee stepped down from his position in the campaign to accept an Ontario government tribunal appointment. He had dedicated himself to the head tax campaign from the start, serving as national president of the CCNC and then chair of the CCNC–NRC. Gary graduated from Osgoode Hall Law School and had served as the executive director of the Metro Toronto Chinese and Southeast Asian Legal Clinic. He remained a redress strategist in the background but could not be a public figure for the campaign due to his new job. I knew Gary to be a very passionate and diplomatic spokesman for the Chinese Canadian community. I would not have had as much patience and I would have suffered a lot more frustration in dealing with the government if it weren't for his moderating and calming influence.

Amy Go, national president of the CCNC, filled in for Gary as chair of the National Redress Committee until February 1994 when Victor Wong of the BC Coalition replaced her. I remained the vice-chair of the CCNC–NRC.

* * *

As a parting gesture before leaving office, Brian Mulroney, through Gerry Weiner, offered a lame attempt to appease the three communities seeking redress with similar proposals.

On May 18, 1993, Weiner met with CCNC representatives in Toronto and presented the government's unilateral redress settlement, which did not address any of the demands that we had proposed in October 1991. What Weiner offered was laughable, if not sad, but apparently his bureaucrats must have gotten wind of the March 1991 Tommy Tao memo requesting the government present each head tax payer and family with a certificate of honour or a gold coin. That was exactly what the government offered to settle this long-standing injustice: a certificate, a medal, a statement of apology, and plaques or displays at the National Archives.

The Chinese community immediately held consultation meetings in Vancouver, Toronto and Montreal, and we overwhelmingly rejected this insulting offer. At the Montreal public meeting on May 26, 1993, James Wing spoke eloquently, as my notes attest:

> What did I do to deserve a medal? I won't go to Ottawa to accept it. We will just be used by the government. Why did we spend so much time to get nothing? We can't let them off the hook. If they don't want to settle, then let history be the judge!

I said at the time that our head tax payers already had a certificate—the head tax certificate—so we didn't need another one. Kenda Gee would later call the medal "the Tommy Tao gold coin."

The other communities in the National Redress Alliance—the Ukrainian and Italian Canadians—also rejected the government proposal. Mulroney's attempt at a redress legacy was ignominiously inadequate.

The CCNC–NRC sent a strongly worded formal response to Mulroney on May 27, 1993, after the community consultation meetings with head tax registrants in the three largest cities. "As we expected, your proposal has been strongly rejected," we wrote. "Many of our elderly head tax payers and widows have labeled it an insult. ... We have not fought for redress since 1984 in order to accept a piece of paper and a little trinket before an election."

However, the National Congress of Chinese Canadians did not reject the government offer. At its Executive Committee meeting, on May 29–30, 1993, the NCCC passed a resolution endorsing the "issue of commemorative coins, plaques and stamps" and requested the government establish an endowment fund of a "reasonable amount" for taking care of the surviving head tax payers, promoting racial harmony, and promoting other activities that would benefit the Chinese Canadian community.[211] In a letter sent to Gerry Weiner, Ping Tan wrote, "The Congress is pleased that the Federal Government is moving toward a resolution of the issue."[212]

The national media had extensive coverage of redress following the government proposal, with many editorials supporting the community's just demands for financial compensation. Mulroney stepped down as prime minister in June 1993 and Kim Campbell assumed power. Monique Landry, the new minister of Canadian Heritage, would be in charge of the redress issue. We had to start over again with the new players on the scene.

I came to the realization at the time that it was the federal bureaucracy that was holding back any redress. I sensed that they had been burned with the Japanese internment redress settlement, in which they grossly underestimated the amount to be paid out to Japanese Canadian victims. (The total compensation due to the unjust internment was $416 million.[213]) That is why, at my final meeting with Gerry Weiner, he talked about the "floodgates." But, at the same time, he told me that for us to win redress we needed "to light a fire under the pants of government."

We needed bold political leadership in Ottawa to overcome the bureaucratic resistance. In the final analysis, redress would have to be, above all, a significant political act.

Chapter 14

Shutting the Floodgates
(1994–2000)

"Retreat temporarily when your enemy is strong. ... Attack when the enemy forces are unprepared."
—Sun Tzu, *The Art of War*

The Chinese Canadian head tax payer plaintiff to sign on for our court battle was ninety-four-year-old Shack Jang Mack of Toronto. His story is typical of the Gold Mountain men. He was born in 1907 and came to Canada from China in 1922. The court document stated that he had gone back to China to marry Gat Nuy Na in 1928, but the Chinese Immigration Act had prevented him from bringing her to Canada. He was able to travel back to China again, but if he had stayed longer than two years at a time he would have lost the right to return to Canada. He sold his café business every time he left Canada and opened another one on his return. In 1950, his wife and family were finally able to join him in Canada.[214]

K im Campbell's short-lived government was kicked out in the October 25, 1993 federal elections and Jean Chrétien assumed the office of prime minister. During the election campaign, we participated actively in canvassing the candidates of the three major parties and urged them to support redress. Many promised their support during the campaign, including Sheila Copps, who would be appointed deputy prime minister in the Chrétien government. Sheila Finestone was appointed secretary of state responsible for multiculturalism. Again, the Chinese Canadian National Council–National Redress Committee (CCNC–NRC) had great hope and faith in the newly elected Liberal government, despite the narrow-mindedness towards redress that Pierre Trudeau's Liberal regime had shown a decade ago.

We set to work on informing the new government players about the head tax redress issues and requesting meetings with the prime minister. Finally, Sheila Finestone—in charge of the dossier—agreed to meet with us. On May 13, 1994, a CCNC–NRC delegation went to Ottawa to meet her at the Confederation Building. The delegation had nine members, including head tax payer James Wing and myself.[215]

At this initial meeting, our objectives were to give the new minister a first-hand briefing; explain our desire to negotiate a fair settlement, and express both our sense of urgency and our expectation of action for our elderly head tax payers. Finestone didn't have much to say; she simply nodded her head during our presentation. As we were leaving, I presented her a copy of *Moving the Mountain*, which she promptly handed to an aide. I don't know if she or her staff ever watched the film.

During 1994, CCNC–NRC chair Victor Wong and I, together or individually, met with Finestone a total of three times. Sensing no movement from the government, we later revised our redress proposal to cap the compensation at the symbolic $23 million. We officially sent the new proposal to Finestone's office on October 19 and then released it to the public. In his confidential memo to the CCNC–NRC, Victor projected that "We are still at least two meetings away from the possibility of real negotiations."[216]

Victor also urged CCNC chapters to send letters to the prime minister prior to Chrétien's upcoming trip to China. We were hoping that Canada would take advantage of this occasion to announce a redress settlement. We did not expect anything less.

There was no indication of the bombshell Sheila Finestone was about to throw at the communities seeking redress.

On December 13, 1994, Finestone announced in Parliament that the government would not continue discussions with ethnic communities on redress issues. Furthermore, there would be no apology and no compensation.

What appeared to be a form letter under Finestone's department letterhead was sent to eight ethnocultural community organizations, ranging from the CCNC and the National Congress of Chinese Canadians to the Canadian Jewish Congress and the Ukrainian Canadian Civil Liberties Association.[217] The December 14, 1994 copy of the letter, addressed to CCNC president Alan Li, made no mention of the head tax and was signed by Finestone. It read in part:

> We wish we could rewrite history. We cannot. We can and we must learn from the past. We must assure that future generations do not repeat the errors of the past. ... We believe our only choice lies in using limited government resources to create a more equitable society now and a better future for generations to come. Therefore, the Government will not grant financial compensation for the requests made.[218]

Condemnation of the government stand was fast and furious from Canada's ethnic communities. Bryce Kanbara of the Toronto chapter of the National Association of Japanese Canadians fired off a letter to Finestone on December 15 that included the following:

> The surprise announcement—just before Parliament's Christmas break—is the product of insidious calculation. It destroys any steps that were made over the past several years towards mutual understanding and trust among individuals, communities and institutions. All this we will have to rebuild.
>
> The rationale you presented to the Canadian people is damagingly simplistic and diminishes the enormity of the injustices perpetrated by Canada.[219]

We were in a state of shock and felt betrayed and abandoned. The very people we looked to for justice had turned their backs to us. This was a hard lesson for many in the movement. Victor Wong issued a confrontational statement on December 16, in which he noted that "the new Liberal government had promised to redress the issue while in opposition and during the election campaign. What the government has done is actually perpetuate another indignity on our seniors."

My personal reaction in the face of this brutal rejection by the government was to follow the advice James Wing gave me: "Let history be the judge." In a letter I wrote to the *Montreal Gazette* on December 15, as the vice-chair of the CCNC–NRC, I said that Chrétien might want to sweep the country's history of government racism under the rug "but future generations of Chinese Canadians will remember that Canada profited from racism to the tune of $23 million. That will be the moral debt and legacy left by Jean Chrétien to future generations."

* * *

If a government does not redress past oppressions, it can be easy to repeat and maintain those oppressions.

In February 1995, two short months after Finestone stated that we "can and we must learn from the past," Paul Martin, the finance minister, imposed a $975 right-to-landing fee on each adult immigrant and refugee. The landing fee is another form of head tax directed at new immigrants, many of whom now come from Asian countries. Prospective immigrants and refugees were powerless to fight this new levy. The government was saying to new immigrants, as it said to the head tax payers, "Give us your money and your labour."

In another letter to the *Montreal Gazette*, published on March 6, 1995, I wrote:

> It is only fair that a head tax be applied to all new immigrants! That seems to be the logic of the federal government. ... By not correcting an injustice against one group of immigrants to Canada, the government feels free to apply an odious policy against all immigrants.

The Canadian government closed all possibilities of redress and didn't even want to talk about it. We were at a loss as to what to do; public meetings were held in different cities to discuss this new development. We needed to take it to the next level and looked at a more confrontational approach. Then the ever-creative and fiery Kenneth Cheung in Montreal proposed the idea of internationalizing the campaign; he suggested paddling canoes down the Hudson River to demonstrate in front of the United Nations Headquarters. Kenneth had borrowed the idea from the Cree and Inuit Nations of Northern Quebec who paddled their *Odeyak* to the UN in protest of the Hydro-Québec project encroaching on their traditional lands. The lawyers who ran the CCNC in Toronto went with a less flamboyant tactic and issued a lawyerly submission to the UN Commission on Human Rights.

The presentation of this submission to UN High Commissioner Jose Ayala Lasso in Toronto on March 21, 1995—International Anti-Racism Day—received extensive media coverage across Canada and even as far as Hong Kong. The *Vancouver Sun* reported that the CCNC submission accused the Canadian government of being in breach of the Universal Declaration of Human Rights and several other UN covenants by refusing to redress head tax payers.[220]

The submission to the UN, signed by Alan Li, national president of CCNC, and Victor Yukmun Wong, chair of the CCNC–NRC, stated,

> The inadequate response of the Canadian government and its inaction in resolving this matter has continued the injustice, and it constitutes a denial of an effective remedy to affected individuals for the nation's violation of human rights.[221]

The submission requested that the commission, "through its appropriate body," take the matter before the Canadian government "and inquire as to why Canada has not adequately and appropriately met its international human rights obligations to Chinese Head Tax payers and their families." Further, "the CCNC calls upon the Canadian government to enter into good faith negotiations immediately to resolve this longstanding grievance."[222]

People seemed to have forgotten that two years earlier, on August 23, 1993, Amy Go, as national president of the CCNC, had also drafted a submission to Theo van Boven, UN Commission on Human Rights special rapporteur, on the right to restitution, compensation and rehabilitation for victims of gross violation of human rights and fundamental freedoms. (Amy and her sister, Avvy, were leaders of the redress campaign in Toronto.) Amy had made the case for redress, included the CCNC–NRC's proposal to the Canadian government, and exposed the government's paltry offer of certificates and medals as totally inadequate. The submission had requested that the commission "intervene in this urgent matter and inquire as to why Canada has not adequately and appropriately met its international human rights obligations to Chinese head tax payers and their families."[223]

* * *

The government's intransigence cast the redress movements in Canada into a dark morass for the rest of the 1990s. The Liberal government's contempt for the ethnocultural communities began to eat away at the political support they previously took for granted. The results would manifest themselves in future elections.

However, the redress activists kept the fire going and began to strategize other ways to force the government to do the right thing. We continued making contacts and recruiting people to the redress committee in Montreal through petitions and small meetings.

In November 1995, I was contacted by May Lui, whom I had met at the meeting with Gerry Weiner in Ottawa in 1991. May was now the public education officer of the Nova Scotia Human Rights Commission. She invited me to be a speaker at the United Nations and Human Rights Conference to be held in Halifax on December 9, 1995. I was to speak about the CCNC–NRC's March 21 submission to the United Nations.

In my speech I tried to personalize the effects of the Head Tax and Exclusion Act on my family. I spoke about how the legislation violated the human rights of the entire Chinese Canadian community, and how, by not redressing these violations, the Canadian government continues to perpetuate these infringements of human rights. I made the link between the past and the present and the ongoing legacy of racist legislation.

"I feel very badly," I said, "that our community was not able to win redress for the Head Tax and the Exclusion Act, not only for ourselves but for today's immigrants who are forced to pay a new $975 head tax (Landing Fee). In 1903, when Sir Wilfrid Laurier spoke in support of the head tax against the Chinese, he said it would be a good source of revenue for the government. In 1995, Paul Martin says the same thing about the new head tax. How much have we progressed in ninety-two years?"[224]

* * *

An interesting sidebar related to my speech in Halifax was a paper that I read much later. It was written by Matt James, professor at the University of Victoria, and presented at the meeting of the Canadian Political Science Association on May 31, 2003. James' excellent paper was titled "Redress, Recognition, and Redistribution: The Case of the 'Chinese Head Tax.'"[225] James introduced the redress struggle into the academic milieu and this paper introduced me to a little-known field of academic study that connects cultural recognition with class redistribution of wealth. James quoted American political philosopher Nancy Fraser as saying:

> Group identity supplants class interest as the chief medium of political mobilization. Cultural domination supplants exploitation as the fundamental injustice. And cultural recognition displaces socioeconomic redistribution as the remedy for injustice and the goal of political struggle.[226]

This may make intriguing academic scholarship but it is a false dichotomy. The fundamental struggle for human rights unites racial, cultural and social-economic class battles. One cannot pit the struggle for reparation of slavery in the US against the economic struggles of unionized workers for better wages. US capitalism is built on the genocide of one group of people (Indigenous Americans) and the economic exploitation of slavery, without which the American workers would not have the present standard of living. James cited American scholar Todd Gitlin in criticizing group identity, with this statement, which does not address white privilege, "A Left that was serious about ... reducing the inequality of wealth and income would stop lambasting all white men, and would take it as elementary to reduce frictions among white men, blacks, white women and Hispanics."[227]

James tried to show how the campaign for head tax redress in fact united the recognition with the redistribution aspects of the struggle by posing Avvy Go's words on "whether it is okay for our Government to benefit from racist laws." James quoted Edmonton's Kenda Gee as saying, "Being forced to offer reparations means that the nation is being forced to 'confront its past so such things do not happen again."[228]

James went on to say,

> May Chiu and William Ging Wee Dere of the Chinese Canadian National Council used media space that they garnered as movement leaders to draw connections between the racist exploitation that underpinned the head tax and Ottawa's 1995 immigration changes, which imposed a 'head tax of $975 on all adult immigrants entering the country, including refugee claimants.' As Dere also explained in an address to a conference sponsored by the Nova Scotia Human Rights

Commission, 'If we had won our redress, it would have been impossible for the government to attack new immigrants with another Head Tax.' Yew Lee has also made the link between the system of racialized economic exploitation buttressed by the head tax and contemporary Canadian immigration policy....

The head tax campaign performs valuable service in helping to place contemporary Canadian immigration policy in its highly revealing historical context. And, to turn specifically to the question of redistribution, using media attention to highlight policies that exploit immigrants is vital to advancing the interests of workers in general.

* * *

In November 1997, Montreal's Jewish and Chinese communities came together to mark the fiftieth anniversary of two historical events—the 1947 repeal of the Chinese Exclusion Act and the reopening of Canada's doors to Jewish immigration.

Cynthia Lam, executive director of the Chinese Family Service and co-president of Quebec Citizenship Week, was one of the speakers at the commemoration, which was held in Chinatown's Poon Kai Restaurant. She noted that once the Exclusion Act had been repealed, Chinese women gradually came to join their husbands in Canada. "They came to nurse their husbands who were in poor health because of the working conditions.... When the husbands died ... the bachelors' society became the widows' society," my personal notes record her as having said.

Bernard Finestone was quoted in a newspaper article as saying:

"I remember my father telling me about the Jews fleeing from Hitler in 1930. Canada was very unreceptive then. It turned away refugees, including my grandfather's relatives and cousins, who were all killed. We are celebrating with the Chinese because we have something in common—respect for family and elders, willingness to work hard and determination to succeed. We're two communities who suffered a lot."[229]

* * *

When all reasonable avenues to approach the government were blocked, the confrontational method saw the lawyers in the CCNC office in Toronto quietly preparing for a court case. We'd already taken to the streets with the Parliament Hill rally in 1992. It would be quite an effort to ask our elderly pioneers to march again five years later.

In 1997, the CCNC applied and received $5,000 in case development funding from the Court Challenge Program. After two years of inactivity, the redress committees hoped that the court case and the preparations around it would revitalize the CCNC–NRC. However, the CCNC Working Group that was created to steer the court case consisted of Torontonians only, including lawyers Gary Yee, Avvy Go and Cynthia Pay and, later, May Cheng, who also became the chair of the National Redress Committee and the national president of the CCNC.

Phillip R. Pike, formerly of the African Canadian Legal Clinic, was commissioned by the CCNC to study the legal issues for a Charter challenge for discrimination flowing from the Head Tax and Exclusion Act. In his conclusion, Pike wrote:

> I am of the view that the strongest and most persuasive argument to be made using s. 15(1) of the Charter to base a claim for redress is one which views the government's failure to redress for the on-going effects of past discrimination as a present act of discrimination which has the effect of perpetuating the past discrimination.[230]

He recommended commencing legal action based on this argument. At the April 9, 1999 national meeting, the CCNC and its member chapters unanimously passed a resolution to bring the case to court and to consult with the head tax payers and widows in order to find plaintiffs in the categories of head tax payer, widow and descendant of head tax payers. Through the efforts of the CCNC legal team, the Court Challenges Program granted $45,000 to pursue the court case.

At this time, Jonas Ma had moved to Toronto and became the CCNC National executive director. He contacted me to see if James Wing would be willing to be a plaintiff as the head tax payer in the case. I wanted assurances from the CCNC that James would be indemnified against any legal expenses or liabilities in case they lost. May Cheng responded that everyone involved must be prepared to take a risk.[231] I was not happy with this response, because

I wanted to shield James against court costs; after discussing the matter with him, I advised the CCNC that they should find a head tax payer who lived in Toronto and would be able to participate locally without having to travel from Montreal.

The CCNC then set out to select a team of plaintiffs in the class action case to represent the head tax payers, the widows and the descendants of head tax payers.

Avvy Go and Winnie Sanjoto, both from the National Redress Committee, met with Mary Eberts on March 22, 2000, and she agreed to act as counsel for the plaintiffs. A Harvard Law School graduate, Mary specialized in Charter and public law litigation related to human rights cases on behalf of women and minorities. In the meeting, Avvy brought up the concern of the possible financial burden to the plaintiffs and their families if they were assigned any court costs. Mary's opinion was that there would be no damage awarded against a losing plaintiff that was funded under Court Challenges. To further isolate the plaintiff against liability, it was proposed that Avvy's Chinese and South East Asian Legal Clinic be retained by the plaintiffs, and the clinic then retain Mary Eberts. Mary insisted that Avvy Go would act as co-counsel.

With Shack Jang Mack of Toronto signing on as the head tax payer plaintiff in the case, Quen Ying Lee of Ottawa signed on as the widow of a head tax payer. The court document stated that she was born in China in 1911, and was the widow of Guang Foo Lee, whom she had married in China in 1930. "Guang Foo Lee was born in China in 1892 and immigrated to Canada in 1913, paying a Head Tax of $500. He died in 1967."[232]

As for the descendant:

The plaintiff Yew Lee is the son of the late Guang Foo Lee and the plaintiff Quen Ying Lee. He was born in China in 1949. Because of the Chinese Immigration Act, 1923, the plaintiffs Quen Ying Lee and Yew Lee were unable to enter Canada until after the repeal of that statute in 1947. They immigrated to Canada in 1950 together with two other children in the family.[233]

After many years in the doldrums following the government's refusal to consider redress, we saw the court case as an opportunity to get the redress struggle back on track in front of our community. Public forums were held in Vancouver, Toronto and Montreal to sign people up for the three classes involved in the class action suit. Kenda Gee of the Edmonton Redress Committee started participating in the National Redress Committee, circulating a petition and obtaining more than two thousand signatures. NDP MP Libby Davies (Vancouver East) tabled the petition in Parliament on October 28, 2002. Sid Tan documented the public meetings and aired the footage on his cable TV program. Fundraising was undertaken in the community for the court case and to support the three plaintiffs. We got a second wind as the court case started to blow the redress sail forward.

Chapter 15

Coming in from the Wilderness (2001–6)

"Though fierce as tigers soldiers be,
   Battles are won by strategy."
   —Luo Guanzhong, *Romance of the Three Kingdoms*

On the morning of March 24, 2006, as I entered the lobby of the elegant, stately George Brown House in downtown Toronto, I noticed a statuesque woman in a flowery dress looking at her cell phone. I recognized her as Susan Eng,[234] a high-profile member of the Chinese community in Toronto. I walked towards her and introduced myself. "It's an honour to meet you," I said. "For those of us who've been struggling in the wilderness all these years, it's great to have someone like you getting involved. This is like coming in from the wilderness."

After three years of legal research and preparations, including numerous meetings with the plaintiffs, a court date was finally set for the class action suit on behalf of head tax payers, spouses and descendants—April 24–25, 2001. Much interest was stirred up in the media, especially the Chinese language press. Even the National Congress of Chinese Canadians had retained a

Toronto lawyer, Richard Woolsford, for the possibility of intervening in court during the Chinese Canadian National Council–backed case.[235]

In court, Mary Eberts and Avvy Go, the lawyers for the plaintiffs, argued that the discriminatory legislation "created profound and enduring racial prejudice against persons of Chinese descent in Canada," in violation of the Canadian Charter of Rights and Freedoms. Second, the government had benefitted from "unjust enrichment" due to the discriminatory laws for the head tax paid by 81,000 Chinese immigrants. (The face value of the $23 million in head tax is estimated at $1 billion today.)

The government lawyers contemptuously asked that the case be thrown out on the grounds that it was "frivolous, vexatious, or an abuse of power."

On July 9, 2001, Justice Peter Cumming rendered his judgment. The Charter, he said, "cannot apply retroactively or retrospectively." On the second argument of "unjust enrichment," the judge ruled that the various forms of the Chinese Immigration Act through the years were constitutional and therefore the enrichment was legal.

The case was dismissed. However, the justice also concluded that the legislation had been "patently discriminatory against persons of Chinese origin" and continued:

> By contemporary Canadian morals and values, these pieces of legislation were both repugnant and reprehensible. . . .
> It may well be that Parliament should consider providing redress for Chinese Canadians who paid the Head Tax or were adversely affected by the various *Chinese Immigration Acts*.[236]

The dismissal was not unexpected but we were encouraged by the judge's comments. However, to complete the legal process, the judgment was appealed to the Ontario Court of Appeal, which heard the case a year later, on June 10–11, 2002. It was then, on June 10, that Justice James Macpherson made an infamous remark from the bench: "The Chinese head tax payers were happy to be here and had already received redress through their ability to remain in Canada," he said. "Paying the head tax is made all worthwhile when one can see their granddaughter playing first string cello for the Toronto Symphony Orchestra."[237]

The stereotyping of the Chinese in Canada seemed to have reached the level of a learned judge.

The CCNC lodged a complaint to the Canadian Judicial Council against Justice Macpherson for his remarks. The council dismissed the complaint on October 28, 2002, stating:

> It is understandable that litigants who have experienced an injustice would be dismayed to see their attempt to seek redress aggressively questioned by the very judges who must rule on the matter. It is understandable, but it is an inevitable consequence of adversarial appellate advocacy. To the extent they (the remarks) have offended "any individual or group", he (the judge) has apologized.[238]

The Ontario Court of Appeal agreed with Justice Cumming's judgment and the appeal against the verdict in the class action suit was dismissed on September 13, 2002. As in the original case, no costs were awarded which meant that the plaintiffs did not have to pay court costs. The plaintiffs and their lawyers decided to ask for leave to argue the class action case at the Supreme Court of Canada, but on April 24, 2003, the Supreme Court issued a ruling not to hear the case. The legal process terminated at that point.

That was not the end of the Macpherson matter, however. In her excellent paper, "Playing Second Fiddle to Yo-Yo Ma," Avvy Go later wrote about how she felt at the time of Justice Macpherson's comments:

> While Ms. (Mary) Eberts, the plaintiffs' lead counsel, was trying her very best to point out to the learned judge that his comments were nothing more than "happy immigrant" stereotype, the other counsel, yours truly, a Chinese Canadian immigrant, was in so much anger that I had to control my urge to start screaming at the top of my lungs as if in doing so, I could make the judge understand how much his words were hurting me and the people in his courtroom.
>
> How ironic that it is at the very moment when members of a minority group are appealing to the conscience of our court to hear their sufferings and heed their call for justice, that they have to witness in first hand the utmost failure of our legal system to even acknowledge their status as a minority group and hence the inequality that they have experienced and continue to experience in our society.[239]

Further, Avvy wrote, "If Chinese Canadians were indeed doing well, perhaps it would have been easier to swallow this line of reasoning." But, she said, the reality was a lot different from the model minority myth:

> Just like all immigrants of colour, many Chinese immigrants are struggling in low-waged, non-unionized jobs. Those who came with professional background and post-secondary education are unable to practice the professions … because of systemic discrimination in the Canadian job market.[240]

* * *

Those involved in the Head Tax and Exclusion Act redress movement had all supported going to court. We had been feeling politically powerless without any access to government, and this method, we had felt, would garner some publicity and gain some sympathy from the public. People associated with the court case agreed that it was a long shot and had hoped that the use of the courts was a process that would rejuvenate the redress movement—which it did.

Working in parallel with the legal process, others were looking beyond the courts, believing full well that the litigation would produce empty results. Using the medium of email, a new generation of activists[241] with fresh energy was impatiently calling for a revival of the campaign in the political arena. This new group was untainted by the personal hostility between the CCNC and the NCCC.

In early 2001, feeling frustrated with the lack of progress at the national level, Alice Leung of the Edmonton chapter of the CCNC and Kenda Gee proposed a Redress Foundation composed of people from across the country free from the history of allegiances to either of the two existing national organizations. As was typical for Canada's regional divisions, they wanted to shift the centre of the redress universe from Toronto and put it in the Prairies and Quebec.

In a March 21, 2001 email to me, Avvy Go was quick to dismiss this idea. Avvy was an "old guard" of the CCNC and there was no way that she would work with people from the NCCC, which she believed was formed to undermine the CCNC and its redress and human rights work.[242] The critical mass of the redress movement was still in Toronto and Vancouver, where the majority of head tax families resided. Without their participation, an independent redress organization would not succeed. However, the idea percolated with me and other people who wanted a more aggressive approach to redress. This thinking would shortly result in a different organizational form.

In 2000, I had stepped back from the CCNC National Redress Committee (CCNC–NRC), feeling burnt out and disappointed with a lack of results. Walter Tom and Kenneth Cheung stepped up admirably as representatives from Montreal and Quebec in the CCNC–NRC.

In February 2001, Joseph Du, co-chair of the NCCC for the Prairies, phoned me from Winnipeg; he was coming to Montreal and wanted to meet May Chiu and me. He had read an article that May and I wrote calling for unity within our community around the redress issue. Meeting us with Jack Lee of Montreal, Joe Du wanted to know if we could form some kind of working relationship between the CCNC and the NCCC.

Joe Du and Jack Lee were well known among the NCCC organizations in Montreal's Chinatown, so every time Joe came into town, we would meet just outside Chinatown at the St. Hubert BBQ at Complexe Desjardins, as he feared being seen conspiring with CCNC operatives. We told Joe that we did not represent the CCNC and in fact, by this time, May and I had been very critical of the CCNC's lack of leadership and direction in the redress campaign.

We didn't think much would come out of this meeting, but we didn't know that in the NCCC, Du was waging a campaign to form a broader unity around redress. He invited me to address the tenth-anniversary annual conference of the NCCC in Toronto on September 1, 2001. I was rejuvenated with the thought of building a united front.

Prior to the conference, Du and I continued our discussions and agreed to a resolution that he would present. Du's resolution called for a common front of Chinese Canadian organizations around redress and the basis of this common front would include individual compensation for the surviving head tax payers or widows and compensation to a community foundation. Unfortunately, Du was not at the conference to defend his resolution. I suspected things hadn't gone his way with the national leadership.

In my speech, I urged conference delegates to take this opportunity to come together and push the government for justice for the individual head tax payers as well as for the community as a whole, trying to marry the positions of the CCNC and the NCCC. I tried to make it clear that I was there as the son and grandson of head tax payers and not as a member of the CCNC.

Immediately after the conference, I wrote a report that I circulated to the CCNC and independent redress activists. In the conclusion, I tried to put a positive spin on the conference:

> There is internal dissent inside the NCCC on redress, on the united front, and compensation issues. There are NCCC people in individual cities that we can work with, Montreal, Winnipeg, Edmonton and even Vancouver. The Vancouver delegate in his regional report mentioned the work of Victor Wong and the VACC (Vancouver Association of Chinese Canadians) as activities on the west coast.
>
> ... It is important to talk to people on the ground, face to face contacts with all spectrums of the community to develop a working relationship and to enhance unity.

Joe Du, Jack Lee, May Chiu and I continued to collaborate to develop a statement of unity, which we originally dubbed the "Quebec–Manitoba Declaration" and later renamed the "Unity Declaration" when other regions of Canada participated in the unity effort.

On the international front, Walter Tom went to the UN World Conference Against Racism in Durban, South Africa, in September 2001 to further publicize the redress campaign and to win international support. Edmonton's Kenda Gee kept the international redress flames burning with Poll Tax redress activists in New Zealand. The Edmonton Redress Committee issued a press statement on February 8, 2002, calling on the Canadian government to follow the example of New Zealand and apologize to Canadian head tax payers. A few days later, on the Lunar New Year (February 12), New Zealand Prime Minister Helen Clark formally apologized to Chinese New Zealanders for the Poll Tax.

I had made a mistake in *Moving the Mountain* in saying that Canada was the only country that had a head tax, as Kenda pointed out. He noted that both New Zealand and Canada took the idea of the racist tax from Australia, which he believed violated the treaty between China and the British Empire. "If Canada can borrow the white supremacist policies from another in history," he wrote, "surely, it can make the same effort to reconcile its mistakes from the action of another nation."[243]

Among redress events in 2002, the redress community was active in pursuing political action, with Kenda nurturing relationships with Canadian Alliance and Conservative politicians in Edmonton and Calgary.

Even though I didn't take part in many CCNC conference calls, I was still getting the minutes. The CCNC had firmed up the individual compensation at $20,000, which was a precedent number set by the Japanese Canadian redress and other settlements, such as for merchant seamen. The CCNC concentrated their efforts on Sheila Copps, heritage minister, who had promised to work on redress while she was in Opposition. Inky Mark, Canadian Alliance/Conservative MP for Dauphin, Manitoba, was collaborating with the NCCC to draft a private member's bill on redress. I convinced the CCNC leadership to contact Inky or they would be left behind. May Cheng, CCNC president, eventually did urge Inky to include compensation for the head tax payers and families in his bill (but he didn't do so).

* * *

"Demonstrations and rallies are the actions of the politically powerless,"[244] Gary Yee once said to me. He operated with the view that redress could only be won if we could win over to our side a political champion powerful enough to affect change. Nevertheless, a determined group of seniors from Montreal saw the need to take some action.

It was time for another head tax rally on Parliament Hill. This time, there were no head tax payers involved; now the marchers were the elderly descendants who were seeking redress for their families. New activists in Toronto, Ottawa and Montreal began organizing and mobilizing for the October 29, 2002 rally. May Chiu, who was at the time the executive director of the Montreal Chinese Family Service, organized the volunteers to fill up a bus, paid for

Demonstrators gather at an Ottawa head tax rally, October 29, 2002.

(Photo courtesy of CCNC)

by our activist businessman, Kenneth Cheung. The rally drew more than one hundred people.

May was critical of the CCNC speakers, who spoke only in English—she had to translate the speeches into Chinese for the elderly. The rally, though, drew a number of politicians, including Heritage Minister Sheila Copps, Multiculturalism Minister Jean Augustine and NDP MPs Margaret Mitchell and Alexa McDonough. Inside the House that afternoon, the rally was the subject of intervention by James Moore from the Canadian Alliance, and Bloc Québécois' Madeleine Dalphond-Guiral, who took the opportunity to again demand the Chrétien government resolve this long-standing issue.

After the rally, May Cheng and Yew Lee met with Copps and Augustine to try to convince the ministers to review the government's policy of "no apology, no compensation." At the meeting, the two ministers said they would be "willing to receive a proposal for redress from the CCNC."[245] Cynthia Pay, the new national president of the CCNC, sent a letter to Copps, attaching the latest CCNC proposal, which was similar to the one given to Sheila Finestone back in 1994, with the exception that the demand for compensation for widows and descendants was not explicitly stated. The issue of compensation for descendants had always been problematic for the CCNC and that led to various ambivalent positions throughout the years.

The 2002 CCNC proposal requested:

- Individual financial redress in the amount of $21,000 per claim, with specific eligibility criteria to be negotiated;
- Further individual redress of a symbolic nature, including:
    a. Letter of acknowledgment and regret from the prime minister of Canada to each holder of a head tax certificate, including the surviving spouse or descendants in circumstances where the head tax payer is deceased; and
    b. Gold Mountain coin in the denomination of $500; and
    c. Other non-financial redress to be negotiated; and
- Community or collective redress—with a focus on educational, social and cultural activities or programs, and in particular, projects which are beneficial to seniors or which promote anti-racism and cross-cultural understanding.

A month later, on December 10, Inky Mark tabled his private member's bill C-333, calling on the government to negotiate with the National Congress of Chinese Canadians on restitution, without any mention of other organizations and without raising the issue of individual compensation to the victims of the Head Tax and Exclusion Act. Derek Lee, a Liberal MP from Toronto, had also proposed a private member's bill to resolve head tax redress a decade beforehand without any success.

By late 2002, the Montreal Redress Committee had grown weary of the Toronto-centric CCNC leadership and met to discuss what needed to be done to move the struggle forward.[246] Nevertheless, we affirmed the legitimacy of the National Redress Committee and the participation of the CCNC as an equal member of the national committee, since we knew unity at this time was critical. We set to work on coalition building with organizations and individuals in our community to support the NRC. This coalition would include individual members of the NCCC and local organizations belonging to the NCCC that shared our views.

We reaffirmed our position to demand redress and compensation for the head tax payers, as well as for the widows and first-generation descendants or to the estate of the deceased head tax payers. This latter point of the estate was at Kenneth Cheung's insistence; he asserted that descendants of the head tax payers also suffered from the immoral laws and deserved compensation.

We disagreed with the CCNC's November 12, 2002 position paper that seemed to be soft on the demand to compensate widows and descendants. We knew there were only a handful of head tax payers still alive across Canada, so we wanted to maintain the individual human presence of the widows and direct descendants as living survivors of the Head Tax and Exclusion Act and to present their names and faces to the public. We pegged the dollar amount for individual compensation at no less than $20,000, an amount awarded in other redress situations. We didn't think much of Inky Mark's private member's bill, and preferred just to let it die a natural death. We tried several times to get Paul Martin to visit James Wing, who was now residing at a seniors' residence in Martin's LaSalle riding.

* * *

Strategists in the redress movement saw 2003 as a good year to build momentum by taking advantage of the federal government's gradual decline into disarray. Prime Minister Jean Chrétien was embroiled in the sponsorship scandal early in the year, and in a bitter internal struggle with supporters of Finance Minister Paul Martin. Chrétien was becoming a lame duck.

May Chiu and I continued our discussions with Joe Du through his frequent visits to Montreal, telephone calls and emails. I drafted a declaration, which I asked Joe to endorse. He still maintained the position that by not asking for individual compensation, we could unite the community around collective redress. May and I were just as stubborn that the actual victims of the Head Tax and Exclusion Act must be compensated as a matter of justice. I remember in a moment of exasperation I said to Joe, "If we don't win redress for our elders, the community deserves nothing."

May, from her position at Chinese Family Service and as a leader in Chinatown, continued to work with individuals and organizations associated with the NCCC. After a meeting with some NCCC people from the Chinese YMCI and the Montreal Chinese United Centre, she was convinced that we should be working with them on redress based on two simple principles of unity:

1. Support the Congress demand for an apology and collective compensation;
2. Congress will not oppose the head tax payers and descendants' efforts to claim individual compensation.

In an email to May, I said, "The problem lies with the Toronto people from both sides, Congress and CCNC with animosity going way back." Ever the naive optimist, I added: "If we can break the Toronto stranglehold, then we have a good chance of success before Chrétien leaves office."[247]

Meanwhile in Toronto, the CCNC leadership was intensifying its lobbying efforts with the Liberal leadership hopefuls, targeting Paul Martin as the heir apparent. Yew Lee and Jonas Ma were based in Ottawa so they had some access to Martin's political aides. They had set up a meeting with Paul Martin on March 25, 2003. (The day before that, the CCNC delegation met with Sheila Copps, another leadership hopeful, but nothing much came out of that meeting.)

Before the Martin meeting, we did our homework. Yew and Jonas met with Kevin Bosch, director of research for Martin, and the CCNC people in Toronto met with Carolyn Bennett, a Toronto MP who was a strong supporter of Martin. Bennett was a friend of Mary Eberts and sympathetic to the CCNC.

Both Bosch and Bennett told us to stress nation building and the legacy of Paul Martin Sr.

We met in Martin's office; Bosch was with him. In the CCNC contingent were Yew Lee, Avvy Go, Winxie Tse, Victor Wong and, from Montreal, Kenneth Cheung and me. From my notes, this is how I recall the thirty-minute meeting, with Martin asking basic questions like how many people were affected by the Head Tax and Exclusion Act and when did it end:

> Then he asked, "Your definition of redress is a cash payment?" It was obvious that he was ill informed about this aspect of Canadian history. The delegation proceeded to explain to him the history of the HTEA and the urgency of redress for the Chinese Canadian community and for Canadian society. Martin's response, "The Chinese are not the only people to whom a wrong was done. I do not want this to be the flavour of the month where Government is making an apology to a different group each week. I do not want to have cheapened apologies."
>
> Martin talked about the nation-building legacy of his father and that his greatest pride was in the work Martin Sr. did on the Citizenship Act.

If I'd known then what I know now, I would have confronted him on Order in Council (PC) 2115, retained by the Liberal cabinet, of which Martin Sr. was a part. It stipulated that only Chinese immigrants who were citizens (not a requirement for other immigrants) were allowed to bring their immediate families to Canada, and it was kept in place after the repeal of the Exclusion Act. But, to continue with my notes:

> I raised again the possibility of meeting with James Wing, a constituent in his LaSalle riding. He asked me to contact his riding office. Then he said, "I think Mr. Wing has been wronged. ... Whatever we do, it has to involve a change in the Canadian psyche; I don't think a cash payment does a lot for the Canadian psyche." The meeting concluded with Martin challenging us to frame redress in terms of nation building.

Not much came out of the Martin meeting other than presenting the redress issue to him in person. But we got the measure of the man; he was

Meeting with Paul Martin, March 25, 2003. Standing in front of Martin, front left to right, are Kenneth Cheung, Winxie Tse, Yew Lee, Avvy Go, William Dere and Victor Wong. (William Dere Collection)

not sympathetic. Paul Martin was still stuck in the mindset of "no apology, no compensation."

Two months later, May 2003 proved to be an inauspicious time for Asian Heritage Month. Sheila Copps' Heritage Canada produced and distributed a poster with Asian caricatures, one with a coolie hat and several with slanty, slitty eyes. There was uproar from the Asian Canadian communities, who demanded the withdrawal of the poster and an apology from the minister. Writing in *The Globe and Mail*, Susan Eng said:

> Now that I see the poster, I understand why this government has been so recalcitrant on the head-tax issue. A mindset that infantilizes and caricatures whole communities of people sets the stage for easy dismissal when some of them make claims for redress. ... Our government has not yet learned from its past."[248]

Susan also had some choice words for Vivienne Poy, former governor general Adrienne Clarkson's sister-in-law and a Liberal appointed senator, who had pushed to implement May as Asian Heritage Month. "Luckily, Senator Poy also thought it a good idea to e-invite community groups to join in this month's celebrations and circulate the poster with a helpful link to the Heritage Canada Web site," she wrote, "so more of us saw the disgraceful poster than would have otherwise. ... For her part, Senator Poy assured the readers of the *Edmonton Journal* that she does not have 'slit eyes.'"[249]

Tony Chan, author of *Gold Mountain: The Chinese in the New World*, also commented on the poster controversy through an email to the redress network, in his usual colourful style, saying in part:

> if you assess the poster closely, it reveals an overt attempt to infantize asian canadians.
>
> representing visible minorities or women [as] children is at the heart of white colonialism and an attempt to reinforce dominance of *whiteness* as the arbiter of acceptability.
>
> so the asian canadians who suggest that this is merely a "small" matter have already bought into the notion that *whiteness* rules."[250]

* * *

The CCNC reaction to Montreal's efforts at building a redress coalition was lukewarm. There was concern that the CCNC would lose the leadership in the redress campaign. "If we are going to form a Coalition, the key determination for participation must be whether or not the groups/individuals support individual compensation," a CCNC document stated.[251]

Instead of looking within the community to build a coalition, the CCNC decided to look outside to form a new group, Canadians for Redress. The CCNC leadership was counting on Jack Layton, the newly minted head of the NDP, to headline this loosely knitted assembly of redress supporters. This was not what May Chiu and I had in mind.

Upon the recommendation of Kenda Gee, Karen Cho, a recent graduate from the Concordia film program, approached me in March 2003 to be a subject in a film she hoped to make about the head tax. It was to be an update on the redress movement since *Moving the Mountain*. I thought this would be a great opportunity to get the redress story into the mainstream public media and I helped to link up Karen to the redress network.

Throughout the spring, I worked with Joe Du to finalize the important sounding Quebec–Manitoba Declaration. The five points of the statement, later to be known as the Unity Declaration, were:

1. The Canadian government shall immediately and unconditionally begin negotiations with the National Organizations and representatives of the Chinese Canadian community to redress the Head Tax and Chinese Exclusion Act. This includes the CCNC and the NCCC.

2. The Canadian government shall offer an apology and redress by providing community compensation, the nature of which shall be negotiated between the government and Chinese Canadian community representatives.

3. The Canadian government shall offer an apology and redress the individual effects of the Head Tax by compensating the surviving Head Tax Payers and the surviving spouses of deceased Head Tax Payers.

4. We call on all Chinese Canadian community organizations and individuals to respect the rights and actions of all those affected by the Head Tax and Exclusion Act who may want to seek individual compensation from the Canadian government.

5. We call on all Canadians to support the redress campaign of the Chinese Canadian community. In winning redress of this long-standing injustice, our community will contribute to building justice and equality for all Canadians.

The negotiation centred on point number four. Joe Du wanted to soften the words related to respecting "the rights and actions" of the victims to seek individual compensation. In the end, the wording as it stood prevailed. I distributed the declaration to the CCNC affiliates and Du did the same with the NCCC organizations. Winxie Tse, president of the CCNC, responded, "We are concerned that there does not appear to be consensus on this issue with some of the member chapters as well as with some members of the Redress Committee.[252]

In the end, CCNC National never signed the unity document. Gary Yee later told me that there was heated debate over the statement but there was no support.[253] Nevertheless, May Chiu got Chung Tang, executive director of the Toronto Chapter of the CCNC,[254] to endorse it.

The NCCC National also did not sign on, but Joe Du and Jack Lee had better success with their local associations. Du received the endorsement of Philip Lee, chair of the Winnipeg branch of the Chinese Benevolent Association. (Lee was to become Manitoba's lieutenant governor in 2009.) Philip Chang of the Winnipeg Chinese Cultural Centre also endorsed the agreement. In Montreal, Timothy Chan of the Hoy Sun Association signed on and Walter Tom did his magic with the Hum/Tom/Tam family associations to get their endorsements. We also received support from Cynthia Lam of the CCNC affiliate in Montreal, the Chinese Family Service.

Despite CCNC's past groundbreaking work in the redress movement, Montreal, Edmonton and Winnipeg did not think the CCNC had anything new to offer or that it could lead the community to the next level of the redress campaign. In mid-2003, via email and teleconference, we began to discuss forming a new redress coalition based on the principles stated in the Unity Declaration. Kenda Gee won over May Lui in Halifax and I contacted the redress activists in Newfoundland. Around the beginning of September, we formed the Chinese Canadian Redress Alliance (CCRA) as a united front coalition. We had representatives in Halifax, Montreal, Toronto, Winnipeg, Edmonton, Calgary and Vancouver.

* * *

The Chinese Canadian Redress Alliance came into being just in time to attach its name to a report prepared by May Chiu and presented to Doudou Diène, the United Nations special rapporteur on contemporary forms of racism, racial discrimination, xenophobia and related intolerance. The special rapporteur was on a ten-day tour of Canada to hear cases related to his purview.

In her September 17, 2003 submission, May laid out the history of the Head Tax and Exclusion Act and the modern-day struggle for redress including the court action. She included the Unity Declaration to show the demands of the community and the names of the supporters. Since the Chinese community had exhausted all local remedies in the two decades since the campaign started, the CCRA submission asked the UN special rapporteur to

1. *Receive and Investigate* complaints from the Chinese Canadian community, head tax payers, wives, widows, and family members, and their representatives about the violations of their basic human

rights caused by various *Chinese Immigration Acts* and *Chinese Exclusion Act* whose effects continue to this day;

2. *Inquire* why the Canadian Government has neither acknowledged that it had violated the basic human rights of the Chinese Canadian community and individual head tax payers and their families nor entered into negotiations to begin reparations;

3. *Recommend* that the Canadian Government immediately enter into negotiations with the Chinese Canadian community, individual head tax payers and their families, and their representatives on the form of redress they have the right to receive for the human rights violations they have suffered.

Unbeknown to us at the time, the CCNC and the Metro Toronto Chinese and Southeast Asian Legal Clinic also presented a submission when the special rapporteur reached Toronto on September 25.[255] It urged the special rapporteur to

recommend to the Canadian Government to redress this historical injustice as it was perpetuated against the Chinese Canadian community, particularly on the individuals who have paid the $500 Head Tax, and were subject to the 24 years of discrimination under the Exclusion Act.

I later discovered that there was a third submission to the special rapporteur by Noah Novogrodsky of the University of Toronto Faculty of Law, International Human Rights Clinic.[256] It asked the special rapporteur to recommend that Canada offer restitution for the $23 million rightfully belonging to the Chinese Canadian head tax payers.

* * *

The National Congress of Chinese Canadians held its twelfth Annual Convention on Joe Du's home ground, on September 12–14, 2003. Once again, he invited me to attend as a speaker on redress. Thinking about what happened at the NCCC convention in Toronto two years earlier, I asked myself whether I was a glutton for punishment.

Du finally convinced me when he said Kenda Gee, May Chiu and Walter Tom were also invited to speak in order to strengthen our numbers. In the end, both Kenda and May decided not to go, although their names were left on the speakers' list. May wanted us to stress our role as a "third way" instead of unifiers of old rivals.

Walter and I were committed to go; we saw it as an opportunity to build the redress coalition. I would also get a chance to meet Daniel Lai from the University of Calgary who contributed to the final wording of the Unity Declaration. I got the organizers to invite Karen Cho, who around this time won the NFB's Reel Diversity Competition to make her film on the redress movement.

I spoke at the plenary session "Head Tax – Re-visit." The title of my speech was "The Unity Declaration and New Strategies for Redress." I went all out to gain as much support as I could around the unity statement and to forge a redress united front. I even name-dropped Paul Martin, knowing that this audience would be suitably impressed even by our fleeting get-together with the soon-to-be prime minister. "The first step in responding to Paul Martin's challenge to our community is to come together and present a united front to the government," I said, continuing:

> Many in our community who have dedicated many years in fighting for redress are doubtful about being able to unite. They are telling me that I am wasting my time here. But how can we respond to Martin's challenge of nation building if we cannot build unity within our community?
>
> I have been working on Redress for over 15 years because I owe it to my father and grandfather. ... I owe it to my mother who is still alive. She suffered through 3 decades of separation from my father due to the Exclusion Act. My father was a founding president of the Chiu Lun Gong Sol in Montreal. This family association is part of the NCCC today. In the streets of Montreal's Chinatown, I have been able to work with members of both the NCCC and the CCNC. There is no reason why this working relationship and coming together of our community cannot continue at the national leadership level.

Raymond Yao, the Chinese language *Ming Pao* Ottawa correspondent, asked me for an advance copy of my speech for "a story on this historic alliance amongst the like-minded leaders from both the CCNC and NCCC."[257]

I was pleased to receive Karen Cho's reaction to my speech, too. She was unburdened with the baggage of Chinese community politics. "Your speech on Sunday was very powerful and moving," she said. "I believe you succeeded in influencing and educating a lot of people. A step in the right direction."

As in 2001, I wrote a summary of the 2003 convention, including the following:

> Overall, I thought we took one step forward. Dr. Du is more convinced that we are doing the right thing, although heavy pressure was put on him. Raymond Yao told me that the Congress leadership met late into the night on what they should do. They were saying that they would have to change the 1991 resolution of no individual compensation. But they needed to hang onto that resolution because they staked their whole redress career on it. ...
>
> I met Moe Levy of the Museum for Human Rights that got a grant of $30M from Heritage Canada and a potential for $70M more for a total of $100M. I asked him how, when the Chinese couldn't get a paltry $23M symbolic refund. He said united political pressure. I used that in my speech, but I didn't say that most of that pressure came from [well-connected media magnate] Izzy Asper.

* * *

A breath of fresh air blew through the redress movement when the CCNC National kicked off its Last Spike campaign, centred around a donation from prominent author Pierre Berton.

Berton donated a railroad spike to the CCNC in 2003; it was one of three hundred that were distributed to VIPs at the CPR's last spike ceremony at Craigellachie, marking the completion of the cross-country railway, in 1885. The Last Spike campaign kicked off in Halifax on September 12, 2003, then travelled across Canada with meetings along the way and wrapped up in Vancouver on November 7, the date of the original last spike ceremony in 1885.

In a news release to launch the campaign, Berton said:

> The last spike marked the end of a nation-building project in Canada. It also signified the beginning of a shameful era of the exclusion of Chinese immigrants. Let this new journey of the last spike bring about the rebuilding of our nation by redressing our past wrongs towards Chinese-Canadians.[258]

Avvy Go travelled with the spike to Western Canada, stopping in Calgary and Winnipeg, where a meeting was held on October 26, with several organizations[259] participating and the support of the Winnipeg mayor. Joe Du also attended, with a group of NCCC members.

The year 2003 ended with a flurry of activities in Montreal. The Last Spike finally arrived and Walter Tom organized a student debate on redress around the symbolic spike. On November 26, we organized a luncheon to honour our pioneers in the family associations and the tongs in Montreal. The highlight was a stirring speech by James Wing, now a frail ninety-one-year-old. CCNC, NCCC members as well as "the third option" CCRA attended the luncheon. Kenneth Cheung, now the national chair of the CCNC, and Christian Samfat of the Chinese Neighbourhood Society proudly displayed the spike. The event was filmed by the NFB for Karen Cho's film as well as by the Global TV series *Past Lives*, which was featuring my family in one of its episodes.

At a Center for Research-Action on Race Relations luncheon, May Chiu and I met with two of the more progressive senators, Mobina Jaffer of BC and Donald Oliver of Nova Scotia. Both were very sympathetic and urged us to continue our efforts to put united political pressure on the government. May also met with Marlene Jennings, who was rumoured to be in Paul Martin's cabinet, to prep her on redress.

I distributed the Unity Declaration as widely as I could, proposing a National Redress Conference to map out a two- to three-year plan to win redress. I pursued Victor Wong, now national executive director of the CCNC in Toronto, to support the Unity Declaration. Victor insisted that we support another proposal called the CCNC Last Spike Resolution, with demands similar to the 2002 CCNC proposal mentioned above. However, I knew that the Last Spike Resolution would not garner much support outside CCNC circles and that the Unity statement was more inclusive of other opinions. Looking back with hindsight today, it seems somewhat ridiculous that the community organizations were divided over such small differences.

I can't move on from this time without telling a very revealing story of the behind-the-scenes antagonists who pulled the strings to oppose the settlement of redress. A Canadian Press article reported in 2003 that federal bureaucrats had advised Heritage Minister Sheila Copps not to apologize or compensate Ukrainian Canadians for their internment during World War I. "Documents obtained under the Access to Information Act show federal officials were concerned that a deal with the Ukrainians would spark demands from other ethnic groups."[260] I should point out that back in 1990 when Copps was still young, idealistic and untainted by power, she voiced strong support for head tax redress.[261] But it seems she didn't have the ability to act against her deputy ministers. Again, it would take some bold political leadership to overcome the resistance of the federal bureaucracy.

In a year-end email touting the third path of the CCRA, I wrote that the campaign "belongs to the community and all those who wish to get involved and push it forward. … We must all have the freedom to participate and speak out on behalf of the head tax payers and their families."

* * *

In 2004, federal politics was in turmoil and people were getting tired and dragging their feet around redress. Paul Martin had become prime minister on December 12, 2003, when Jean Chrétien resigned in the midst of the sponsorship scandal.[262] Martin then lost his majority in the June 28, 2004 elections, but returned as prime minister with a minority government. The Martin administration was wearing us down by simply refusing to talk. Paul Martin revealed his true self by not even acknowledging our invitations to meet with the only surviving head tax payer in his riding, James Wing.

In April, UN Special Rapporteur Doudou Diène released his report, part of which discussed the Head Tax and Exclusion Act. He recommended that "the Canadian government consult with members of the Chinese Canadian community to examine possibilities of compensation with the people who were affected, including the head tax payers, descendants and other members of their families."

This report received national and international attention.

As the *Pacific Citizen*, the national publication of the Japanese American Citizens League, reported: "The government's response to the UN recommendations was the same as it has been for the last ten years: No." It continued:

Minister of Multiculturalism Jean Augustine (said) to the Pacific Citizen, "In terms of the section dealing with the redress, I can only repeat that Canada decided to put closure to the issue and that being no financial compensation for historical acts."

"The pictures that the government is giving of racial harmony is different from the community's," Diène said. "They (the community) have expressed experiences of racism."[263]

You can imagine the reaction to the government's stonewalling and ongoing policy of no talk, no redress from the redress campaigners. The *Pacific Citizen* article quoted Kenda Gee, chair of the Edmonton Redress Committee, as saying, "Jean Augustine's parrot of the 'official government' policy is completely unacceptable" and that "the remarks ... merely underline the ignorance or willful blindness of this issue that is prevalent among our Ottawa bureaucrats and officials."[264]

As we plodded along, I felt that every bit of national and international pressure and exposure would help to move the campaign forward.

By September, Karen Cho, a fifth-generation Canadian of mixed heritage, was wrapping up her documentary, the final title of which became *In the Shadow of Gold Mountain*. Through the film, Karen discovered how the Chinese half of her family wasn't welcome in Canada, while this country encouraged and rewarded the European half of her family to settle here. The documentary featured James Wing, Chow Quen Lee and Vancouver's Gim Wong, a World War II veteran who witnessed his parents' "brutal struggle" to pay off their head tax debt.

The film premiered in Montreal on September 24 in a joint presentation of the National Film Board and the Chinese Canadian Redress Alliance at the Chinese Catholic Mission in Chinatown. The event attracted four hundred people who jammed into the mission's auditorium. The audience was a cross-section of the community with many elderly and many young people. Yew Lee drove in from Ottawa, James Wing said a few inspiring words, and Karen was there to answer questions and to animate the discussion afterwards. There were representatives from the city and from Quebec's Ministry of Immigration. Parti Québécois MNAs Louise Harel and Elsie Lefebvre attended in person. Montreal MPs Irwin Cotler, Marlene Jennings and Raymonde Folco sent support letters.

CCNC National also sent a message of solidarity. We saw the momentum building as the evening well on; after the screening, 292 people signed the petition circulated by the Edmonton Committee. Many people signed up to join the CCRA or asked to be kept informed.

The National Film Board worked with the CCRA to organize screenings across Canada. Much to our chagrin, CCNC National did not organize a screening in Toronto. In the Greater Toronto Area, Nancy Siew and Simon Cheng stepped in to present the film as part of the United Way of York Region fundraising.

Maybe it was because May Chiu had withdrawn the Chinese Family Service from the CCNC, or because the Edmonton chapter had pulled out of the CCNC National, but at a screening of the film at the University of Alberta, there was a run-in with a white supporter of the CCNC who came in from Toronto. He would not allow literature from the CCRA or the petition from the Edmonton Redress Committee to be distributed at the event, saying that it was from "outsiders." Needless to say, we were quite upset with this sectarian action.

Kenda, who was chair of the Edmonton Redress Committee, was moved to pen an email to Gary Yee, who was no longer officially associated with the CCNC but was still considered the elder statesman of the redress movement. Kenda informed Gary that the Edmonton Committee would regrettably stop supporting future CCNC activities.[265]

In the Shadow of Gold Mountain gave people a boost in the campaign and became a tool for organizing.

While May Chiu and I were distributing leaflets to attract people to the Montreal presentation, we ran into Jonas Ma, who was in town to visit his mother. Jonas joined us in the leafleting and we had a long discussion on what steps to take to move forward. In an email to me later, Jonas noted that we had spoken about "the urgency, priority and time-framework" for all stakeholders. "Most urgent, highest priority and immediate," he said, were the surviving head tax payers and their spouses—"so that they can see justice in their life." He continued:

> 2) Second most urgent: HT descendants to present a position to the government after a funded and self-managed process of consultation within a year or so;
> 3) Third in term of urgency, priority and probably long-term: community compensation with community-wide consultation. ... [T]his kind of discussion is only meaningful if the government is willing to negotiate.[266]

In responding to Jonas—and agreeing with his three points and priorities—I noted that if we didn't achieve redress for the surviving head tax payers and widows, his points two and three would be irrelevant because what right would the community have to take this money? "Compensation, first and foremost must go to the direct victims, the ones who built our community and won the right for all of us to be here," I wrote, continuing:

> Now the question is how do we win justice for our elders in the short time we have. … We want justice for our pioneers who were direct victims of racism and who suffered tremendous hardship due to that racism. This is clear. There is no other way of seeing this.[267]

The Ottawa film screening was set for November 3 at the Library and Archives Canada screening room. The National Film Board sent out invitations to all the MPs and senators. Jonas and the organizers didn't want to feature any politicians as speakers since Karen Cho and Yew Lee would be on hand to carry the discussion. Ray Yao followed the Montreal and Ottawa events closely and gave the film extensive coverage in *Ming Pao*.

In the Shadow of Gold Mountain was a tool to help galvanize the community around redress from its premiere in September 2004 to well into 2005. Public screenings were organized from Halifax to Vancouver, and people used the film to educate themselves on the Head Tax and Exclusion Act redress and to begin local mobilization to join the redress efforts. In addition, the film received national media exposure with its broadcasts on the CBC and its cable TV news channel, Newsworld. Even though *Moving the Mountain* was a groundbreaking film that kick-started some activists to become involved in the movement, *In the Shadow* was a timely film and became the tool for the redress movement that *Moving the Mountain* never was. Due to its patronage by the National Film Board and the CBC, it reached more Canadians and brought the history of the head tax into the mainstream.

* * *

In the second half of 2004, those of us in the redress movement began debating among ourselves whether to revise our stand on fighting for compensation for descendants. By this point, we had been banging our heads against government obstinacy and cold-heartedness for twenty years.

The first descendants were people like Yew Lee and me, the sons of head tax payers. The second descendants were the grandchildren like Gary Yee,

Victor Wong, Walter Tom and Kenda Gee. We knew that, as the many lawyers in our movement would say, time was of the essence for our surviving head tax payers and widows. By this time we had become more pragmatic and flexible. Even May Chiu—who was not a descendant, but who waged the good fight because of the principles of equality—agreed and she put the thoughts down articulately in an email:

> I feel like I'm cutting off a leg, but at this late stage of the game, I'm prone to say let the descendants fight for their own compensation. We don't have much time left for the survivors and adding descendants would leave the door wide open to the floodgates argument. In speaking with the community, when we say that our priority is the survivors and widows, there is a lot more sympathy because there are so few left.... Maybe when all the survivors and widows have died, you can advocate compensation for the descendants.[268]

Around this time, I learned from Joe Du that Raymond Chan, the newly appointed secretary of state for multiculturalism, would be attending the annual convention of the National Congress of Chinese Canadians in Victoria on September 18. My suspicious nature led me to fire off an email of warning to redress activists.

In the email, I stated that Chan seemed to be cozying up to the NCCC and that he and the NCCC might strike a symbolic deal on redress (community funds, medals, trinkets, etc.) at the expense of the head tax payers and widows. I wrote further that this was the most opportunistic and expedient course of action for the government and it would use the NCCC as the conduit to legitimize the deal. The government would parade its Chinese contingent of Vivienne Poy and Raymond Chan to tout this "historical" settlement. I stressed that if the government did offer this kind of proposal, which the community had rejected twelve years ago, we would need to develop an appropriate response.

I repeated the CCRA priorities that I had expressed to Jonas Ma: (1) immediate settlement and justice for the surviving head tax payers and widows, and (2) future negotiations with community representatives for eventual community redress. I finished the email by saying, "This is the kind of pre-emptive position we need to get through to Raymond Chan before he misleads the community into a symbolic settlement."

Joe Du boasted to Kenda in a September 18 email: "We control Raymond Chan now." But a short year later, we would discover how Chan, Paul Martin and the NCCC had struck a deal; we would not be sure then who was controlling whom.

Towards the end of 2004, we were getting a little impatient with our lack of results. In an email to Kenda and others, I listed a couple of items that had come out of a Montreal HTEA redress committee meeting. Paul Martin, in meeting with the editorial boards of the Chinese media in Montreal, had given "the same evasive answer he gave nearly two years ago when I met him" on redress, I wrote, claiming that the community was divided on the issue, and that he didn't know what the community wanted. I added: "Looks like the message has not yet gotten through his thick head or the collective thick-headedness of his staff." The other item was about "the scuttlebut" that when Raymond Chan and Viv Poy attended the NCCC meeting in Victoria, "a proposal was floated to give a settlement package of $23M–$25M to the community as an endowment fund, which would dish out some money to the surviving HT payers and spouses." The NCCC, I added, was "hoping this compromise would settle individual and community compensation."

Others, like Walter Tom, weren't feeling as burnt out as me. With enthusiasm, Walter continued to make the rounds with the elected politicians, including Liberal MP Raymonde Folco, who, Walter wrote in an email, "understood the urgency of the situation and supported our position that the survivors and their widows should not be held hostage to community politics." In a Montreal community forum with Raymond Chan, Walter joined Jack Lee and Tim Chan of the NCCC in presenting a "united front requesting individual and community redress for the HTEA." He also reported that the City of Montreal administration had "accepted to put forward a resolution recognizing the contributions of early Chinese Canadian pioneers ... and supporting Redress, using as a basis the CCNC resolution adopted by BC and Vancouver in 1992."[269]

* * *

The year 2005 would be a pivotal year for the redress movement. (Foreseeing this, Kenda Gee had told me by email at the end of 2004: "In 2005, redress will be won or lost."[270])

By February 2005, James Wing's health had deteriorated noticeably. He was now 93. On Valentine's Day, May Chiu sent another letter to Paul Martin to inform him of James' failing health and ask him to visit James—now the only surviving head tax payer—in Martin's LaSalle riding. I don't know if Martin ever responded to that letter, but I do know that he never visited James.

On March 27, through Walter Tom's hard work, the Chinese Canadian Redress Alliance, along with a number of other organizations including NCCC members, held a ceremony at city hall to recognize the contributions of the early Chinese pioneers to the city. Montreal had formally passed a resolution of support calling for redress and compensation for the Head Tax and Exclusion Act. More than two hundred guests from the different Chinese ethnocultural organizations as well as representatives from the three levels of government attended. A representative of the Chinese embassy was also there.

Mayor Gerald Tremblay made a strong and passionate speech recognizing the contributions of Chinese Canadian pioneers and lent his voice in support of redress. Certificates of honour were presented to the various institutions and individuals from the community. My mother was one of those awarded a certificate. Now in her hundredth year, she was too weak to attend the ceremony, so my daughter, Jessica, received the certificate and spoke on behalf of her grandmother.

Gim Foon Wong also made a mark in 2005. A passionate, outspoken man with an unquenchable thirst for justice for the head tax families, he wanted to make his contribution to the redress movement, so he decided to ride his motorcycle across Canada at age eighty-three, to publicize the redress campaign.

Gim was a World War II veteran. During the war, he wanted to be a fighter pilot and tried several times to enroll in the air force. Initially, he was refused, as Canada did not want to accept Asians into the armed forces. Eventually, short of manpower, the air force accepted Gim in 1943 and trained him as a tailgunner, one of the most dangerous jobs. Gim excelled in his training and was later promoted to flight engineer, a commissioned officer. He chuckled to himself every time a non-Chinese person had to salute him.[271]

Gim's feisty, scrappy personality was shaped by his humble beginnings. His father arrived in Canada in 1906 and paid the $500 head tax. His mother arrived in 1921 and also had to pay the $500. Like most other Chinese immigrants at the time, the burden of repaying the head tax debt kept the family in poverty. (Gim was featured in Karen Cho's 2004 film, *In the Shadow of Gold Mountain*, and Kenda Gee's 2012 award-winning documentary, *Lost Years*.)

In June 2005, Gim and his son Jeffrey began their preparations for the "ride for redress." Jeffrey would follow Gim in a camper van. They estimated about a month on the road at a cost of about $5,000, which they hoped the sponsor CCNC would help to fundraise.

As he had planned, Gim reached Ottawa on Canada Day; he stopped his motorcycle at the steps of Parliament, and unfurled a small banner that simply said, "I am Canadian." He then waited for Prime Minister Martin to arrive. Miro Cernetig, in the *Vancouver Sun*, described the scene:

> "I got within 15 feet of him," says Wong, shaking his head ruefully at the memory of his one-man effort to penetrate the prime ministerial bubble. "We let his office know I was coming. But the RCMP pounced on me. I never got to meet Paul Martin."[272]

The next day, Martin missed another golden opportunity to show his respect for the Chinese Canadian community when Gim arrived in Montreal. He was a unifying force for the redress activists of the CCRA, CCNC and the NCCC as well as local politicians, as they all came out to welcome him. Montreal had raised enough money to pay for this last leg of his ride plus the airfare to take him home. Gim was physically and emotionally wiped out when he

Gim Wong on his motorcycle in front of Montreal's city hall on July 2, 2005. At left Kenneth Cheung, national chair, CCNC; second left is Jack Lee, co-chair, NCCC; fifth left is Timothy Chan, president, Hoy Sun Association; next to Gim, Marcel Tremblay, city councillor; front right, Walter Tom, co-chair, CCRA. (Photo courtesy of Walter Tom)

reached Montreal and he was in no condition for a road trip home. His son drove the camper towing the motorcycle back to Vancouver.

Despite the opposition of other Chinese Canadian veterans, Gim felt strongly that fighting for redress of the Head Tax and Exclusion Act was the Canadian thing to do. The fact that he was a veteran, lending his voice to redress, gave the campaign credibility and a different profile to counter the fear of backlash emanating from the more timid sectors of the community. We all agreed that Gim's ride invigorated the movement to continue its efforts for the next crucial stage of the struggle.[273]

The excitement of Gim Wong's ride for redress would sustain us into the autumn.

In August, the CCRA began to discuss our demands and to develop a work plan because we were hearing within the community that something was afoot. Our old friends Raymond Chan, Inky Mark and his accomplice Bev Oda were engaged in behind-the-scenes discussion with the NCCC. The cozying up of Chan and the NCCC was producing some results. Conservative Bev Oda on November 4 introduced her private member's bill, Chinese Canadian Recognition and Redress Act, C-333, a revival of Inky Mark's bill that called for the government to negotiate with the NCCC only, without any mention of compensation for the head tax payers or their families. Mark's original bill had died in 2002.

The CCRA vigorously denounced C-333 when it was first revived, calling it the "Chinese Canadian Non-Recognition and Non-Redress Act." In a press release, we said it represented a "devious and cynical attempt to curry favour with some members of the Chinese Canadian community," and went on to say that the bill did not redress "the actual victims" who had suffered due to the Head Tax and Chinese Exclusion Act. "There are head tax payers and widows still alive today. They have not been consulted in this process. They are victimized and excluded once again."[274]

We said this was an attempt of the government to divide the Chinese community by singling out only one organization.

Oda's bill did not pass but the Martin government tried to use it as a cover to cut a deal with the NCCC and hoodwink the Chinese Canadian community. The Acknowledgement, Commemoration and Education (ACE) program was a slush fund of $25 million over three years, built into the February 2005 federal budget. It was hoped that, with this money, Martin would do away with the nuisance of the different ethnocultural groups demanding redress for various "wartime measures and/or immigration restrictions," as Heritage Canada put it. Seeing it as a "blanket act of redress," the CCNC, CCRA and other ethnocultural groups rejected the ACE proposal.[275]

By September 2005, talk of a general election was in the air, and May Chiu asked me to meet her. She informed me that the Bloc Québécois had asked her to be a candidate in the elections, but she wasn't sure in which riding. I postulated that the party would not offer her a winnable riding, reserving those for the *pure laine* candidates. She would be put into a throwaway riding as a token candidate. She told me that she had the idea of running in LaSalle, Paul Martin's riding. I said that was a great idea; LaSalle had a sizable Chinese population and the campaign would do the most damage to Martin and his wrong-headed stand on Head Tax and Exclusion Act redress.

Seeing that, no matter what the community said, the government was bulling ahead to sign the ACE agreement with the NCCC, I sent an open letter to Paul Martin and with the power of email, I copied it to all the MPs. In part, I wrote:

> You are planning a photo opportunity at the end of November with some members of the Chinese Canadian community who are willing to accept your government's paternalistic gesture.
>
> In the wake of the Gomery Commission into the sponsorship scandal, your government is willing to hand out $12 million to an obscure group in the Chinese Canadian community ....
>
> You have not consulted the actual victims of the Head Tax and Exclusion Act, the elderly pioneers, the "gold mountain widows," nor their families. ... They need recognition of their history, struggles and contributions to Canada. They want acknowledgement of the pain and suffering the HTEA caused themselves and their families. They want sincerity which can only come in the form of an official apology.[276]

On November 24, an agreement in principle was signed in Ottawa by Raymond Chan, representing the government, and Ping Tan, who was billed as representing the Chinese Canadian community—as represented by, it noted in parentheses, "the National Congress of Chinese Canadians." The agreement pointedly said: "The Government of Canada and the Chinese Canadian Community have developed this Agreement-in-Principle, premised on the principles of 'no compensation' and 'no apology.'"[277]

The agreement provided for an initial funding of $2.5 million to be given to the NCCC and in return the organization would not seek an apology or any compensation for the head tax payers. The $2.5 million later grew to $12.5 million.

There was immediate outrage that the government had so little consideration for Chinese Canadians, and that the NCCC would sell out the head tax payers and their families for such a paltry sum.

Four days after signing the agreement, the Martin government lost a vote of no confidence in the House of Commons. This vote followed months of wrangling, with the opposition parties accusing the Liberal government of corruption in the aftermath of the Gomery Commission into the sponsorship scandal. Martin was forced to call a general election for January 2006.

The Chinese language media voiced the community's outraged response to the agreement in principle as they daily reported the denunciations from call-in shows on radio and TV. On the popular Toronto First Radio call-in show, twenty-five-year-old host Simon Li doggedly asked Martin about the ACE agreement. It was an unprecedented display of defiance by speaking truth to power. Here are some excerpts from the interview (transcript provided by Brad Lee):[278]

> **Li**: My callers would like to ask you this question, Mr. Prime Minister: What is so wrong with saying sorry to those who paid the head tax?
>
> **Martin**: You're dealing with a government policy that has been established for a long time. … not only have we put up the original $2 million but there's more money to come and this was done by Raymond Chan …
>
> **Li**: But what's so wrong in saying, "Sorry"?
>
> **Martin**: We're acknowledging what happened. …
>
> **Li**: Mr. Prime Minister, I've met a 100-year-old man who has paid the head tax. What is wrong with you giving him back his money?
>
> **Martin**: I also met with a person who was somewhere between 93 and 98, who paid the tax. What he said to me was, "What I want you to use this money for is to educate … Canadians in the wider community what happened."
>
> **Li**: So in a nutshell, the 100-year-old-man that I talked to would not get his money back?
>
> **Martin**: What he is going to get is that Canadians for generations to come are going to know what a terrible thing happened to him. …

Li: What do you have to say to my callers who have said that your party has taken the tax payers' money (and given it) to political cronies?

Martin: I was the person who put in place the Commission of Inquiry that called in Judge Gomery …

Li: I'm talking about the head-tax issue here and the National Congress [of Chinese Canadians].

Martin: Well … we met with the National Congress and they're the ones who said that we should deal with this issue. They're the ones who said this is the way to deal. … Deal with it in terms of education. …

Li: Let me put it a more direct way. Why, Mr. Prime Minister, on the eve of a federal election was so much money given to a single organization that sent out squads of volunteers to campaign for Liberal candidates in Toronto's Chinatown in the last election?

Martin: Uh, this money is being given to the wider Chinese community. It's not being given to any single organization and we met with leaders right across the country on this. …

Li: … We were just talking about the representation of the National Congress, and the government's list of supporting organizations for the proposed settlement consists of over 200 organizations, some of which are not even aware … [that they] have been included such as CCNC, which was deleted from the list after filing complaints to Raymond Chan, Family Services of Greater Montreal, Amitié chinoise, the Chinese neighbourhood association in Montreal, et cetera, et cetera. [Has] your government done the due diligence in your announcement and could you provide evidence to show all the listed organizations have indeed supported the proposed settlement?

Martin: … we dealt with the leadership. …

Li: How could, as I said before, your government and Raymond Chan send out the list, saying that your settlement has the support of 200 organizations? Several of them, they said they were not aware. … how could this happen?

Martin: The fact is that we did consult with as wide a part of the community as we possibly could …

Li: They don't think so.

Martin: Well … you can speak to Raymond Chan …

Li: My last question, Mr. Prime Minister. Some of my callers …

a number of them believe this is another Liberal sponsorship scandal, but it's in the Chinese community … . Given the money you've given to the National Congress, do you agree?

Martin: … I think that what we're doing is the right thing.

Even Jan Wong, who was at the time a *Globe and Mail* columnist, was moved to comment on the ACE agreement. Jan had not previously shown any public support of the redress movement, but now she asked the right questions in an article:[279] "Why did the deal exclude an apology? Why was there no compensation to those who paid the head tax? And why, on the eve of a federal election was so much money given to a single organization?"

The indignation of the Martin deal with the NCCC could be seen on Chinese TV and heard on the Chinese call-in radio programs, as my Toronto brother-in-law Xia Yang, who had immigrated to Canada a few years earlier, told me. He said redress was the topic most widely discussed on the current affairs programs. There was something qualitatively different happening in Canada's Chinatowns. People started talking about the head tax payers and how they were getting screwed by this sponsorship type deal between the NCCC and the Martin government. There was a backlash to the deal, not from the mainstream, but from within the community. Many people in the community saw through the agreement and accused the Liberal government of being paternalistic and taking them for fools.

An air of defiance, excitement and expectation in the redress movement carried us into 2006. Head tax redress had now become an election issue.

In the lead up to the January 23 voting, we did our usual canvassing of the politicians to get their stand on redress. There was movement on the part of the Conservatives. They read the mood of the Chinese Canadian community and they promised an apology if elected.

Kenda Gee worked tirelessly to defeat the Liberal incumbent, Anne McLellan, the deputy prime minister, in the riding of Edmonton Centre. He developed a good relationship with Laurie Hawn, who eventually won the seat. Kenda provided Hawn with information on the redress campaign and Hawn became an advocate of head tax redress within the government caucus.

During the heated debate around head tax redress during the election campaign, two timely broadcasts of *In the Shadow of Gold Mountain* on CBC Newsworld—on January 3 and 7—explained the head tax issue to a vast audience of Canadians.

My brother-in-law was well aware that I was active in the redress movement, so he would ply me with accounts of how the Chinese media were covering redress and the ACE agreement. The media turned from occasional reporting of redress to taking an active editorial stand sympathetic to the elderly head tax payers. The media played up Chinese sentiments of respect for the elderly by featuring interviews and images of surviving head tax payers and spouses. I thought this was one of the turning points in the campaign.

However, Ray Yao, the Ottawa correspondent for *Ming Pao*, later disagreed with me.[280] Ray, who with his white goatee could be mistaken for David Suzuki, gave me an in-depth analysis of the Chinese language media. He had come to Canada in 1976 from Hong Kong, where he was the assistant editor of the *Far Eastern Economic Review*. Prior to that he was the deputy chief editor of the oldest English newspaper in Asia, the *China Mail*. Ray covered the Vietnam War from Bangkok. In Canada, he was a special advisor to the CBC on Hong Kong and China, a regular contributor to the *Financial Post*, then the *Ming Pao* correspondent in Ottawa. He retired from that post in 2008.

Ray told me that the history of Chinese language newspapers in Canada started with Sun Yat-sen, the Kuomintang and the Chinese Benevolent Associations in the early twentieth century. The modern-day Chinese media were owned by the private sector, were motivated by profit and were generally conservative. The younger second and third generations did not read Chinese; they lacked the communication skills to influence the Chinese press. The people who operated the Chinese media were from Hong Kong, Taiwan and even China, so they were generally removed from the *lo wah kiu* generation. "The *lo wah kiu* did not oppose redress," Ray said. Instead, they said "'we paid with our tears, sweat and blood, but we had the opportunity to raise good families here, Canadian society provided us with mainly political and social stability—our kids could go to schools; our kids went to universities with the *gwailo*.'"[281]

And how did the Chinese media cover the two competing organizations, the NCCC and the CCNC, and redress in general? Ray told me that the Chinese media didn't willingly show preferences. The NCCC, though, was closer to the new immigrants and the Chinese media. The CCNC was more mainstream in focus, and it used English more than Chinese.

"The media lack editorial commitment, [and they have a] lack of resources for background or understanding of the redress issues," he said. The number of news releases and conferences was what determined coverage. "NCCC issues releases in Chinese and can speak Cantonese," he continued. "The NCCC is more Liberal, Hong Kong leaning, the CCNC more NDP and PC. Political agenda got in the way of unity. Raymond Chan and Paul Martin couldn't care less about the Head Tax, only getting the vote."

Ray went on to say that the Chinese media got more involved only when "the issue of compensation became more of a reality." The turning point had come when the mainstream media began discussing this and politicians turned it into a social justice issue to solicit Chinese support.[282]

I had the sense that Ray was talking as a critical, hard-biting journalist with a cynical view of the Chinese media establishment.

Paul Martin's dithering and hard-headed handling of the head tax issue cost him many votes in the Chinese Canadian community. The over one million strong community was flexing its electoral muscle as it engaged the participation of a new generation of articulate and politically savvy activists to push the Martin government up against the ropes.

George Lau, co-chair of the Ontario Coalition of Chinese Head Tax Payers and Families, was quoted as saying that Chinese Canadians over the age of fifty had in the past tended to vote Liberal "because we are grateful immigrants." Now, though, "this issue of the Chinese head tax is changing our minds."[283]

The day after the general elections, the CCRA issued a press release claiming credit for helping to defeat the Martin government.

The Chinese community in Montreal succeeded in helping to defeat Liza Frulla (Jeanne-Leber), Minister for Heritage Canada. Frulla's Department was instrumental in formulating the "no apology, no compensation" policy towards Chinese Canadian pioneers, ...

In LaSalle-Emard, Bloc Québécois candidate, May Chiu, a long time HTEA activist shamed Prime Minister Paul Martin for not agreeing to meet 92 year old Mr. James Wing, LaSalle constituent and Head Tax payer. Mr. Martin's margin of victory was greatly reduced ... Right across Canada, Chinese Canadians were galvanized by the Liberal betrayal of their early pioneers.... This flexing of political muscle is felt in many ridings: the election victory of NDP's Olivia Chow in Toronto, the defeat of Deputy Prime Minister Anne McLellan in Edmonton, the reduction in the margin of victory for Liberal Raymond Chan in Vancouver.[284]

We were buoyed by the results of the elections. It didn't matter whether we would normally have voted NDP or Liberal. Harper promised to issue an apology and some form of redress. He was astute to see how the community had denounced the Liberal deal with the NCCC. It was an opening for the Conservatives into the ethnocultural communities and they took full advantage. We felt we had turned the corner in the redress campaign. However, we were still concerned that the ACE agreement in principle was legally signed and still had validity until the new government decided to abrogate it.

Raymond Leung phoned from Vancouver in the evening of February 28 to inform me that he had issued a statement on the agreement in principle and asked me to help him circulate it. Raymond was the acting president of the Chinese Benevolent Association of Canada, the venerable organization that was founded in 1889. It was very significant that one of the most respected organizations representing the *lo wah kiu* generation had come out to oppose the agreement.

The statement from the CBA labelled the agreement "unworkable," for several reasons:

1. The NCCC was "not a total representative of the spectrum of [the] Chinese Canadian community in Canada."
2. The agreement did not include a formal apology in Parliament or direct payments to head tax payers, their families or descendants.
3. Since the agreement, the Chinese community had been more divided than before on the Head Tax issue.

The CBA in Vancouver believed the head tax issue needed to be revisited, and it called for a modified agreement to be drawn up between the new federal government and "all factions" of the Chinese Canadian community, "with the following undertakings":

1. That a formal apology be made in Parliament to the Victims, or their Families or Survivors or Descendants of the Head Tax;
2. Redress must include a direct compensation to individual Victims, or their Families or Survivors or their Descendants as a token of regret for the past Injustice;
3. That a Compensation Fund be set up with a program to commemorate and educate Canadians about past Injustice done to a vital member of our great Canadian Community;

4. A Head Tax Redress Committee be formed to include all major Chinese Associations, Government Representatives and Head Tax Victims or their Representatives.[285]

I immediately distributed the CBA statement to my mailing list of Head Tax and Exclusion Act activists and organizations and the major news outlets, and emailed the new Conservative cabinet and all other MPs.

I received an invitation to attend a March 24 head tax consultation meeting at George Brown House in Toronto, all expenses paid, with Heritage Minister Bev Oda and Parliamentary Secretary to the Prime Minister Jason Kenney. The invitation came from Canadian Heritage by fax to my office late Friday, March 17. Luckily I went to the office on Saturday morning to catch up on some work and noticed the fax; I had the rest of the weekend to consult with people about the proposed meeting and I had until Tuesday to accept.

I was the only one invited to the meeting from Quebec; Montreal people urged me to attend, even though it was so hastily arranged. I was one of several dozen people invited from across Canada who were associated with either the CCNC or the NCCC.

When I arrived at the meeting venue in Toronto and saw well-known Chinese Canadian lawyer Susan Eng inside the building, it really felt as though we were coming in from the wilderness.

Chapter 16

Half Victorious

"Now the emperor listens to deceitful ministers and sends me poisoned wine!"

—Shi Naian, *Water Margin*

Sitting in the parliamentary gallery looking down at the members of Parliament reminded me of sitting in the nosebleed section of the old Montreal Forum. I'd gone there once to watch hockey with my father and I wondered what he would say now. He never came to the seat of power, where punishing legislation was passed to tax him when he came to Canada and where another cruel law was passed to keep my mother from joining him. Nevertheless, with three hundred other Chinese Canadians, I was there to listen to the prime minister of Canada apologize to my father and my mother.

As lawyer Susan Eng and I were standing outside the meeting room, waiting for the government entourage to arrive for the 10 a.m. start, we peered inside and saw Ping Tan and a group from his National Congress of Chinese Canadians talking with bureaucrats from the Department of Canadian Heritage. One of the government officials quickly walked over and closed the door. It seemed the NCCC had gotten an extra, early meeting with the Heritage functionaries; we assumed the congress was still lobbying to salvage the Acknowledgement, Commemoration and Education (ACE) agreement.

News of the hastily called consultation that Heritage Minister Bev Oda and Parliamentary Secretary Jason Kenney would be holding with "leaders of many head tax redress groups" had broken publicly in a dispatch from the *Ming Pao* Ottawa bureau dated March 21, 2006.[286] The article quoted a "Senior Conservative source" as saying that "the two main community organizations" were not expected to reach an agreement soon on the issue of compensation to the community or to the individual head tax payers. It was "very probable," the article said, that Prime Minister Stephen Harper would, "via Oda and Kenney," first discuss agreeing to an apology and then look into suggestions regarding the form compensation might take. MP Inky Mark was quoted as saying that he felt "deeply surprised" that Oda hadn't invited him to the meeting.[287]

Leading up to the March 24 meetings, the two major organizations began preparing and jockeying for space in both the Chinese and mainstream media. I participated in the conference calls that the Chinese Canadian National Council organized to prepare for its Oda/Kenney meeting. Toronto CCNC people had access to some inside information on the composition of the NCCC delegation and we discussed how we could take advantage of the *rapport de force*. It was in one of these calls that I got carried away with my rhetoric, calling on people to unite against our common enemy—the government. Victor Wong chided me, saying that we should not consider the government as the enemy but we must work with it to resolve redress.

For its part, the NCCC issued a press release on March 22, trying to salvage the ACE agreement in principle it had with the old Paul Martin government. More importantly, it also relented on the issue of individual redress, saying the NCCC "expresses support for government to make appropriate compensation for Head Tax survivors and spouses." Joe Du had finally succeeded in getting the NCCC leadership to agree to this concession.

The CCNC-affiliated meeting with Oda and Kenney at George Brown House was scheduled to last an hour and a half. Our contingent was composed of people mainly from Vancouver and Toronto. A total of fourteen people had been officially invited, and three or four others joined in. Some of these people had recently become active in the redress campaign as a result of their opposition to the ACE agreement in principle that they felt had sold out the head tax payers and their families.[288]

The ministers had scheduled the NCCC delegation for after lunch, at 1 p.m.

The NCCC-affiliated contingent seemed to have an even bigger group than we did. Susan Eng, who apparently had some access to Heritage Canada or Jason Kenney's office, provided us with a list of the NCCC participants, and it had two dozen or so names[289]—we believed that at least four or five of them would support the two-stage redress.[290]

Our morning meeting began with a round of introductions. Bev Oda was there with three senior bureaucrats from Heritage Canada.[291] Due to the number of people sitting around the table, we were asked to keep our interventions short. Oda spoke first for the government and said the prime minister had charged her and Jason Kenney "with a clear mandate to work with the Chinese Canadian community to carry out the commitment made during the election campaign." Kenney added, "The government is seeking community consensus on the appropriate means of redress." The two ministers used the word "redress" throughout the meeting.

Susan Eng spoke first for our side and presented the framework and timetable for redress. She proposed the first stage approach of parliamentary apology and immediate redress for the surviving head tax payers and spouses. There would then be a second stage of consultation regarding descendants and community compensation. Kenney asked how long the second stage should be. The answer was the New Zealand model of two years. He said that was too long; maybe one year.

I then put forward the position of the Chinese Canadian Redress Alliance in support of the framework laid out by Susan. I mentioned that the CCRA had worked diligently to unite with people like Joe Du and Raymond Leung of the NCCC to achieve agreement on redressing the head tax survivors and widows and that there was consensus in the community on that issue. I added that the Chinese community had spoken out passionately for an apology and compensation during the recent elections, and that the Liberals had paid the price for their intransigence on redress. Knowing that Kenney was once head of the Canadian Taxpayers Federation, I pointed out that the early Chinese immigrants were subjected to "taxation without representation." He gave me an ironic smile. I urged him to have the first stage settled by July 1, 2006, for the sake of our elderly head tax survivors.

Unanimity was expressed on the redress framework—the two-stage approach and the two basic demands of apology and immediate compensation to the survivors. I felt a unity among the people representing our position to the government and a sense of achievement and solidarity.

Minister Oda then asked about the amount of compensation. Even though we had agreed the night before in our conference call not to be baited into giving a number, Susan hesitatingly gave a low-ball number, "$10,000 to $15,000." Since this opened the money talk, Avvy Go noted that the Japanese redress was $21,000. I upped the ante with the CCRA's figure of $30,000. Sid Tan read a letter from ninety-nine-year-old Charlie Quan, Vancouver head tax payer, asking for $35,000. Since the government had not said whether it was willing to negotiate compensation, I didn't see any harm in stating a high starting position. Oda said she would take all this into consideration. Joseph Wong, the founding president of the CCNC, summarized the financial redress: "The compensation must be meaningful in relation to the suffering inflicted by the Head Tax and Exclusion Act."

Both Oda and Kenney asked questions about the second stage for descendants and community compensation. Unfortunately, we had not had any deep discussions or developed any talking points on this. Due to the absence of any consensus, this issue was the weakest as people volunteered their own positions. Joseph Wong proposed again gold coins for descendants, this time two gold coins per head tax family, each valued at $500. However, he also added the need for community services for seniors. Ray Lee wanted community participation in long-term commemoration and education. Kenney would later pick up this suggestion and implement it as the low-cost Community Historical Recognition Program.

Bill Chu called for education of the larger public on racism. Yew Lee wanted reconciliation with descendants as part of the healing process. I stated that this issue remained open and we needed greater community consultation, especially with head tax families, on the most appropriate form of redress for descendants, to be negotiated with the government. Someone brought up the principle of "one certificate, one claim" for the head tax families. There was a suggestion to relax immigration rules for head tax descendants. Oda shut that down and said the government would not tie redress to immigration policy.

Our meeting ended at 11:45 a.m. with our side stating that we were looking for a quick resolution and we would help the government in whatever way possible to achieve stage one of redress by July 1. Oda and Kenney stated that the meeting was positive and thanked everyone for being so frank and open. We felt the response from the government was promising. They got the consensus they were looking for. There were no criticisms of any other groups, and the ACE agreement was not mentioned.

A large contingent of mainly Chinese media gathered outside the meeting hall. Susan Eng and Joseph Wong easily stepped forward to field the questions in English and Chinese. The government consultation meetings were front-page news in the Chinese dailies, and breaking news on Chinese TV and radio. They also made headlines in the mainstream *Toronto Star* and Canadian Press wire services.

As I wrote in my summary, "For those of us who toiled in obscurity for the past 20 years, I am glad we have a media star like Susan Eng to speak prominently for the cause."

During the media scrum, I approached Diane Fulford, the assistant deputy minister to Oda, and asked her who was in charge of the redress portfolio, Jason Kenney or Bev Oda? She looked at me with some irritation and tersely responded, "Canadian Heritage is in control of the portfolio." I thought to myself, maybe she is one of those bureaucrats who cautioned the government on redressing the ethnocultural communities for fear of the floodgates opening. Canadian Heritage had also been responsible for formulating the ACE deal[292] with the NCCC so we knew which way they were leaning and probably why the NCCC people had the early morning meeting with them. On the other hand, I knew that Kenney, being the prime minister's parliamentary secretary for multiculturalism, had Stephen Harper's ear. And so did everyone else. It was said that Susan Eng had direct access to Kenney by having his cell phone number. Furthermore, Oda had been opposed to individual compensation in the past with her support of the Inky Mark private member's bill, so it would be more beneficial for our campaign if Kenney drove the redress policy for the prime minister.

The afternoon session between the government and the NCCC contingent did not go as well as our morning meeting, as I later learned from Raymond Leung, Donald Chen and Ray Lee. Ray was a friend of Kenney's from Calgary and the minister had invited him to attend the 1 p.m. session.

Ping Tan, the NCCC executive co-chair, apparently did most of the talking. He stated three points: the government must implement the ACE agreement in principle, a formal apology and a community foundation. Joe Du spoke in favour of the two basic demands of apology and individual compensation for the surviving head tax payers and spouses and he also added the third point of a community foundation. As if he wanted to placate the leadership of the NCCC for his stand on individual redress, Joe spoke against any compensation for descendants and he went on to say that there was no working with any other group on the question of compensating descendants. Others, including the Chinese Benevolent Association, spoke in favour of the two basic demands.[293] Altogether, five spoke in favour of the apology and compensation for the surviving head tax payers and spouses; five spoke against.

Raymond Leung told me later that Ping Tan declared the NCCC spoke for the Chinese Canadian community, representing 280 organizations. Raymond had responded that the figure was actually 280 minus 120—the number of organizations represented by the CBA. "You just lost 40 per cent of your membership."

Both Oda and Kenney saw through the division within the NCCC. Oda said to Ping Tan, "If we implement the AIP (agreement in principle), then the Prime Minister cannot apologize." The NCCC old guard had conveniently forgotten that Tan had given up any right to an apology or compensation when he signed the 2005 agreement with Raymond Chan of the Liberal government. Tan had no response to Oda. Kenney said, "Do you people not recognize the outcry from the community during the elections? The government recognizes it." Kenney saw the different opinions and said, "You better talk among yourselves."[294]

At 2:30 p.m. some of us returned to George Brown House to listen in on the media scrum. Minister Oda and Jason Kenney met the press and said the two meetings had been positive. "The government is committed to acting quickly and keeping the promise of head tax redress." They would recommend to the prime minister to include redress in the Throne Speech. Direct redress compensation was possible. Timing was important because they recognized the age of the survivors. The July 1 target was possible.

So Oda and Kenney seemed to have taken up our position for stage one.

When asked by a reporter, Ping Tan said that the NCCC was not opposed to the government giving compensation to the survivors, although, according to the debriefing, he never stated this position in the meeting with the two ministers.

The CCNC side debriefed over lunch and at a scheduled 4 p.m. meeting at the CCNC office, to which we invited Raymond Leung and Donald Chen of the Chinese Community Centre of Ontario, both of whom had been in the NCCC contingent that met with Oda and Kenney. The main consensus was that it was a very positive day and we congratulated each other for the hard work that had gotten us to this point. We were optimistic that the government would accept the two-stage solution. There was some discussion about forming a broader united front ad hoc committee to further negotiate with the government and build on the momentum in the community for an all-inclusive redress.

The only criticisms of our morning meeting I heard were about Joseph Wong's gold coins and Susan Eng downplaying the amount of compensation. Since both of them were not at the 4 p.m. meeting, I asked Victor Wong to express these comments to Joseph and Susan. Victor agreed with the criticisms but he was hesitant to be the bad guy giving negative feedback to the two community luminaries.

* * *

The Conservative government moved quickly. As I said at the time, it did more in its first one hundred days in office on the Head Tax and Exclusion Act issue than all previous governments combined over the previous twenty-two years.

On April 4, Governor General Michaëlle Jean delivered the Speech from the Throne. We were disappointed that the head tax was mentioned in only one sentence: "The Government will act in Parliament to offer an apology for the Chinese Head Tax." Nevertheless, for many in the Chinese Canadian community this was an acknowledgment of the suffering caused by exclusion and recognition of our history in this country. Harper was living up to his election promise of apology, but we were still looking for the "appropriate redress."

Feeling left out of the process, Inky Mark tried to revive his private member's bill to ask for an apology and individual compensation. He asked for the support of the CCNC by including it and the NCCC as the Chinese Canadian organizations with which the government should negotiate. Victor Wong asked for my opinion on this latest maneuver. I responded that I didn't feel we needed this bill to get redress. "We need to apply the pressure to the government, not to spend energy in trying to save Inky Mark's face," I said. "Where was he when we were fighting for genuine redress with apology and compensation?" People on the CCNC side agreed with the stance to work on the government instead of being sidetracked.

The Montreal chapter of the Chinese Canadian Redress Alliance issued a press release on April 15 to announce that it would start registering claimants for the head tax families as a way to continue putting pressure on the government. The press release also reiterated the CCRA's proposal for a two-stage resolution for redress, starting with an official apology and direct compensation to the surviving head tax payers and the surviving widows of head tax payers (target date for completion: July 1, 2006). The second stage would involve a broad consultation of Chinese Canadians to work out the best way to redress the descendants of head tax payers and the community.

Through the months of April and May, people eagerly went to the three designated Chinatown locations—Hoy Sun Association, Ming Wah Hong and the Chinese Family Service—to register their claims, even though we strongly cautioned with bold print on the registration form that "The government has not yet agreed to any compensation at this time."

We registered 135 head tax claims in Montreal. Almost all of them had photocopies of the head tax certificate attached; some even included poignant notes on how their families were affected by the years of separation and deprivation. Among the registrants, there were two surviving head tax payers, nineteen surviving spouses and 114 descendants.

As the government maintained a public silence on the redress proposal, we had an internal debate as to whether to forward the registration forms to Canadian Heritage. The CCNC was forwarding their registrations to Ottawa. But some of us wanted to hold on to the registrations as a way of pressuring the government to negotiate and not providing them with any numbers. Kristina Namiesniowski, the Canadian Heritage official who was at the March 24 consultation, told Victor Wong that the government would not want to receive any registrations but would instead develop its own official application process, if and when redress was offered.[295] Finally, towards the end of May, we decided to mail copies of the 135 registrations to Canadian Heritage.

Then the Canadian government did an astounding thing—it organized consultation meetings in the Chinese Canadian community. During the month of April, either Oda or Kenney attended consultation meetings organized by Canadian Heritage in six cities across the country—Halifax, Montreal, Toronto, Winnipeg, Edmonton and Vancouver—attended by over two thousand people.

Minister Bev Oda was at the April 29 consultation in Montreal where three hundred people packed into the auditorium of the Chinese Cultural Centre. We were the only city in which the consultation was held in Chinatown. Victor Wong was there with a CCNC delegation from Ottawa and Toronto. Raymond Leung of the national CBA had decided to attend all the consultation sessions across the country at his own expense. Ping Tan of the NCCC was also present. He asked me if I still supported compensation for descendants since the government could not afford the $1 million[296] payout for each descendant. I told him that we had never put forward such a number and that since he had no family ties to the head tax, he should just step aside and let those who were affected fight the battle.

The overwhelming majority of the people who attended the session in Montreal were seniors, the sons and daughters and family members of deceased head tax payers. A Chinese Canadian Redress Alliance news release included some of their testimonials:

> "Because of the Exclusion Act, I was not able to reunite with my father until I was 17 years old," said Lee Ming Fung, while holding up a copy of her father's head tax certificate. She then unfurled the old bag that her father used to collect dirty laundry and explained how difficult his job was. "My father died soon after I arrived and I demand redress for what my father suffered and for what I have suffered, having been robbed of my relationship with him."
>
> As the son of a head tax payer, Jack Lee insists also on community compensation, "The Head Tax and Exclusion Act took a terrible toll on the development of the Chinese community, and there also needs to be a collective compensation."[297]

My daughter, Jessica, and my son, Jordan, stood side by side at the microphone as Jessica spoke for their hundred-year-old grandmother, about how she had suffered through the Exclusion Years, and saying that she deserved the justice that could only come about through recognition and redress. Jessica added, "This legacy profoundly impacted multiple generations of Chinese Canadian families, and the community as a whole, and it can be felt to this day. ... While discrimination is always painful and divisive, legislated, institutionalized discrimination is all the more so. ... I have watched my father fight for this cause for most of my life, and feel that redress for the Head Tax and Exclusion Act is long overdue."

I also spoke about how important it was, for the sake of our surviving head tax payers and spouses, for the government to act quickly. The government moderator and translator for the minister reminded me, and everyone in the room, to keep each intervention to under two minutes. I shot back that people have been waiting a long time to let the government know how they felt about the suffering that was inflicted on their families and if they had to take more than two minutes, so be it.

The government functionary never brought up the time limit again, as many of the seniors, mainly women, got up one after the other to emotionally express their long personal suffering caused by the separation of families. They all spoke in Cantonese or Toishanese, so the Mandarin-speaking translator had to concentrate and worked extra hard. We really didn't know what she translated to the minister.

The women, almost all of them speaking in public for the first time, told heart-breaking stories of family separation—the endurance and suffering of their parents and themselves during the Exclusion Years. The audience was brought to tears several times. Walter Tom gave an impassioned account of his grandfather who paid the head tax. May Chiu talked about her election campaign running against Paul Martin. If the Conservatives didn't settle redress by the next election, she warned, she would run against a Conservative minister to raise the issue again.

This unprecedented public outpouring of the community's grievances on the Head Tax and Exclusion Act came to a resounding close with Raymond Leung getting up to the mic and asking all those who supported individual redress for the head tax families to stand up and clap. The audience responded with a thunderous standing ovation for several minutes.

If nothing else, these public consultations had made my two-decade involvement in the campaign worthwhile. Our community had been mobilized; the people had stood up, spoken up to challenge the government and demanded justice. I felt a very warm feeling as I went home that night.

After a couple of hours, though, I reminded myself that we had not won anything from the government yet and there was much work left to be done.

* * *

Even after listening to the heart-wrenching emotional and personal stories from the children, grandchildren and families of head tax payers on how the Chinese Exclusion Act affected all of them, we feared that the Conservative government was still stalling on a settlement when Jason Kenney said in Vancouver, "There are groups that are miles apart on this, so it's going to be difficult to come up with a consensus."[298] The CCRA organized a press conference to remind people of the voices of the Montreal Chinese community at the April 29 public consultation. We accused the government of using community "division" as an excuse for inaction.

However, Kenney may have had a dilemma, or even two, on his hands. First, the various pro-compensation organizations were demanding different amounts for head tax payers and descendants. The CCNC National put forward $20,000 for surviving head tax payers and spouses, with $10,000 going to the estate with no surviving head tax payer or spouse; the CCRA, including Edmonton, Halifax and Newfoundland, asked for $30,000/$20,000; ACCESS (Association of Chinese Canadians for Equality and Solidarity Society) in Vancouver wanted $35,000 based on one certificate–one payment; the BC Coalition of Head Tax Payers, Spouses and Descendants wanted $39,000 based on one certificate–one payment. Second, Kenney and Oda heard from the two thousand participants in the cross-country consultation that descendants were very forceful in wanting redress to apply to them as well; we were well into stage two of the redress framework. I am sure the Canadian Heritage bureaucrats were churning the numbers to see how much this would all cost the government.

The NCCC stood firm on its position of opposing compensation for descendants. This was the government's safety valve.

Those of us within the movement were faced with the same dilemma. We could not agree on the financial amount for the survivors, although we made a last-minute attempt for agreement at $25,000 across the board, and we still were not able to come to agreement on compensation for the descendants. Many thought that we would have more time to consult and discuss the descendants situation, whether compensation should go to the first, second or third generation or to the estate of the deceased head tax payers and spouses based on one certificate–one payment for each family. Based on the sentiments of the head tax families expressed at the consultation meetings, we were moving from compensation for the first generation to legal successors. We were timid on this question due to the subconscious fear of being seen as being greedy, resulting in a backlash and the concern of government finding the money. I said the money would come from the same place that the head tax went into. If the government had given the slightest hint that it would be willing to negotiate, I am sure that we would have been able to arrive at a united position on the financial amount for the survivors and the families.

As we entered May, there was still no concrete information from the government, nor any signs that they were willing to negotiate or even meet. However, rumours abounded—there was talk that compensation would only go to the surviving head tax payers but the surviving spouses would be left out.

The reason floated for that minimalist position was racist and sexist. Either the Canadian Heritage bureaucrats or Conservative bagmen on the Hill had apparently said that compensating widows would be complicated due to the Chinese practice of having multiple wives and concubines.[299] We did not directly address such an absurd assertion but we stuck to our position that the Gold Mountain widows had suffered just as much if not more than the Gold Mountain men. Right up to the end, we fought for equal rights for the surviving spouses—they needed to be compensated. If the bureaucrats got their way, with fewer than fifty surviving head tax payers, the financial compensation would be chump change and they would have done their job well in guarding the floodgates.

At about this time I received a phone call from James Wing. His son Simon had informed him on the progress of the campaign. He wanted to tell me that he was very thankful to all of us who have been working on his behalf. I told him that the government had not officially offered anything but we would continue struggling until justice is done. At ninety-three, James had suffered a mild stroke and he was not physically able to participate in any of the activities, but he was hopeful that we would win justice soon. I passed James' message to the redress network; they were all very appreciative of his encouragement.

"That really is a heart warming reminder of who this is really for," Susan Eng wrote in an email, continuing:

I'm grateful that he has lived to see it (and given the age of so many in this group—fully aware). All of us who have fathers or grandfathers (who) have passed away will take a moment to reflect on how they would have felt and Mr. Wing stands in for all of them.[300]

The redress organizations were issuing press statements almost daily, hoping that some of them would influence the Prime Minister's Office. We were fighting to keep the surviving spouses on an equal footing as the head tax payers. One of the statements, released by the Ontario coalition, was written by Susan Eng and opened by saying: "Please do not discriminate against the Golden Mountain widows who already suffered once before under the Head Tax and Exclusion Acts." She went on to quote me:

"I can see the pain and loneliness still in my mother's eyes. She is entitled to justice not just for my father but also for herself. Nothing can compensate for the lost years of their youth, but redress will finally recognize their contributions to building Canada and that they did not suffer in vain."[301]

Prime Minister Stephen Harper personally took part in a roundtable session with elderly head tax payers, spouses and descendants in Vancouver on May 25. In the ninety-minute meeting, Mrs. Quon Chang Shee Dere, 102, asked Harper in Toishanese, "I am going to stay alive as long as it takes to get justice. How much longer would you expect me to live?"[302]

The meeting was organized with the BC Coalition of Head Tax Payers, Spouses and Descendants, which took the opportunity to reiterate its position, asking for an all-inclusive redress to the head tax families based on one certificate–one payment.

There was much excitement throughout Canada's Chinatowns as Harper said the final decision on head tax redress would be made before the end of the current session of Parliament, by the end of June.

There was also speculation and skepticism as to what this decision would be as the government had kept us in the dark and were not open to negotiations.

There was a rumour that the government wanted a meeting of the redress-seeking groups for June 3. We worked overtime to try and get a consensus of demands in time for this possible meeting. The emerging consensus was:

- Equality between head tax payer and spouses
- Redress amount of $25,000
- Inclusion of sons and daughters of deceased head tax payers and spouses
- Inclusion of descendants born in the Exclusion Years, before the May 17, 1947 repeal date of the Exclusion Act

When the June 3 meeting fell through, the redress organizations reverted to their previous positions on compensation. The government was still in control of the process, so we had no negotiating input.

* * *

In the meantime, Christine Nassrallah of Canadian Heritage was asking for the list of people who registered in Montreal along with their addresses. It appeared that something big was coming up and I suspected the government wanted to get in touch with the head tax families. Christine wouldn't divulge any information when I tried to bargain the list for information about the proposed government package. All she would say is that the government wanted to invite head tax payers and spouses to Ottawa for a ceremony on June 22. I didn't want the Montreal head tax families to be left out, so I finally sent the list to Ottawa.

The Chinese dailies *Sing Tao* and *Ming Pao* were reporting that the possible July 1 ceremony of acknowledgment and apology was being moved up to June 22 and that compensation would be given to the surviving head tax payers and possibly spouses but nothing for the descendants. The government was getting ready to impose a unilateral redress package without negotiations. Canadian Heritage desperately wanted lists of head tax families to invite to Ottawa for the ceremony.

On the weekend of June 2, frantic telephone calls were made across Canada from Newfoundland to BC; I was receiving fresh emails asking what we should do or offering suggestions on how we could still influence the government before it was too late. There was talk about boycotting the ceremony and holding a parallel event in protest. Kenda Gee and the Edmonton Committee were taking a hard line and refused to send their list to Ottawa until Canadian Heritage was more forthcoming in revealing what the redress package contained. The BC coalition was talking boycott, as they fired off a letter to Oda and Kenney requesting an immediate meeting.

Yew Lee of the Ontario coalition drafted a letter to Oda and Kenney calling for an emergency meeting the next weekend with all redress organizations to negotiate a settlement package. Edmonton, Regina, Montreal, Newfoundland, BC and the CCNC signed off on the letter. I also drafted a letter to Oda and Kenney on behalf of the CCRA to support the other redress-seeking organizations' call for a meeting and to reemphasize our stand of inclusive redress for the head tax payers, spouses and descendants.

However, according to a *Ming Pao* report on June 6, it was all over but the shouting as far as the government was concerned. June 22 would be the date: 3 p.m. for the apology after Question Period, 4 p.m. for the ceremony in the Railway Committee Room, then a reception and photo ops. The article also reported $16 million for individual redress and $8 million for community projects.

Jason Kenney responded in the Chinese press to our letters requesting a meeting. *Sing Tao* quoted Kenney as refusing any meetings with the redress groups, saying there had been extensive consultations and the government would make its decision without "negotiations." He said, in a paternalistic tone, that the last (Liberal) government had negotiated with one group, the NCCC, and that ended up dividing the community.

The CCNC and the Ontario coalition of head tax families were uneasy about the calls from the west for a boycott of the June 22 ceremony. They decided to work with Heritage as they saw the apology to be a victory. Victor Wong put a positive spin to Kenney's message in the media—he had accepted the CCNC suggestions to apologize in Parliament and hold a reconciliation ceremony. I wrote back to Victor,

> The point is to get the government to treat us and the HTEA families with some respect instead of releasing "information" through the media and disrespecting us for asking for a say in the final outcome.
>
> Once we accept their bluff, the game is over .... My voice may be one in the wilderness, but I want the government to treat our seniors with some respect, rather than have them paraded around without knowing what is in store for them. If we have combative 95 year olds willing to go to Ottawa to shake their fingers at Harper, all the power to them.

Gordon Jin, co-chair of the Newfoundland and Labrador Head Tax Redress Committee, also weighed in with a June 6 email to Victor Wong and others, asking whether the nation-wide consultations were all for naught if a settlement was imposed by the government without any negotiations. He agreed that getting the head tax survivors, spouses and descendants to go to Ottawa might just be a public relations exercise. Jin and Robert Hong headed up the redress work in Newfoundland out of St. John's. (Robert Hong is the son of a Newfoundland head tax payer.)

In an email, Yew Lee wrote: "William, you are not a voice in the wilderness. ... Gordon and I are here with you, amongst many others."[303]

The CCRA saw the expected apology as a half victory and although we did not call for a boycott we did not encourage people to attend because the government had not offered any redress proposal.

At about this time, Susan Eng appeared to have accepted the non-disclosed redress package from the government, as she planned a "Redress Express" in which seniors would ride the rails from Vancouver to Toronto and transfer from there to Ottawa. This would be a gruelling trip for ninety-year-olds. As a railroader with some knowledge of train travel in Canada, I did not encourage anyone, regardless of age, to take such a tiring journey. Nevertheless, Susan pushed ahead with her plan and approached VIA Rail for sponsorship.

Even Ping Tan of the NCCC couldn't go against the tide of community opinion. He stated his support of individual compensation for the head tax survivors and spouses during an interview on Simon Li's *Power Politics* radio program on June 6. Avvy Go pointed out on the same program that the government could not play the "division" card on redress as the two major organizations were calling for an apology and compensatory redress for the survivors. The NCCC chairman added that he didn't know what sort of division Kenney had been referring to, but he didn't answer when asked about descendants.[304]

Montreal also contributed to the flurry of activities leading up to June 22. We called a press conference for June 13 to dispel Jason Kenney's pronouncement of division in the community. The press conference would be a bipartisan affair featuring Quebec head tax families united in seeking financial redress; members of the CCRA and Jack Lee, co-chair of the Quebec branch of the NCCC, would also speak. We urged the federal government to meet with the direct victims so they would have a say in the final settlement. When we issued the press release for the conference, there were immediate howls of criticisms from BC and Toronto that the NCCC could not be trusted and that we needed to work with the grassroots. May Chiu, organizer of the press conference, aptly responded to the derision in an email to the redress network, stating that we had been "working with Congress members for several years to promote unity." Further, she said, "I take my cue from the HTEA families and victims."[305]

Kenda Gee informed me that he was getting emails from CCNC's Victor Wong and Sid Tan of ACCESS asking if the CCRA had gone over to the NCCC and whether we supported the agreement in principle deal between the NCCC and the former Liberal government. As I told Kenda, it was laughable that after working on redress for so many years, people were still suspicious of our stated positions and intentions.

In the crucial days before the June 22 ceremony, Ray Yao was extremely helpful to Kenda and me: he asked us for comments on new information he had gathered on the Hill as the Ottawa correspondent for *Ming Pao*. In our response, we informed him of the positions the various factions were taking.

He was politically astute and did an excellent job in deciphering the "truth from facts" from the myriad number of press releases sent out by the different redress-seeking organizations as well as the NCCC-affiliated groups. His coverage of the Montreal press conference highlighted the first ever joint conference of the CCRA and the NCCC (Quebec) to ask for redress for the head tax payers, spouses and descendants, as well as community compensation. Ray advised that Stephen Harper, seeking Quebec votes, would pay more attention to the French media than the English. May went all out to attract the French press, which had a reputation of not covering minorities. The two major French dailies, *Le Devoir* and *La Presse*, were at the press conference.

On the same day as the Montreal press conference, the government confirmed that the prime minister would formally apologize in Parliament to Chinese Canadians for the Head Tax and Chinese Exclusion Act on June 22. However, there was no information on any redress proposal and the government did not give any indication that it would meet with the community to discuss any redress settlement before the apology date.

Susan Eng and the Ontario Coalition publicly announced the Redress Express Train on June 13. The plan was to have head tax payers, spouses and descendants board the train in Vancouver on June 16, pick others up along the way and reach Toronto by June 21 to join a "major group" before arriving in Ottawa for June 22.[306] Susan asked me if Montreal would participate. At the time we were not even certain if we would participate in the government's June 22 ceremony, but I responded politely that it would only take two hours for people to drive from Montreal to Ottawa so it didn't make sense to take a five-hour train ride to Toronto and then another five hours to come back up to Ottawa.

I was not the only one questioning the idea of the train ride; the BC coalition and ACCESS also voiced doubts. "I would prefer to see them (seniors) go on a first-class airplane ride," the *Vancouver Sun* quoted Karin Lee of the BC coalition as saying. "It's ridiculous to bump around for five days when you're 101 years old. How many people have enough time to gather up their life ... and take a five-day trip?"[307] After she saw the headline of the article alluding to dissent around the Redress Express, Karin emailed the redress network saying she had been misquoted—she supported the train initiative and she would be at the station to see the group off with lion dancers.[308] Sid Tan was also unimpressed and he questioned the "lack of detail about the form of apology," before embarking on such a trip.[309] Sid suggested that we could accept or reject the apology depending on the redress details; we would lose all leverage by willy-nilly accepting the apology.

However, with the grand plan to transport seniors to Ottawa by train, it was plain to see that the Ontario coalition and the CCNC had decided to participate wholeheartedly at the apology ceremony without knowing what the redress proposal would be. The Last Spike was brought to Vancouver to ride the train to Ottawa, where it would be presented to Stephen Harper as a token in response to his apology. The CCNC was already preparing celebratory dinners in Ottawa (June 22) and Toronto (June 25).

Gordon Jin of the Newfoundland and Labrador Head Tax Redress Committee questioned the enthusiasm shown by Central Canada. He pointed out the lack of dialogue or communications from the government since the nation-wide consultation meetings in April. He asked if it is just an apology without any substantive redress. He added that it would be a shame if the elderly head tax survivors went to Ottawa without any information on a settlement.[310]

The government mailed out invitations to head tax payers and spouses that were on the lists provided to Canadian Heritage. Government functionaries also started to contact these people by phone to gauge how many people would be attending the ceremony and to drum up a good turnout. Robin Tom, son of a deceased head tax payer, called me to say that a Sylvie Campeau from Canadian Heritage had contacted him several times to make sure his mother would attend the apology ceremony in Ottawa. Robin told her that his mother used a wheelchair and would not easily be able to travel and asked whether he could go in her place. He was told no. Robin then told the functionary to ask Harper to come to Montreal and apologize to his mother in person.

The invitation did not extend to descendants or family members; this was the first clue that descendants were being left out of the redress package. Canadian Heritage finally clarified that caregivers accompanying the survivors were also invited; in addition, invitations were sent to organizations like the CCNC and the NCCC to ensure a crowd of Chinese faces.

Yew Lee requested a last-minute meeting with Bev Oda and was told that the minister was unable to meet with him. Reacting to this rejection, Yew said he had "very mixed feelings" as June 22 neared. "I can only foresee that we can only accept the apology on a 'conditional' and 'qualified' basis," he said. "There are too many unresolved issues, and voices that have not been heard."[311]

On June 15, *Ming Pao* gave an excellent account of the mood of the community under the headline, "Strong and negative reactions from Head Tax payer families and claim groups—On the eve of conclusion to Headtax redress, several groups jointly blast: Harper forces elders to the capitol for a political show." The article quoted a ninety-year-old widow in Montreal as saying that a government official was pressuring her to attend the ceremony in Ottawa and that she's been told family members could not represent her. In the end, the family decided not to participate.[312]

By this time Kenda Gee and the Edmonton Committee, thinking that it was not fair to keep Alberta seniors from getting an invitation, relented and emailed their list of head tax families to Canadian Heritage.

My mother, who was then 101, received her invitation; I explained to her that the government had not offered anything other than an apology and she agreed it was not worthwhile to attend such a gruelling event. I was able to wrangle invitations from Canadian Heritage for my siblings, but I had not decided whether I would go. Simon Wing also told me that he wouldn't be subjecting his ailing father to such a tiring affair.

On June 19, the CCRA (Montreal), the Edmonton Redress Committee and the Newfoundland and Labrador Head Tax Redress Committee issued a press statement, which read in part:

> Until we know further details, we are not encouraging people to go to Ottawa," said May Chiu, member of the Redress Alliance. "It would be devastating for our seniors to go to Ottawa only to have their photos taken and then return home without having their Head Tax money returned to them.
>
> It is disgraceful that the sons and daughters of head tax payers, who spoke most vocally in the Canadian Heritage consultations, are not invited," said Walter Tom, grandson of a head tax payer. "My father is bitterly disappointed he has been excluded from the ceremony. It's not his fault that his father, who paid the head tax, died years ago while waiting for redress from the government.[313]

The release of this statement brought us a lot of flack and "friendly fire" from the CCNC-centric people in Toronto and BC, for raining on the apology parade. Only ten years later did I get a positive assessment of our stance when Yew Lee said, "I felt there should have been a stronger voice from the left. ... If Quebec didn't come together, it would have been difficult for Toronto to spearhead it all."[314]

* * *

On June 20 at around 9 a.m., I got a call in my office from a caregiver at my mother's nursing home. She informed me that Mother had suffered a stroke during the night and was rushed to the hospital. After calling my siblings, I dropped everything and went straight to the emergency room. Mother was in stable condition but her whole right side was paralyzed. I held her left hand and she squeezed mine; it was at this point I decided that I had to go to Ottawa to represent her in Parliament. My sister Pui Yung agreed, "Yes, we have to go on Mother's behalf."

The next day, June 21, Ray Yao informed us of a leak from Canadian Heritage that the redress package consisted of the apology and compensation only for the surviving head tax payers and the surviving spouses, nothing for the descendants and no community compensation. I took the news in stride, feeling emotionally tired and not combative enough to react. May Chiu was the first to fire off a strong reaction: "I am very disappointed," she wrote in an email to the redress network. "Once again, the Harper government has proven its commitment to lack of accountability, transparency, openness, and fairness." May continued:

> During its own consultations, the majority of the speakers were first-generation children who suffered tremendously from the Exclusion Act. It is a shame that the government would turn its back on these victims. No wonder the government deliberately excluded the first generation from tomorrow's ceremony! Shame on all who sold out our own people![315]

Other members of the CCRA came out to criticize the government stand, including Daniel Lai of Calgary:

> One key point that may be considered is that if no compensation is given to descendants, this government is sending out a message to future governments that as long as they can stall and delay as long as possible until as many victims of discriminatory policies pass away as possible, they are able to get away with it. The government, by not providing descendants compensation, is sending out this message, loud and clear.[316]

There was no immediate reaction from the CCNC people; they may still have been on the Redress Express without access to email.

* * *

On the morning of June 22, my sister and I drove to Ottawa. It was a hot, sunny day. According to the instructions in the invitation, we were to meet at a downtown hotel and shuttle buses would take people to Parliament Hill. As I got on the bus, Susan Eng called out to me, "I thought you were boycotting this." I responded that I was there to represent my mother. The only person I told in Ottawa that my mother had suffered a stroke was Gary Yee and he offered his heartfelt sympathy.

CCNC leaders received five invitations from Canadian Heritage and they rode the last leg of the Redress Express from Toronto to Ottawa along with the head tax families who came from the West. The NCCC received the same number of official invitations but there was talk in Montreal that a bus was being organized by the NCCC to take people to Ottawa. As Canadian Heritage targeted, three hundred people jammed into the Railway Committee Room and the public gallery of the House of Commons. Many people I saw were not members of head tax families, but they were invited in order to fill up the seats.

It turned out to be a long, taxing day. It must have been exhausting for the seniors. After lining up in the muggy heat to clear the security check, we were ushered up to the gallery where we patiently waited for Question Period to finish. On cue, Prime Minister Stephen Harper stood up to deliver his apology speech, interspersed with the Cantonese words, "*Ga na da do heep*—Canada apologizes."

It was a moving moment for me and many others in the gallery, which was filled with Chinese men and women, old and young. Tears flowed down many faces; I also teared up. Being there physically, I was carried along with the emotionally laden atmosphere. It was a landmark moment; the prime minister of Canada recognized our history, our contributions and our suffering, as he apologized for the wrongs inflicted on our pioneers, who included my grandfather, my father and my mother. I was moved more by the emotional reaction of our community in the gallery and by being among my people than by the speech itself. I felt I was truly Canadian and that I belonged here. After twenty-two years of struggle for redress, I felt our community had come of age and I was proud to have been part of that process and proud of our achievements.

"The ground felt firmer under my feet," Yew Lee said afterwards. "The apology accomplished that. I had to embrace my identity throughout the campaign."[317]

Gary Yee, one of the trailblazers in the redress movement, was in two minds about the day. "Although there was a special feeling in the Chamber when the P.M. made the apology, it felt disappointing when more details were stated at the follow-up ceremony," he wrote later. "It was not even a symbolic sum of $23 million returned to the Head Tax families or Chinese Canadian community. ... I know I was supposed to feel happy perhaps, but I think I had mixed feelings." He added:

> I realize now that my feeling at the time was more like numbness. I am not overjoyed but nor am I bitter. There is some sense of relief, but only partially; and there is some sense of accomplishment and success, but only partially; and there is some sense of closure, but only partially.[318]

Lost in the euphoric moment of the apology were Harper's words on redress: "To give substantial meaning to today's apology, the Government of Canada will offer symbolic payments to living head tax payers and living spouses of deceased payers."

Ray Yao's source had been right: there was no mention of descendants. Despite all our submissions to the government, despite all the heartfelt presentations from head tax families at the Canada-wide consultations, the Government of Canada had remained unmoved and the descendants and families of head tax payers were excluded. I had expected the descendants to be left out, so I was not surprised. So on that day, the second stage struggle to redress the descendants and head tax families began.

If we put a positive spin on the events of June 22, 2006, however, we did get the apology and we did get individual compensation for the surviving head tax payers and we established the equality of the widows who received the same compensation.

My sister was pensive on the drive home from Ottawa and I recall her saying that, although she was grateful for the apology and the return of the head tax money to the survivors, the apology was "only words if there is no concrete redress for the families who unfortunately have parents who passed away over the last 20 years." Her own father-in-law had passed away during that time.

After hearing the apology from the prime minister, with my sister Pui Yung in
the Railway Committee Room, June 22, 2006. (William Dere Collection)

I spoke with other head tax families who went to Ottawa from Montreal
and they echoed my sister's sentiments. "The government has created two
classes of people, those who are still alive and those families whose parents
have died," was one comment. Another said, "Everyone suffered; this symbolic gesture should apply to everyone. I hope the different organizations continue to fight for the other families whose parents have died. I hope they move
quickly before it is too late."

The day after the apology, I went to the Hôtel Dieu Hospital in Montreal
and told Mother that the prime minister and the Canadian government had
apologized for the head tax and the Exclusion Act. There was a faint smile on
her dry lips. After a lifetime of sacrifice for her children and family, she wasn't
thinking about what this meant for her, she was thinking of me. "You must be
happy," she said. "You worked so long for this. You can rest now."

* * *

What happened on June 22 was not a redress agreement. It was more of a
redress announcement, a proclamation by Harper—nothing was negotiated,

although the government did adhere to two of our demands, an apology and financial redress for the survivors.

Yew Lee later relived a conversation he'd had with Jason Kenney, shortly before June 22. Yew had said, "It would be preferable if the government negotiates a settlement with the Chinese community." Kenney had looked at Yew sternly and simply said, "This is not a negotiation."[319] The federal bureaucrats had done the calculation. The unilateral settlement cost the government one-tenth the price of an F-35 fighter jet.[320] The Canadian government won the war of attrition against our head tax payers and their families.

Forty-nine head tax payers were compensated, with each receiving an ex-gratia amount of $20,000, which was also paid to 736 surviving widows. The payment applied to all those who were alive on February 6, 2006, the date that Stephen Harper was sworn in as prime minister. It was an arduous application process for many of the seniors and their families; certified documents had to be dug up to be submitted, including difficult to obtain copies of birth, death, marriage (or proof of conjugal relationship), citizenship and, of course, head tax certificates. In total, 856 applications were received by the March 31, 2008, deadline; 785 were accepted with payments made for a total value of $15.7 million.[321] As the deadline neared, an enlightening email (March 13, 2008) came from Bill Chu, the head of Canadians for Reconciliation, as he chastised Victor Wong for not communicating with the First Nation Chiefs about the head tax compensation. Bill estimated that there were about twenty to thirty surviving Indigenous spouses of deceased head tax payers. I also learned that Saskatchewan Indigenous Senator Lillian Eva Quan Dyck's father was a head tax payer.

There was no compensation for head tax payers or spouses who did not survive long enough to see Stephen Harper become prime minister. Over 99 per cent of Chinese Canadian families who suffered under the Head Tax and Chinese Exclusion Act were not compensated. The $15.7 million figure was amazingly close to the $16 million that the June 6, 2006, *Ming Pao* article predicted the government was planning to grant for individual compensation. The federal bureaucracy must have tabulated the numbers with the information that the redress movement had provided on the surviving head tax payers and spouses. The survivor compensation was a no-brainer. Despite the apology and the symbolic payments—it was less than the $23 million collected in head tax—we shouldn't lose sight of the fact that the Canadian government still profited from racism.

The apology was not something to accept or reject. June 22, 2006, was a historical, landmark moment for the Chinese Canadian community.

Like most landmark moments, what happened afterwards became anticlimactic; we had spent our energy and lost our momentum. Despite brave words, we looked Jason Kenney in the eyes and we blinked. I don't recall many people who said at the time that we could have rejected the apology; it would not have been fair to the survivors and it was not our choice to make. We cautioned people about June 22 and got soundly criticized. Some of us soldiered on towards stage two; others who came aboard to push the last six months of the campaign over the top went back to their respective causes and interests, thinking to themselves, "A job well done."

We took to the streets on July 1, 2006; Humiliation Day continued for the descendants and families who were excluded from the unilateral redress settlement. It was to be the last Canada-wide protest for the direct family victims, and pickets and demonstrations took place in front of federal buildings in Vancouver, Edmonton, Ottawa and Montreal. Toronto was notably absent from this action.

"This [redress] decision was not addressed to the community... but plunged ahead against the will of many across the country including major centres like Montreal & Vancouver," Kwoi Gin, filmmaker and head-tax descendant, noted in an email to me. "It's ironic that our forefathers managed to build the railroad that eventually connected this country together from coast to coast but we as a sorry excuse of a community still cannot stand together on this fight."

Gin expressed the disappointment and anger of the head tax families excluded from the redress. "This direct redress was not going to include those already dead, which is the majority," he noted. "How can a small group of individuals measure the degree of oppression & decide the value of who gets compensated & who doesn't? I guess that was just 'another Chinaman's chance' as the White railroad bosses use to say." The excluded group of pioneers, he added, included his great-grandfather. In his email, written on June 26, 2006, he continued:

> As I ponder at my Great Grand Dad's crinkled head tax certificate this morning, I was thinking how worthless it was. But then I realize that it is still an important reminder ....
>
> I'm happy for those old timers who did get compensation. ... But the only real winner was Mister Harper who has gained a few votes ...

I still feel that we could have pushed for a better deal while the political gift lay in our favour. I hope everyone counted their teeth just to make sure they were all still there before Harper left the room!

A hundred years later, I'm still asking myself 'when will we stop building the railroad for the White man?' Great Grand Dad said never settle for "it's better than nothing". I'll be @ Great Grand Dad's grave making mega apologies for failing his generation with Johnnie Walker in hand so he can stop turning.

* * *

Just a few weeks after the Harper apology, my mother passed away, on July 13, 2006. She was 101.

Two years after the apology, on November 8, 2008, we lost a star of our redress movement when James Wing passed away too. He was ninety-six. Alan Hustak wrote an obituary for the *Montreal Gazette*, which included quotes from the eulogy James' son Simon gave at this father's funeral.

Simon talked about the wide range of his father's interests. "He was sympathetic to Chairman Mao and the Communists in China but not dogmatic about it," he said. "He was liberal in his thinking, which sometimes got him into trouble with his peers, many of whom supported the Nationalist Chinese."

The *Gazette* article quoted Simon as saying that James had "an uncanny knack for bringing justice and mercy together when they sometimes seemed to demand opposite conclusions. He applied the same approach to his involvement with the movement for the redress of the head tax." Simon's eulogy went on to say:

> (My father) participated actively in this movement for redress, offering to share his own personal story wherever it would help. He truly thought that Canada was a great country and was thankful for its many blessings to him and his family.
>
> However, he believed that for the sake of honesty, to honour truth and righteousness, that it was necessary that we acknowledge this aspect of our history and make some form of apology.

The *Gazette* obituary even quoted me on James' contribution to the redress movement and to our 1993 film, which brought his story to a wider audience: "'It was through James Wing that a younger generation was able to get a glimpse of the hardship and racism our parents and our grandparents had to suffer,' said William Dere, who wrote and directed Moving the Mountain." Further, I was quoted as saying, "'There was no bitterness in him. He opened up about his past when others of his generation wouldn't talk about it.'"[322]

In the space of a few short years, I experienced emotional highs and lows. We achieved a half-victory with the apology and the semi-redress. It was heart-warming to see the surviving head tax payers and spouses receive justice in their lifetime. There was enough credit to go around for those that participated in the two-decades-long campaign. Nevertheless, I was emotionally drained. Winning the apology coincided with losing my mother. My mother's death and the passing of an elder statesman of the redress movement severed my personal ties to the era of the Exclusion Years. I wondered then and I still wonder today whether the experience of my parents' generation will have any meaning for a new generation.

* * *

More than a decade has passed now since the 2006 apology. Evaluations of the redress campaign by some of us who participated in the trenches are not all kind.

May Chiu says we were "dishonest" with the two-stage proposal, when we had no intention of carrying out the second stage once the surviving head tax payers and widows were redressed. The families of Kwoi Gin, Walter Tom, Kenda Gee, Sid Tan and twelve thousand other head tax families were never compensated as the campaign faded out. May started me thinking that the two-stage proposal might have been a strategic mistake. Tactically, we got what we wanted—a government apology and an immediate redress for the surviving seniors; but it also gave Kenney and Harper an easy way out at the minimal cost. They opportunistically offered the first stage and then walked away. We may have pursued the two stages in principle but not in practice. We united with the less conservative part of the NCCC on redressing the survivors but we couldn't win them over to an inclusive redress for the descendants. We needed the CCNC as the major force in pushing for full redress, but without their active participation, we did not have a plan to pursue compensation for the families. Despite this failure, I don't think history will judge us too harshly.

Kenda Gee, probably the angriest of all of us during the campaign, had a kinder evaluation. "I've personally had no regrets about our efforts," he told me in 2016. "The redress campaign had always been a delicate balancing act. How do you negotiate and counter two decades of political stall tactics by Ottawa with ensuring that at least one surviving head tax payer could some day see and hear an official apology from government?

"The two-stage strategy was much better and effective than anything else that had been proposed beforehand. We often lamented that 'government' played the divide and conquer game. ... We played the divide and conquer game in our own way. That is why our strategy was good."[323]

Walter Tom spoke about the difficulty of hindsight when I talked to him in 2016. Back in 2006, "a certain amount" of head tax payers were still alive, he noted, "and widows as well. There was a real possibility that there would be nothing. They would all pass away but there wouldn't even be an apology. We had to take the deal at the same time we had to press for more. I understand why there are parts of the community that said, 'Let's just take that and move on.' Our stance in Montreal, we wanted it for the sons and daughters as well. But where was Toronto? It was [all] being controlled by Toronto at the time."[324]

Kenda thinks the two-stage strategy was probably "the ugliest compromise." It got the redress issue to the table "due to our efforts at the turn of the millennium," he told me in 2016. "If we didn't have people in Toronto like Susan Eng and Victor Wong being so eager, we could have stopped it and we could have negotiated."[325]

I share Kenda's and Walter's assessments. After twenty-two years, the community had managed to unite around the demand for justice for the handful of survivors, including my mother. It was the best to hope for after two decades of Ottawa intransigence and indifference, aided by a portion of the community acting as a fifth column for the government. The two-stage strategy was able to neutralize the community naysayers and pressure the government into seeing that there was no choice but to give in to the unified demand of redress for the survivors. There comes a time in long-term struggles when you need to realize that time and reality have diminished the original goals and what you are left with would be the best outcome.

"I was a strong proponent of the two-stage strategy," Gary Yee noted in a

2016 conversation with me. "We had some heated discussions in Toronto and emails across the country. It was a huge strategic issue. ... I don't think we were deceptive or trying to fool people, we were very aware that by doing the two-step strategy we would reduce the chance of settling for the descendants but we would increase the chance of settling with our priority people, the head tax payers and widows. ...

"I think it was neither dishonest nor a mistake. It was a deliberate decision that was made with our eyes open—that would be the consequences that it would reduce the chances of further settlement but given the situation we had, it was the best way to go, and the only practical way to get a settlement within the life time of our HT payers and widows."[326]

Sid Tan and the Vancouver-based Head Tax Families Society of Canada are keeping the torch burning. They are in a never-ending campaign for full inclusive redress based on the principle of one certificate–one claim. As I write, the Chinese Canadian National Council[327] exists in name only, so there is not much help there.

We are looking for the next generation of head tax activists but the reality of today's Chinese Canadian community will not easily attract new energy to this cause. The living legacy of the Head Tax and Exclusion Act has kept the Chinese Canadian community an immigrant community.

By 2018 we numbered 1.5 million people, with the origins and languages of new arrivals making us one of the largest and most diverse ethnic groups in Canada. We have gone from the early Toishanese to the Cantonese of the Hong Kong immigrants, to the Taiwanese, the Vietnamese, those coming from Southeast Asia and French-speaking Mauritius, and more recently the Mandarin speakers from Mainland China—all with different cultural backgrounds. All of this has been changing the nature of the Chinese Canadian community. The different immigrant groups are not even all aware of the historical contributions and sacrifices of the early Chinese Canadian pioneers who built the footings of our foundation in this country, so they don't feel the passion of my generation for the redress struggle.

Perhaps Ray Yao best reflected the attitude of the new community in his uncompromisingly colourful style when he told me: "For the Hong Kong people, for the Taiwanese people, for the Indochinese Chinese people who are working ten hours a day in a noodle shop making minimum wage ... 'You are a lawyer and driving a bloody SUV, and then you want your $20,000? You didn't suffer, your grandparents suffered and you reap the benefit?'"[328]

Ray knows that not all head tax descendants are lawyers with SUVs; there are many who still suffer the consequences of legislated Chinese exclusion.

Although I was going around interviewing people like May, Kenda, Walter and Gary in 2016, the tenth anniversary of the 2006 apology generally passed without any notice in the Chinese Canadian community.

When I ran into Jack Lee on Father's Day, June 19, 2016, having dim sum at the Ruby Rouge Restaurant in Montreal, I asked him, "Is the Congress commemorating the tenth anniversary of the apology?"

"The tenth anniversary?" he asked.

"Yes, Harper's apology for the head tax."

"Oh yes, nobody's talking about it. You know, we should get Justin Trudeau to implement the ACE agreement."

In Toronto, Avvy Go remembered and tried to organize something with Walter Tom in Montreal, who in turn contacted Sid Tan in Vancouver, but in the end she only got the city of Toronto to commemorate June 22 as Chinese Head Tax and Exclusion Act Redress Day.

Ten years earlier, following the apology, Toronto City Council passed a similar motion moved by Councillor Paula Fletcher and supported by Mayor David Miller on June 28, 2006, to proclaim June 22 as Chinese Canadian Head Tax Redress Day. At that time, the reaction from our community was lukewarm. Harvey Lee of the BC coalition and a head tax descendant succinctly put it: "Don't get sucked in again. Redress has been only partially done. Let's not agree on Redress Day until all of the redress, including families, has been completed."[329]

I don't know if there was an expiry date on the proclamation of Redress Day in 2006, but Toronto did it again in 2016. There were no celebrations or commemorations within the Chinese Canadian community for the tenth anniversary. People were still seeking a full and inclusive redress.

PART FOUR

Identity, Love and Belonging

Chapter 17

Being Chinese in Quebec

"The kind of racism the Chinese in Montreal have been subjected to is a systemic, institutional, collective one, a kind that has gone beyond the trivial fact of one person ill-treating another person."
—Chan Kwok Bun, *Smoke and Fire: The Chinese in Montreal*

My son, Jordan, resisted when he received a document from the Quebec government that unilaterally placed accents on our family name, turning it into Déré. "They imposed a name on Grandfather when he came to Canada," he said, incensed, "and now they once again want to nationalize our name."

Once the redress struggle ended for much of the Chinese Canadian community, I was able to start weighing up the circumstances of my own life in the unique province that I've lived in for more than sixty years. Being Chinese in Quebec is not like being Chinese in Canada as a whole or in any other part of the country. For one thing, you are a minority within a minority because this is the province where Canada's French-speaking minority is trying its hardest to maintain its language and culture within a largely English-speaking country. You come up against the "national question" and "identity politics," which simply put mean that the rights of the Quebec nation take precedence over all other minority rights in the province. You cannot avoid belonging to a group that is regarded as socially marginalized; that notion is always there, with values imposed by the dominant culture, as illustrated in the little story above about my son's experience with our family name. Resist as we might, the forces of assimilation are relentless.

Discussions about all this in Quebec are fraught with perils and traps, and even raising the subject in this book might be seen in some quarters as Quebec-bashing. That speaks to the dilemma that minorities face in claiming their own cultural space here. Quebec is actually about a generation behind the rest of Canada in terms of race relations and in the development of minority culture. Next door in Ontario, for example, however effective it may or may not be, the provincial government acknowledged the problem when it created an Anti-Racism Directorate with a three-year strategic plan to administer the province's Anti-Racism Act, 2017, under a minister responsible for combatting racism.

In Quebec, aside from everyday racism, racialized minorities face systemic racism. I'll let the numbers speak for themselves: one-third of Montreal's population is composed of visible minorities, but in 2017 there were no people of colour among the councillors of Projet Montréal's new municipal government, the year before that, only 6.9 per cent of Montreal's police force were from racialized minorities.[330] Only 1.6 per cent of the work force at Hydro-Québec, one of the province's biggest employers, were from a racially defined minority (312 out of 20,000) in 2016. Even in early 2018, at the top of the provincial ladder, only one out of the twenty-eight members of the Quebec cabinet, or 3.5 per cent, was a member of a racialized minority, in a province where the last census (2016) showed that 13 per cent of the population belong to a racialized minority. I think you get the idea.

According to the 2016 census, Montreal is the most trilingual city in Canada with 21 per cent of the population being able to speak at least three languages. I, for one, celebrate this diversity. Fighting for diversity, though, is only the start of the fight against systemic racism. I was reminded of this on February 11, 2018, when I attended a conference organized by the Center for Research-Action on Race Relations at the Union United Church, a beacon in Montreal's Black community. Nelson Mandela visited the church in June 1990, a few months after gaining his freedom from twenty-seven years of imprisonment in South Africa on February 11 of that year. The Quebec National Assembly passed a motion in 2015 declaring February 11 Nelson Mandela Day after an initiative pushed by a group of racialized minority citizens. Systemic racism and violence affect many Black lives, as speakers at the 2018 conference testi-fied; a recent example was the 2017 police killing of Pierre Coriolan, a Black man with mental health issues. The conference launched a petition drive to demand that the city of Montreal establish a consultation process on concrete ways and means to fight systemic racism. Once again, the Black community was showing the way for all racialized minorities, tackling these difficult issues through unity and organization.

Attending this conference stimulated me all over again to consider how my community, the Chinese community, could participate actively in the struggle to move Quebec forward towards becoming an equitable and inclusive soci-ety. In the years immediately after we won the apology and partial redress from the federal government in 2006, I was still stuck in the mindset of Head Tax and Exclusion Act campaign politics. But as this book was heading towards publication, I was forced to stretch my thinking in the difficult task of writing about my identity and belonging in Quebec within the specific constraints of life in this province. Actually, the process began when I worked on the film *Être chinois au Québec* (Being Chinese in Quebec) from 2009 to 2012.

* * *

When I first became involved in the advance planning for a film focusing on the Chinese in Quebec, I had no way of knowing that the political and artistic struggle over the vision of the film would end up giving me a fresh perspective on my community.

The idea for the film was born after a fund of $5 million was allocated to the Chinese community under the Community Historical Recognition Program. This was something the federal government had grudgingly provided in the wake of its June 2006 apology in Parliament for the Head Tax and Exclusion Act. In late 2008, Yat Lo—now on the Chinese Canadian Advisory Commit-tee of the recognition program for Quebec—contacted me to say that there was money left and very few projects were coming out of Quebec.

In early January 2009, Walter Tom, May Chiu and I met at the Arahova Restaurant on St. Viateur in Montreal and, over souvlaki, discussed how we could take advantage of the funding to bring the story of the Head Tax and Exclusion Act to the Quebec population. We settled on proposing a video project as a follow-up to *Moving the Mountain*—twenty years later. I approached Malcolm Guy, my co-director of the original film, and he agreed to participate under the auspices of his production company, Productions Multi-Monde.

At this time I didn't have a good grasp of the circumstances or the views of the 102,000 Chinese living in Quebec (92,000 of whom lived in the greater Montreal area). I visualized the film treatment as being rooted in the redress movement. The Head Tax and Exclusion Act campaign politics had actually become less and less relevant over time, with the underlying legacy of the head tax not that apparent to the next generation of Chinese Québécois. Nevertheless, I persisted in this thinking, as the proposal I prepared to submit for the funding reflected, with questions such as: "How will the new generation of Chinese Canadians face the tough issues of equality and social justice in the wake of the Apology hard won by their elders… in their ongoing struggles for self-identity … and integration?"

The fault lines of the Chinese community and Quebec society were not that obvious to any of us at the outset. We submitted the proposal in April 2009, and after Malcolm haggled for many months with recognition program officials, the $180,000 funding we had requested for the project was finally approved. Shooting began in the summer of 2011 with a 600-mile road trip up to the Gaspésie, or Gaspé Peninsula, to look for the sparse number of Chinese who had settled in the outlying regions of Quebec.

By nature I am an agitator, a propagandist, and my style is to provoke people to think out of the common thought. I believed this would be a good opportunity to deal with racism in Quebec and how it affects the Chinese community. However, I was about to experience first-hand just how difficult it is to challenge the "model minority" myth that has so long applied to Chinese Québécois, a myth based on the idea that the Chinese have all done exceptionally well for themselves in the province, learned French and declined to fight the system. Even my production partners on the film were worried by the prospect of challenging the myth. It's possible there may have been some concern that this could harm the film's chances of being broadcast or getting widespread distribution. But my position was that it was necessary to look at all angles. Some countered with the argument that not all Québécois are racist, xenophobic or Islamophobic—a typical line used to avoid or deflect discussion of these issues in Quebec. For my part, I did not see how anyone making a serious film or offering any kind of honest commentary about the contemporary Chinese in Quebec could do so without dealing with the issues of "national oppression" and "big nation chauvinism," terms used by the

Québécois to describe their situation, but which could just as well be applied to the minorities in the province. Ultimately I was unable to win this argument and in 2012 had to dissociate myself from the project, although my name remains in the film credits.

I didn't object that my shooting script was not followed, since I did what I do best and enjoyed doing: organizing public meetings with young members of the Chinese community. I organized two focus meetings, at the Young Chinese Professionals Association offices and at the Montreal Chinese Alliance Church, where the "provocative" 1993 video I'd made called *Gens du pays: The Chinese of Québec* was shown and discussed. It was through these discussions that I began to reshape my thinking of what young Chinese were facing in Quebec. Each of these meetings drew about twenty people, mostly in their twenties, including students and young professionals, all very smart and confident of their place in Quebec society and all either bilingual or trilingual, being Bill 101 kids—that is, born since the 1977 Quebec legislation made French the official language in the province and required immigrant children to attend French-language schools. It was this energy and confidence in staking out their place in Quebec that I wanted to project in the film. At the same time, I could see that they still felt unsure about their place here; the reticence came from the lack of opportunities to build their sense of belonging and acceptance.

I recruited two bright, photogenic young Chinese Montrealers, Bethany Or and Parker Mah, to act as the conduits for the film. They represented the new generation of Chinese youth who did not participate in the redress campaign, but they were community conscious enough to understand the significance of the Head Tax and Exclusion Act.

Parker, originally from Vancouver, is a fourth-generation Chinese Canadian whose grandfather and great-grandfather paid the head tax. Bethany is also fourth generation. Not all their four generations were born in Canada but all of those forebears lived in and contributed to Canada and paid the head tax. Parker, with English as his first language, was more comfortable in expressing his Chinese-ness, even though his parents sacrificed his learning of Chinese to allow him to learn French as a second language. Bethany was less confident in her Chinese skin. She had become somewhat assimilated due to Bill 101 and felt more comfortable speaking French in the trendy neighbourhood of Mile End. These two were typical of today's young generation in our community in Quebec.

The process of making the film was an awakening for me, in terms of both how we are seen in Quebec and, more importantly, how we see ourselves.

During the filmmaking, I wrote a piece in the film blog about the responsibilities of minority filmmakers. I had hoped to influence the film crew, but some perceived it as an example of Chinese "narrow nationalism." Minority filmmakers "must answer for what they produce," I said, "because what they do is a reflection of the community they live in and they must take responsibility for the end product and be accountable to that community." And I went on to say that "primarily we must tell and show the truth and do it honestly and passionately. We must tell the stories that the mainstream ignores or refuses to acknowledge as important." Further, "we must tell it in such a way that is not tripe, cliché, stereotypical or to fit certain expectations of the mainstream."

I went on to note that minorities are acutely underrepresented in the dominant news media, films and public discourse in Quebec. Minorities must develop our own presence and representation. We must promote and be proud of our cultural works and not be afraid to confront the issue of under-representation. We must also demand access to the mainstream media and not remain a kind of exotic other.

My blog entries have since been deleted from the film website, and of course in the end this film was not my kind of film, and I left after I started feeling uncomfortable working on a project for which I could not take responsibility. But the resulting political debate and struggle around the film helped me gain new insights into being Chinese in Quebec. You might say that I'm just tossing out sour apples, but since walking out on the film at the beginning of 2012, I've been freed up to examine where the Chinese stand in this province through the experiences and tangible examples that came my way because I was engaged in this film. Now, I can see the film as a kind of transmission belt, something that helped move us all forward by pointing out the problems that the Chinese population faces in Quebec.

* * *

Être chinois au Québec – un road movie debuted in May 2013. The film follows Bethany and Parker as they meet other Chinese youth and explore how these young people feel about themselves, living as they do in Quebec, and what they know about the history of their community. The film is mostly in French and it received favourable reviews in the media, in my opinion because it did not challenge any of the preconceived mainstream notions of the Chinese minority.

I've avoided commenting publicly on the film in the years since it was made because I respect the Chinese Canadians who worked on it—they had high hopes of making a difference—and because I also did not want to damage Malcolm's efforts in distributing the film for broadcast, since he put a lot of time and energy into getting it produced. But enough years have passed for me to express sadness that the huge impact we had hoped to make on Quebec society didn't come about; mainstream society was not provoked into considering the Chinese as a long-established part of the fabric of Quebec.

Issues that weren't covered included the underlying malaise that the Chinese community faces when it comes to getting jobs and access to services. The film could also have been relevant in terms of current events in Quebec around then. The governing Parti Québécois was trying, through its proposed Charter of Values, to outlaw any open signs of religion for public workers, such as wearing the Muslim hijab, the Jewish yarmulke or the Sikh turban. A few years later both separatist parties with seats in the National Assembly—Québec solidaire, after its merger with Option nationale, and the Parti Québécois— put independence at the forefront of their public discourse. In Quebec, the voice of the Chinese population tends to be lost in all this political noise. The film did not expose the rift between the majority and the struggles of the minority fighting for a more pluralistic and inclusive Quebec society.

A shorter made-for-TV version of the film that had a potentially wider audience, on cable TV's French documentary channel Canal D, was safe, inoffensive and cuddly, with a hint of the exotic. (This is the version I am focusing on in my comments.) In it, the French-speaking Chinese had become the "model minority" in Quebec.

It was not a film of struggle from the heart of the community, dealing with the legacy of the racist Head Tax and Exclusion Act and the Laundry Tax— Quebec's own unique law. Nor did it confront head-on the exoticization of the community; the act of exoticizing renders you stereotypical, different and not a part of the Quebec fabric. The film did include a segment on the "buying" of Chinese babies—the Association de la Sainte-Enfance raised funds for its missionary work by collecting from schoolchildren in Quebec under the rubric of saving the little souls in China; donating 25 ¢ meant you could get a small medallion that depicted a Chinese child, thus you were "buying" a

Chinese baby. This practice meant that for many in the mainstream Québécois generation of the 1950s and '60s, this was their first introduction to Chinese people. I can imagine that "saving" Chinese babies would have had a strong effect on the mainstream perception of the Chinese people. That was an era of an all-white environment, with minorities unwelcome in French schools. None of this was explained in the film, so watching *Être chinois au Québec*, you would think all this was benign because the racism is couched behind the façade of nationalism and in defence of the national culture and identity.

But there are real day-to-day struggles in Quebec against systemic racism. Chinese immigrants still face difficulty in finding work and getting employment equity. They are under-represented in Quebec government institutions,[331] and they struggle to access social services when they face problems like gambling addiction or depression. The elderly struggle to find housing and health care with adequate translation services. Young people face insufficient youth and educational services. Among younger people, the job situation is a big issue, as is the constant struggle against assimilation and for cultural identity and self-expression. These day-to-day struggles are not glamorous, but they are real. They are a far cry from reflecting a model minority.

As I feared, the only portrayal of struggle in the film was cut for the Canal D broadcast that I saw. I suppose it was cut to fit the time slot. I need to write a few words about this part of the full film. It involved the Chinese immigrant workers at Calego International Inc., a backpack manufacturer in Ville St-Laurent. It was a struggle that gained widespread support in the Montreal Chinese community but very little coverage in the mainstream media.

The following paragraph is a summary of the 2011 Quebec Human Rights Commission judgment:[332]

The matter dated back to July 11, 2006. On that day, only workers of Chinese origin had been summoned to a meeting in the company warehouse to hear the criticisms of owner Stephen Rapps. Through an interpreter, he told the workers: "This is Canada, not China. We take showers and shampoo every day, wash hands with soap, flush the toilet after use. Don't piss on the floor… This is my kitchen, not yours. My kitchen, I want it clean. You Chinese eat like pigs." The Chinese workers demanded an apology from the owner. When the owner refused to apologize, the workers walked out and resigned en masse and they filed a complaint with Quebec's human rights commission. On April 19,

2011, the Human Rights Tribunal ruled in favour of the fifteen Chinese workers and ordered Calego to pay $150,000 in damages.

The factory owner appealed the ruling, claiming he had a right to "freedom of expression." The fifteen Calego workers had to wait until February 28, 2014, when the Quebec Court of Appeal ruled in their favour and awarded them $130,000.

Xiang Ma was a professor in a university in China when she decided to immigrate to Canada. She was one of the leaders of the Calego workers who confronted the employer. "We are educated people," she said in an interview. "We know how to live." Xiang Ma and Yong Shan He led the walkout and filed the complaint with the Commission des droits de la personne et des droits de la jeunesse (there is no official English name but it is essentially the Quebec human rights commission). Yong Shan He was physically assaulted for his leadership role, but he was not intimidated; the tribunal awarded him additional compensation.

Nowadays, Ma owns and operates a dry cleaning establishment, and He, who was a mining engineer in China, is working in another factory as a numerical control machine operator. Both Ma and He believe that workers, especially minorities, should stick together and oppose any form of discrimination. As recent immigrants, they are determined to stand up for their rights and make a good life for themselves and their families here. Their struggle for justice united the Chinese community behind them. Through their actions, they set a good example for Chinese and other minorities to fight against discrimination.

In September 2011, I met He and Sheng Liu, a supporter who initiated the community campaign in solidarity with the workers. In our discussion, he said he believed this was the first time the Chinese people had waged a struggle of this type in Quebec. "We hope with our actions, we have shown to all Chinese and Asian people in Montreal that one should never be afraid to stand up for civil rights and to fight racism," he said. Liu was moved to take action when he read about the case in the Chinese newspapers. "We have the right to speak out. Supporting fellow Chinese workers was the right thing to do. I didn't know the Calego workers, but I had a sense of shared responsibility to defend them."

The Calego workers and other new immigrants had learned the lessons of the Chinese Revolution during their socialist education in China, and they knew about the struggle for rights and the importance of solidarity. For them,

322 · CHAPTER 17

unity, organization and solidarity were necessary to win their extraordinary victory against racism. The story of their victory and ongoing need for solidarity deserved to be told to the wider society, especially in the Francophone media which disdains to cover minority struggles. These were role models in our community, but none of the viewers who watched *Être chinois au Québec* on Canal D saw them, and Quebec society generally remains blissfully unaware of the Calego workers' struggle.

There is another issue—about a quintessential stereotypical livelihood—that I believe is worth discussing.

The film shows Zhou Jinn, who has two PhDs but could not get a job in his chosen field of biology because his French was not good enough. He now operates a *dépanneur*—a convenience store. The dépanneurs are the classic immigrant family businesses today in Quebec. They are like the hand laundries of a previous era. Through hard work and long hours, dépanneur owners want to make a good life for their families, especially their children. This is the aspect I find of interest. Many Chinese-trained professionals fall back on going into business for themselves due to the discrimination of a closed society, but that is only one aspect of a much more complex dynamic of operating a dépanneur. I am not sure what the film showed in this regard—happy convenience store operators? Someone from the community with a more organic appreciation of the complexity of immigrant life would see things differently. The majority of Quebecers don't see the struggle aspect since dépanneur operators, like the old laundrymen, remain in the background and go unnoticed.

The other perspective sees them as being wealthy investor immigrants buying into small businesses. In reality, some were professionals in China with the skills required to get into Canada, but they have to labour in factories here, as in the case of the Calego workers. Once the family saves enough money, they can purchase a dépanneur to work for themselves. This is the clash of cultures that I was hoping to expose.

* * *

The road trip with the film crew to find Chinese living in Quebec's outer regions stirred me to consider the role Chinese immigrants have had in the historical development of other parts of Canada.

The economic growth of this country (in other words, Canadian capitalism) has strong ties to the racist exploitation of Chinese immigrants. We know about the contribution of the Chinese in building the iconic Canadian Pacific Railway (CPR); the head tax, which totalled over $23 million, nearly matched the $25 million[333] Canada granted the CPR to build the railway, so Chinese immigrants helped build the transcontinental railroad *and* helped finance it. But when the film entourage visited the Jardins de Métis—known in English as the Reford Gardens—near Matane on the south shore of the St. Lawrence River in 2011, I heard about a less well-known example of economic exploitation: Through some kind of historical alignment of the stars, an element of Canadian capitalism was helped off the ground by the food preferences of early Chinese arrivals in Canada.

The Reford family owns the Reford Gardens. The summer home of Lord Mount Stephen (George Stephen), first president of the CPR, is built inside the grounds of the gardens, overlooking the majestic St. Lawrence. Stephen's sister married into the Reford clan. The Chinese pioneers unwittingly contributed to establishing the Reford family empire in the rice business because they were major customers. Family scion Alexander Reford, who in 2011 was director of the gardens, told me that Robert Reford established the Mount Royal Rice Mills, today's Dainty Foods,[334] in Victoria in 1885 to mill unprocessed rice from the Far East to supply the Chinese population in BC. Ottawa imposed a tariff on foreign milled rice to keep the price of rice milled in Canada artificially high. The Chinese had no choice but to pay the higher prices.[335] By 2018, Dainty Foods was, according to the *Canadian Food & Grocery Industry Guide*, "Canada's preeminent supplier of value-added rice products to North American markets."[336]

* * *

I can't write about the *Être chinois au Québec* story without touching on a clear example of the competing visions for the film, reflecting different perspectives on the Chinese minority. This involved two Chinese missionaries in the Cree community of Oujé-Bougoumou, in Northern Quebec. Malcolm thought it would be an interesting scoop to show Chinese Christian missionaries working among the Cree people. Our researcher, Doris Ng, had a friend who is the daughter of the missionary couple and she thought this would be a great story. I was hesitant to get caught up in the excitement of starting our road trip by driving eight hours from Montreal up to Oujé-Bougoumou, and pointed out that we would be publicizing a colonizing religion's ongoing influence in

Northern Quebec. The fact that the proselytizing was done by Chinese missionaries did not make it any more palatable to me.

Upon digging further into the situation, here's what I found: The Chinese missionaries, Pastor Enoch Hall and his wife, Frieda, had been serving the Cree community for thirty years since immigrating to Canada from Hong Kong. Apparently they changed their family name from Ho (He in the Pinyin system of transliteration) to Hall, since some of the local people had trouble pronouncing Ho. They belong to the evangelizing Pentecostal denomination, as part of the Chinese Christian Church network. The only place of worship in Oujé-Bougoumou is their church.

A classic struggle between Indigenous spiritualism and Christianity was taking place in Oujé-Bougoumou, as I said to the film crew when I told them that I refused to take part in this story.

Due to complex colonial events in history, Christianity got a foothold among the Northern Cree in the first half of the twentieth century with the arrival of the Anglican, Catholic, Evangelical and Pentecostal churches and residential schools. As described in a *Globe and Mail*[337] article, Oujé-Bougoumou was created out of the desolate wilderness after the Cree Band survived years of dislocation, poverty and adversity. The modern village was formed in the 1990s and recognized by the United Nations as a model community.

Oujé-Bougoumou has a population of 725 (2011 census), 95 per cent of whom are Cree. One of the most modern and imposing structures in the community, built in a stylized teepee, is Reverend Hall's Pentecostal church.

In the months before our intended trip to Oujé-Bougoumou, a news story broke that underlined my discomfort about telling the story of these Chinese missionaries: the Oujé-Bougoumou Band Council dismantled a *mitutsaan*, or sweat lodge, that band member Redfern Mianscum had built in a friend's backyard. The council had passed a resolution that an article in *Indian Country Today* described this way:

Citing [the] vision of their elders, the Oujé-Bougoumou Council adopted a Resolution … banning sweat lodge ceremonies and all traditional Native spiritual practices on the reserve.

The Council hereby unanimously declares that the sweat lodge is to be dismantled and removed, and that all sweat lodge practices in the community immediately cease. Oujé-Bougoumou will continue to uphold its faith in and guidance by God.[338]

The same article reported Redfern Mianscum's defence of his spiritual practices:

"The sweat lodge helped me turn away from alcohol and things that were hurting my family," said Mianscum, who returned to Cree traditions four years ago after his family suffered the loss of a baby. "I went back to the healing methods of our ancestors, and it turned me around for the better," he said. "I wanted to share that with my family and others who believe this way."

Redfern Mianscum believed that no government—including a tribal government—should deny its citizens the right to religious freedom. "I have the right to practice my spiritual beliefs using the methods of our ancestors. These ceremonies helped me with my healing journey," the article quoted him as saying. "These traditions should be respected and protected."

After enduring years of hardship and displacement because of James Bay hydroelectric projects, the Oujé-Bougoumou Cree received formal recognition from the Canadian government in 1992, with land granted to establish a permanent village and with inherent rights of self-government and self-determination. These are the rights that the band council cited to determine the fate of the sweat lodge.

Oujé-Bougoumou Chief Louise Wapachee was inaugurated in 2007, with Pastor Enoch Hall presiding at the event.

These are issues for the Cree people to decide. My argument prevailed and subsequently, the roadtrip to Oujé-Bougoumou never took place. Perhaps one day I will drive up there myself and say hello to Reverend Hall.

At the other end of the spectrum, earlier in this chapter I mentioned there were areas I wanted to venture into in the making of *Être chinois au Québec* that others were not keen on exploring. Interviews and parts of interviews that I regarded as important ended up on the cutting-room floor. The issues involved are significant and have yet to be addressed in the Chinese community, and without access to government services we will not receive help any time soon.

There was the story of May Chiu's mom. It was a concrete example of the ongoing struggles among Chinese immigrant women—struggles of isolation, loneliness, mental health problems, the lack of services and support for their situation. Many in the Chinese community have lived through this with our moms and these stories need to be revealed and the women's contributions brought to light. May described her mother's poignant personal story, but it was left out of the film.

Then there was the segment in the film that involved a group that at the time was known as the Chinese Social Club, which would go on to become the core of an anti-racist organization called the Progressive Chinese Quebecers (PCQ). The social club aimed to critically analyze Quebec society and take action. Many of its members were young, and young people have the natural ability to break through old and moribund conventions—the baggage of conventional wisdom does not burden them. The social club wanted to operate from within the Chinese community with its own content to avoid becoming assimilated into the larger social movement. The club had that great potential to question—and to change—things as they are. Ainsley, one of the participants, touched on the need to organize when she said, "In the face of racism, I need to be with my people." The film gave short shrift to these views.

The club went on to develop into a Facebook page with over 280 members, who later organized the PCQ to take part in the ongoing struggle against systemic racism in Quebec. Activists in the PCQ include May Chiu, Alan Wong, Janet Lumb, Bethany Or, Parker Mah, Amy Ma and some old-timers like Jonas Ma, Walter Tom and me. A positive role of the film was that it stimulated some Chinese activists in Quebec to network on social media and to get organized.

May and Walter spoke for themselves. Why they became activists was edited out of the film. They had spoken about existing social injustice affecting the community, immigrant struggles, ongoing discrimination, social services and cultural identity. These are the struggles that May and Walter were implicated in and these struggles are ongoing and others needed to learn from their example.

Another issue involves one of my earlier scripts, that was not followed, in which I wanted to address how ex–Parti Québécois leader André Boisclair slurred Chinese people and got away with it. He used the French term *"les yeux bridés"* to describe Asians. It means slanted eyes.

Boisclair said that when he was at Harvard, a third of the students were "slanted eyes." He said he meant it as a compliment because these slanted eyes were the overachievers. Following a barrage of condemnation from the Chinese media and community organizations, he hid behind the nuance of the French language, saying that those who were offended do not understand how the language is used. PQ officials then blamed the Chinese community for always making racism an issue. You could say that being nationalist means you don't have to say sorry.

This exposure in the film would have placed the Chinese community within the Quebec context and illustrated how the dominant society has a way to go in being more sensitive to the reality of minorities. But, alas, this was also swept under the rug.

While we were preparing to shoot the film, a controversy on Quebec cinema broke out as Quebec actor and director Jacob Tierney said in an interview in *La Presse* that Quebec cinema was *"blanc, blanc, blanc*—white, white, white" which did not reflect the reality of immigrants and minorities here.[339] The largely nationalist cultural community denounced Tierney and circled the wagons to bluntly declare that Québécois films naturally reflected the history and culture of the Quebec people. However, these historical and cultural depictions do not include immigrants and minorities. To be fair, some people, like Quebec filmmaker Philippe Falardeau, came to Tierney's defence.

In the context of the Quebec elections in 2012 and the xenophobia stirred up by the Parti Québécois position on limiting minority rights, we needed to hear the views of minorities, including the Chinese community. The ruling majority was trying to legislate people's values and social behaviour. The line between pluralism and nationalism could not have been more acute. Who would stand up for us? Who would represent our point of view? The film was still being edited, and it could have addressed the issue of xenophobia from the PQ, but it did not. Again, this was an opportunity lost.

Such criticism of the PQ may have been construed as Quebec-bashing by the hard-core nationalists who control the mass media through, for example, Québecor Inc. (owned by ex-PQ leader Pierre Karl Péladeau). The voice of the minorities, especially the Chinese minority in Quebec, is minuscule in comparison, like a peashooter against a cannon.

Être chinois au Québec avoided any criticism of the xenophobic nationalism. It did not show the Chinese community standing up to this xenophobia.

In the film, Sophie Zhang cites the protection of the Francophone language and culture to explain why Quebec is not as welcoming to other cultures, but that falls into the category of justification for not dealing with minority struggles. Sophie, a medical student who grew up in small-town Quebec, Ste-Geneviève-de-Batiscan, has internalized the arguments of the nationalist

Québécois on the need to protect the French language, culture and values. Twenty years earlier, Cynthia Lam, in my film *Gens du pays: The Chinese of Québec*, gave the same explanation but she concluded that the Quebec insecurity complex is no justification for ignoring minority rights: "We cannot wait for the majority to resolves its problems. We need to address our own problems too." Cynthia put forward a line of struggle.

Some of the examples above demonstrate an atmosphere of victimization in Quebec. The nationalist media and politicians assail the majority population about the constant threat to their cultural values, language and way of life that seemingly come from the cultural minorities. On the other side, the minority communities feel the oppressive atmosphere of racial profiling and systemic racism. Psychologically, we seek acceptance and validation from the majority. The result is that I find it difficult to carve out some space to articulate my cultural need to freely express myself as a Chinese Québécois in order to fully participate and contribute to a pluralistic society.

Some of us refuse to be just add-ons to the dominant culture. Some claim that we suffer from an identity crisis because of our inability to assimilate. Some of us like to display the acceptable "song and dance" culture that offends no one; our attitudes are still defined by the dominant culture and we tend to be defensive for being different. The "in your face" cultural consciousness will hopefully advance, once we stop defining ourselves in reaction to the dominant society and express ourselves on our own terms. There is little of the in-your-face attitude in *Être chinois au Québec*, but the model minority syndrome came through.

The subjects in the film are mainly overachievers from the Chinese community. I tried to counter this by finding working-class or struggling immigrants who had less language skills and less confidence to talk about their situations. Without building a degree of trust or friendship with these individuals, it was not possible to have them speak about their personal situation in front of the camera. However, the Chinese workers at Calego were the ideal counterpoint to the model minority image. They were actual workers resisting racial discrimination and they won their battle against corporate interests. But their story was not told to the general audience in prime time.

In the larger picture, Quebec has tried to imitate the European model of the traditionally "pure" nation-state, notably France. However, time and reality march on. Quebec needs to recognize the hybrid nature of its society. The First Nations are true nations, but they do not have the outlook of the European nation-state. Their nature is to live in collaboration with others, which they showed in teaching the early French colonials how to survive the harsh Canadian winters, as John Ralston Saul eloquently pointed out in his book, *A Fair Country*.[340]

Quebec's reality is being transformed into an intercultural and hybrid one by new immigrants marrying into Quebec society. However, some of our young Chinese Québécois are stuck in the narrow nationalist mentality of Quebec self-preservation. We need to get our young people to think about our own community's struggles.

I support the Quebec nation's right to self-determination and I embrace the French language, Quebec history and culture. However, most minorities here do not share the nationalist passion for an independent country of Quebec. Separation is seen as being divisive and the struggle for the rights of minorities would be more effective in unity with others across Canada. Some old nationalist militants still hold to the theoretical position that Quebec is an oppressed nation because it does not have the constitutional right to secede. But old revolutionaries would say a nation cannot free itself if it oppresses others.

Alas, *Être chinois au Québec* could have been an opportunity for our youth to explore and express the needs and struggles of the Chinese community in relation to the larger issues of Quebec society. This could have been the legacy of the head tax redress struggle.

Cultural minorities in Quebec have been so absorbed in the implanted ideas of the need to protect the French language and Québécois culture that there hasn't been too much space left for these minorities to develop and exert themselves independently on their own cultural terrain. However, Quebec is changing, and changing for the better. Independent of the wills of the *pure laine* nationalists, Quebec is becoming more diverse, mixed, multicultural, multiracial and, dare I say it, more multinational. Optimistically, I see Quebec becoming a pluralistic society where people are willing to live inclusively with others who are different.

As *Être chinois au Québec* was being edited, I wanted to write the narration, thinking that a tone of struggle could transform the overall film, but I was told not to and to allow the editor to work without my influence. It was at that point that I walked away from the film. One reason why I have brought all this up now is that there were people apart from me who were hoping to see the film unveil issues that still need addressing. For example, May Chiu, one of the most integrated members of our community, wrote to me after watching the final few minutes of the nearly completed edit that "whatever you do, I'm sure the finished product will be very provocative!"[341]

Sorry, May, I wasn't able to be there to make this film provocative.

* * *

The provincial Liberal government under Philippe Couillard took an unprecedented step in July 2017. Pushed by a petition of 2,700 names and recognizing that there was a problem with systemic racism in Quebec, it called for a Commission on Systemic Racism. Immediately, there were howls of opposition from the nationalist Parti Québécois about "putting Quebec on trial," and from the Coalition Avenir Québec, which said that Haitian migrants fleeing the US were a threat to Quebec's "language and values."[342] Both groups called for the commission to be cancelled. People on Quebec's nationalist left were also divided. Some said that the commission would cause divisions along racial lines or that there was no systemic racism since we never had a slave trade in Quebec, unlike the United States.

Overnight, the Progressive Chinese Quebecers (PCQ) went from a virtual organization on Facebook to a physical reality as a dozen activists came together to develop a position paper to deliver at the Commission on Systemic Racism. There was much excitement among the racialized communities as over thirty different organizations received promise of funding from the government to hold community consultations. The PCQ reached out to other Asian communities, such as the Koreans and Japanese. We formed a coalition with Ciné-Asie, PINAY (Filipino Women's Organization) and the South Asia Women's Centre. As an Asian bloc, we were preparing to participate fully in the government commission.

In the meantime, the Quebec government in October 2017 passed Bill C-62 targeting Muslim women, forbidding them from wearing face covers while receiving or giving government services. This led to the fear that Muslim women wearing a face cover would not be able to ride on public transit, until the justice minister was forced to clarify that this should not be the case. There was a big outcry from the Muslim community and civil libertarians. In December 2017, a Quebec Superior Court judge temporarily suspended this aspect of the law. Many of us linked this attack against the Muslim community to the systemic racism in Quebec society. One of the many lessons I had learned from the Head Tax and Exclusion Act is that when the government legislates against one group of people and treats them as "others," it creates a less accepting atmosphere in society.

So it was not surprising that also in October 2017, a month after the Commission on Systemic Racism was to start, the government pulled the ground out from under us. It caved in to the opposition and scrapped the commission, saying it would focus instead on a one-day forum on "valuing diversity and fighting discrimination." The more than forty anti-racist organizations (including the PCQ) that formed the Table de concertation contre le racisme systémique vowed to carry on and to establish a People's Commission on Systemic Racism. On November 15, 2017, more than five thousand people marched through downtown Montreal in a demonstration against hate and racism that was endorsed by 170 different organizations.

As I write, the fight against racism, systemic or otherwise, is ongoing in Quebec. The Quebec Chinese community, often perceived as being dormant and apolitical, has also been organizing to participate in this battle.

Chapter 18

"Listen to Your Mother"

"Being deeply loved by someone gives you strength, while loving someone deeply gives you courage."
—Laozi

---

*Before coming to Canada at the end of our honeymoon, we had an early
morning domestic flight from Kunming to Guangzhou, China, on the way
out to Hong Kong. On the bus to the Kunming airport, Dong Qing checked
that she had all her Canadian immigration papers in her bag. She had had
to leave her Chinese identification documents at her old workplace when
she left her job, but she had her Chinese passport. At security, a guard
demanded to see her residency card or she would not be allowed to pass.
Dong Qing impressed me by showing the fiery and combative side of her
personality. The guard was about to tear open the immigration envelope,
which announced in large writing that it was not to be opened except by a
Canadian immigration officer. "Go ahead and open the envelope and I will
have you arrested, not just in China but also by Canada!" she said. The
official backed down and we were the last ones to board the flight.*

It was a snowy evening, the last day of January 1989. I was sitting in front
of the TV watching some forgettable program and convalescing from an

operation for a burst appendix. I had developed appendicitis on the long journey home from a holiday in Fiji. Initially, the doctor misdiagnosed it as the flu
and fatigue from the lengthy flight. Three days later I checked into emergency
and they operated on me straight away. Although I was not overly preoccupied
by the seriousness of this health problem, everyone told me that it was serious
and I could have died.

The telephone rang.

"William, do you know who this is?" the woman at the other end of the
receiver asked. "Do you remember me?"

I knew that voice and I did remember her but in my surprise I hesitated in
saying yes and only blurted out, "Well, ah … ."

"It's GG!"[343]

"Of course, I remember you! Are you in town? Are you in Canada?"

The last time I'd seen GG was in 1976. She was a Chinese Malaysian student completing her degree in international studies at McGill. We had met at
meetings of the Afro-Asians or the Canada-China Society. We had attended
various political activities together and had gone to some social functions with
mutual friends from Malaysia and Singapore. At the end of the summer term,
she was going to Boston to see a friend. I remember it was a hot, sultry night
in August as I drove her to the Voyageur Terminus at the corner of Berri and
de Maisonneuve to catch the midnight bus. In front of the bus door, she stood
close to me for a long moment, looking straight at me with her big brown
eyes and her moist, full, sensuous lips, inviting a kiss. Cowardly, I hugged her
goodbye. On the way back to my one-room apartment in the McGill Ghetto, I
kicked myself several times for not kissing her.

Thirteen years later she was back—on a six-month sabbatical at McGill—
and she wanted to see me. We had dinner the next night. She told me that she
had been thinking about us and asked if I knew that she was crazy about me. I
didn't know what to say. I knew she was very expressive but I didn't expect her
to be so bold. I admired her for being able to reveal her feelings so strongly. I
wished I could. I was stunned; I was excited; I never thought a woman would
feel that way about me. We had a very close and personal discussion over dinner. I am not normally an emotionally accessible person, but I was able to
open myself to her. She told me that she was married. Her husband was back
in Malaysia but they had an open marriage. I didn't know what that meant and
I became hesitant. Sensing my hesitation, she took the initiative and gave me
the kiss that I should have given her thirteen years earlier.

"Let's go back to your place," she whispered in my ear.

It was a thrilling and passionate time with GG. Her vulnerability brought out the vulnerability in me; it was very intimate, but the intensity started to cool off after five months, towards the end of June. We ended it over lunch in a restaurant across from her apartment near McGill. It was the moralist in me speaking, as I questioned why, as a married woman, she wanted to have this relationship. She didn't answer. I was afraid of a long-term emotional entanglement with a married woman, so I said I felt uneasy about continuing. She said she was going home to Malaysia the following week. One of the last things she said to me was, "Listen to your mother; find yourself a good wife."

* * *

I had contracted peritonitis from the burst appendix and I had adhesions surrounding my intestine from the surgery. All this resulted in a three-week stay at St. Mary's Hospital. Upon leaving the hospital, I was alone in the house. My mother and sisters, Pui Yung and King Sin, took turns cooking for me as I spent the month of January recovering and feeling sorry for myself.

My mother was wearing her worries on her face. "Ah Wee, this situation is not good for you," she said. "You need to have a wife to take care of you. Listen to your mother."

Without my knowledge, my mother and sisters had been complicit in pursuing Dong Qing Chen after my mother and King Sin met her during their visit to China in 1987. Pui Yung must have written to Dong Qing pretending to be me because in April 1989, I received a letter from Dong Qing thanking me for my photo and she enclosed a photo of herself. The photo showed a very pretty, happy young woman, innocent and vibrant. My sister wanted me to go to China to meet her.

I told GG about Dong Qing, and when I showed her the photo, I expected some recrimination, but I got the opposite reaction.

"Oh, I am so excited for you. She's so attractive—just perfect for you."

GG had a way of making me feel positive about myself.

My whole family was on my case to visit China to meet Dong Qing. Then the Tiananmen Incident happened in June of that year. China was in turmoil and I had a convenient excuse to put off the trip. My mind was in its own state of turmoil. I was under too much mental stress, trying to intellectualize and analyze the situation. What do I do? Am I ready for an arranged marriage?

None of my close friends, who were all non-Chinese, were much help. They all believed in the notion of romantic love. They advised me to be careful. Not to get fooled by pretty looks. Once I brought Dong Qing to Canada, her whole family would follow suit. Did I want that kind of responsibility?

Aside from organizing head tax redress activities and working on *Moving the Mountain*, my mind was preoccupied with Dong Qing for the rest of 1989. Well, not just her specifically, but the idea of her and the idea of going to China to marry her. I even discussed my situation with Charlie Chin, who was in Montreal for the head tax benefit concert in November of that year. Charlie was staying with me and during a late-night chat he gave me his words of wisdom.

"What's so bad about marrying someone over there?" he asked. "It's been going on for generations. It's worked for our parents and grandparents. If you hang on to that Western mentality, you'll never be true to yourself."

Sound advice, but I was still conflicted in my mind, heart and soul. I wasn't ready to let go of that Western mentality.

I wondered how my father felt when he went back to China to marry my mother in 1925. Those were simpler times, and I am sure he did what was expected without much rumination, and he was probably excited to take a wife as an act of responsible maturity.

Dong Qing and I were exchanging letters on a monthly basis. Finally, at the end of 1989, I decided I would go to China to meet her. I used the excuse of doing some filming for *Moving the Mountain* as a cover for the trip. (I ended up shooting the opening sequence of the Fong Dang village kids with a Hi-8 camera I bought in Hong Kong on the way.) My sister King Sin arranged to join me in Vancouver, coming from Edmonton, for the flight to Hong Kong; her two sons, Stanley and Pat, originally from Edmonton, were now successful businessmen there. I really appreciated her willingness to travel with me and give me moral support and encouragement.

I would be in China for Chinese New Year; that was when Dong Qing would be on holiday.

Chinese marriages are truly family affairs. Dong Qing's sister, Dong Ling, was living in New York as a visiting scholar. She asked if she could visit me during the 1989 Christmas holidays, to which I consented. I knew she was protective of Dong Qing and wanted to check out the man that *mingyun* (destiny) had in mind for her little sister. Since arriving in the US in August, Dong Ling had been having a hard time. For one thing, her stipend from the Chinese government was late in coming and she survived by getting a job as a dim sum cart pusher in a Chinatown restaurant. On top of that, she had to leave her two-year-old son back in Guangzhou with her husband and in-laws, and she cried for him every night.

To take her mind off her problems for the few days that she was here, I introduced her to Canadian winter activities, tobogganing and snowshoeing. It must have been a successful visit. Dong Qing later wrote to me saying that Dong Ling hadn't had so much fun in such a long time. I had passed the sister test.

I was starting to warm up to the idea of marriage again. It had been five years since my divorce. I missed the companionship and the security of being in a marriage. I missed the idea of being in love. As I prepared to go to China, I had no expectations. Friends cautioned me, but I tried to clear my head of any confusion, trepidation or doubt. I wanted to keep an open mind and an open heart as I entered into this uncharted territory. It would be the adventure of a lifetime but I still feared the unknown emotional prospect that this journey would entail.

My sister and I arrived in Hong Kong on January 21, 1990. We stayed in the British colony for two days to acclimatize and to buy gifts to take into China. The night before we were to enter China, I had the strangest dream: I was skating on Beaver Lake, on Montreal's Mt. Royal, and I started sinking and falling through the ice. I woke up in a cold sweat. I told King Sin about the dream and she tried to reassure me that I didn't need to rush into anything, that I should just do what I felt was right. On the train to Shenzhen, we got off at the border station, Lo Wu. I had flashes of memories of my last trip to Lo Wu fifteen years earlier. Then it had been a frontier border crossing; now, it was a modern busy commuter station, part of the Hong Kong mass transit system.

After entering into China, we hopped onto a bus to go to the branch of the Agricultural Bank of China where Dong Qing was working. She would be expecting us. After an hour on the bus, we realized that we were going in the wrong direction. The driver let us off at another branch of the bank. Fortunately, a bank employee knew Dong Qing and phoned her. Dong Qing worked in the accounting department at the head office, so many people knew her. We were told to wait at the branch and Dong Qing would come to get us. I decided to wait outside and take in the atmosphere.

There was a cacophony of automobile horns, bicycle bells and whistles; the street was crowded with people, bikes, carts and vehicles all competing for the same square foot of space. I thought about the China that I visited fifteen years ago and the idealism that had clouded my perception. It was much more orderly then, as people marched in step; today, it was chaotic but vibrant and full of energy.

When I saw Dong Qing approaching, after all the anticipation, I was overwhelmed. She looked like a gorgeous movie star—*and she still does*, with wavy light brown hair flowing in the breeze. She wore no makeup—she *always* looks more beautiful without makeup. With well-formed lips, and when she smiles, little dimples form at the corners of her mouth. Her laughter is so refreshingly sweet and infectious. When I hear that laugh, it makes me happy because I know she is enjoying life. She spoke to us laughingly, saying that it was difficult for anyone to find their way around Shenzhen with so much construction. At first impression, I thought she had dyed her hair. When I'd visited New York's Chinatown a few years back, I'd seen Chinese girls who had dyed their hair blond; I was under the naive belief that all Chinese people had naturally black hair, so I immediately assumed a version of the New York fad had caught on in China. I discovered, though, that Dong Qing's chestnut brown hair colour was natural.

We met up with Dong Qing's mother for lunch at a local restaurant. After lunch we saw my sister off. She would spend Chinese New Year with her sons in Hong Kong. On the way back to Dong Qing's apartment, we shopped for the evening meal. She turned out to be a great cook. She shared a two-bedroom apartment with a fellow bank worker who had left to spend New Year's with her family. Dong Qing and her mother slept in the roommate's room while I took her room.

Even though Dong Qing's mother was from Toishan and Dong Qing knew the dialect, we had some problems communicating, since my vocabulary was from the era of my parents. Dong Qing also spoke Cantonese and Mandarin, so we used a mixture of Toishanese and Cantonese.

Dong Qing cooked a delicious meal with fresh produce bought at the market. After supper, her mother suggested that we go out while she cleaned the dishes.

Shenzhen in 1990 was one big construction site, a fishing village turned boomtown, after Deng Xiaoping had designated it as a Special Economic Zone in 1980. There were people who obtained official status to work in Shenzhen and there were others who migrated from the regions who were there illegally trying to ride the economic tide of development; some made it and many others did not.

As we walked near the train station, I stood out as a foreigner with my clothes and bearing. An aggressive beggar carrying a baby accosted me, shouting loudly at me, grabbing onto my sleeve and refusing to let me go. I didn't know what to do. I couldn't shake free and I didn't want to get physical because of the baby. Dong Qing quietly and sympathetically spoke with the man; this calmed him down. She gave him some money and urged him on his way.

We then carefully navigated our way around construction debris and the crowded streets and we ended up inside the quiet tranquility of Lychee People's Park, named for the many lychee trees growing there. We sat on a bench and we talked, and talked and talked, about life and aspirations. We talked about life in China and life in Canada. We talked about the surprises that life brings us and we talked about how we'd arrived at this moment. We both blamed it on our mothers. With long moments of silence, we were engrossed in each other's thoughts and had not noticed that darkness had fallen. There were no lights in the park, and attendants with flashlights were walking around shooing young lovers and other stragglers out; they were to lock the gates at 10 p.m.

On the way back to her apartment, I felt a warm connection with Dong Qing. My fears and anxieties were slowly evaporating.

The next morning, Dong Qing, her mother and I went to the station to take the train to Shaoguan, their hometown. The city, with a population of 700,000, was the northern gate of Guangdong province, just south of Hunan.

Nothing could have prepared me for what I experienced at the train station. It was the day before the Chinese New Year and the building was jammed with people hauling luggage and packages to take home, parents hanging onto their children as they struggled to get on trains to go visit the grandparents. Dong Qing, being experienced in these situations, had purchased the tickets days in advance but it was not early enough to get "soft" seats and we ended up in the regular cars. We were squeezed shoulder-to-shoulder as we inched our way to the platform. Timidly, I hung on to Dong Qing and her mother, as I feared being separated in the crowd. Everyone else seemed to take it in stride as they patiently pushed and jostled their way forward without the orderliness I was used to in Canada or even in Hong Kong. This was no time to be courteous; if you let up for one second, you would be left behind.

Inside the train car, it was the same bedlam. None of the seats were reserved; it wouldn't have mattered even if they were. Seats meant for two people bore four, each perching a piece of rear end on the vinyl. The aisles were packed, and if people found space underneath a seat, they would crawl into it. The man standing next to me joked, "Better not go to the toilet; you'll never get back and you will lose your seat."

We arrived in Shaoguan in the late evening; the temperature was unusually cold at four degrees Celsius. Dong Qing's father and brother met us at the station with a government-provided van and driver.

The year 1990 was auspiciously the Year of the Horse, *Ma*. It is also Dong Qing's mother's family name. Ma Peiqing is from a head tax family. Her father and grandfather were Gold Mountain men and both paid the head tax when they immigrated to Canada in the early 1900s to settle in Edmonton, which remains an enclave for the Mah (Canadian version of Ma) clan. Ma Peiqing was born in Basha, Toishan, in 1930. Shortly after her one-month birthday celebration, her father returned to Canada. Due to the Exclusion Act, the Chinese Revolution, the Cultural Revolution and other historical circumstances, her father never saw her again. After Liberation, Peiqing studied medicine and became an obstetrician/paediatrician to serve the new China. She had an opportunity to leave China with her three children during the Cultural Revolution when her husband was sent to the countryside. Even though her parents were waiting for her in Hong Kong, and despite the hardships caused by the Cultural Revolution, Peiqing could not leave her husband.

Dong Qing's father, Chen Zhongshu, was an old Communist revolutionary. He had joined the anti-Japanese resistance at age fourteen as he travelled through Guangdong looking for his older brother, whom he discovered had been captured and killed by the Japanese. His brother was a well-respected Communist cadre, so the comrades took in the young Zhongshu and trained him to be a resistance fighter and Communist organizer. Although the People's Liberation Army did not have official rankings, based on his responsibilities it seems Zhongshu eventually rose to the equivalent rank of a colonel. Zhongshu's older sister was also a Communist revolutionary and she organized students at the Whampoa Military Academy in Guangzhou. She was betrayed, captured and executed by the Kuomintang.

After the anti-Japanese war, Zhongshu, in his early thirties, ascended in the administration to become the mayor of Shaoguan. During the Anti-Rightist Campaign in the late 1950s, he ran afoul of the Party leadership when he criticized cadres from other regions of China who took up leading positions in Shaoguan, saying that they did not understand local conditions.[344] He was sent to a factory for reform through labour.

Already labelled as a dreaded rightist, he was again targeted for criticism during the Cultural Revolution and sent to the countryside. Throughout these ordeals, Zhongshu never wavered in his loyalty to the Communist Party. When the Cultural Revolution was repudiated, he was rehabilitated and appointed to the Agriculture Commission and then the United Front Commission, working with other political parties, overseas Chinese and foreign organizations. In 1981, Zhongshu was nominated to run for mayor of Shaoguan again. This time his name was put on the ballot with seven others, but the people of Shaoguan voted him in as their mayor once again. He remained at this post until retirement in 1990. The Chinese government then designated him an Old Revolutionary Hero for his contributions to the revolution.

Since June 4th was still fresh in people's mind, I took the opportunity to ask my prospective father-in-law what he thought about the Tiananmen incident. He gave me a pat Party response. China had gone through much social and political upheaval over the past half century: foreign occupation, anti-Japanese resistance, civil war, political campaigns and the Cultural Revolution. The Chinese people were wary of more turmoil leading to chaos, especially with ideologies borrowed from the outside. The people mainly supported the government's efforts to maintain a peaceful order and to prevent anarchy.

I told him about my participation in the Marxist-Leninist movement in Canada. He seemed to be familiar with the international movement and the role played by the Chinese Communist Party. He said China has learned not to meddle in the internal affairs of foreign countries. He also gave a harsh assessment of the people who participated in the Marxist-Leninist movement in the West. He said those people were just "playing at revolution." I didn't question his appraisal; he had gone through an earth-shaking revolution that claimed the lives of two of his siblings.

* * *

It seemed people didn't sleep much on New Year's Eve, as firecrackers sounded all night long to scare away the bad omens and welcome the good spirits. After a hearty New Year's breakfast of *jook* with pork and thousand-year-old egg, *mantou* and fried dough, I got up the nerve to ask Dong Qing for our first date.

She suggested that we bicycle and take in the sights around Shaoguan. They were a two-bicycle family, so each of us had a bike. We pedalled out of town and through the countryside for about fifteen miles to Nan Hua Di, a thousand-year-old Buddhist temple where we stopped for a *luo song* vegetarian lunch. Then we headed for the Maba Man Museum.[345]

On the way back to Shaoguan, we got lost and ended up at one of the hot springs for which Shaoguan was famous. We decided to try the therapeutic baths. The bath section for men was separated from the women's section. I decided to bathe in the hot spring water where I was lulled to sleep by the pleasant sensation of the geothermal bath. After over an hour, I realized it was getting late and quickly got dressed and rushed out to the lobby where Dong Qing was patiently waiting. She was worried about me but the attendant assured her that I was still inside. She explained that most Chinese did not use the baths because the tubs were not clean. She had just had a shower and come back out. I was impressed by her patience and consideration.

Dong Qing asked people along the way for directions to the road for Shaoguan. The locals kept saying, "It's not too far," to encourage us to keep going. We finally found our way back to the main road and we reached home at dusk. Altogether we biked thirty miles that day and Dong Qing was suitably impressed that at my age I had the stamina to do such a long bike ride. Little did she know that I was training in Hung Gar kung fu and had trained extra hard before any overseas trip to build up my conditioning. Nevertheless, Dong Qing must have thought about the difference in our ages: I was forty-one and she was twenty-eight.

Dong Qing had grown up during the Cultural Revolution; she was the youngest of three children and had developed an independent and self-reliant spirit in the midst of instability.

I was starting to learn her family story. Her father had been sent to the countryside for re-education and he only got permission to go home for a few days at a time, sporadically. Her mother worked long hours at the hospital, shifts lasting up to thirty-six-hours, because many of the staff were criticized and sent away for re-education, thus causing a personnel shortage. Dong Qing spent her early years in the hospital's nursery and daycare and when she started school, she, her sister and brother were left to take care of the household. On top of the long hours, Peiqing had to attend political study sessions that went late into the night.

The Chen family had little money but it didn't matter; everyone else was in the same boat. The children did all the housekeeping and Dong Qing learned how to cook the meals. Being the youngest, she was assigned to do the shopping and queued up every month with the ration coupons to buy the necessities of rice, oil and the limited amount of 250 grams of pork per person per month. Starting at age six, she had to wake up in the middle of the night to queue up at 4 a.m. for the shop that opened at 6 a.m. She was grateful for an aunty next door who roused and accompanied her for the pre-dawn trek to the government store. If she was late, the shop could run out of supplies and they would have to go without for the month. Families also raised chickens and ducks for the eggs and the occasional poultry dinner. Dong Qing recalled the children would be given two boiled eggs to celebrate a birthday.

Even though her brother, Xia Yang, later entered culinary school and became a professional chef, Dong Qing's creative talents in the kitchen earned her the title of cook for the family.

The same year that Dong Qing turned eighteen, Deng Xiaoping announced the Special Economic Zone in Shenzhen. Many young people saw this as a great opportunity for their careers and there was fierce competition for jobs in the southern city bordering Hong Kong. Dong Qing had enrolled in the accounting program at the local university in Shaoguan. One of her mentors was offered a posting in Shenzhen; he saw the industriousness in Dong Qing and asked if she wanted to work at the Agricultural Bank in China's new boom-town. She jumped at the opportunity to exercise her free spirit, to leave home and to create a new life 250 miles away. While working at the bank, she completed her degree in accounting.

* * *

We had a delicious and plentiful New Year's meal with all the traditional dishes—including the mandatory chicken, complete with beak and feet. The Cantonese word for chicken is *gai* which sounds like the word for life as in *hau sai gai*—a good life. Later I noticed that one of the two chickens that Dong Qing's paternal grandmother was raising on the balcony was gone. The chicken had sacrificed its life so we could have a good life. It must in fact have been the rooster, since there was no more crowing after New Year's Day.

The next day, Dong Qing's father displayed his Communist style of work and sat the whole family down, including grandma, to meet with me as he poured steaming hot tea for everyone and passed around watermelon seeds. Dong Qing's brother welcomed me to the family. I realized that they wanted to know my intentions towards Dong Qing, as they were very concerned for her happiness. Sensing my unease, Zhongshu said, "You don't have to rush into anything but you have come a long way to meet Dong Qing so you must have some feelings for her."

Unlike the old days of my father, we actually discussed the pros and cons of marrying a *Gim Shan Haak*[346] and what it would be like for Dong Qing to re-establish her life in Canada and how difficult it would be for her. She said very little during the meeting. Finally, after about an hour, Zhongshu brought the meeting to a close by saying that it was now up to Dong Qing and me.

That afternoon, Dong Qing and I went out to do some shopping. It was raining, so I held the umbrella for both of us. She hung onto my arm to stay dry. It felt cozy and affectionate. In the evening, as she sat on the bed in her room, I asked if she wanted to marry me and move to Canada. For a long moment, she kept her eyes looking at the floor and then finally murmured, "*Hau*" (yes). I sat on the bed and held her, but she turned her head away when I tried to kiss her. Her modesty would not allow it; she did not know me well enough to be kissed.

This was the last day of January; my flight back to Canada was on February 9, so the next eight days would be a whirlwind as we scrambled to make the marriage official.

Dong Qing had to go back to Shenzhen for work, and we would register the marriage there, since she had to obtain permission from her work unit for marriage and to change her civil status. She wrote out the application letter for the bank and showed it to her mother. Peiqing scolded her for making the letter so dry—"You need to add some words of love and affection!" I chuckled and said that I would have written it the same as Dong Qing.

There were many forms to be completed, photos to be taken for the marriage certificate and a medical examination with the doctor attesting that I did not have AIDS or suffer from any mental disorder before the marriage would be approved. We were on tenterhooks waiting for the red tape to be cleared.

One evening, Dong Qing and I went back to the Lychee Park and I brought out the diamond ring that my mother had given me for her. As I placed it on her finger, she asked me if I was having second thoughts, and said that we didn't have to go through with this if we didn't want to. Despite the uncertainty and not knowing what the future would bring, I told her that I wanted to go through this with her. She said she had the same feelings.

She wanted to tell me about her shortcomings. She mentioned some words in Chinese that I didn't understand, so she brought out her electronic translator whose synthesized voice squeaked "capricious." I didn't even know what capricious meant in English, so I said that's not a bad trait. Then she asked about my shortcomings. I said I was moody. She replied that was probably from not being able to discuss my feelings with my family and that I kept a lot of things inside myself. She had hit the mark. I thought to myself, "She understands me, she's my soul mate. Now, I have to marry this woman."

On February 7, all the paperwork and medical certificates were approved. The marriage was registered and the marriage certificates issued; it was official. The next day would be my last in China. We woke up early to go to the government offices to obtain Dong Qing's exit papers. We were happy as we held hands walking down the street and feeling that everything would be fine.

When I arrived back in Montreal, I applied to bring Dong Qing to Canada.

It would take a year and a half for the Canadian government to grant her the immigration papers to join me. But in 1991, I was finally able to go to China to accompany Dong Qing on her journey to her new home. Before leaving China, we decided to take our belated honeymoon in the city of Kunming, in the southwestern province of Yunnan. It was the first time we'd been alone, without the support of family and friends. We spent a week touring around Kunming and in that time started to bond as a couple, relying on each other to get around. She translated from Mandarin for me. I only had my Lonely Planet guidebook to offer.

* * *

Before Dong Qing came to Canada, I discussed with my nephew Stanley in Hong Kong how things would be tough for her: she would be starting all over again, learning a new language, making new friends, finding work. What Stanley said still sticks with me to this day, "Then why don't you move to China and you take the burden of doing all those things?"

More recently I asked Dong Qing, "How do you think we would have done if I had moved to China, instead of you moving to Canada?"

"I think you would have done fine, with a master's degree in engineering, you could have taught at the university; if we had bought my apartment at that time for $10,000, it would be worth a million dollars today; and like my colleagues, I would have become a multi-millionaire during the boom years, with my contacts in the banking business."

Instead, we happily settled into a somewhat unorthodox middle-class life in Canada.

Chapter 19

Identity and Belonging

"We're still here/ we're going strong/ and we're getting tired of proving we belong."
—Chris Iijima, "Asian Song"

Why am I so drawn to Chinatown? Some people say it's smelly and dirty, but I like the smell. It reminds me of my childhood when my father brought me here every Sunday. The dirt shows that lively and energetic people populate the place. As I shop for Chinese greens at the grocery stores, the clerks no longer call me gaw-gaw (older brother). Now it is shok-shok (younger uncle) or bak-bak (elder uncle) to reflect my age. I love Sunday dim sum and joking with the women cart pushers, one of whom once teased me, "Shok-shok, you must have been in a hurry to come here today." I had worn my T-shirt inside out, and I told her that I had done so purposely because the label was scratchy. We both guffawed. Chinatown has a village feeling and this is my village.

When I first arrived in Canada in 1956, you could say that I was a Chinese immigrant, even though I was the third generation of my family to be here. Over the next few years, people in Chinatown started identifying me as a *jook sing*,[347] a not so endearing term used by the *lo wah kiu* to describe those young people who were losing their Chinese culture and identity. I was losing my ability to speak Cantonese and resorted to the Toishanese spoken by my parents and the people in Chinatown. More seriously, my mental functions were being taken over by the English language and the dominant culture.

The three hours of formal Chinese language training every Saturday was not enough to stem the powerful attraction of English from school and the popular cultural media of TV, radio and comic books. I abandoned the Monkey King for Superman.

I was impressionable; my mind absorbed any cultural stimulus like a sponge. The TV programs like *Father Knows Best* and *Leave It to Beaver* showed me an idyllic family life far beyond living in the back of a laundry. Every Sunday night, my father and I watched *Bonanza* on the eight-inch black and white Admiral TV, small enough to be taken from beneath the ironing table and placed on top when the day's ironing was done. My mother never watched TV, not because she didn't understand the language but because she was always busy in the background, keeping the laundry clean and preparing the next day's chores.

On *Bonanza*, there was a character named Hop Sing—the loyal Chinese servant and houseboy to the Cartwright family. Veteran actor Victor Sen Yung, who was born in San Francisco in 1915 and a University of California, Berkeley, graduate, played the role. After a while, I started to look at Hop Sing differently. His pidgin English rendered him a stereotypical comic character. Even at eleven, I sensed that the Chinese characters on TV were inferior to the white characters; there was no pride to being Chinese.

* * *

There is a generational particularity to the Chinese diaspora. As the Chinese wandered around the world and settled in the far corners of the earth, we carried with us the regional cultural, social, political, dietary and linguistic baggage of the era. My father's and grandfather's world was that of early twentieth century China when they came to Canada. Their world-view—that of the Chinese peasant—was formed in the villages of the southern, semi-tropical countryside. Unprecedented events were happening in China that would shake their world outlook to the core; despite these vicissitudes, they managed to cling to their age-old belief system as peasants everywhere would.

In dynasties past, it is believed, the emperor did not allow his subjects to travel abroad. When they made their perilous journey across the Pacific to Gold Mountain, my grandfather and father felt they had no other choice if their family was to survive. As Cho-yun Hsu wrote in *Daedalus*:[348]

Many Chinese began to be aware of their Chinese identity only after leaving China to live overseas where they were often treated as aliens by the indigenous population of their host country. Such bitter rejection trained Chinese to view non-Chinese with distrust and suspicion and only strengthened their own sense of connection with China and other Chinese.

Throughout the world, there are more than fifty million people in the Chinese diaspora. I have read that the "search by disaporic Chinese for an authentic Chinese meaning is inherently flawed and futile."[349] However, as the first overseas Chinese pondered their existential significance, they also expressed the angst of living in a foreign land. Edith Eaton, a Eurasian, in the early 1900s wrote sympathetically, under the pen name of Sui Sin Far,[350] about the diasporic lives of the Chinese men, women and children in Canada and the US. Many since then have enriched our souls and minds with the cultural and political expressions of our collective experiences in Gold Mountain.

The idea of the Chinese model minority, though, is a construct of the media, politicians and academics to depict how a minority should behave and function in the dominant society. The premise is that the model minority is an example for other minorities, does not create trouble, overachieves and accomplishes within the parameters of the prevailing social order; all this assumes that the group is homogeneous and limited only by the abilities of its members, and that everyone has equal opportunities.

The model minority is not real; it is a bogus construct to divide minorities—setting one against another. The Chinese Canadian community is not homogeneous; like any other community, it reflects the class nature of society and, therefore, the term "model minority" is meaningless. There are the few who make it to the top of the economic strata but the majority earn a living working in day-to-day jobs.

You only have to walk the laneways behind the restaurants and the curio shops of Chinatown and look into the sweatshops to see the Chinese immigrant working class. The majority of Chinese immigrants to Canada are now coming from Mainland China. Many of them have professional skills but fall into low-paying unskilled jobs once arriving here. They have not forgotten the socialist education they received in China, though, and as Justin Kong writes in *New Canadian Media*, they retain "a basic understanding" of the concepts of class, capitalism and exploitation.

"Labouring in the deskilling, dehumanizing and precarious Canadian economy," Kong writes, "reignites in the Chinese worker the earlier internalizations of working class consciousness."[351] Once these contradictions are exposed and brought out into the open and discussed, the concept of the model minority will finally be debunked.

Pierre Trudeau's state policy of harmonious Canadian multiculturalism was less an attempt to promote minority cultural identity than it was an effort to contain Quebec nationalism and the independence movement in the 1970s. People today criticize multiculturalism as an ideology from the right, left and centre depending on their political stand. Multiculturalism, nevertheless, offers a cultural space for minorities to participate in Canadian society in whatever form they choose.

The Chinese identity in Canada has ranged from the model of the sojourner to the assimilationist depending on historical circumstances and on how welcoming the policies of the Canadian government are at the time. However, a distinct identity has developed within the Chinese community, manifesting itself in the 1970s and 1980s. This identity was born out of the struggle to establish a sense of belonging and out of resistance to assimilation. But more importantly, it was based on a hundred-year history of struggle in Canada.

Some may say that we drew inspiration from the Asian American civil rights movement in the US, which in turn drew encouragement from the Black Power movement. I would say that modern-day Chinese Canadian cultural identity came of age in the late 1970s, as emerging Chinese Canadian writers penned words to express our experiences, and during the anti-racism campaign that ensued after CTV aired an episode called "Campus Giveaway" on its *W5* program in 1979. The grassroots movement that came out of that battle against racism firmly planted Chinese Canadian faces in front of the media and Canadian society.

Before, during and after that anti-racism campaign, cultural creations from young people within the community started blooming to portray Chinese Canadian history and everyday life.

I was excited to see the first issue of the *Asianadian* magazine back in 1978. Tony Chan and Cheuk Kwan founded the periodical in Toronto. It spoke to me as the voice of a new generation of Chinese Canadians who proudly and resolutely advocated an anti-racist, anti-sexist, anti-homophobic and pro-struggle perspective. It spawned a number of influential Asian Canadian writers like SKY Lee, Rick Shiomi, Jim Wong-Chu, Paul Yee, Maryka Omatsu and Richard Fung. There has been no other magazine like it since its demise in 1985.

Ten years later, Vancouver's Jim Wong-Chu and the Asian Canadian Writers' Workshop founded *Ricepaper*, which is still being published, and Edmonton's Kenda Gee produced the short-lived *Chinacity*, but they never became the hard-hitting, righteously spoiling for a fight kind of journal that was the *Asianadian*.

In the late 1970s, I was still caught up in the Canadian Maoist movement; my Chinese Canadian identity consciousness was just beginning to sprout. When Siu Keong Lee of the Montreal Anti-W5 Committee tried to recruit me to this anti-racist struggle in 1979, I didn't see the immediate significance of the issue; I was looking at the bigger class struggle and I tried to recruit Lee to the Workers Communist Party. The anti-W5 movement has become a watershed in the struggle of the Chinese Canadian community, whereas the WCP has become a footnote.

The refreshingly creative works of Chinese Canadian artists in literature, music, stage and film were in stark contrast to Pierre Trudeau's multicultural song and dance. They put into context the struggles of my father, grandfather and other Gold Mountain men and women, and gave flesh and blood to their experiences. It may be a search for roots, but some of the firmest roots are within Canadian soil. All these works stirred in me a pride that I had never felt before as a person of Chinese background living in Canada. This identity consciousness ushered me from the margins and firmly planted me in this country as a Chinese Canadian.

The percentage of Chinese-ness and Canadian-ness is always shifting and under constant negotiation depending on the circumstances in society and within my life. Nevertheless, it is uniquely Canadian.

The partial victory of the redress campaign established our collective place in Canadian history. My twenty-year involvement in the redress movement was as much a pursuit for identity and belonging as a pursuit for collective justice. My travels across Canada to meet dedicated and fascinating Chinese

Canadians from all walks of life gave me a sense of community that has cemented over the years. The friendships that I built through this long campaign have nourished my Chinese-ness. Although there were political and tactical disagreements in pursuing redress, there were no enemies among us, as we came together within the rubric of being Chinese in Canada, which held a bigger connection than any transient differences.

Winning the apology and recognition of our history in this country has solidified in me individual pride as a Chinese Canadian, as well as in the community's bond to Canada. The enrichment of this experience and the friends that I made in the common pursuit of justice have contributed more profoundly than I can express to forming my Chinese Canadian consciousness.

With each new wave of immigration, however, the Chinese Canadian identity that I know is being submerged. The diverse groups of Chinese now living in Canada are creating new Chinese Canadian identities through their own experiences. This evolution does render the search for "an authentic Chinese meaning" futile, as that Chinese meaning is always changing.

* * *

It is a burden, but I resist assimilation of my mind and spirit, however subtle the forces of assimilation may be. It seems I've been chasing that elusive identity in the abstract—as an intellectual exercise. I am concluding that identity is a state of being, challenging to define and always in flux. But I don't need to be defined by others; certainly, I don't need to be validated by the norms of the prevailing society. Once I realized that I could define myself, that's when I became comfortable in my own identity. I've discovered that cultural identity is as personal and unique as one's experiences. I've realized that my Chinese Canadian identity may not be the same as that of another Chinese Canadian; however, there are similar strains within the framework of our common heritage.

Whatever we feel about our identity, the only important aspect for me is that I can be proud of who I am. Identity consciousness for me is shifting from the realm of the political to that of the personal.

I've been able to live my life with a sense of purpose and meaning. I don't understand everything, but I have the ability to question why and how things happen. I've lived in pursuit of dreams; these dreams have evolved over the years but they remain slightly beyond the reality in which I live.

I am a lucky man. I have a loving, beautiful and supportive wife; I have two wonderful and intelligent children who are compassionate, socially aware and know right from wrong. When it comes down to it, my wife, Dong Qing, my daughter, Jessica, and my son, Jordan, have provided my sense of personal identity.

As I write this, I am in my late sixties and feeling comfortable in my own skin. There is a Toishanese expression, *on lock*—to be content, calm and at peace. I am starting to enjoy my *on lock* as I settle into my own Chinese Canadian identity. Dong Qing's love has given me my sense of personal belonging.

ACKNOWLEDGMENTS

There are many people who encouraged and supported me through this writing process. They all contributed their knowledge and wisdom.

The late Dr. Daya Varma first inspired me to write with his wry humour: "Old men write books." Steve Orlov gave me the initial push and encouragement to write this book. In the course of writing, during our regular luncheon dates the late Dr. Philip Taylor gave me his sage advice, critique and warm encouragement to carry on. Philip was a "Coloured" South African, as designated by the former apartheid regime, so he provided a unique perspective on the struggle for identity and belonging.

I am truly appreciative of James Wing, Eileen Hum, Hum Yue Teng and the ladies of my mother's mah jong circle—Mrs. Lee Suey Toy, Mrs. Wong Hang Hong, Mrs. Jang Eng Ling, Mrs. Eng Tang and Mrs. Mak Yu Hai. They all provided flesh and blood stories of their difficult times.

I wish to thank Kenda Gee, May Chiu and Walter Tom, who sustained me through the redress struggle and in the effort to get this seminal story to the Canadian public.

Thank you to all those who agreed to share their experiences through their interviews and reminiscences: Gillian Taylor, Roger Rashi, Alan Silverman, Yvette Matyas, Herman Rosenfeld, and James (Maoist days); and Gary Yee, Avvy Go, Chung Tang, Sid Tan, Yew Lee, Raymond Yao, Jack Lee, May Chiu, Kenda Gee, Walter Tom and Simon Wing (redress movement).

Thanks to Marty Fisher and John Iwanic, of our dinner group, who graciously agreed to read and give me their comments on some of the chapters. A special thanks to Anita Malhotra for her initial research of the parliamentary debates on the Chinese Head Tax and Exclusion Act.

I am grateful for the help provided by the staff and editors of Douglas &

McIntyre, Brianna Cerkiewicz, Nicola Goshulak, Peter Robson, Anna Comfort O'Keeffe, copy editor Caroline Skelton, and Howard White. I especially want to thank Cheryl Cohen, my substantive editor, who did an excellent job in trying to keep my rhetoric in check in order to make the book more appealing to the general public. She stimulated and challenged me to bring out the best in my writing. They all guided me through the publication process.

A special thank you to Leila Lee, non-fiction editor, and Allan Cho, editor of *Ricepaper Magazine*, and to Madeleine Thien, co-editor of *Granta 141: Canada*, for their helpful and encouraging words. Thanks to Arden Ford, Ray Beauchemin, Denise Roig and Mark Abley for their publishing advice.

Thank you to Amin Kassam, Frank Chin, John Kuo Wei Tchen, Simon Li, Avvy Go, Susan Eng, Kwoi Gin, Justin Kong, Matt James, Ingrid Peritz and Alex Norris for the kind permission to reproduce their work. Thanks to Paul Jones for providing old copies of *Third World Forum*.

Finally, I wish to thank my sisters, Pui King, King Sin and Pui Yung, and my brother, Ging Tung, who dug into their collective memories to talk about Grandfather Tan Suey Der and our parents, Hing Dere and Yee Dong Sing, to whom we are all grateful. I am thankful for the support of my children, Jessica and Jordan; and my deepest gratitude to my wife, Dong Qing Chen, who inspires and nourishes me every day.

ENDNOTES

Introduction

1   I finally discovered many things about my father while researching
     for *Moving the Mountain*. *La Presse* journalist Jooneed Khan called the
     documentary a homage to my father. "Un film sur une ignominie que le
     Canada doit assumer...," *La Presse*, October 20, 1993.

Chapter 1

2   Accessed April 19, 2018. http://www.okthepk.ca/dataCprSiding/spike/
     spike.htm.
3   Patricia E. Roy, *The CPR West*, Hugh A. Dempsey, ed. (Vancouver:
     Douglas & McIntyre, 1984), 292.
4   Hansard, Commons Debates, May 31, 1887.
5   Accessed June 16, 2018. http://www.bac-lac.gc.ca/eng/discover/
     immigration/immigration-records/immigrants-china-1885-1949/Pages/
     list.aspx?RegistrationDate=1949-09&&p_ID=45.
6   Starting in Confucian times, a courtesy name was conferred on both
     men and women as they reached adulthood. This practice is not so
     common today, but it seems to be having a revival with the growing re-
     acceptance of Confucianism.
7   Denise Helley, *Les chinois à Montréal – 1877–1951* (Québec: Institut
     québécois de recherche sur la culture, 1987), 95.
8   "Les Chinois Ne Veulent Point Payer," *La Presse*, July 31, 1915.
9   Accessed May 25, 2018. http://ici.radio-canada.ca/premiere/emissions/
     le-15-18/segments/chronique/39177/jean-francois-nadeau-chinois-
     quartier-blanchisserie-montreal-histoire.

10   Accessed May 25, 2018. http://bibnum2.banq.qc.ca/bna/lovell/.

11   Denise Helley, 109.

12   Ibid., 278.

13   Hum Yue Teng interview. April 1992.

14   My grandfather wrote this poem in 1944 on the occasion of his sixtieth birthday. It was later published in the *Chinese Young Men's Christian Institution Journal* to commemorate its fiftieth anniversary in 1961.

15   These names are pseudonyms for friends, as is the literary custom.

16   *Ah Ngeen* is the title for the paternal grandmother. *Ah Paw* refers to the maternal grandmother.

Chapter 2

17   This is one of two poems written by my father in the 1940s and published in 1970 in the *Dere Clan Association* journal in Hong Kong.

18   The Canadian Pacific Empress line of ships carried many of the Chinese immigrants to Canada. The *Empress of Russia* was one of those ships; it also transported the Chinese Labour Corps to service the Allied forces fighting in Europe during World War I, and carried Sun Yat-sen from Hong Kong to Shanghai in 1922.

19   Lisa Rose Mar, *Brokering Belonging – Chinese in Canada's Exclusion Era, 1885–1945* (Oxford University Press, 2010), 149. The detention building was located near the waterfront at the end of Thurlow Street. The building had long been demolished when Vancouver began developing the waterfront with Canada Place and the convention centre. It is ironic that the early Chinese were locked up in detention and paid $500 to get out, while today businessmen pay hundreds to stay in an Asian hotel located at the same place.

20   Harry Con, Ronald J. Con, Graham Johnson, Edgar Wickberg, William E. Willmot. Edgar Wickberg (ed.), *From China to Canada, A History of the Chinese Communities in Canada* (Toronto: McClelland and Stewart, 1982), 143.

21   Peter S. Li, *The Chinese in Canada* (Toronto: Oxford University Press, 1988), 78.

22   The Chinese Exclusion Act was passed in 1923.

23   Historically, the *lo fawn* are all those that lived outside the Great Wall. In this case it refers to white people.

24 Con et al., 185. The labour market was very restrictive to the Chinese, especially during the Depression.

25 Betty Lee Sung, *Mountain of Gold* (MacMillan, 1967). Chapter 11, "Laundries – A Haven and a Prison," gives a good description of the hand laundry business in the US.

26 Paul C. P. Siu, *The Chinese Laundryman – A Study of Social Isolation* (New York University Press, 1987). This is a PhD thesis on Siu's research into the hand laundries of Chicago in the 1930s. Siu was the son of a laundryman.

27 Ibid., 130.

28 Thomas Hum had a plaque commemorating his service to the Chinese community at the Montreal General Hospital.

29 Eileen Hum interview. July 8, 1992, at the Laval Street YMCI.

30 John Kuo Wei Tchen, "Editor's Introduction" in *The Chinese Laundryman – A Study in Social Isolation*, by Paul C. P. Siu, xxxiii.

31 The term "sojourner" is controversial among Chinese Canadian activists and academics. Paul Siu's definition is more dialectically nuanced, as quoted by John Kuo Wei Tchen in the introduction to *The Chinese Laundryman – A Study of Social Isolation*. Siu defined a sojourner as one who "clings to the culture of his own ethnic group as in contrast to the bicultural marginal man. Psychologically he is unwilling to organize himself as a permanent resident in the country of his sojourn. When he does, he becomes a marginal man." Tchen added, "Chinese sojourners could also choose to be settlers." In reality, the "sojourners" became immigrants due to a confluence of historical events beyond their control. Even though they remained marginalized, the immigrants became citizens the first chance they got.

32 The *woi* was a unique institution of the early North American Chinese immigrant economy. Each week, one or more borrower would bid for money by secretly writing on a piece of paper the interest he would be willing to pay for the loan. The borrower who bid the highest interest would take the amount of money required, either for a business or a trip home to China. The borrower paid off the loan through weekly contributions. Banks, which few laundry workers trusted, always had higher interest rates. The *woi* did not require any collateral or security since everyone knew and trusted each other. The *woi* still exists in some clan associations.

Chapter 3

33 Former Governor General Adrienne Clarkson and her family took up four of those numbers. Clarkson's father, William Poy, worked for the Canadian Trade Commission in Hong Kong. When the colony fell to the Japanese in 1942, the Canadian staff was repatriated, but the Exclusion Act prevented the Poys from immediately coming to Canada. External Affairs intervened and used an unfulfilled quota in a US–Japanese prisoner exchange agreement, bringing the Poys to Canada under the auspices of the Red Cross.

34 Kwok Bun Chan, *Smoke and Fire—The Chinese in Montreal* (Hong Kong: The Chinese University Press, 1991), 144. With permission of the publisher.

35 Ibid., 209.

36 Ibid., 178.

37 Li, 20.

38 Paul Yee, *Saltwater City—An Illustrated History of the Chinese in Vancouver* (Vancouver: Douglas & McIntyre, 1988), 95.

39 Accessed May 26, 2018. https://www.collectionscanada.gc.ca/chinese-canadians/021022-1400-e.html.

40 Con et al., 183.

41 Yee, 90.

42 Ibid., 90.

43 Edgar Wickberg, ed., *From China to Canada, A History of the Chinese Communities in Canada* (Toronto: McClelland and Stewart, 1982), 167.

44 Yee, 90.

45 Con et al., 193.

46 Ibid., 193.

47 Ibid., 200.

48 "Montreal Chinese Raise $10,000 For Red Cross Work in War Area." *Montreal Gazette*, September 4, 1937.

49 "Chinatown Battle Averted as Police Stage Night Raids." *Montreal Gazette*, January 22, 1934.

50 An article in the French language *La Patrie*, which ran on March 22, 1936, painted a dark and mysterious picture of Montreal Chinatown with this headline: "Randonnée Nocturne dans le Quartier Chinois de la Métropole—Un Guide Peu Banal Lorsque la Nuit Tombe—Le Magasin du Diable—Promenade Souterraine—Un Coin de L'Orient—

Chez les Fumeurs D'Opium—Dans L'Obscurité des Caves—Chez les Chee Kung Tong." It's little wonder that mothers would say to their kids, "Behave, or I will send you down to Chinatown."

51 Patricia Roy, "The Soldiers Canada Didn't Want: Her Chinese and Japanese Citizens," *Canadian Historical Review*, LIX, 3. 1978.

52 Ken Lee interview. May 17, 1992, Vancouver.

53 "The Chinese Immigration Act." *Montreal Gazette*, August 23, 1943.

54 Accessed June 5, 2018. http://www.chinaheritagequarterly.org/features.php?searchterm=030_chronology.inc&issue=030.

55 Accessed May 26, 2018. http://www.chinaheritagequarterly.org/features.php?searchterm=030_1940.inc&issue=030.

56 Shuang Shen postulated in *Cosmopolitan Publics: Anglophone Print Culture in Semi-Colonial Shanghai* (48): "The time of *The China Critic* was one of national resistance to foreign domination and Japanese military aggression, the magazine avoided the label 'nationalist,' the editors tried hard to distinguish themselves from what they considered to be 'narrow-minded nationalism' both within China and in the outside world."

57 George Mar interview. May 17, 1992, Vancouver.

58 Hansard, May 1, 1947. 2646.

59 Hansard, February 11, 1947. 335.

60 Ibid., 313. Thatcher later left the CCF and became the Liberal premier of Saskatchewan. His quote reflected the position of the CCF during the parliamentary debate to repeal the Exclusion Act.

Chapter 4

61 Con et al., 211.

62 Accessed May 26, 2018. https://archive.org/stream/proceedingsofsta1948cana/proceedingsofsta1948cana_djvu.txt.

63 Con et al., 214.

64 Ibid., 216.

65 Ibid., 217.

66 Ibid., 216.

67 Accessed May 26, 2018. https://ccncourstories.wordpress.com/videos/paper-sons-video/.

68 Freda Hawkins, "Canada and Immigration, Public Policy and Public Concern." (Montreal: McGill-Queen's University Press, 1971), 133.

69 Denise Helley, 277.

70 Con et al., 218.

71 Li, 93.

72 The French school system had a policy of not accepting immigrants in those days. Many European Catholics, like the Italians, ended up going to English schools. Immigrants then identified with the Anglophones of Québec. Bill 101 now requires all immigrant children to go into the French system. See the following article on the experience of Italian immigrants with the language of education in Québec: http:// www.pkidd.com/doc/Gazette.2014-02-14.Sabino.Grassi.Echoes_of_ rejection.pdf (accessed May 26, 2018).

73 A dress with side slits worn by socialites, upper class women and showgirls.

74 Upon the suggestion of my godmother, my father transferred me to St. Thomas More primary school for grades 4 to 7 because it was a newer school with young teachers, including Ed Kirk. St. Thomas More was in the more affluent west end of Verdun.

Chapter 5

75 Marlon K. Hom, *Songs of Gold Mountain* (Berkeley: University of California Press, 1987), 146. Used with the permission of University of California Press.

76 Interviews with my mother when she was 85 to 90.

77 Toicheng is the county seat of Toishan.

78 Third Uncle was probably a village cousin or friend of my father. Chinese call males "uncles" whether we were related or not. Third means that the man was the third son in the family.

79 The old-fashioned cast iron weighed up to ten pounds. Laundry work was known as the "ten pound livelihood."

80 Chinese expression meaning "at peace."

Chapter 6

81 Karl Marx, preface to *A Contribution to the Critique of Social Economy* (Moscow: Progress Publishers, 1977).

82 During the anti-colonial and anti-imperialist period of world history, the "Third World" refers to the developing countries of Asia, Africa, Latin America and the Caribbean. These countries were fighting for independence against the domination of the developed capitalist countries of the First and Second Worlds.

83 Frantz Fanon, *The Wretched of the Earth* (New York: Grove Press, 1963), 53.

84 Ibid., 311–315.

85 Walter Rodney, *How Europe Underdeveloped Africa* (London: Bogle-L'Ouverture Publications, 1972).

86 Régis Debray, *Revolution in the Revolution?* (New York: Grove Press, 1967), 21.

87 Edgar Snow, *Red Star Over China* (New York: Grove Press, 1968), 16.

88 Ibid., 95.

89 Sean Mills, *The Empire Within: Postcolonial Thought and Political Activism in Sixties Montreal* (Montreal: McGill-Queen's University Press, 2010). See my review of the book at Rabble.ca: http://rabble.ca/books/reviews/2010/11/montreals-sixties-heyday (accessed May 27, 2018).

90 Pierre Vallières, *White Niggers of America* (Toronto: McClelland and Stewart, 1971). Vallières' "white niggers" are the *Québécois de souche.*

91 SWAPO of Namibia was the national liberation movement that gained independence from South Africa in 1990. Southwest Africa (the colonial name) was a former German colony that was taken over by Britain after World War I. South Africa administered the colony and imposed its apartheid policies. SWAPO waged a guerrilla struggle from 1966 until it gained Namibian independence in 1990.

92 The Patriotic Front was a united front of the ZAPU and ZANU national liberation movements that waged a guerrilla war for independence against the Rhodesian colonial regime. ZANU won the post-independence elections in 1980 and has remained in power ever since.

93 Lin Piao, Mao's heir apparent, was accused of plotting against Mao and died in a plane crash as he fled to Moscow in 1971.

94 Roger Rashi interview. October 27, 2015.

95 This was made up of the CSN, FTQ (Fédération des travailleurs et travailleuses du Québec) and the CEQ (Conseil des enseignantes et enseignants du Québec).

Chapter 7

96 Howard Fast, *Being Red* (Boston: Houghton Mifflin Company, 1990), 101.

97 With the kind permission of the poet, Amin Kassam.

98 For more information on the MPIQ, see Amanda Ricci, "From Acculturation to Integration. The Political Participation of Montréal's Italian Canadian Community in an Urban Context (1945–1990)" (master's thesis, Université de Montréal, 2009).

99 Alan Silverman interview. July 14, 2015.

100 My notes on the meeting with Chai Zemin, president of the Chinese People's Association for Friendship with Foreign Countries, May 31, 1975.

101 Roger Rashi interview. October 30, 2015.

102 J. Peters, *The Communist Party, A Manual on Organization*. (San Francisco: Proletarian Publishers, 1975).

103 Roger Rashi interview. October 30, 2015.

104 Notably, the Azania People's Support Committee (South Africa), Zimbabwe Support Committee, Canada-China Society and Kampuchea Support Committee.

105 Juanita later became the first Black judge in Quebec.

106 CSN, teachers, machinists, metalworkers, oilworkers' unions, Palestine Solidarity, Association of Métis and Non-Status Indians of Saskatchewan, to name a few.

107 Azania was the name the PAC used for South Africa, which they considered to be a colonial name. Although of Greek origin, Pan-Africanists interpret "Azania" to mean "Land of the Black People."

108 Other groups that entered into unity talks with the League and later rallied: Regroupement des comités de travailleurs; Centre de recherches et d'information du Québec; Groupe d'action socialiste; Noyau des petites entreprises; Groupe Abitibi-Témiscamingue (M-L).

109 From Herman Rosenfeld, who took part in the unity talks with the BSG in Toronto.

110 Roger Rashi interview. October 30, 2015.

111 Jean-Philippe Warren, *Ils voulaient changer le monde, le militantisme Marxiste-Léniniste au Québec* (Montreal: VLB Editeur, 2007).

112 Roger Rashi interview. October 27, 2015.

113 Gillian Taylor interview. July 16, 2014.

114 Ibid.

115 Accessed June 5, 2018. https://news.google.com/newspapers?nid=
    1946&dat=19771001&id=Uo8xAAAAIBAJ&sjid=1aEFAAAAIBAJ&pg
    =2970,20032&hl=en.

Chapter 8

116 Manuel Vazquez Montalban, *Murder in the Central Committee* (London:
    Pluto Press, 1984), 59.
117 John Nyathi Pokela helped found the PAC with Robert Sobukwe
    after they broke away from the ANC over armed struggle and other
    nationalist differences. Pokela, upon his release from thirteen years at
    Robben Island, assumed the leadership of the PAC in 1981 to unite the
    various factions of the liberation movement.
118 Accessed May 30, 2018. https://www.marxists.org/history/erol/
    ca.secondwave/bsg-rallies.htm
119 Theoretical journal of the Workers Communist Party (Marxist-
    Leninist), October no. 7, Autumn 1979, 103.
120 "'Multiculturalism' pits immigrants against nationalities." *The Forge*,
    May 23, 1980.
121 The CBW and the CCNC each celebrated its tenth anniversary and
    billed this as "an unprecedented coalition building event" of the two
    communities. It was held at the Negro Community Centre in Montreal
    on December 16, 1990.
122 Statement made during Xi Jinping's visit to Mexico on February 11,
    2009, before he became president.
123 Accessed May 30, 2018. https://www.marxists.org/history/erol/
    ca.collapse/wcp-quebec-serious.htm.
124 Yvette Matyas interview. March 3, 2016.
125 Roger Rashi interview. October 30, 2015.
126 Ibid.
127 Ibid.
128 Mary Gabriel, *Love and Capital* (New York: Little, Brown and
    Company, 2011).
129 Alan Silverman interview. July 14, 2015.
130 Conversations and correspondences with James, who requested that
    his full name not be used in this era of the Internet where Googled
    information can be misused and abused.

131 One of the many studies on Bhopal by Daya Varma was this one, co-written with his wife, Dr. Shree Mulay, and published in the *Handbook of Toxicology of Chemical Warfare Agents* (2009). Daya wrote over 225 scientific publications and two books.

132 Mao Zedong, *On Contradiction: Selected Readings from the Works of Mao Zedong* (Beijing: Foreign Languages Press, 1971).

Chapter 9

133 Daya Ram Varma, *The Art and Science of Healing Since Antiquity* (Xlibris, 2011), 144.

134 World Economic Forum. Accessed May 30, 2018. https://www.weforum.org/agenda/2016/06/7-things-to-know-about-chinas-economy.

135 Xue Muqiao, *China's Socialist Economy* (Beijing: Foreign Languages Press, 1981).

136 June Fourth is synonymous with the Tiananmen Democracy Movement. Today, conflicting reports have emerged from the Western press on whether a "massacre" actually took place at Tiananmen Square on June 4, 1989.

137 Used with permission of *Monthly Review*. Accessed May 30, 2018. http://monthlyreview.org/2013/03/01/china-2013.

138 Accessed May 30, 2018. https://in.reuters.com/article/cuba-castro-quotes/factbox-cubas-fidel-castro-in-his-own-words-idINKBN13L04E.

139 See Chapter 18 for more on my father-in-law, Chen Zhongshu.

140 *Zhaxi Dele* is the Chinese transcription of the traditional Tibetan greeting, loosely translated as "blessings and good luck."

Chapter 10

141 Frank Chin, *The Chickencoop Chinaman/The Year of the Dragon* (Seattle: University of Washington Press, 1990), 29. With the kind permission of the author, Frank Chin.

142 The four classics are: *Water Margin/Outlaws of the Marsh* by Shi Naian; *Romance of the Three Kingdoms* by Luo Guanzhong; *Journey to the West* by Wu Cheng'en; and *Dream of the Red Chamber* by Cao Xueqin.

143 Jim Wong-Chu, *Chinatown Ghosts* (Vancouver: Pulp Press, 1986).

144 Frank Chin, 71. With permission of the author.

145 The essay appeared in *The Big Aiiieeeee! An Anthology of Chinese American and Japanese American Literature*. Edited by Jeffery Paul Chan, Frank Chin, Lawson Fusao Inada and Shawn Wong (New York: Penguin Books, 1991).

146 *The Big Aiiieeeee!*, 2. With permission of the author.

147 Ibid., 3.

148 Ibid., 27.

149 Ibid., 12.

150 Coincidentally, I interviewed her great grand nephew, Charles Laferrière, for my film *Gens du pays: The Chinese of Québec*. He introduced me to *la chinoiserie*, of which he had a big collection.

151 SKY Lee, *Disappearing Moon Cafe* (Vancouver: Douglas & McIntyre, 1990).

152 The term Toishanese (Taishanese) is generically applied to those coming from the Sei-yap (Four Counties) districts of Taishan, Kaiping, Enping and Xinhui.

Chapter 11

153 Louis Chu, *Eat a Bowl of Tea* (Seattle: University of Washington Press, 1979).

154 It's the same Wong Foon Sien who made the annual trip to Ottawa seeking equal treatment for the Chinese community after World War II. Wong founded the Chinese Trade Workers' Association in 1942.

155 Ann Silversides, "Chinese group to press Ottawa for redress over $500 head tax." *The Globe and Mail*, May 5, 1984.

156 *Joong* is cooked to celebrate May 5 each year in commemoration of the Chu Dynasty poet Qu Yuan, who drowned himself in the river after the Chu kingdom fell in 278 BC. As the legend goes, people threw packets of rice into the water to prevent the fish from eating his body. Chinese have been eating *joong* ever since.

157 Ingrid Peritz, "City tearing us apart, brick by brick, says Montreal's Chinese." *Montreal Gazette*, November 18, 1981. Front page.

158 Ingrid Peritz, "Montreal Lobby Dogging Drapeau to Far East." *Montreal Gazette*, May 10, 1985. Front page.

159 Some of the members of the committee were: Helen Jong, Queenie Hum, Johnson Choi, Yat Lo, George Lee, Jonas Ma, Sandy Yep, Thinh-Yien Hua and me.

160 Lilly Tasso, "Trois membres de la communauté chinoise se presentent aux élections scolaires, le but: changer les attitudes, combattre les stéréotypes." *La Presse*, September 30, 1987. A14.

161 "Unmanned polls meant long wait for voters." *Montreal Gazette*, November 16, 1987. Complete with a photo of the elderly women waiting.

162 "Grogne dans le quartier chinois." *La Presse*, November 18, 1987.

163 Clair Balfour, "Impression of possible arrogance was not intended." *Montreal Gazette*, November 9, 1987.

164 Some other members were Queenie Hum, Jonas Ma, Sandy Yep, Fo Niemi, Leung Tom and Tommy Hum.

165 Mémoire présenté au Comité consultatif sur les relations inter-culturelles et inter-raciales de la Communauté urbain de Montréal par un groupe d'individus et d'organisations de la communauté sino-canadienne. William G. W. Dere, Queenie Hum, Kai Lee, Jonas Ma, Min Yi Pang, Service à la famille chinoise du grand Montréal, Association des professionnel(le)s, hommes et femmes d'affaires, Union des chinois du Cambodge au Canada, Communauté catholique chinoise, Chambre de commerce du Quartier Chinois de Montréal, Association des restaurateurs chinois de Montréal, Amitié chinoise de Montréal, Association des chinois du Vietnam à Montréal, Association des chinois volontaires du Québec, Emission chinoise de Radio Centre-ville. 1 et 2 février 1988.

166 Tracy Wong, "Head Tax—benefit draws large support." *Asian Leader*, December 1989. 11.

Chapter 12

167 Program for the Toronto International Film Festival, September 9–18, 1993. 303.

168 Some of these volunteers were: Patty Kwan, Shirley Lo, Connie Ho, Nicole Lemire, Melinda Young, Belle Kei Wing Wong, Anita Malhotra, Lisa Wong, Raymond Foo and Mary Sui Yee Wong. In Vancouver, there was Barry Wong, Peter Mah, Seline So and Shelly Cheung.

169 Cynthia Lam was the executive director of the Chinese Family Service of Greater Montreal for many years. She was a recipient of the Order of Canada.

170 Kenneth Cheung was a community activist who took on Montreal's city hall. He was a leader in the HTEA redress movement.

171 Queenie Hum was the former assistant executive director of the Chinese Family Service. She was the first Chinese to be elected to office in Quebec as a school commissioner in 1991. Queenie was later appointed a Refugee Board judge.

172 Taishan is the Pinyin name for Toishan. While one million people live in Toishan today, there are 1.5 million Toishanese scattered in ninety-one countries. The majority of Toishanese are in North America.

173 Letter to the CBC from Ms. Priscilla (Pat) Fong, which was copied to me, Gary Yee and Walter Tom, December 3, 1993.

174 Jooneed Khan, "Un film sur une ignominie que le Canada doit assumer …." *La Presse*, Montreal, October 20, 1993.

175 In Victoria, a detention centre for Chinese immigrants was built at the corner of Dallas Road and Ontario Street. Immigrants were questioned, given a medical examination and made to pay the head tax there. Many poems written by the detainees were discovered on its walls before the centre was torn down. https://www.uvic.ca/library/featured/collections/about/Victoria-Chinatown.php (accessed June 5, 2018).

176 "Chinese Players Give Performance at Gayety Theatre," *Montreal Daily Star*, May 1, 1923. 6.

Chapter 13

177 For an excellent account of the Japanese Canadian redress campaign, read Maryka Omatsu's *Bittersweet Passage: Redress and the Japanese Canadian Experience* (Toronto: Between the Lines, 1992).

178 *Economic Losses of Japanese Canadians after 1941: a study conducted by Price Waterhouse* (Winnipeg: National Association of Japanese Canadians, 1986). https://search.library.utoronto.ca/details?652012&uuid:31042f28-62464e92-b863-1d043abb44a3.

179 Debbie Parkes, "Chinese-Canadians call for compensation." *Montreal Gazette*, November 4, 1988.

180 Editorials supporting head tax redress appeared in the *Vancouver Sun, Toronto Star, The Globe and Mail* and *Montreal Gazette*.

181 SUCCESS is the original acronym for United Chinese Community Enrichment Services Society. Now it is just known by its initials.

182 Reports gleaned from Wikileaks exposed some of the fabricated "eyewitness" reports from Tiananmen on that fateful night to be "pack

journalism" to fit the Western narrative on China. See the following, all accessed May 31, 2018: http://www.telegraph.co.uk/news/worldnews/wikileaks/8555142/Wikileaks-no-bloodshed-inside-Tiananmen-Square-cables-claim.html; http://tiananmenmyth.blogspot.ca/; http://www.cbsnews.com/news/there-was-no-tiananmen-square-massacre/.

183 Gary Yee interview. June 9, 2016.

184 "From CCNC monthly bulletin," *Asian Leader,* July, 1989. 10.

185 Correspondence from Amy Go, national president, CCNC, May 2, 1991.

186 For a good account of the anti–W5 struggle, see Anthony B. Chan, *Gold Mountain: The Chinese in the New World* (Vancouver: New Star Books, 1988).

187 http://www.ncccanada.ca/PageNCCCStatement.htm (page no longer accessible).

188 "Chinese group urges apology, endowment fund for head tax." Canadian Press, May 20, 1991.

189 Ping Tan is a Malaysian-born Toronto lawyer. He was the chairperson of the Confederation of Metropolitan Toronto Chinese Canadian Organizations (CTCCO) when he wrote his letter critical of the CCNC to the prime minister. The CTCCO unites the various family and other *lo wah kiu* associations in Toronto. Tan was later the founding executive co-chair of the National Congress of Chinese Canadians.

190 Memo to the CCNC-NRC from Gary Yee, May 7, 1992.

191 "Canada fields controversial delegate in China trip." *The Globe and Mail,* November 7, 2014.

192 "Chinese Canadians demand explanation from CSIS head." CTV News, July 2, 2010.

193 The letter stated in part: "The Chinese Canadian war veterans (Pacific Unit 280) expressed their view that an official apology should be sufficient; while the Chinese Freemasons as well as some prominent individuals such as Dr. Wally Chung expressed the view that the apology should be accompanied with some funding set aside for the community, but not individual financial compensation. ... If you remove the individual compensation component from the redress package, we believe strongly that you will easily win majority support."

194 Kevin Griffin, "Chinese Head Tax: Rally draws 500 compensation supporters." *Vancouver Sun,* July 6, 1992.

195 Letter from Gary Yee, CCNC national president, to Prime Minister Brian Mulroney, December 21, 1990. The letter refuted Joseph Du's July 19, 1990 letter of criticism of the CCNC, which was also sent to the prime minister.

196 Du was a Vietnamese Chinese born in Haiphong in 1933. He immigrated to Canada after graduating from Taiwan National Medical School in 1961. He served as a pediatrician in Manitoba's northern reserves for thirty-three years. He received the Order of the Buffalo, the Order of Manitoba and the Order of Canada. He was the co-chair of the National Congress of Chinese Canadians. He died in Winnipeg in 2017.

197 Correspondence from Gary Yee to Raymond Wong, president, Montreal Chinese Community United Centre and head of Les Aliments Wong Wing, April 10, 1991.

198 Correspondence from Amy Go, national president, CCNC, May 2, 1991.

199 In an email sent March 20, 2001, Gary disclosed that he was indeed hurt when the "National Congress and some of the Chinese newspaper articles and some elders in our community attacked me personally and questioned my motives for leading the redress campaign from 1987 into the early 1990's. ... My response to their letters to the PM was mildly critical of two Toronto-based groups and I copied these two groups—they then used my letter as the basis for an entire campaign against the CCNC and me for disrespecting the family associations and for using redress to further myself and the CCNC. Eventually, they started the National Congress of Chinese Canadians to oppose us. ... And it hurts to be criticized for volunteering your time and energy."

200 Memo to NRC Policy Subcommittee, from Yantay S. Tsai, Re: Draft Discussion Paper (dated June 13, 1991), June 25, 1991.

201 Other cities that responded: Ottawa, Hamilton, Victoria, Regina, Edmonton, Calgary, Winnipeg, Clearwater, Halifax, London and Charlottetown.

202 Chinese Canadian National Council, *National Survey on Redress (1991), Phase II: Report of the Survey* (June 12, 1991).

203 Memo to Gary Yee, chair, CCNC-NRC, from Victor Yukman Wong, on the CCNC-NRC Position Proposal, August 19, 1991.

204 Letter from Paulina Zillman, president, Manitoba Academy of Chinese Studies, C.M. Wong, president, CCNC-Winnipeg Chapter; Yantay

Tsai, editor, *Manitoba Chinese Post*; H.C. Lim, president, Chinese Community Council of Manitoba; and Otto So, president, Manitoba Chinese Fellowship, Winnipeg, to Prime Minister Brian Mulroney, May 14, 1991.

205 Other delegates: CCNC President Alan Li, Executive Director Shana Wong, and Avvy Go from the Toronto Redress Committee. From Ottawa there was Lewis Chan, CCNC executive member and president of the Canadian Ethnocultural Council, and from the Halifax Chinese Canadian Association, May Lui.

206 The National Redress Alliance was composed of the CCNC-NRC, the National Association of Japanese Canadians, The National Congress of Ukrainian Canadians and the National Congress of Italian Canadians. Gary Yee actively tried to build the redress network with the other affected communities. He participated at the In Justice Conference in Vancouver organized by the NAJC and Simon Fraser University at the end of April 1992, where he met with Art Miki of the NAJC and Dmytro Cipywnyk, president of the Ukrainian Canadian Congress.

207 Walter Tom interview. May 6, 2016.

208 Mrs. Lee's full name is not known, because upon her marriage to Mr. Lee, her identity was subsumed into his, in keeping with Chinese Confucian tradition.

209 Memo to CCNC-NRC, from Gary Yee, May 7, 1992.

210 Gary Yee, "The legacy of a racist law." *The Globe and Mail*, April 30, 1993.

211 Resolution of the National Congress of Chinese Canadians, adopted at the National Executive meeting, Toronto, May 30, 1993.

212 Letter from Ping Tan, executive co-chair, NCCC, to Gerry Weiner, covering the NCCC resolution, May 30, 1993.

213 Thanks to research provided by Kenda Gee. The compensation of $415,908,000 was broken down as follows: $21,000 each went to 17,948 survivors including descendants alive on September 22, 1988, totalling $376,908,000; $24 million to the Canadian Race Relations Foundation; $12 million to rebuild Japanese Canadian community institutions, such as community and cultural centres; $3 million to administer the redress settlement.

Chapter 14

214 Shack Jang Mack, Quen Ying Lee and Yew Lee v. The Attorney General of Canada. Judgment of the Ontario Superior Court, Justice J. Cumming, July 9, 2001.

215 The CCNC delegation was composed of: James Wing, head tax payer from Montreal; Victor Yukman Wong, chairperson, CCNC-National Redress Committee, Vancouver; Amy Go, chair, CCNC National Board of Directors, Toronto; Alan Li, president, CCNC National Executive, Toronto; Gary Yee, former chair, CCNC-NRC, Toronto; Melina Young, vice-chair, CCNC National Board of Directors, Ottawa; and me, who was then vice-chair, CCNC-NRC.

216 Memo to CCNC-NRC members from Victor Yukman Wong, October 19, 1994.

217 The other organizations were the German Canadian Congress, the National Association of Canadians of Origins in India, the National Congress of Italian Canadians, and the Ukrainian Canadian Congress.

218 Letter from Sheila Finestone to Alan Li, December 14, 1994.

219 Letter to Sheila Finestone from Bryce Kanbara, director, Greater Toronto Chapter NAJC, December 15, 1994.

220 Kim Bolan, "Chinese group asks UN to act on redress." *Vancouver Sun*, March 22, 1995.

221 Chinese Canadian National Council submission to the United Nations Commission on Human Rights, March 21, 1995.

222 Ibid.

223 CCNC-NRC submission to Theo Van Boven, special rapporteur on the right to restitution, compensation and rehabilitation for victims of gross violation of human rights and fundamental freedoms, UN Commission on Human Rights. August 23, 1993.

224 For a transcript of the speech: http://www.asian.ca/redress/sp_19951205.htm (accessed May 31, 2018).

225 Matt James, "Redress, Recognition, and Redistribution: The Case of the 'Chinese Head Tax.'" *Canadian Journal of Political Science/Revue canadienne de science politique*, December 2004. Originally presented at the Annual General Meetings of the Canadian Political Science Association, May 31, 2003, Halifax. With permission of the author.

226 Ibid., 885.

227 Ibid.

228 Ibid., 895, 896, 897.

229 Wilfred Quiambao, "A cruel separation—Jews, Chinese remember racist immigration barriers." *Montreal Gazette*, November 15, 1997.

230 Memo to CCNC and members of the Head Tax/Exclusion Act Charter Challenge Working Group from Phillip R. Pike, June 5, 1998.

231 May later wrote to the Court Challenges Program of Canada expressing "concerns that any process we engage should not create a new financial burden on the head tax payers and their families." Letter from May Cheng, chair, Head Tax Redress Committee, to Sarah Lugtig, director, Equality Rights Program, August 17, 1999.

232 Shack Jang Mack, Quen Ying Lee and Yew Lee v. The Attorney General of Canada. Judgment of the Ontario Superior Court, Justice J. Cumming, July 9, 2001.

233 Ibid.

Chapter 15

234 Susan Eng is the daughter of a head tax payer and a prominent Toronto lawyer, who was the former chair of the Metro Toronto Police Services Board.

235 Minutes of National Redress Committee teleconference. March 7, 2001.

236 Shack Jang Mack, Quen Ying Lee and Yew Lee v. The Attorney General of Canada. Judgment of the Ontario Superior Court, Justice J. Cumming, July 9, 2001.

237 Avvy Go, "Playing Second Fiddle to Yo-Yo Ma." (Presentation to Fourth Colloquium on the legal profession, March 2005, Toronto.) With permission of the author.

238 Canadian Judicial Council, "Judicial Conduct Committee Vice-Chairperson closes file involving Mr. Justice Macpherson of the Court of Appeal for Ontario." October 28, 2002.

239 Go, 15.

240 Ibid., 17.

241 Some of these people were Chung Tang, executive director of the CCNC Toronto Chapter, Kenda Gee of the independent Edmonton Redress Committee, Walter Tom and May Chiu from Montreal, Daniel Lai of Calgary, May Lui from Halifax, among others.

242 Avvy Go interview. June 13, 2015.

243 Accessed June 1, 2018. http://www.asian.ca/redress/nr_20020208. htm-.

244 Gary Yee interview. June 9, 2016.

245 Letter from Cynthia Pay, national president, CCNC, to Sheila Copps, December 2002.

246 Minutes of Montreal HTEA Redress meeting. December 20, 2002.

247 Email exchange with May Chiu, March 13, 2003.

248 Susan Eng, "If this is 'inclusive,' count me out." *The Globe and Mail*, May 13, 2003. A19.

249 Ibid. A copy of the offensive poster and the *Edmonton Journal* article are available on the Asian.ca website, http://www.asian.ca/posteroffends/ ahm_poster_offend_ej.jpg (accessed June 1, 2018).

250 Tony Chan's email to me and many others in the redress community, May 8, 2003.

251 Minutes of CCNC redress conference call. January 14, 2003.

252 Winxie Tse email response to me and twenty-five others in the redress network.

253 Gary Yee interview. June 9, 2016.

254 Chung told me that the Toronto chapter of the CCNC supported the Unity Declaration because it was the right thing to do. Even though they shared the same office, there was little communication between Victor Wong's CCNC National and the Toronto chapter. Chung didn't know that CCNC National did not endorse the declaration.

255 Submission to the United Nations special rapporteur on contemporary forms of racism, racial discrimination, xenophobia and related intolerance by Chinese Canadian National Council and Metro Toronto Chinese and Southeast Asian Legal Clinic on Redress for Chinese Head Tax and Exclusion Act, September 25, 2003.

256 Submission to United Nations Special Rapporteur Doudou Diène, by Noah Novogrodsky, University of Toronto Faculty of Law, International Human Rights Clinic, December 22, 2003. https://www. law.utoronto.ca/documents/ihrp/UN_headtax_brief.pdf (accessed July 4, 2018).

257 Email from Raymond Yao, September 10, 2003.

258 Warren A. Maily, "Redressing the Past of the Lo Wah Kui." *Pacific Rim*, 2005. http://langaraprm.com/2005/culture/redressing-the-past-of-

the-lo-wah-kui-chinese-canadians-demand-compensation-for-past-injustices/ (accessed June 1, 2018).

259 Canadian Race Relations Foundation, Ukrainian Canadian Congress and the National Association of Japanese Canadians.

260 Paul Samyn, "Documents show bureaucrats told Copps not to apologize to Ukrainian Canadians." Canadian Press Newswire, December 21, 2003.

261 Shelley Page, "Chinese Canadians deserve head tax redress, Copps says." *Toronto Star*, March 7, 1990. A17.

262 The sponsorship scandal was the outcome of the sponsorship program by the Liberal government to promote Canadian industries in Quebec, to counter the influence of the Parti Québécois. The program ran from 1996 to 2004. It was the subject of a judicial inquiry by Judge John Gomery, who found broad corruption where people and companies connected to the Liberal Party were given public money for doing little or no work.

263 Lynda Lin, "Canada Maintains No Reparations Stance For Chinese Canadians—But UN Report Recommends It Pay Reparations." *Pacific Citizen*, April 2–15, 2004.

264 Ibid.

265 Kenda Gee email to Gary Yee, October 14, 2004.

266 Jonas Ma email, September 20, 2004.

267 My email response to Jonas Ma, September 20, 2004.

268 May Chiu email to leaders of the CCRA, October 16, 2004.

269 Walter Tom email, December 10, 2004.

270 Kenda Gee email, December 15, 2004.

271 Rod Mickleburgh, "Obituary: Gim Foon Wong's motorcycle ride turned the tide on Chinese head-tax redress." *The Globe and Mail*, October 1, 2013.

272 Miro Cernetig, "Gim Wong's motorcycle diaries." *Vancouver Sun*, January 14, 2006.

273 For more on Gim Wong's fascinating story, go to the Chinese Canadian Military Museum Society website: http://www.ccmms.ca/veteran-stories/air-force/gim-wong/ (accessed June 1, 2018).

274 CCRA press release, March 21, 2005.

275 Letter from Colleen Hua, national president, CCNC, to Paul Martin, March 4, 2005.

276 Open letter to the prime minister, November 14, 2005.

277 http://www.cic.gc.ca/english//department/laws-policy/agreements/ china/china.asp (page no longer accessible).

278 Simon Li's interview with Paul Martin, *Power Politics—Yet Boon Jing King* on Toronto First Radio, AM 1540, December 6, 2005. Reproduced with the kind permission of Simon Li.

279 Jan Wong, "Give the money to us—who gets the $2.5 million federal payout announced this week for Chinese Canadians?" *The Globe and Mail*, November 26, 2005. M2.

280 Raymond Yao interview. August 7, 2014.

281 Ibid.

282 Ibid.

283 Jennifer Forhan, "Chinese Canadians seek apology, could sway election." Reuters, January 6, 2006.

284 CCRA press release, January 24, 2006.

285 Raymond Leung, Chinese Benevolent Association of Canada press release, February 28, 2006.

Chapter 16

286 The consultation meetings were called with less than a week to fly Chinese Canadians involved in redress from across Canada to Toronto. According to Ray Yao, Stephen Harper needed these meetings to honestly say that discussions were underway with Chinese Canadian groups on redress for the April 4 Throne Speech.

287 "Harper expected to agree to an apology first and discussion of compensation later." *Ming Pao*, March 21, 2006. A2.

288 Those invited by Canadian Heritage were: CCNC—Colleen Hua, Joseph Wong, Victor Wong; Ontario Coalition—Susan Eng, George Lau, Yew Lee, Har Ying Lee, Doug Hum, Avvy Go; BC Coalition—Bill Chu, Karin Lee; ACCESS (Vancouver)—Sid Tan; CCRA (Montreal)— William Dere; Sien Lok Society (Calgary)—Ray Lee.

289 Susan Eng email, March 23, 2006.

290 Members of the NCCC delegation: Ping Tan—executive co-chair; Jack Lee—Quebec co-chair; Gordon Joe; David Chuenyan Lai—Victoria co-chair; Man Wai Yu—Montreal Chinese Cultural Centre; Lena Wong—Toronto Chinese Cultural Centre; Howe Lee—Chinese Canadian Military Museum Society; K.W. Chang—Alberta Cultural

Community Centre; Joseph Du—Manitoba co-chair; Yung Quon
Yu—CBA; Chuck Chang—Chinese Freemasons of Canada; Tak Nam
Foo—SUCCESS; Raymond Leung—CBA of Canada; Jun K. Wong—
Montreal Chinese United Centre; Hughes Eng—Confederation
of Toronto Chinese Canadian Organizations; Steve Yang—Regina
Chinese Business Association; John Lam—Shon Yee Benevolent
Association of Canada; Kitty Mar—Vancouver Chinese Cultural
Centre; Ming Tat Cheung—Toronto Chinese Cultural Centre.

291　They were: Susan Peterson, associate deputy minister; Diane Fulford, assistant deputy minister; and Kristina Namiesniowski, director general.

292　February 3, 2006 letter from Luc Rouleau, director, Ministerial Correspondence Secretariat (I didn't make up the title) of Canadian Heritage in response to my November 14, 2005 letter to Paul Martin, which was forwarded to Raymond Chan. In the response, they were still touting the ACE program, "In the coming weeks, the new Government will decide both the direction of the ACE Program and how to address related issues."

293　Others in favour were: Ontario Community Centre, Calgary Sien Lok Society, Vancouver's SUCCESS and James Pon, a head tax payer, who said he would donate his money to the Chinese Railway Workers Museum.

294　The information on the NCCC meeting with Oda and Kenney came from Ray Lee, Raymond Leung and Donald Chen who attended the meeting.

295　Victor Wong email, April 18, 2006.

296　The $1 million amount was reported in an article covering a public meeting in Vancouver where a descendant said the pain and suffering caused by the government to his family was worth $1 million. The Congress mischievously latched onto this number.

297　CCRA press release, June 13, 2006.

298　*Vancouver Sun*, June 8, 2006.

299　Researcher Ken Rubin discovered in 2007, through access to information, that Canadian Heritage bureaucrats floated this drastic speculation in a briefing paper. Canadian Heritage reinforced its original advice to the Martin government to shut tight the floodgates by warning against possible huge payouts. https://www.usherbrooke.ca/sodrus/fileadmin/sites/sodrus/documents/polygamie35.pdf (accessed June 14, 2018). Thanks to Kenda Gee for the link.

300 Susan Eng email, May 8, 2006.

301 "Chinese Canadians ask PM Harper: Please do not discriminate against the Golden Mountain widows." Press Statement, May 24, 2006.

302 Bruce Campion-Smith, "Harper hears first-hand of suffering caused by Chinese head tax." *Toronto Star*, May 26, 2006.

303 Yew Lee email, June 7, 2006.

304 CCNC National press release, "No Division on Head Tax Issue." June 8, 2006.

305 May Chiu email, June 11, 2006.

306 Ontario Coalition of Head Tax Families press release, "Chinese Canadians Ride the Redress Train." June 13, 2006.

307 Mike De Souza et al, "Cold water poured on redress train." *Vancouver Sun*, June 14, 2006. A1.

308 Karin Lee email, June 15, 2006.

309 De Souza, A1.

310 Gord Jin email to redress network, June 15, 2006.

311 Yew Lee email, June 16, 2006.

312 *Ming Pao*, June 15, 2006. A2.

313 "Chinese Canadian Redress Alliance Demands More Than an Apology Calls for Government Accountability and Transparency in Redress Settlement." June 19, 2006. Press release issued by May Chiu, Kenda Gee, CCRA and Gord Jin, Newfoundland and Labrador Head Tax Redress Committee.

314 Yew Lee interview. August 7, 2014.

315 May Chiu email to the redress network, June 21, 2006.

316 Daniel Lai email to the redress network, June 21, 2006.

317 Yew Lee interview. August 7, 2014.

318 "Personal Reflections from the Redress Express." Gary Yee, May 2012.

319 Yew Lee interview. August 7, 2014.

320 A bare bones version of each fighter jet had a price tag of $150 million.

321 Thanks to Kenda Gee for his research. http://www.cic.gc.ca/english/resources/publications/multi-report2009/booklet.asp (page no longer accessible).

322 Alan Hustak, "Montrealer fought to right wrongs of Chinese head tax." *Montreal Gazette*, November 23, 2008.

323 Kenda Gee interview. April 25, 2016.

324 Walter Tom interview. May 6, 2016.

325 Kenda Gee interview. April 25, 2016.

326 Gary Yee interview. June 9, 2016.

327 I tried several times to reach Victor Wong for an interview for this book but he was unavailable.

328 Ray Yao interview. August 7, 2014.

329 Harvey Lee email to CCNC National, June 27, 2006.

Chapter 17

330 I tend to prefer the term "racialized minority" over "visible minority" for reasons that the Ontario Human Rights Commission has expressed: "Recognizing that race is a social construct, the Commission describes people as 'racialized person' or 'racialized group' instead of the more outdated and inaccurate terms 'racial minority', 'visible minority', 'person of colour' or 'non-White.'" (From "Racial Discrimination, Race and Racism," accessed at www.onhrc.on.ca on February 28, 2018.) The old terminology is generally defined in terms of whiteness, whereas "racialized" is based on historical and institutional racial prejudice and not necessarily on the colour of skin.

331 According to a CBC report from September 17, 2013, only 7.1 per cent of government workers come from the "cultural communities," which make up 12.3 per cent of the general population. And 95 per cent of senior government jobs are held by white Francophones who make up 79 per cent of the population. The inequality is even starker with the median income of visible minorities in Quebec at $19,551 while the median for Francophones is at $29,432. http://www.cbc.ca/news/canada/francophones-still-dominate-quebec-s-public-service-1.1856933 (accessed June 1, 2018).

332 Accessed June 1, 2018. http://www.cdpdj.qc.ca/Documents/COMM_Calego_avril2011_En.pdf).

333 Robert Chodos, *The CPR, A Century of Corporate Welfare* (Toronto: James Lorimer & Company, 1973), 22. "The total value of government aid is impossible to estimate." There was $37.8 million worth of government built lines turned over to the CPR and a grant of 25 million acres of prime land along with the right of way upon which the track was built, among other subsidies.

334 Accessed June 1, 2018. http://www.daintyrice.ca/en/subcontent.php?page=D12000.

335 Accessed June 1, 2018. http://www.biographi.ca/en/bio/reford_
robert_wilson_14E.html.

336 Dainty Foods entry, *Canadian Food & Grocery Industry Guide*.
https://www.contactcanada.com/database/freesearch.
php?portal=0a10&action=view_profile&id=2240 (accessed April 25,
2018).

337 Ingrid Peritz, "Dismantled sweat lodge exposes rift in Christian,
traditional teaching." *The Globe and Mail*, June 17, 2011.

338 Valerie Taliman, "Christian Crees Tear Down Sweat Lodge." *Indian
Country Today*, July 2, 2011. http://indiancountrytodaymedianetwork.
com/2011/02/07/christian-crees-tear-down-sweat-lodge-15500
(accessed on June 1, 2018). With permission of Indian Country Media
Network.

339 Nicolas Bérubé, "Jacob Tierney: <<Les anglos et les immigrants sont
ignorés>>." *La Presse*, July 6, 2010.

340 John Ralston Saul, *A Fair Country*. (Toronto: Viking, 2008).

341 May Chiu email, February 23, 2012.

342 Marian Scott, "Setback for Diversity." *Montreal Gazette*, December 28,
2017.

Chapter 18

343 GG is a pseudonym. I don't feel I have the right to reveal her identity.

344 This policy is still in practice today to ensure centralized leadership is
followed and to prevent local cronyism.

345 The Maba Man Museum is the site where the relics of a settlement
dating back 150,000 years were found.

346 *Gim Shan Haak* means "Gold Mountain guest": the name for Gold
Mountain men returning to China to marry.

Chapter 19

347 *Jook sing* literally means "bamboo pole," which is hollow on the inside.
It is a derogatory term for those Chinese who have lost their culture and
identity.

348 Cho-yun Hsu, "A Reflection on Marginality." *Daedalus, Journal of the
American Academy of Arts and Sciences*, Spring 1991.

349 Loong Wong, "Belonging and diaspora: The Chinese and the Internet." http://firstmonday.org/ojs/index.php/fm/article/view/1045 (page no longer accessible).

350 Sui Sin Far means "narcissus flower" in Cantonese. *Mrs. Spring Fragrance* (1912) is a collection of short stories featuring "The Story of One White Woman who Married a Chinese."

351 Justin Kong, "The New Chinese Working Class and the Canadian Left." *New Canadian Media*, November 6, 2015. http://newcanadianmedia. ca/item/31450-the-new-chinese-working-class-and-the-canadian-left (accessed June 5, 2018).

INDEX